At Cambridge Milton was whipped and Wordsworth got drunk, Tennyson met Arthur Hallam, and Ted Hughes met Sylvia Plath, Macaulay was hit by a dead cat and Henry James was nearly concussed by a punt pole. Nowhere in England outside London is richer in literary associations than Cambridge, yet this is the first complete history of creative writers in the town and University. First published in 1985, the 1995 revised edition contains much new or corrected material and a new introduction by Peter Ackroyd.

Graham Chainey begins with the legends that surround Cambridge's foundation, and traces through the centuries a crowded story rich in engrossing and often amusing incident. Here are the great names that have brought Cambridge fame throughout the world, and many lesser writers not usually linked with the place who have contributed to its history or have been affected by it – for better or worse. Besides discussing those born or educated in Cambridge and those who have taught there, Graham Chainey describes memorable visits by Dr Johnson, Oscar Wilde and Sherlock Holmes, among many others. The final chapters take the story up to the present day and give a picture of a literary city that in this century has produced A. A. Milne as well as E. M. Forster, the Bloomsbury Group as well as *Beyond the fringe*, and not only Rosamond Lehmann, Thom Gunn, and David Hare, but also P. D. James, Tom Sharpe and Salman Rushdie.

This book is an affectionate, amusing, but unsentimental account of an important part of England's literary history. Numerous appendices and a detailed bibliography help make it a valuable reference work as well, and there are over sixty illustrations. *A literary history of Cambridge* will appeal to everyone with a taste for literary anecdote, as well as those interested in how a single place can have inspired so much hatred and so much love in so many talents.

A LITERARY HISTORY OF CAMBRIDGE

A LITERARY HISTORY
of
CAMBRIDGE

Revised edition

GRAHAM CHAINEY

CAMBRIDGE
UNIVERSITY PRESS

Published by the Press Syndicate of the University of Cambridge
The Pitt Building, Trumpington Street, Cambridge CB2 1RP
40 West 20th Street, New York, NY 10011–4211 USA
10 Stamford Road, Oakleigh, Melbourne 3166, Australia

First published by The Pevensey Press 1985
and © The Pevensey Press 1985

This edition published by Cambridge University Press 1995
and © Cambridge University Press 1995

Printed in Great Britain at the University Press, Cambridge

A catalogue record for this book is available from the British Library

Library of Congress cataloguing in publication data applied for

ISBN 0 521 48244 5 hardback
ISBN 0 521 47681 X paperback

On the title page: 'Colinet resting at Cambridge by night': a woodcut by William Blake illustrating Ambrose Philips' 'Imitation of Virgil's First Eclogue', as published in Robert Thornton's *The Pastorals of Virgil* (1821). Colinet is an unhappy shepherd, drawn by 'fond desire strange lands and swains to know'. The 'strange lands' include Cambridge: Blake shows King's College Chapel on the far side of a broad winding Cam. Ambrose Philips (?1675–1749) was a Fellow of St John's College and a poet best remembered for his rivalry with Pope and his nickname 'Namby-Pamby', earned by his adulatory verses addressed to all and sundry.

Quam male Phoebicolis convenit ille locus!
– *John Milton*

Cambridge is a delight of a place, now there is nobody in it.
– *Thomas Gray*

Oh! dark asylum of a Vandal race!
– *Lord Byron*

. . . you that do profess to teach
And teach us nothing, feeding not the heart.
– *Alfred Tennyson*

An asylum – in more senses than one.
– *A. E. Housman*

I went to Cambridge and hated it beyond expression.
– *D. H. Lawrence*

Cambridge exceeded our most macabre expectations.
– *Christopher Isherwood*

Not a place in which a writer ought to remain.
– *E. M. Forster*

Uninhabitable.
– *Kingsley Amis*

Contents

List of contents

Foreword by Peter Ackroyd

The history of Cambridge University is also the history of English literature. John Skelton was the first poet to be educated there, and he was followed by Thomas Wyatt, Edmund Spenser and Christopher Marlowe. Marvell was almost seduced by the Jesuits, and Milton was mocked by the undergraduates of Christ's for his effeminate appearance. Christopher Smart was confined to his rooms in Pembroke for debt, but William Wordsworth walked among the colleges in reverie upon ground 'which had yielded to the steps of generations of illustrious men'. Samuel Taylor Coleridge took opium in his damp rooms, while Lord Byron careered around the narrow streets of the town in a carriage-and-four. Alfred Tennyson played with his pet snake in Trinity, and Siegfried Sassoon dreamed within Clare. The university was known to Chaucer's Miller, as well as to Conan Doyle's Sherlock Holmes. Pepys drank in Magdalene, Ronald Firbank smoked drugged cigarettes in Trinity Hall and Malcolm Lowry boozed at St Catharine's.

Characteristically it has been a university of verse rather than of prose, and in the solitary and reserved atmosphere of this place (quite different from the gregarious and metropolitan Oxford) there is some note or tone which encourages the sublimities of poetry rather than the frivolities of the novel – in fact it comes as something of a surprise to be reminded that William Makepeace Thackeray and Laurence Sterne were also members of the university. Certainly it is the perfect locale for solitary walking, and the flat landscape has always been conducive to the contemplation which precedes poetical composition. How many young or aspiring writers have made the journey to Grantchester, beside the sluggish waters of the Cam, and on that pilgrimage sought their true voice?

But if poetry derived from solitary brooding, it may also spring from ill-health and suffering. Cambridge has not necessarily been a kind nurse, and writers as diverse as George Herbert and Samuel Taylor Coleridge have suffered from the damp and the mist which rise from the circumambient fens; for many centuries various forms of rheumatism, consumption, and feverish ague have afflicted the undergraduates toiling in their cold rooms. It used to be said that the wind came straight from the steppes of Siberia, and there are many who wished that it had stayed there.

But the relative isolation and discomfort of the university have also encouraged sterner virtues; for many years the tone of Cambridge has been one of high seriousness, of moral earnestness and intellectual enquiry which are as evident in the Apostles of the nineteenth century as in the Leavisites of the twentieth. Perhaps I may be allowed a brief passage of autobiography in this place. I remember my own intoxication with poetry when I was an undergraduate at Clare College; with a great friend from King's, Kevin Stratford (a wonderful poet who died too young), the streets and alleys of the town, the walks by the meandering river, and the rooms of our contemporaries, became the setting for discussions which lasted long into the night. We shared our enthusiasms, and acknowledged our ambitions. That early period in my life still summons up for me the enduring atmosphere and permanent enchantment of the university. Mr Chainey's book has rekindled those memories in a delightful way; his is a work of scholarship and learning, but one that effortlessly and wittily conveys the central importance of Cambridge in the literary life of the nation. Here, in these pages, is our true inheritance.

Preface

Many books have been written descriptive of the buildings of Cambridge, or chronicling the development of the institutions of its university and town; fewer attempts have been made to chronicle the imaginative life that gives any place its most significant value and that in its peculiar richness makes Cambridge so seminal an influence on the literature of the nation. Yet there is a special fascination in chronicling the way in which a particular locality – its landmarks and innate characteristics only slowly changing over the centuries – can exert different influences over different people and different periods, and itself be reinterpreted through the eyes and words of those who pass through it. For, as much as a place moulds those who live in it, those who live in it make the place, and this must be especially true when they possess some of the most gifted and original minds in the nation's history.

This book is for all those for whom the bricks and stones of a place are nothing until they are invested with the spirit and remembrance of those who have inhabited them, and who share Wordsworth's imaginative feeling for the spirit of place:

> I could not print
> Ground where the grass had yielded to the steps
> Of generations of illustrious men,
> Unmoved.

I am grateful to the following for the help they have provided during my research for this book: Mrs Muriel Brittain (Assistant Keeper of the Records, Jesus College), Mr Richard Burns, Dr Glen Cavaliero, Mrs E. E. Duncan-Jones (*née* Phare), Dr Robert Gittings, Mr Thom Gunn, Miss Olwyn Hughes, Miss Kate Leavis (for information about the Leavis family), the late Mr Nicholas Moore, Mr Frederic Raphael, Mr Peter Redgrove, Miss Constance Babington Smith, Mr D. A. Steel (for information about André Gide), Miss Anne Stevenson, Mr Edward Upward, and Mr Clive Wilmer. I have also greatly benefited from the editorial skills of Mr Michael Hall of the Pevensey Press. I alone, however, am responsible for any factual or interpretative errors.

G.R.C.

NOTE TO THE REVISED EDITION

I have taken the opportunity offered by this new edition to correct some errors, rectify some omissions, and bring the book up to date with regard to more recent writers and with those published sources which have appeared since 1985.

Graham Chainey
Brighton, 1994

Acknowledgments

The author and publishers are grateful to the copyright holders for permission to reprint from the following works: Kingsley Amis, *What Became of Jane Austen?* (1970), Jonathan Cape Ltd; E. F. Benson, *As We Were* (1930), © Executors Estate of Rev. K. S. P. McDowell, and Chatto and Windus Ltd; John Berryman, *Love and Fame* (1971), Faber and Faber and Farrar, Straus & Giroux, Inc.; Rupert Brooke (ed. G. Keynes), *Letters* (1968), Faber and Faber; Lord Byron (ed. L. A. Marchand), *Letters and Journals* (1973–82), John Murray Ltd and Harvard University Press; S. T. Coleridge (ed. F. L. Griggs), *Collected Letters*, vol. 1 (1956), Oxford University Press; Frances Cornford, *Collected Poems* (1954), Hutchinson Books Ltd; Donald Davie, *These the Companions* (1982), Cambridge University Press, and *Collected Poems*, Routledge and Kegan Paul plc; Gavin Ewart, *The Collected Ewart* (1982), Hutchinson Books Ltd; E. M. Forster, *The Longest Journey* (1907) and *Goldsworthy Lowes Dickinson* (1934), Edward Arnold Ltd and Harcourt Brace Jovanovich, Inc.; Thom Gunn, *The Occasions of Poetry* (1982), Faber and Faber and Farrar, Straus & Giroux, Inc.; Christopher Isherwood, *Lions and Shadows* (1938), Curtis Brown Ltd (on behalf of Christopher Isherwood, © 1938 Christopher Isherwood) and Candida Donadio & Assoc., Inc.; D. H. Lawrence (ed. H. T. Moore), *Collected Letters* (1962), Copyright © 1962 by Angelo Ravagli and C. Montague Weekley, executors of the Estate of Frieda Lawrence Ravagli, reprinted by permission of Laurence Pollinger Ltd and Viking Penguin, Inc.; F. R. Leavis, *Two Cultures?* (1962), the Estate of F. R. Leavis, and Chatto & Windus Ltd; Shane Leslie, *The Cantab* (1926), the Estate of Shane Leslie, and Chatto & Windus Ltd; Malcolm Lowry, *Ultramarine*, © 1962 by Margerie Bonner Lowry, and *Under the Volcano*, the Executors of the Malcolm Lowry Estate, and Harper & Row, Publishers, Inc.; Rose Macaulay, *Three Days* (1919), A. D. Peters & Co. Ltd; A. A. Milne, *It's Too Late Now* (1939), Curtis Brown Ltd (on behalf of the Estate of A. A. Milne); Samuel Pepys (ed. R. Latham and W. Matthews), *The Diary* (1970–83), Bell & Hyman Ltd; Sylvia Plath, *Letters Home* (1975), Faber and Faber, and Harper & Row, Publishers, Inc.; John Cowper Powys, *Autobiography* (1934), Laurence Pollinger

Ltd and the Estate of John Cowper Powys; Siegfried Sassoon, *Memoirs of an Infantry Officer* (1930) and *The Old Century* (1938), Faber and Faber and Viking Penguin Ltd; W. M. Thackeray (ed. G. N. Ray), *The Letters and Private Papers* (1945), Belinda Norman-Butler, Oxford University Press and Harvard University Press; H. G. Wells, *The New Machiavelli* (1911), the Literary Executors of the Estate of H. G. Wells; Leonard Woolf, *Sowing* (1960), the Estate of Leonard Woolf, The Hogarth Press and Harcourt Brace Jovanovich, Inc.

Christopher Isherwood kindly gave his permission to publish for the first time his poem printed on pp. 240–1.

Grateful acknowledgment is made to the following for permission to reproduce illustrations: *Titlepage* Tate Gallery, London; 1, 25 photo: Ernest Frankl, The Pevensey Press; 2, 3 photos: Charlotte Hall; 4 The Master, Fellows and Scholars of Corpus Christi College, Cambridge; 5, 7, 12, 13, 15, 17, 22, 26, 34, 38, 41, 45 The National Portrait Gallery, London; 6, 19 The Master and Fellows of Trinity College, Cambridge; 8 Dr D. E. Coombe; 9, 11 The Master and Fellows, Magdalene College, Cambridge; 10, 14 The Cambridgeshire Collection, Cambridgeshire Libraries; 16 The Master and Fellows of St John's College, Cambridge; 18, 27, 28 Cambridge University Library; 20 The British Library; 21, 33 The Fitzwilliam Museum, Cambridge; 23 Lincolnshire Library Service; 24 The Tennyson Research Centre Collection, Lincoln, by courtesy of Lord Tennyson and the Lincolnshire Library Service; 30 The Master and Fellows of Trinity Hall, Cambridge; 31, 35, 54 The Provost and Fellows of King's College, Cambridge; 32 Miss F. M. McCormick; 36 The Hogarth Press; 37 Mr Timothy Moore; 39 The Hulton Deutsch Collection; 40 Miss Ursula Bickersteth; 42 Mr John Schroder; 43 Mr Peter Ward; 44 Mrs Sophie Gurney; 46, 51, 52, 53 Mr Peter Lofts (Ramsey & Muspratt); 47 from V. Nabokov, *Speak, Memory* (1967), by permission of Mrs V. Nabokov; 48, 49 Mr Edward Upward; 50 Miss Kate Leavis; 54 Mr Thom Gunn; 56 photo: John Haynes; 57, 58 Cambridge Newspapers Ltd; 59 photo: Julian Calder (*The Daily Telegraph*); 60 photo: Glynn Griffiths (*The Independent*).

Some myths and a tale

Francis Brackyn, Recorder of Cambridge, greeting King James I on the outskirts of the town on 7 March 1615, expatiated grandiloquently on the origins of the university the king had come to visit.

> Touchinge the antiquitie and denomination, historians testifie it was builded before Christs incarnation, with a castle, towers, and walls of defence, by Duke Cantaber, the sonne of the Kinge of Spayne, who was entertained in England by Kinge Gurguntius . . .
>
> The Muses did branch from Athens to Cambridge, and were lovinglie lodged in the houses of Citizens untill Ostles and Halls were erected for them without endowments, and nowe the materials of the castle, towers, and walls are converted into Colleges, beautifieing this famous universitie.

It is not recorded whether Brackyn, more than once the subject of personal lampoon in student plays, spoke with subtle sarcasm or simple obsequiousness; but fables such as the one about Duke Cantaber had already enjoyed centuries of acceptance among more scholarly minds than his, and were far from being discredited yet. For though Cambridge University is old (it traces its origins to the early thirteenth century) and Cambridge town older (the Romans settled in the area around Castle Hill), according to medieval writers there existed a fabulous Cambridge of legendary creation which had risen and flourished in the remotest depths of antiquity.

The authentic early history of Cambridge is obscure, episodic, violent. Sited at a crossing of road and stream and on turbulent territorial borderlands, the town was a military and commercial station that prospered and decayed, was fortified and sacked, under Roman, Dane and Norman. The earliest references to it in literature are accordingly vague and fragmentary. Bede tells how in 696 the monks of Ely were sent to find a stone with which to make a tomb for their foundress, Queen Etheldreda. They boarded boat and 'came to a small abandoned city, not far from thence, called Grantacaister', where, finding the very thing, 'a white marble tomb, most beautifully wrought', they carried it off, thanking God.

'Grantacaister' is presumed to be the abandoned Roman town rather than the present-day village of Grantchester, two miles upstream. Two centuries later, the 'Anglo-Saxon Chronicle' speaks of a Danish army wintering here in 875. The town is now called 'Grantabrycge', the first recorded use of the word 'bridge' in the English language. In 1010 the Danes again ravaged the area and burnt the town, the men of Cambridgeshire gaining lasting repute for their resistance.

The sound of the monks of Ely singing, according to the twelfth-century 'Liber Eliensis', touched the heart of the Danish conqueror Canute (who ruled England 1016–35) as he arrived there by boat, causing him to burst into an impromptu song with English words, of which the first verse is preserved, and which is possibly the earliest literary composition connected with the area:

> Merie sungen the muneches binnen Ely,
> Tha Cnut ching reu ther by.
> Roweth, cnites, noer the land,
> And here we thes muneches saeng.

('Merrily sang the monks of Ely, when King Canute rowed thereby. "Row, knights, near the land, and let us hear these monks' song."')

After the Norman Conquest, Domesday Book (1086) records 'Grantebrigge' as having ten wards and four hundred houses. Just as the Romans had to contend with Boudicca, the Normans had to suppress the Saxon resistance organised by Hereward, who carried out guerrilla operations from Ely's watery fastnesses. His deeds inspired local folk legends, many of which were enshrined in such chronicles as the 'Gesta Herewardi', the 'Liber Eliensis', and a late-fourteenth-century forgery, the 'Historia Croylandis', purporting to be from the pen of Hereward's contemporary Ingulf, Abbot of Crowland (d. 1109). This tradition provided the basis for two Victorian novels, Charles MacFarlane's *The Camp of Refuge* (1844) and Charles Kingsley's *Hereward the Wake* (1866). Kingsley in passing gave new life to a story in another forgery, the continuation of Ingulf's chronicle attributed to Peter de Blois, that it was Joffrid, Ingulf's Norman successor as Abbot of Crowland, who first established, in 1109, a school of learning at Cambridge. 'Peter de Blois' relates:

> He sent to the abbey's manor at Cottenham, near Cambridge, Gislebert, his fellow monk and Professor of Divinity, with three other monks who had accompanied him into England; who, being learned in philosophical theorems and other primitive sciences, journeyed daily to Cambridge and there publicly taught their sciences in a barn they had hired, rapidly attracting a great concourse of scholars. By the second year after their coming the number of scholars had grown so great, coming from all over the country as well as the town, that neither the largest house or barn, nor any church, could contain them.

'Peter de Blois' is engagingly circumstantial about the times of day at which the various subjects were taught and the names of the four good monks who had unwittingly founded the university. 'And thus from a small fountain which grew into a great river, we behold the city of God enriched and all England made fruitful, by so many Masters and Doctors proceeding from Cambridge.'

Other accounts were more ambitious. For, once Cambridge began to have real pretensions to academic standing, its largely unromantic early history could not satisfy the imaginations of medieval authors. The absence of genuine documents was a gift rather than a hindrance to monks with time on their hands and a desire to gild their university's reputation. Thus a 'Charter' signed by King Arthur in 531 turned up to give the university a useful royal founder, while 'Papal Bulls' dated 624 and 689 accorded it the blessings of popes.

The poet John Lydgate (c. 1370–1451) appears to have been one of the first to celebrate Duke Cantaber. Born at Lidgate near Newmarket and spending much of his life in the monastery at Bury St Edmunds, Lydgate in about 1440 wrote some 'Verses on the Foundation of the University of Cambridge' in which, citing Bede and Alfred of Beverley, he attributes the university's foundation to Duke Cantaber in the year 4348 from the beginning of the world (c. 373 BC).

> Fower thowsand complete by accomptes clere
> And three hundreth by computacion
> Joyned therto eight and fortie yeare,
> When Cantebro gave the fundacion
> Of thys cytie and this famous towne
> And of this noble universitie
> Sett on this ryver which is called Cante.

Cantaber, who had studied at Athens, brought with him the philosophers Anaximander and Anaxagoras. Later, according to Lydgate, Cambridge was visited by Julius Caesar himself, who was so impressed he took many 'clarkes of famouse renowne' back to Rome.

Nicholas Cantalupe (d. 1441), prior of a monastery at Northampton, in a Latin work of about the same date on the university's origins, tells how Duke Cantaber, exiled from Cantabrigia in Spain, married the daughter of King Gurguntius of Britain and was awarded the eastern part of the realm. In token of gratitude, 'he built on the River Cante a great city to which he gave his name, and summoned astronomers and philosophers thither from Athens'. (Cantalupe gives the year as 4321.) Under King Cassibelan, the university entered an idealistic, expansionist, and devoutly Christian era; but the Romans destroyed 'that glorious city, the mother of philosophy, beautiful in its habitations, defended on all sides by towers, girt with walls made of squared stone', and slaughtered its priests and scholars, including the 'athlete of God, Amphibalus, rector of the schools of Cambridge.' The epithet 'athlete of God' happily combines the classical and Christian features of this dreamt-up city of antiquity. Cantalupe's version was transcribed c. 1509 into a manuscript known as the 'Cambridge Black Book', along with some of the spurious Charters and Bulls, which he may also have concocted. His precise connection with Cambridge is not known. The legend is further recounted in the 'Historia' of John Rous (c. 1411–91), chantry priest of Warwick, who is scrupulous also to report that the town of Oxford (but not its university) was founded by Mempricius in the days of Samuel.

Though Cantaber was the preferred founder of the university, he was not without rival. The Italian historian Polydore Vergil, for instance, in his *Historia Anglica* of 1534, assigned the honour to Sigebert, King of the East Angles, in 630 – an alternative tradition followed by, among others, John Leland, the Tudor antiquary. For centuries such legends retained general credence, being paraded, with suitable rhetoric, on ceremonial occasions such as royal visits, often by those who should have known better. In 1507 John Fisher, Chancellor of the University and the mainspring of Cambridge's great Renaissance expansion, repeated the Cantaber tradition in an oration before Henry VII and the Lady Margaret; in 1564 Queen Elizabeth heard it from the lips of the Public Orator, whose boast that Cambridge, whether founded by Cantaber or Sigebert, was certainly older than Oxford (whose university could unearth no founder more ancient than King Alfred), evoked anger in the sister university. Thomas Caius, Fellow of All Souls, at once wrote a defence of Oxford to which John Caius (no relation), second founder of Gonville and Caius College, responded in 1568 with a weighty treatise *De Antiquitate Cantabrigiensis Academiae*, in which he displayed both great erudition and, for someone who was also a genuine historian of Cambridge, astonishing credulity. Thomas Caius replied again, their books went into fresh editions, and a controversy was fanned that by the mid-seventeenth century had become a heated political issue. Sir Symonds D'Ewes (1602–50), antiquarian and staunch Cantab, defended Cambridge's precedence in a speech to the House of Commons in 1640 in high style:

> If I do not therefore prove that *Cambridge* was a renowned Citie at least 500 yeares before there was a house of *Oxford* standing and whilest bruite beasts fed, or Corne was sowne on that place where the same Citie is now seated: And that *Cambridge* was a Nursery of Learning before *Oxford* was knowne to have a Grammar Schoole in it, I will yeeld up the bucklers.

As late as 1753, Edmund Carter began his *History of the University of Cambridge* with a muddled résumé of the legends, confusing Cantaber with Sigebert, Romans with Saxons, and Grantchester with Cambridge, and printing a letter supposedly from the Anglo-Saxon writer Alcuin to the scholars of Cambridge, recalling his student days at Cambridge under Bede. (In reality Bede died the year Alcuin was born, 735, five centuries before Cambridge University existed.)

An unconnected and perhaps more interesting medieval legend is that associated with Wandlebury, the Iron Age fort that crowns the Gog Magog Hills just south-east of Cambridge. Gervase of Tilbury reports in his 'Otia Imperialia' of about 1211:

> In England, on the borders of the diocese of Ely, there is a town called Cantabrica, just outside of which is a place known as Wandlebiria, from the fact that the

Wandeli [Vandals], when ravaging Britain and savagely putting to death the Christians, placed their camp there. Now, on the hill-top where they pitched their tents, is a level space ringed with entrenchments and with a single point of entry, like a gate. A very ancient legend exists, preserved in popular tradition, that if a warrior enters this level space at dead of night by moonlight and calls out 'Knight to knight, come forth', he will at once be faced by a warrior armed for fight, who charging horse against horse, will either dismount his adversary or himself be dismounted.

According to Gervase, a knight called Osbert, staying with friends in the town, heard this legend and decided to test it. Dressed in full armour, he entered Wandlebury and called out the challenge. The magical opponent duly appeared, they jousted, and Osbert won; but as he was leading away the captured horse, his fallen foe hurled his javelin and wounded him in the thigh – a wound that subsequently gave pain on every anniversary of the tournament. Although Osbert proudly displayed the horse that night 'with its fierce eyes, erect neck and black mane', at cockcrow it burst its reins and vanished.[1] Sir Walter Scott acknowledged Gervase's story as the source for an episode in his poem *Marmion* (1808) in which King Alexander III jousts with a Goblin Knight in a similar location (Canto III, stanza XXIII). Sir Thomas Malory in *Le Morte Darthur* (1470) refers to 'Wandesborow castle', which has been identified with Wandlebury Ring; a recent theory suggests Malory himself may have lived at Papworth St Agnes, fifteen miles north-west of Cambridge, rather than in Warwickshire as tradition-ally believed. The ancient figure of a giant, cut into the turf at Wandlebury, was apparently visible until the nineteenth century. T. C. Lethbridge, who excavated the site in the 1950s, published his interpretation (not accepted by other archaeologists) in *Gogmagog: The Buried Gods* (1957).[2]

No doubt legends such as these, with their Christian knights, enlightened princes, magnificent towered walls, and epochs of Athenian scholarship, served as compensation for the medieval reality: a huddled, unwalled town on a capriciously flooding river, visited by plagues and leprosy, hedged by fens and bandits, stricken by fires and riots. It is not definitely known whether Geoffrey Chaucer (c. 1340–1400) ever came to Cambridge, but his 'Reeve's Tale', set in the village of Trumpington just south of Cambridge, shows convincing familiarity with actual medieval life in the area.

Among the pilgrims portrayed in Chaucer's *Canterbury Tales* are a drunken miller, who contributes a bawdy tale set in Oxford, and a choleric reeve from Norfolk, who replies with an equally bawdy one of Cambridge. Reeves (estate stewards) were all too familiar with the trickster ways of millers, and

---

[1] The legend is retold in the fourteenth-century 'Gesta Romanorum' (Tale no. 155) and in William Harrison's *Description of England* (1577).

[2] According to Lethbridge, 'Gogmagog' was a generic name applied by later generations to any such giant figure. The earliest recorded use of the name Gog Magog Hills is 1574 (C. H. Cooper, *Annals of Cambridge*, ii. 321). The name Wandlebury is infinitely older.

Chaucer's reeve clearly relishes telling how a particularly bumptious miller gets his deserts.

Simkin, the miller in his tale, lives at Trumpington, where his mill stands by a bridge across the Cam (which Chaucer calls a 'brook', in contrast to Lydgate's 'large brode ryver'). This mill, which actually existed and is recorded in Domesday Book, is last mentioned in 1467, but its ruins were still visible in 1753, according to Carter's *History of Cambridgeshire*. It stood beside what is now known as Byron's Pool, and in pre-Byronic days was still called Old Mills.

> At Trumpyngtoun, nat fer fro Cantebrigge,
> Ther gooth a brook, and over that a brigge,
> Upon the whiche brook ther stant a melle;
> And this is verray sooth that I yow telle:
> A millere was ther dwellynge many a day.
> As any pecok he was proud and gay.

Simkin is an extrovert, swellheaded character, thieving and impudent, with knives and daggers stuck in his belt and a constant eye to the main chance.[3] His wife, full of fancy airs, is in fact the local parson's daughter (and so illegitimate). Their daughter Malin, snub-nosed like her father, is buxom and twenty. The parson is being particular about whom this granddaughter marries: he wants someone well-to-do who can inherit his living – a typically scandalous state of affairs that probably mirrors historical truth in fourteenth-century Trumpington.

The whole family, in short, is ripe for comeuppance; and one day two poor scholars, John and Aleyn, come to the mill from the college known as 'the Soler Halle at Cantebrigge'. Soler Hall is probably based on the actual King's Hall (founded in 1326, later merged into Trinity College), which at the time Chaucer was writing the *Canterbury Tales* (between 1387 and his death) was both the largest and, through its royal connections, the most important of the seven or eight existing foundations. The details accord: the original buildings of King's Hall did have upper rooms called solars; the college had a large number of northern students; and it placed greater emphasis on civil law than other colleges – and John and Aleyn suggest by their speech that they are from the north and studying law. But King's Hall was never known as Soler Hall (though real foundations, such as Garret Hostel at Cambridge and Oriel College at Oxford, were often named after architectural features) and Chaucer's scene-setting is plausible rather than literal.

With its sluggish stream, Cambridge had few mills and it was not unusual for a college to send its meal as far as Trumpington to be ground. But the manciple of Soler Hall is ill and unable to oversee the milling and Simkin is stealing even more

---

[3] Simkin's pugnacity is interesting in view of the fact that a miller of Trumpington was killed c. 1375. Cooper's *Annals of Cambridge* has references under 1406 and 1420 to the deceit of Cambridge millers.

than usual. John and Aleyn, however, volunteer to go in the manciple's place, and arrive at Trumpington with the college's weekly sack of wheat to try and outwit the miller. But though they position themselves where they can watch the corn go in and the flour come out, Simkin causes a diversion by releasing their horse, which they have to chase all over the neighbouring fen. By the time they get back it is nightfall and Simkin has filched half a bushel of the college's flour for himself. Knowing the town gates will be closed, they have to beg him to let them stay the night – a situation he makes satirical use of:

> Myn hous is streit, but ye han lerned art;
> Ye konne by argumentes make a place
> A myle brood of twenty foot of space.

His tone changes, however, when they produce good silver. Sending Malin to fetch ale from the village, he roasts them a goose, foreseeing a merry evening at their expense. He does not foresee, as he solicitously prepares them a bed with sheets and blankets in the family bedroom, that they in the night will get their revenge.

> And in his owene chambre hem made a bed,
> With sheetes and with chalons faire yspred
> Noght from his owene bed ten foot or twelve.
> His doghter hadde a bed, al by hirselve,
> Right in the same chambre by and by . . .

The 'Reeve's Tale' is unusual among Chaucer's tales in being set in a specific locality, and it would be interesting to know how exactly he came by his local detail. His family had East Anglian connections (a John Chaucer is mentioned as a bailiff of Cambridge in the records of a court case of 1411);[4] he may often have passed through the area on his way to attend to business in Norfolk; and he may have visited Cambridge in 1388 when parliament was held there as part of the authorities' clampdown in the wake of the Peasants' Revolt. On the latter occasion Richard II lodged at Barnwell Priory but the court was entertained at King's Hall itself, where, however, according to Thomas Fuller's *History of the University of Cambridge* (1655), 'all things were so conveniently contrived, that the courtiers all had lodgings and offices by themselves, without meeting with the scholars, save only in the passage towards the kitchen'. Though not actually a member of this parliament, Chaucer may well have come on business.

   Even if Chaucer lacked first-hand experience of the locality, he certainly must have known many graduates of King's Hall, since many of them entered the royal service. In addition, a contemporary of his in the household had been Sir Roger of Trumpington himself, whose wife Blanche was a fellow lady-in-waiting with Chaucer's wife Philippa to Constance of Castile. Sir Roger, who died in 1378 and

---

4 Cooper, *Annals of Cambridge*, i. 153.

was the great-great-grandson of the crusader whose brass is in Trumpington church, inherited the manor in 1368, though he resided in Bedfordshire. The mill was for long rented by the Trumpingtons from the more important Cayley manor.

But it is tempting, and not too fanciful, to imagine Chaucer himself in Cambridge on one or another occasion: supping in King's Hall and absorbing local gossip, paying a visit to friends at Trumpington, stopping by with his keen and enquiring eye to examine the imposing mill by the pool before riding back beside the meandering river into the crowded medieval town. Neither Chaucer nor even the wildly imaginative authors of medieval legends could have foreseen the centre of learning that the town would eventually grow into.

2

Heretics' Hill

About 1491 a 'poet' is recorded as employed by the university. An Italian named Caius Auberinus, his job was to write Latin orations and letters at twenty pence a time. 'Such was the conception of poetry at Cambridge', comments Arthur Gray, 'at the beginning of the century which in its closing years saw the production of the *Faerie Queene* and *Doctor Faustus*'.[1]

The previous century, following Chaucer's death in 1400, had indeed been blank, almost its only poet of note being the satirist John Skelton (c. 1460–1529), who was also possibly the first poet to be educated at Cambridge ('Alma parens, O Cantabrigiensis', he exclaims in his last poem) – perhaps at Peterhouse. Records mention a Skelton about to graduate in 1480, and a 'Scheklton' proceeding MA in 1484. A tradition that he was curate of Trumpington and, like Caius Auberinus, composed official documents for the university has not been confirmed; the curate of Trumpington *was* a university copyist, and in 1507 is known to have translated two of Skelton's Latin squibs into English, which possibly led to his later being confused with Skelton himself.

After a life at court as cleric-poet and tutor to the infant Henry VIII, Skelton spent his later years as rector of Diss in Norfolk, gaining a certain notoriety for his unclerical lifestyle there (he was married and had children). But he himself always considered that his chief claim to glory was his appointment as 'poet laureate' at Oxford in about 1488. This was an honorary title, quite distinct from the later royal appointment, and was roughly equivalent to a doctorate in grammar, the main test of eligibility apparently being the composition of one hundred lines of Latin in praise of Oxford University. The University of Louvain awarded him the same honour in 1492, Cambridge in 1493. Henry VII, who admired Skelton, gave him a special dress of green and white embroidered in gold silk with the name 'Calliope', the ancient muse of epic poetry; and at Cambridge he was accorded the privilege of wearing this dress in place of academic robes.

[1] *Cambridge and its Story* (Methuen, 1912), p. 157.

In many ways the last poet of medieval England, Skelton was a cantankerous, unconventional figure, not afraid in his earlier days to pen satires on the court and on the powerful Cardinal Wolsey, yet at the end proving a reactionary opposer of the new Renaissance learning that was beginning to permeate England from Italy. In his poem 'Speak, Parrot' (1521) he castigates the introduction of Greek studies at Cambridge as upsetting the time-honoured scholastic studies of the 'trivium' (grammar, logic, and rhetoric: the BA course) and 'quadrivium' (arithmetic, geometry, music, and astronomy: the MA course):

> In *Achademia* Parrot dare no probleme kepe;
> For *Greci fari* so occupyeth the chayre,
> That *Latinum fari* may fall to rest and slepe,
> And *silogisari* was drowned at Sturbrydge Fayre;
> Tryvyals and quadryvyals so sore now they appayre
> That Parrot the popagay hath pytye to beholde
> How the rest of good lernyng is roufled up and trold.[2]

His last poem, 'A Replication Against Certain Young Scholars Abjured of Late' (1528), is an even more blistering attack on two of the growing group of Cambridge reformers, Thomas Bilney and Thomas Arthur, whose public censure of certain Romish practices had brought them into serious conflict with Wolsey. (Bilney was eventually burnt at Norwich for heresy.) Dedicated to Wolsey, the poem is a splenetic stream of invective against modern Cambridge students.

The aging Skelton, however, was a lone rock amid the incoming tide not only of the Renaissance but also of the Reformation, in which Cambridge was to be especially important. In addition to Bilney and Arthur, the university produced many celebrated members of the movement for reform. Thomas Cranmer (1485–1556), compiler of the English Prayer Book and Archbishop of Canterbury, was made a Fellow of Jesus College in 1515 (he lost his fellowship when he married the niece of the landlady of the nearby Dolphin tavern, but regained it when she died in childbirth). Nicholas Ridley (1500–55), who studied at Pembroke and was later Master of the college, remembered Cambridge in his farewell letter written on the eve of his execution as the place 'where I have dwelt longer, found more faithful and hearty friends, received more benefits . . . than ever I did in mine own native country wherein I was born'. Hugh Latimer (c. 1485–1555) of Clare, who began as an opponent of reform, owed his spiritual conversion to Bilney, with whom he walked daily about Castle Hill, which gained the soubriquet 'Heretics' Hill' in consequence. Others included Miles Coverdale (1488–1568) and William Tyndale (d. 1536), translators of the Bible. It was men like these, meeting in such places as the long-vanished White Horse Inn near

---

[2] The annual Sturbridge Fair, founded in 1211, was held just outside the town and usually completely interrupted the university's studies. 'Trold' means 'trundled away'.

King's College ('Germany' as it became called from their Lutheran proclivities), who made Cambridge the main driving force for church reform in England, despite opposition from the authorities (Luther's books were publicly burnt by the university, on Wolsey's orders, in 1521) and the mortal risk their avocations incurred: almost all of them in time went to the stake for their beliefs – Cranmer, Latimer, and Ridley perishing at Oxford during the reign of the Catholic Queen Mary. In Macaulay's words, 'Cambridge had the honour of educating those celebrated Protestant Bishops whom Oxford had the honour of burning.'

Among a number of eminent Continental scholars invited to Cambridge, none so added to the lustre and expanded the range of Cambridge learning as the Dutchman Desiderius Erasmus (c. 1466–1536), who arrived in 1511 at the invitation of his friend John Fisher, Chancellor of the University. For Cambridge, Erasmus's two-and-a-half-year stay was a tremendous boost: the first professor of Greek at Cambridge and the first person to teach Greek there at all, he was later additionally appointed Lady Margaret Professor of Divinity. Erasmus lived in Queens' College, of which Fisher had been President, probably in the tower in Pump Court overlooking Silver Street which still bears his name; and among the projects he worked on during his stay were his Greek edition of the New Testament – the first accurate one in the original language – and his edition of St Jerome.

For Erasmus, Cambridge meant one or two friends, tolerable libraries, and a reasonable salary; but the tone of the thirty-one letters that he wrote from Cambridge is largely one of complaint. The first, written on arrival to his friend Andrea Ammonio, an Italian in the papal service in London, complains of the horrors of the journey down, and sniffs: 'I expect I shall stay at this college for a few days, anyway.' The college ale, he laments at once, does not suit him at all (Erasmus suffered from the stone) and he begs Ammonio to send him a cask of Greek wine. In fact Ammonio sent Erasmus four casks during his stay, but two arrived unsealed and spoilt, eliciting rage against the boorish and thieving natives. To his friend John Colet, the founder of St Paul's School and the leading English humanist of the day, Erasmus wrote that he hardly expected to get rich in Cambridge – 'what can I filch from people without a rag to their backs?' Full of personal gripings and Continental politics, the letters are disappointingly silent on any of the positive aspects of the scenes around him. There is no mention of such building projects as St John's College (founded, largely on Fisher's initiative, the year Erasmus arrived) or King's College Chapel (now nearing completion), nor of meetings or discussions with any of the reforming spirits.

Despite the diet, the climate, the barbaric Latin of the scholars, the perfidy of the locals, and the recurrent outbreaks of plague, Erasmus stuck Cambridge out as long as he could, finding excuses to stay away in the winter or shutting himself up in his turret with his books. But at last he had had enough.

Then winter came on, and, towards the close of each shortening day, Erasmus could mark from his window the white fogs rolling in from the surrounding marshes, reminding him of the climate he most of all disliked, – the climate of his native Holland; while day after day, the sound of footsteps, in the courts below, grew rarer and rarer. At last the gloom, the solitude, the discomfort, and the panic, became more than he could bear; and, one night, the customary lamp no longer gleamed from a certain casement in the south-west tower. And when the fear of the plague was over, and the university returned, it was known that Erasmus had left Cambridge; and no doubt many a sturdy defender of the old learning said he was very glad to hear it, and heartily hoped that all this stir about Greek, and St Jerome, and errors in the Vulgate, was at an end.[3]

In January 1514, after the college ale had brought on a particularly alarming attack of the stone, he rode back to London, as ill-tempered and ill-disposed as he had come.

A short work by Erasmus on the art of letter-writing, brought out in a pirated edition in 1521 by John Siberch (who had come over from Siegburg, near Bonn), was one of the first books to be printed in Cambridge. (The first English press was that started by Caxton at Westminster in 1477; the first book printed in Oxford appeared in 1478.) Siberch stayed about two years in Cambridge, printing about ten books in all, the very first being the text of a speech of welcome given by Henry Bullock of Queens' (one of Erasmus's favourite pupils) on the occasion of a visit by Wolsey in 1520. After Siberch's departure, no books were printed at Cambridge for sixty years.

One of the first students at St John's when it opened its doors in 1516 was a precocious twelve-year-old, later to become the illustrious courtier-poet Sir Thomas Wyatt (c. 1503–42). Together with the Earl of Surrey, Wyatt was to lead the fashion for importing Italian forms and metres into English. At Cambridge he became a close friend of John Leland of Christ's (c. 1506–52), who was later appointed 'King's Antiquary' by Henry VIII and travelled the country at the dissolution of the monasteries expropriating the choicest manuscripts for the royal libraries. Two other antiquaries of the day were also Cambridge men: Raphael Holinshed, whose *Chronicles* provided source material for the plots of many of Shakespeare's English history plays, was at either Trinity Hall or Christ's in about 1544; while William Harrison (1534–93), whose college is not known, wrote in his *Description of England* (1577) that 'for uniformity of building, orderly compaction and refinement, the town of Cambridge exceedeth that of Oxford . . . by many a fold.'

Among the first students at Trinity College, founded by Henry VIII in 1546, was George Gascoigne (c. 1525–77), who was to make his mark as a poet,

---

[3] James Bass Mullinger, *The University of Cambridge*, i. 506. A fictional recreation of the Cambridge of the time is to be found in N. M. Wilby's novel *Alexander Tomlyn* (1933), in which both Erasmus and Fisher appear. The novel's hero is the first scholar at Christ's College.

playwright, and critic. One of the foundation fellows there was the mysterious Dr John Dee (1527–1608), who, after graduating from St John's in 1545, taught Greek for a while at Trinity. Here he undertook a production of Aristophanes' *Peace* in the college hall, in which amazement was caused when a winged scarab flew through the air with a man and a basket of victuals on its back. By this clever stage effect, Dee first acquired the reputation as a magician that was later endorsed by his scientific and astrological experiments in London.

Thomas Tusser (1525–80), the farmer–poet known for his verse anthology of practical wisdom, *Five Hundred Good Points of Husbandry* (1557), in which many proverbial sayings had their origins, came up from Eton to Trinity Hall, as he tells in his 'Metrical Autobiography':

> From London hence, to Cambridge thence,
> With thanks to thee, O Trinitee,
> That to thy hall, so passing all,
>   I got at last:
> There joy I felt, there trim I dwelt,
> There heaven from hell I shifted well;
> With learned men, a number then,
>   the time I past.

Thomas Fuller in his *Worthies of England* (1662) recounts how Tusser 'was successively a musician, schoolmaster, serving-man, husbandman, grazier, poet; more skilful in all than thriving in any vocation; he spread his bread with all sorts of butter, yet none would stick thereon'. Unsuccessful, despite his own fund of good advice, as a Suffolk farmer, Tusser returned to his old college in about 1574 as singing clerk in the chapel:

> When gaines was gone, and yeres grew on,
> And death did crie, from London flie,
> In Cambridge then, I found agen,
>   a resting plot;
> In college best of all the rest,
> With thanks to thee, O Trinitee,
> Through thee and thine, for me and mine,
>   some stay I got.

But he was destined to die in a London debtors' prison.

A writer who was to give an important impetus to English prose was Roger Ascham[4] (1515–68), who entered St John's in 1530. Ascham was made a fellow soon after graduating and went on to lecture in Greek, but his promising academic career was frustrated by college politics and illness. It was during his convalescence that Ascham began to devote himself to a sport not favoured by the university authorities – archery – and in 1545 he published a treatise on the

---

[4] Spelt in the fashionable Greek style, but pronounced *Askam*.

subject, *Toxophilus: The School of Shooting Contained in Two Books*, dedicated to the king. In it, Ascham argued that physical exercise should be promoted as an accompaniment to study, not condemned as dissipating a scholar's abilities. Even the assiduous Erasmus, not easily parted from his books, accepted this 'when he was here at Cambridge; which when he had been sore at his book (as Garrett our bookbinder hath very often told me)[5] for lack of better exercise, would take his horse, and ride about the Market Hill'. Like a good bow, Ascham says, the dedicated scholar profits from regular 'unbending'. Although it was one of the earliest prose treatises to be written in English instead of Latin, in style and structure *Toxophilus* is soundly classical, comprising a Platonic dialogue between two Cambridge scholars strolling in the fields after dinner on a sunny spring day. The king, himself a keen bowman, rewarded Ascham with a pension.

In 1546 Ascham was appointed Public Orator, a post first established in 1522, the duties of which included not only the delivery of Latin orations on ceremonial occasions but also the drafting of official university letters – a function previously fulfilled by 'poets' like Caius Auberinus. Two years later, however, he left Cambridge to become tutor to the Princess Elizabeth, who as queen appointed him her Latin secretary. At his death he left unfinished the other work for which he is remembered, *The Scholemaster*, an exposition of Renaissance educational ideals. In it he glances back with fondness at St John's – 'such a company of fellows and scholars . . . as can scarce be found in some whole University' – but laments the effects of Mary's reign, when progressive scholars were supplanted by bogus upstarts and by 'hedge priests, fetched out of the country'. He laments, too, the influx of the courtly rich set (young blades like Wyatt, presumably) who first began to frequent the university at this time. 'Then began simplicity in apparel to be laid aside, courtly gallantness to be taken up, frugality in diet was privately disliked, towngoing to good cheer openly used.' The university, formerly an ascetic training ground for clergy and schoolteachers, had now additionally become a finishing school for courtiers and aristocrats. However, since the accession of Queen Elizabeth,

> the young spring hath shot up so fair, as now there be in Cambridge again many goodly plants . . . which are like to grow to mighty great timber, to the honour of learning and great good of their country, if they may stand their time . . . and if some old doterel trees, with standing over-nigh them and dropping upon them do not either hinder or crook their growing.

[5] Erasmus's fellow Dutchman Garrett Godfrey was one of three official booksellers in the town. The others were Nicholas Speryng and Sygar Nicholson.

3

Hatchery of wits and roaring-boys

'If doterel trees do not crook their growing' – Ascham's premonition seems at first sight not inapplicable to the case of Edmund Spenser (1552–99), who came up to Pembroke College[1] in May 1569 as a sixteen-year-old sizar.[2] At the Merchant Taylors' School in London Spenser had already learnt Italian and French and that same year he contributed translations of Petrarch and Du Bellay to a small anthology. (Another Merchant Taylors' boy, Lancelot Andrewes, later Master of the college, Bishop of Winchester, a translator of the Authorised Version of the Bible, and the author of celebrated sermons, followed Spenser to Pembroke.)

Pembroke was small – there were about forty undergraduates and the Old Court where Spenser lodged was the smallest in the university – and the young poet was soon drawn into the circle around one of the Fellows, quirky, egoistical Gabriel Harvey (c. 1545–1630). Harvey, a notable Cambridge 'character' of his day, combined genuine scholarship and progressive ideas with bombastic conceit and censorious puritanism, and was disliked by many of his colleagues. Spenser and Andrewes may have been present on the occasion when he was about to deliver his first Greek lecture in the college hall and the junior proctor, one of his particular enemies, came 'swelling in . . . and commandeth the scholars from the table, saying in his proctor's voice that I should read no lecture there'.

Spenser was drawn into intimate friendship with Harvey – a friendship sometimes depicted as threatening the development of his poetry, for Harvey was full of fashionable notions about rhyme being barbaric and the only proper metres for English poetry being the (quite alien) ones of classical Latin, which now seem

---

[1] Until the nineteenth century, Pembroke, Clare, and St Catharine's called themselves Hall rather than College. The modern style is followed throughout this book.

[2] Until the nineteenth century, students other than scholars were divided into three classes: the majority were fee-paying 'pensioners', but those from aristocratic or wealthy families entered as 'fellow-commoners', gaining, in return for extra fees, the right to wear special gowns and to eat on high table with the fellows; those too poor to afford a pensioner's fees, on the other hand, could enter as 'sizars', paying for their education through such menial tasks as waiting on high table and washing up. Spenser, Marvell, Dr Bentley, Christopher Smart, Wordsworth, and Henry Kirke White were all sizars.

merely to indicate how thoroughly the understanding of English versification had been lost since Chaucer's day. These ideas were widely discussed at the time, however, particularly at Cambridge (Ascham in his *Scholemaster* was one of their proponents), and although Spenser's true destiny was to channel English poetry back into its proper course, for the moment he explored this classical-metres cul-de-sac with Harvey, with whom he exchanged a number of letters on the subject that were published in 1580. (The specimen English hexameters Harvey sent for Spenser's edification included some apparently addressed to a bay tree at Trinity Hall.) Spenser tried his own hand at English hexameters but his natural sense of English prosody was not perverted ('Why a God's name may not we have the kingdom of our own language?' as he demanded of Harvey) and he went his own way and eventually produced *The Shepheardes Calendar* (1579) and his allegorical epic *The Faerie Queene* (1590) – a work which Harvey at first censured for its rhyme and archaic style but finally praised.[3] Spenser remained attached to Harvey, later dedicating a flattering sonnet to him, beginning

> Harvey, the happy above happiest men,
> I read; that, sitting like a looker-on
> Of this worldes stage, doest note, with critique pen,
> The sharpe dislikes of each condition . . .

and going on to praise his critical power. Harvey is also depicted as the shepherd Hobbinol in *The Shepheardes Calendar*, which was published with an introduction and glosses provided by 'E.K.' – probably Edward Kirke, Spenser's fellow sizar at Pembroke and another member of Harvey's circle.

There is little official record of Spenser's university career. It was usual at that time to study for seven years, students coming up at a much younger age than nowadays and studying three years for their BA, then four more for their MA. After taking his MA in 1576, Spenser obtained through Harvey's influence a place in the household of the Earl of Leicester, through whom he met Sir Philip Sidney. Sidney, Spenser, Harvey, and Sir Fulke Greville (1554–1628) of Jesus College formed a literary coterie called Areopagus, debating the classical-metres question and similar matters. Though Spenser did not return to Cambridge, in a stanza of *The Faerie Queene* (Book IV, Canto XI, stanza 34) he celebrates the river Ouse with its many tributaries, which, he says,

> Thence doth by Huntingdon and Cambridge flit,
> My mother Cambridge, whom as with a Crowne
> He doth adorne, and is adorn'd of it
> With many a gentle Muse and many a learned wit.

[3] Harvey indeed loved Chaucer, and was probably one of a group of Cambridge Chaucer enthusiasts which included Thomas Speght of Peterhouse (who published an early edition of Chaucer in 1598), Francis Beaumont of Peterhouse (father of the dramatist), and possibly John Whitgift of Peterhouse (later successively Master of Pembroke and of Trinity). So Spenser was in good company at Cambridge in his passion for Chaucer.

Though Spenser had left, Harvey's lean, black-suited figure continued to haunt the Cambridge scene. Forever stoking up quarrels and controversies, intimate with students but at loggerheads with colleagues, Gabriel Harvey was a don of a certain recurrent type (Oscar Browning was a later example) – lovable to some, obnoxious to others, mingling charm and vanity, ability and absurdity.[4] His commonplace book and the marginalia jotted in the books he read reveal him to have been far from the 'happy above happiest men' of Spenser's sonnet, content to be a 'looker-on'. He was a figure of curdled ambitions, longing to stride the world stage like a Machiavelli, Alexander, or Caesar, but inept at furthering himself beyond his Cambridge niche. Even there his disputatiousness served to debar him from advancement: in 1581 he was passed over for the post of Public Orator, and in 1585, though actually elected Master of Trinity Hall (to which he had migrated when Pembroke became too hot for him), his election was overruled by mandate of the queen. Finally, it was as a notorious pedant and figure of fun that he became widely known outside the university, having embroiled himself in a desperate paper war with two younger Cambridge writers, Robert Greene (1560–92) and Thomas Nashe (1567–1601).

Greene, born in Norwich, went up to St John's in 1575; Nashe, born in Lowestoft, entered the same college in 1581. Greene took his BA and roamed Europe before returning to study for his MA at Clare; after that, his career was a dizzy descent. In a deathbed pamphlet, *The Repentance of Robert Greene, Master of Arts*, written in a miserable London garret where he had been carried, so the story goes, dying of syphilis, dropsy, and a surfeit of pickled herring and Rhenish wine consumed in the company of Nashe, Greene looked back through his dissipated years at the origin of his fall. 'Being at the University, I lit among wags as lewd as myself, with whom I consumed the flower of my youth, who drew me to travel into Italy and Spain, in which places I saw and practised such villainy as is abominable to declare.' During his brief rakehell existence, Greene supported himself by producing enough pamphlets, low-life tracts, romances, and plays (including *Friar Bacon and Friar Bungay*) to fill fifteen volumes of collected works.

Though Nashe was to follow a similar path, he always retained a scholar's pride and fond memories of his college. In the preface he wrote to Greene's romance *Menaphon* (1589), he called it

---

[4] Was Harvey homosexual? In *The Shepheardes Calendar* Hobbinol laments the loss of the love of the shepherd boy Colin Clout (= Spenser), who has transferred his attention to a maiden. E.K. carefully glosses: 'In this place seemeth to be some savour of disorderly love, which the learned call paederasty: but it is gathered beside his meaning.' Hobbinol's passion is purely platonic, E.K. says. Possibly the friendship between Spenser and Harvey is the first example of the sort of *amor platonicus* that was to be common so long as the university remained an exclusively male institution.

that most famous and fortunate nurse of all learning, Saint John's in Cambridge, that at that time was an university within itself, shining so far above all other houses, halls and hospitals whatsoever, that no college in the town was able to compare with the tithe of her students; having (as I have heard grave men of credit report) more candles lit in it every winter morning before four of the clock than the four-of-the-clock gave strokes.

Ten years later, in his last book, *Nashe's Lenten Stuff*, he again referred to St John's, 'in which house once I took up my inn for seven year together lacking a quarter, and yet love it still, for it is and ever was the sweetest nurse of knowledge in all that University'.

When Nashe left Cambridge in 1586 (he did not take his MA) he embarked like Greene on a prolific writing career in London, turning his hand to anything that offered. In 1588 he and Greene were drawn into the Martin Marprelate controversy, rather curiously on the side of the Church and Establishment against the anonymous puritan pamphleteer (who may have been another Cambridge man, John Penry); and Richard Harvey, one of Gabriel Harvey's brothers, also a Fellow of Pembroke, could not resist suggesting in a pamphlet of his own that their dissolute lives scarcely qualified them for such opinions. Greene retorted in *A Quip for an Upstart Courtier* with aspersions on all three Harvey brothers as well as their father (an aged rope-maker of Saffron Walden) which were so virulent that the offending passages had to be suppressed. Suddenly the battle grew viciously personal.

Gabriel Harvey, enraged at Greene's attack, sought legal redress, but by then Greene had already died in his garret. There was still Nashe, however, who in a passage of *Pierce Penniless* (1592) assumed the cudgels, warning Gabriel: 'off with thy gown and untruss, for I mean to lash thee mightily'. In reply to Richard Harvey's insolent identification of him with one Thomas Nash, master butler at Pembroke, Nashe retorted that even the butler is 'a far better scholar than thyself . . . and one that sheweth more discretion and government in setting up a size of bread, than thou in all thy whole book'.

Gabriel Harvey stuttered back in *Four Letters and Certain Sonnets, Especially Touching Robert Greene* (1592) that Greene was 'the stale of poules, the Ape of Euphues, the Vice of the stage . . . a wild head full of mad brain and a thousand crochets . . . a pettifogger, a player, a cozener, a railer, a beggar, an omni-gatherum, a gay nothing; a store-house of bald and baggage stuff, unworth the answering . . . an image of idleness; an epitome of fantasticality; a mirror of vanity'. In one of the sonnets Harvey calls Greene

> Sir reverence, a scurvy Master of Art,
> Answered enough with a Doctor's fart

while in another, the black-humoured 'John Harvey's Welcome to Robert Greene', he imagines his brother John, himself recently dead, beckoning the dying Greene to join him:

Come, fellow Greene, come to thy gaping grave:
Bid vanity and foolery farewell:
Thou overlong hast played the madbrain'd knave,
And overloud hast rung the bawdy bell.
Vermin to vermin must repair at last.

Nashe received all this with glee: Harvey was setting himself up perfectly as a target. In *Strange News* (1593) Nashe satirised Harvey's boast to have invented English hexameters and condemned his influence on Spenser: 'Immortal Spenser, no frailty hath thy fame but the deputation of this idiot's friendship.' He eulogised Greene:

A good fellow he was, and would have drunk with thee for more angels than the lord thou libeledst on gave thee in Christ's College; and in one year he pissed as much against the walls as thou and thy two brothers spent in three.

In a night and a day would he have yarked up a pamphlet as well as in seven year, and glad was that printer that might be so blest to pay him dear for the very dregs of his wit.

Harvey's tone grew apoplectic – 'I will batter thy carrion to dirt, whence thou camst; and squeeze thy brain to a snivel, whereof it was curdled' – but Nashe's most brilliant onslaught was yet to come. In a masterpiece of character assassination, *Have with You to Saffron Walden: or Gabriel Harvey's Hunt Is Up* (1596), he fashioned a satirical biography of his victim that is a *tour de force* of styles – subtle, snide, punching, teasing, hyperbolic – dancing at arm's length and with endless verbal invention around his lumbering prey. Depicting Harvey's student days at Christ's, for instance, he invents a letter from his tutor to his father lamenting how Harvey is

distractedly enamoured of his own beauty, spending a whole forenoon every day in sponging and licking himself by the glass; and useth every night after supper to walk on the market hill to show himself, holding his gown up to his middle, that the wenches may see what a fine leg and a dainty foot he hath in pumps and pantoffles.

Again, describing how Harvey in 1578 presented some verses to the Queen at Audley End, the great house near Saffron Walden, Nashe depicts him as 'ruffling it out, huffty-tuffty, in his suit of velvet'. At the queen's remark that he looked something of an Italian (a fashionable compliment), Harvey 'quite renounced his natural English accents and gestures and wrested himself wholly to the Italian punctilios, speaking our homely island tongue strangely, as if he were but a raw practitioner in it'. When, more recently, Harvey and he both chanced to be staying at the Dolphin, with only a nailed-up wainscot door between them, Nashe couldn't help noticing that Harvey spent a fortnight in the inn's best rooms without paying, and dined every day in Trinity Hall (where he had lost his fellowship) without settling his commons. Nashe dedicated the book to Richard

Lichfield, barber at Trinity College,[5] which inspired Harvey to call his next reply *The Trimming of Thomas Nashe* and sign it with the barber's name. But the scandal had gone far enough, and in 1599 the Bishop of London ordered 'that all Nashe's books and Dr Harvey's books be taken wheresoever they may be found, and that none of the same books be ever printed hereafter'. A hard sentence for someone like Nashe who lived by the pen.

The Nashe–Harvey controversy gave entertainment, but was scarcely great literature. But in age midway between Greene and Nashe and presumably at one point contemporary with them at Cambridge was the most meteoric and original wit of the period. Christopher Marlowe (1564–93), the son of a Canterbury cobbler, came up to Corpus Christi in 1580 with one of the scholarships that Archbishop Parker, former Master of the college, had endowed for boys of the King's School, Canterbury, the award requiring that the holder be able to sing 'and, if it may be, such as can make a verse'.

Harvey has portrayed in one of his letters to Spenser the Cambridge of 1580 that Marlowe found himself in – teeming with Renaissance ideas, some of them heretical to puritanical Harvey but the very stuff of Doctor Faustus's imaginings; permeated with a new worldliness and opportunism that Marlowe would have absorbed; populated increasingly with courtly types whose dazzling presence must have whetted the scholarship boy's ambition. Harvey noted

> An exceeding great difference between the countenances and ports of those that are brave and gallant and those that are basely or meanly apparelled: between the learned and unlearned, Tully and Tom Tooly, in effect none at all . . . Machiavelli a great man . . . the French and Italian when so highly regarded of scholars, the Latin and Greek when so lightly? . . . All inquisitive after news, new books, new fashions, new laws, new officers, and some after new elements, and some after new heavens, and hells too. Turkish affairs familiarly known: castles builded in the air . . . in no age so little so much made of, everyone highly in his own favour, thinking no man's penny so good silver as his own . . . Heresy in divinity, in philosophy, in humanity, in manners . . . The devil not so hated as the pope . . . Not a few double-faced Jani, and changeable chameleons: over-many clawbacks and pickthanks: reeds shaken of every wind: jacks of both sides . . .

The first record of Marlowe at Corpus is a charge of one penny, probably for a drink on arrival, in the buttery books for December 1580. The following week he spent three shillings – extravagant for a scholar on a shilling a week. His college, bursting at the seams with the Renaissance expansion, lodged him with three other Parker scholars in a ground-floor room, a former storeroom converted to receive them, on R staircase in Old Court (then the only court).

---

[5] ' . . . the thrice egregious and censorial animadvertiser of vagrant moustachios, chief scavenger of chins, and . . . special supervisor of all excremental superfluities for Trinity College in Cambridge'. In 1591 Lichfield was instrumental in starting a notorious Cambridge riot outside St John's College (Cooper, *Annals of Cambridge*, ii. 501).

As an undergraduate, Marlowe (or Marlin or Merling as he variously spelt himself) was supposed to subscribe to a closely ruled routine: lectures in logic, philosophy, Aristotle, rhetoric; taverns and fine clothes banned; chapel at five in the morning. But the real life of undergraduates rarely follows the rules laid down for them. In *Doctor Faustus* Marlowe later expressed the opinion that students should be 'bravely clad' in silk, so possibly he did something, like many of those around him, to liven up his own 'black puke' academical dress and to 'ruffle and roist it out'. Though the university forbade public dramatic performances in the town, Marlowe may have witnessed surreptitious shows in the yards of such inns as the Eagle across the street from his college entrance, before the proctors and their men came to break up the entertainment.[6] The college library – thanks largely to Archbishop Parker's generosity – was as well stocked as any in Cambridge with works to feed his imagination. In his shared refurbished store-room, between delivering disputations and intoning plainchant in chapel, Marlowe's brain was busy with epics and exotic adventures. Here he wrote his first play, *The Tragedy of Dido*, based largely on Virgil; Nashe, whom he probably met at Cambridge, may have had some share in its composition. Here also he translated Lucan's *Pharsalia* into blank verse and Ovid's *Amores* into rhymed couplets – an invaluable poetic apprenticeship. And it was probably works in the college library such as Ortelius' atlas of the world that inspired his fascination with Timur of Persia and gave him the historical and geographical background for his first dramatic success, *Tamburlaine the Great*, the first part of which was probably begun at Cambridge.

No Elizabethan writer shows himself more of a university man than Marlowe in his plays: the student's tags and quotes, the learned references, the use of Latin at key points all indicate a scholar's mind. But, like Nashe and Greene, he chafed under the still largely medieval university system, impatient for the wider world. In *Edward II* he advises:

> you must cast the scholar off
> And learn to court it like a gentleman!
> 'Tis not a black coat and a little band . . .
> Can get you any favour with great men.
> You must be proud, bold, pleasant, resolute:
> And now and then stab as occasion serves.

No longer, as in Ascham's day, was it enough to be a gentleman and a wit within the university's bounds, taking up bowmanship or some such classically approved sport to make the whole man. The so-called 'University Wit' of the Elizabethan age needed an infinitely broader stage, needed to attack the very frontiers of

---

6 In 1600 a Corpus graduate was caught taking part in a performance at the Black Bear, 'having deformed long locks of unseemly sight, and great breeches, undecent for a graduate or scholar'. He was ordered to have his hair cut and was suspended from his degrees (Cooper, *Annals of Cambridge*, ii. 598).

experience. At the start of Marlowe's greatest and most personal play, Doctor
Faustus dismisses one by one the subjects of the academic curriculum in favour of
a more dangerous and potent knowledge.

> Is to dispute well logic's chiefest end?
> Affords this art no greater miracle?
> Then read no more, thou hast attained that end.
> A greater subject fitteth Faustus' wit.

'Marley' graduated BA in 1584. Unlike Nashe, he opted to stay on to become
an MA, even though this normally implied a willingness to take holy orders and
it is difficult to imagine Marlowe, later to proclaim himself an atheist and to
blaspheme colourfully against Saviour and saints, having any such intention.
Probably the time gave him a breathing space and cover – breathing space to get
Tamburlaine ready for the London stage, cover for his new sub-career as one of
Her Majesty's agents. For Marlowe was one of the earliest of a waywardly
unscrupulous breed of Cambridge men – often, like him, socially dazzling,
psychologically paradoxical, and with homosexual tendencies – to be recruited
into cynically pragmatic causes.

Some time at Cambridge Marlowe must have met his future patron Thomas
Walsingham, look-out and recruiting officer for his cousin Sir Francis
Walsingham, the queen's spy chief. Catholic Spain threatened invasion; in France
the seminaries at Douai and Rheims were hotbeds for disaffected English
Catholics. Eager for adventure and ambivalent enough about religion (he admired
Catholic ritual), Marlowe was assigned the job of posing as a Catholic convert
and reporting what was happening in Rheims.

Apart from his increased absences from Cambridge, nothing is known of all this
until the time came for him to receive his MA. The university, knowing only that
he had apparently defected to the Catholics, decided to withhold it. It required no
less a body than the Privy Council, with extraordinary but meaningful inter-
vention, to oblige the university to award the degree, informing them:

> Whereas it was reported that Christopher Morley was determined to have gone
> beyond the seas to Rheims, and there to remain, their Lordships thought good to
> certify that he had no such intent, but that in all his actions he had behaved
> himself orderly and discreetly, whereby he had done Her Majesty good service
> and deserved to be rewarded for his faithful dealing. Their Lordships' request was
> that the rumour thereof should be allayed by all possible means, and that he
> should be furthered in the degree he was to take this next Commencement;
> because it was not Her Majesty's pleasure that anyone employed as he had been
> in matters touching the benefit of his country should be defamed by those that are
> ignorant of the affairs he went about.

Marlowe's subsequent career was as crowded and high-pitched as one of his
own plays. A successful dramatist while Shakespeare, his exact contemporary,
was scarcely known, the friend of Raleigh and supplicant of Southampton, he died

in mysterious circumstances, stabbed in a Deptford tavern in the company of other former agents while up for impeachment for blasphemy, leaving Nashe to eulogise yet another prematurely departed friend: 'His pen was sharp pointed like a poniard; no leaf he wrote on but was like a burning glass to set on fire all his readers. Learning he had, and a conceit exceeding all learning, to quintessence everything which he heard.'

In 1953 a portrait was discovered in the Master's Lodge at Corpus Christi of a 'bravely-clad' Elizabethan, 'aetatis suae 21, 1585'. Marlowe was twenty-one in 1585, and it has been conjectured that it is a portrait of him done after graduating BA, though the costume does seem rather fine for a scholarship boy. The picture bears a suitably Marlovian inscription – 'quod me nutrit me destruit' ('what nourishes me destroys me') – and now hangs in the college hall.

A plaque in Old Court commemorates the stay of both Marlowe and a somewhat junior playwright, John Fletcher (1579–1625), one-half of the collaboration of Beaumont and Fletcher that produced so many successful Jacobean comedies. Fletcher came to Corpus about the time of Marlowe's death; but after the death of his father (a former President of the college) seems to have been obliged to give up his studies. John Fletcher was only one of a clan of literary Fletchers, all Cambridge men. His uncle, Giles Fletcher the Elder (c. 1549–1611), Fellow of King's, who probably supported him after his father's death, was the author of sonnets and a book of Russian travels. His two sons, John Fletcher's cousins, were also poets – Phineas and Giles the Younger.[7] Other Elizabethan dramatists with Cambridge connections included Thomas Heywood (c. 1574–1641), who was apparently at one time a Fellow of Peterhouse, and Thomas Preston (1537–98), Fellow of King's and friend of Spenser, who was appointed Master of Trinity Hall on the occasion when Gabriel Harvey was passed over, and who wrote a bombastical tragedy entitled *Cambises, King of Persia* (1569).

Sir Francis Bacon (1561–1626), the great Elizabethan statesman, philosopher, scientist, and essayist, came up to Trinity in 1573, aged twelve, with his elder brother Anthony. They probably lodged with the Master, who was their tutor. Anthony, however, 'paid more for pills and potions, for meat from the Dolphin tavern, and for Dr Hatcher's drugs, than for Latin and Greek', while Francis, already precocious in languages and scientific curiosity, found the dogmatic Aristotelian syllabus constrictive and barren, the dons (as he later wrote in *The Advancement of Learning*) possessing 'abundance of leisure and small variety of reading, their wits being shut up in the cells of a few authors, chiefly Aristotle, their Dictator'. Sensing he was wasting his time, he transferred after three years to Gray's Inn. He remained loyal, however, to the university, which he

---

[7] See chapter 4 below.

represented years later in parliament, and sent gifts of venison to his old college at Christmas.[8]

John Lyly (1554–1606) transferred to Cambridge from Oxford, where he had failed to win a fellowship; part at least of *Euphues*, his exotically styled and highly influential prose romance, was probably written at Cambridge. Sir John Harington (1561–1612), godson of the queen, studied at King's between 1576 and 1581. Harington translated Ariosto's *Orlando Furioso* at the queen's request, but his *Metamorphosis of Ajax* ('a jakes'), a bawdy satire on the theme of indoor sanitation, resulted in banishment from court. (Elizabeth nevertheless had a water closet, the first in England, installed according to his design.) Thomas Campion (1567–1620), musician, poet, and physician, possibly became friendly with Nashe at Cambridge, where he spent three years at Peterhouse. Joseph Hall (1574–1656), Fellow of Emmanuel, theologian, bishop, and satirist, entered on a pamphlet war with John Marston as a prelude to a long and diverse literary career. Henry Peacham (1578–1643), educated at Trinity, wrote *The Complete Gentleman*, for long the accepted manual of polite conduct.

Drama was as vital a part of the literary scene in Cambridge as elsewhere in Elizabethan England. Despite the ban on strolling players, performances continued to take place in inn yards and at Sturbridge Fair. The Lord Chamberlain's company itself (of which Shakespeare was a member) visited Cambridge in 1595 and perhaps again in 1602, on the latter occasion possibly treating the citizens and scholars of Cambridge to one of the first performances of *Hamlet*, the title-page of the First Quarto of which (1603) states that it had been acted in London 'as also in the two Universities of Cambridge and Oxford'. (It has even been suggested that the character of Horatio was altered from a soldier to a scholar as a tribute to the universities, particularly in view of the praise Shakespeare received in the *Parnassus* plays (see pp. 27–8 below). As *Hamlet* apparently had no warrant from the university, it was probably performed in an inn yard. Shakespeare himself was famous in the part of the Ghost.) Ben Jonson's *Volpone* was similarly performed at Oxford and Cambridge in 1606, Jonson dedicating it 'to the most noble and equal sisters, the two famous Universities, for their love and acceptance shown to his poem in the presentation'.

Though professional performances were not favoured, college plays, performed and often written by the students, were considered in those pre-Puritan days to be an educationally valuable way of filling the bleak winter evenings (most students stayed in residence during the short vacations). In some colleges, provision for such plays was even written into the statutes: a statute of Queens'

---

[8] There is a local allusion in a letter Bacon wrote to a friend in 1609: 'Myself am like the miller of Grantchester, who was wont to pray for peace among the willows, for while the wind blew the windmills wrought and the water-mill was less customed. So I see that controversies of religion must hinder the advancement of sciences.'

College in 1546 stipulates that any student who refused to take part was to be expelled.

As early as 1386 a payment is recorded at Michael House (subsequently incorporated into Trinity) 'for an embroidered pall or cloak, and six visors and six beards for the comedy'. Similar payments are recorded at King's College from 1482 onwards. In 1510 a comedy by Terence was acted at King's Hall; at St John's in the 1520s two moralities by one of the Fellows, Thomas Artour, were performed. From then until the Puritans' total ban on stage plays in 1642, scores of plays must have been produced, usually at Christmas but also on royal occasions. In the early days the plays were generally classical works by such authors as Plautus and Aristophanes; later, original Latin and Greek plays were written, and finally original plays in English. Dramatic content correspondingly widened from didactic morality through romantic comedy to satire. Though most colleges had plays, they seem to have been most popular at St John's in the early days, and later at Trinity, which built its own Comedy Room in the 1620s (if not earlier) on part of what is now the Master's Garden. Though the more puritanical looked askance, wise teachers saw the plays' virtues. Ascham approved heartily of them and wrote fondly of the decorated appearance of St John's hall during play time; Sir John Harington wrote in 1597 that 'in stage plays may be much good . . . and I remember, in Cambridge, howsoever the preciser sort have banished them, the wiser sort did, and still do maintain them'.

On the occasion of a college performance, students appointed as 'stage-keepers' (stewards) dressed up in visors and smart suits and carried torches to show guests across the dark courts to their places in the college hall. Music was often provided by the town waits. Performances were apparently accompanied by much smoking and drinking, and often by the breaking of windows and other intercollegiate violence caused by gate-crashers or the angered targets of satire – as when, at a famous riot outside Trinity in 1610, invaders from St John's were repelled by the stage-keepers of Trinity with staves and stones. College plays 'stood the honest stage-keeper in many a crown's expense for links and vizards; purchased many a sophister a knock with a club; and emptied the college barrels', in the words of the Prologue to the second *Return from Parnassus*. They also provided budding dramatists with a chance to try their skills.

St John's had plays from 1520, Christ's from 1531. An anti-papal play, *Pammachius* by the German dramatist Thomas Kirchmeyer, performed at Christ's in 1545, incurred the wrath of the Chancellor of the University. The first play at Trinity was Dee's production of *Peace* in 1546. About 1554, *Gammer Gurton's Needle*, the first college play in English and only the second extant comedy in the language, was performed at Christ's. Possibly the work of William Stevenson, Fellow of the college, it is neither classical in form nor of university-wit standard, being a slapstick affair in rhymed doggerel. The lost needle in question is eventually found – to the uproarious discomfort of Gammer Gurton's man Hodge – in the seat of his breeches.

Plays formed only part of the Christmas entertainments, over which a *dominus ludorum*, or lord of the revels, usually a BA, was elected to preside. (Milton held a similar position at Christ's during the Long Vacation festivities of 1628.) The diary of John Mere, Esquire Bedell of the University, records some of the activity at Christmas 1556: the lord of Christ's College came 'Christmas-like thither with a drum before him'; one of the university waits expired raving of the plague; on New Year's day there was 'a show in Trinity College in their court of the winning of a hold and taking of prisoners, with waits, trumpets, guns and squibs'; on 6 January there was 'a play at the Falcon and another at the Saracen's Head'; on 7 January there was a comedy by Plautus at Trinity. (College accounts show that Trinity often put on as many as eight different productions over the Christmas period.)

In August 1564 Queen Elizabeth thoroughly enjoyed the feast of plays put on for her in King's College Chapel. In 1579 the students of St John's put on a Latin tragedy, *Richardus Tertius* by Thomas Legge, Master of Caius, which was so powerful, wrote Sir John Harington, it 'would move, I think, Phalaris the tyrant, and terrify all tyrannous-minded men from following their foolish ambitious humours'.

In 1581 a celebrated Latin comedy, *Pedantius*, possibly by Edward Forest, Fellow of the college, was put on at Trinity. In effect a satire of Gabriel Harvey, its memory was gloated over by Nashe in *Have with You to Saffron Walden*:

> *Pedantius*, that exquisite comedy in Trinity College, where, under the chief part, from which it took its name, as namely the concise and firking finicaldo fine schoolmaster, he was full drawn and delineated from the sole of the foot to the crown of his head. The just manner of his phrase in his orations and disputations they stuffed his mouth with . . . not the carrying up of his gown, his nice gate on his pantoffles, or the affected accent of his speech, but they personated.

The Harveys were again satirised in Nashe's own *Duns Furens: Dick Harvey in a Frenzy*, performed at Peterhouse at about the same date, on which occasion, according to Nashe, Richard Harvey in anger 'broke the college glass windows; and Doctor Perne caused him to be fetched in and set in the stocks till the show was ended, and a great part of the night after'.

When *Roxana*, a Latin tragedy by William Alabaster (1567–1640), was performed at Trinity in about 1592, it was acted 'so admirably and so pathetically, that a gentlewoman present thereat, upon hearing the last words – *sequar, sequar* – so hideously pronounced, fell distracted and never after recovered her senses'.

Pedantius had been in Latin; it was the ever rumbling dissensions between the university and the town that caused the first satirical plays to be written in English – the only language their victims were likely to understand. In 1583 Thomas Mudde of Pembroke was committed to the Tolbooth for having attacked the Mayor in a comedy, and obliged to apologise. Yet, according to Fuller's

History of the University of Cambridge, a far more humiliating blow to the town dignitaries came in 1599 with the performance of *Club Law*, an anonymous satire which 'sent up' two Mayors, their sergeants, an alderman and the Town Clerk.

> Clare Hall was the place wherein it was acted, and the mayor, with his brethren, and their wives, were invited to behold it, or rather themselves abused therein. A convenient place was assigned to the townsfolk, (riveted in with scholars on all sides) where they might see and be seen. Here they did behold themselves in their own best clothes (which the scholars had borrowed) so lively personated, their habits, gestures, language, lieger-jests, and expressions, that it was hard to decide, which was the true townsman, whether he that sat by, or he who acted on the stage. Sit still they could not for chafing, go out they could not for crowding.

Though the incensed townsmen complained to the Privy Council, the students got off with a slight reproof.

The most interesting student plays surviving from the period, however, are the three *Parnassus* plays, produced as 'Christmas toys' at St John's around the turn of the century. Their authorship is uncertain, though one William Dodd, Fellow of the college, seems on internal evidence a candidate. The first of the trilogy, *The Pilgrimage to Parnassus*, performed in the winter of 1598/9, follows the adventures of two young students, Philomusus and Studioso, on the road to Parnassus – that is, the BA degree. They pass through the Land of Logic ('full of craggy mountains and thorny vallies') and the Lands of Rhetoric and Philosophy – representing the stages of the curriculum. In each there are characters to dissuade them from persevering, like the sponge Madido, dipping his nose alternately in ale and Horace, claiming,

> Why, give me but a quart of burnt sack by me, and if I do not with a pennyworth of candles make a better poem than Kinsander's *Satyrs*, Lodge's *Fig for Momus*, Bastard's *Epigrams*, Lichfield's *Trimming of Nash*, I'll give my head to any good fellow to make a *memento mori* of!

– or the sensuous Amoretto, rhapsodiser and reader of Ovid, who entices them to taste 'wanton merriments' with women. Finally, an indigent graduate scribbler named Ingenioso, closely modelled on Nashe, warns them that 'Parnassus is out of silver pitifully, pitifully'; the graduates he has met have been nothing but 'a company of ragged vicars and forlorn schoolmasters, who as they walked scratched their unthrifty elbows, and often put their hands into their unpeopled pockets'. They only have to look around them to see that uneducated people prosper better in the world than graduates do – look at Hobson the carrier and Newman the cobbler, both of whom have made fortunes without the need of learning.

Nevertheless, Philomusus and Studioso complete their pilgrimage and take their degrees; but in the sequel, *The Return from Parnassus* (1599/1600), they learn the bitter truth of Ingenioso's warnings. Leaving Cambridge, they are obliged to seek employment where they may: Philomusus becomes a country sexton, Studioso tutor to a brat of a gentleman's son. Neither is secure in these lowly positions: Philomusus is dismissed for not polishing the church floor, Studioso for refusing to let a menial servant sit above him at table. They resolve to emigrate.

The final and longest play of the three, *The Return from Parnassus or the Scourge of Simony*, was such a success that it was performed at St John's at two consecutive Christmases (1601 and 1602) and published in 1606. The same two heroes, having failed to prosper on the Continent, are now reduced to swindling and 'cony-catching' (in the steps of Greene?), masquerading as French physicians. They earn little, however, and are sought by the constables, so are brought to what they term 'the basest trade' of all – the stage. They apply for auditions to Burbage and Kemp, the two leading actors of the day. Kemp, portrayed as blissfully ignorant of Latin and other scholarly acquirements, passes censure on university plays and players: 'Few of the university pen plays well, they smell too much of that writer Ovid, or that writer Metamorphoses, and talk too much of Proserpine and Juppiter. Why, here's our fellow Shakespeare puts them all down, ay, and Ben Jonson too' – a touch which bears comparison with Greene's celebrated complaint in his *Repentance* that the university-educated dramatists were being pushed out of business by an 'upstart crow' of an actor, who 'being an absolute Johannes factotum, is in his own conceit the only Shake-scene in a country'.

In an earlier scene, Ingenioso and a printer friend, seen examining a recently published anthology, make interesting criticisms of such contemporaries as Spenser, Nashe, Marlowe, Ben Jonson, and Shakespeare himself. Later, Ingenioso is seen haggling with his publisher over his own latest production, *A Catalogue of Cambridge Cuckolds*.

In the final scene, the Recorder of Cambridge (presumably a lampoon on Francis Brackyn, who had acquired odium by his attempts to overthrow the university's inequitable precedence over the town) is portrayed roistering with a titled friend. Together they run down scholars as 'pestilent fellows', the Recorder sneering of graduates, 'the University breaks wind twice a year, and lets fly such as these are' (BAs generally left at Easter, MAs in July). But the sharp tongue of Ingenioso claims the final word, upbraiding the Recorder as 'you that hate a scholar because he descries your ass's ears; you that are a plaguy stuffed cloak-bag of all iniquity, which the grand serving-man of Hell will one day truss up behind him, and carry to his smoky wardrobe'. Such words were doubtless received with much stamping of student feet in the packed hall of St John's College at Christmas in the first years of the seventeenth century.

4

Mitre College and the Dolphin Schools

The death of Elizabeth and the accession of James I were marked by the university (which since 1584 had had its own press) with a volume of commemorative verse – the first in a long series to be issued on national occasions (nearly fifty were produced between 1603 and 1763). The poems, usually in Latin, Greek, or other scholarly languages, but in later years increasingly in English, were mainly by heads of colleges and professors, though contributions were also gathered from younger men with a reputation for verse, and many writers – including Herbert, Crashaw, Cowley, Marvell, Dryden, Gray, and Smart – made some of their first appearances in print in this way.

Two leading Jacobean influences, John Donne (c. 1571–1631) and Ben Jonson (1572–1637), possibly studied at Cambridge. Donne, a Roman Catholic at a time when Catholics were debarred from degrees, studied with private tutors at both Oxford and (apparently) Cambridge, the latter probably in about 1588–9. Two verse letters of his were addressed afterwards to friends at Cambridge. One, 'to Mr S.B.' (Samuel Brooke, later Master of Trinity), advises him not to neglect his own poetry and to beware of

> those Schismatiques with you,
> Which draw all wits of good hope to their crew

– presumably another reference to the Harvey brothers. The other, 'To Mr B.B.', chides him for staying on to take his MA and exhorts him to hurry and join his friends in London, where they are all now studying law:

> Then weane thy selfe at last, and thee withdraw
>   From Cambridge thy old nurse, and, as the rest,
>   Here toughly chew, and sturdily digest
> Th'immense vast volumes of our common law.

The evidence for Ben Jonson studying at Cambridge is even vaguer. Fuller's *Worthies of England* is the only authority that after leaving Westminster School 'he was statutably admitted into St John's College in Cambridge . . . where he continued but few weeks for want of further maintenance', being obliged to return home to apprenticeship in his stepfather's trade of bricklaying. In 1615 some Fellows of St John's, preparing for a visit from King James, reported from London: 'We have . . . entreated Ben Jonson to pen a ditty, which we expect upon Saturday', which confirms a connection with the college. Both Donne and Jonson were eventually awarded honorary degrees at Cambridge.

One of the principal followers of Donne's 'metaphysical' style of verse was George Herbert (1593–1633), whose mother was a close friend of Donne's. Herbert came up to Trinity from Westminster in 1609, aged sixteen, and pursued a distinguished university career until 1623.

The Cambridge climate, corrupted by the nearness of the undrained fens, was as insalubrious as in Erasmus's day and Herbert was taken ill the moment he arrived. He was to be ill for most of the rest of his life, dying of consumption at forty.[1] His first English poems, addressed to his mother soon after his arrival at Cambridge, announce his intention to dedicate his poetic talent to divine love, not profane – a promise he kept to the end.

A letter to his stepfather, Sir John Danvers, refers to Herbert's delicate health and begs money for books:

> You know I was sick last vacation, neither am I yet recovered . . . Now this Lent I am forbid utterly to eat any fish, so that I am fain to diet in my chamber at mine own cost; for in our public halls, you know, is nothing but fish and white meats . . . Sometimes also I ride to Newmarket, and there lie a day or two for fresh air . . . I protest and vow, I even study thrift, and yet I am scarce able with much ado to make one half year's allowance shake hands with the other. And yet if a book of four or five shillings come in my way, I buy it, though I fast for it: yea, sometimes of ten shillings.

Herbert took his BA in 1613 and three years later he became a Fellow of Trinity. At first he taught grammar at the college, then in 1618 he was appointed university reader in rhetoric. Perhaps dazzled by the king's visit to Cambridge in 1615 and the prospect of a career at court, he seems to have set himself to flatter the royal scholar by analysing in his lectures one of James's speeches to show it was as eloquent as those of the classical masters. The authorities evidently approved of this approach, for in 1620 he was made Public Orator, a chief requirement of the post in those days being an ability to flatter the great and powerful. 'The Orator's place', Herbert told his stepfather,

> is the finest place in the University . . . The Orator writes all the University letters, makes all the orations, be it to King, Prince, or whatever comes to the University; to requite these pains, he takes place next the Doctors, is at all their assemblies and meetings, and sits above the Proctors, is Regent or Non-Regent at his pleasure, and such like gaynesses, which will please a young man well.

---

[1] Laurence Sterne, Henry Kirke White, and James Elroy Flecker also died of consumptions apparently contracted at Cambridge.

One of his first jobs was to thank the king for the present of a copy of his works, and a Latin epigram, attached to the main letter, suggesting that other libraries might have more books but the Cambridge library was complete in one book –

> Quid Vaticanum Bodleiumque objicis hospes?
> Unicus est nobis bibliotheca liber.

– apparently so pleased the king that he called Herbert 'the jewel of the university'. Later, Herbert wrote to thank King James for putting off the proposed draining of the fens, a project which (despite the threat to health) the university bitterly opposed (Cambridge was for centuries dependent on its river trade). He also wrote to thank Sir Francis Bacon for the gift of one of his books, and became by degrees his loyal and admiring friend, helping to translate *The Advancement of Learning* into Latin. Herbert was also active on royal occasions: in addition to his contributions to commemorative volumes, an epigram of his own on Prince Charles's trip of 1622 to woo the Spanish Infanta was borne away with delight by the king to Newmarket; with equal resourcefulness, when Charles returned without a Catholic bride and the bells of Great St Mary's pealed for three days with relief, the Public Orator delivered a thanksgiving speech to the university.

This was virtually the close of Herbert's Cambridge career. In 1624 he was elected to parliament, and politics claimed him for several years until, wearying at last of worldliness and the courtly brilliance that had seduced him, he returned to his inner mission, ending his days as a country parson in Wiltshire. All his life his withdrawing spirituality had been at odds with his love of society, and in the end he achieved neither the high position nor the spiritual attainment he longed for. His poem 'Affliction I' expresses his sense of inner division:

> Whereas my birth and spirits rather took
>   The way that takes the town,
> Thou didst betray me to a lingering book,
>   And wrap me in a gown.

After Herbert's death, the manuscripts of his poems were bequeathed to his dearest friend, Nicholas Ferrar (1592–1637), with instructions to burn them or publish them as he thought fit. Ferrar had been Herbert's contemporary at Cambridge, and had followed a somewhat similar career. After a fellowship at Clare, he too moved into politics and business, before renouncing the world for the service of God. Ferrar and Herbert were made deacons in the same month, but while Herbert remained the rector of an obscure parish, Ferrar set up a celebrated independent centre of worship at Little Gidding in Huntingdonshire. Recognising the sincerity and artistry of his friend's poems, Ferrar had them published under the title *The Temple* in 1633 by the Cambridge University Printer, Thomas Buck.[2]

Like Herbert, Robert Herrick (1591–1674) produced only a single volume, his *Hesperides* of 1648; and he too, after Cambridge, became a clergyman. There the similarity ends. Herrick's lyrics celebrate the very subject Herbert had renounced: brimming with the pastoral names of his mistresses, they evoke the sight and smell and physical presence of women, his line 'Gather ye rose-buds while ye may' summing up the hedonistic philosophy of his verse.

Herrick's father, a wealthy London goldsmith, died when he was one, leaving him in the custody of an uncle. Like Jonson, Herrick was apprenticed to the family trade, and stuck it out for several years before it became plain that he was not meant for a goldsmith (his poems, however, remain full of precious-stone images). Persuading his uncle to let him go to Cambridge, he arrived at St John's in 1613 at the then advanced age of twenty-two. To distinguish himself from the younger students he entered as a fellow-commoner, but the double fees resulted in an endless struggle with debts.

The fifteen letters that survive from Herrick at Cambridge to his uncle, far from describing life at the university, beg repeatedly for payment of his allowance and help with his bills. The money was actually Herrick's own, held in trust by the uncle, but his allowance was churlishly small and irregularly remitted. He had particular difficulty meeting his initial expenses: the silver goblet which fellow-commoners were expected to donate to the college coffers cost him £5, and then there were his embroidered gown, his hose, and bedding to pay for.

> Sir, I know you understand me, and did you but know how disfurnished I came to Cambridge, without bedding (which I yet want) and other necessaries, you would (as I now trust you will) better your thoughts towards me, considering of my forced expense. Sir, I entreat you to furnish me with ten pounds this quarter; for the last money which I received came not till the last quarter had almost spent itself, which now constrains me so suddenly to write for more. Good Sir, forbear to censure me as prodigal, for I endeavour rather to strengthen than debilitate my feeble family fortune.

His chosen college was large and expensive, if academically rather declined from its early glories. Sir Symonds D'Ewes, a diffident freshman of 1618, complained that 'swearing, drinking, rioting, and hatred of all piety and virtue' abounded at St John's, but Herrick, author of the 'Welcome to Sack', no doubt enjoyed (when he could afford) the roistering of its tennis courts and neighbouring taverns.

---

[2] Appointed in 1625 and the first University Printer of importance. Other works to come from his press behind St Bene't's Church included Crashaw's *Epigrammata* (1634), John Donne's *Six Sermons* (1634), the Edward King memorial volume (1638), Thomas Fuller's *History of the Holy War* (1639), Lancelot Andrewes's *Sermons* (1641), and William Harvey's *De Circulatione Sanguinis* (1649).

In 1616, however, Herrick transferred to the smaller and cheaper Trinity Hall (whose first Master, his namesake Robert Eyrick, was an ancestor). Still at a loss for a profession, Herrick toyed with the idea of taking up law (always the traditional study at Trinity Hall) and informed his uncle that he now intended 'to live reclusive, till time contract me to some other calling, striving now with myself both sparingly to live and thereby to shun the current of expense'. It was from Trinity Hall in 1617 that he took his BA, 'with many a throe and pinches of the purse; but it was necessary, and the prize was worthy the hazard'. Although he took his MA in 1620, he did not stay at Cambridge after his first degree, but probably returned to London, where he was gathered into Ben Jonson's 'tribe'. He left several outstanding debts.[3]

As a fellow-commoner of St John's, Herrick must have been present at one at least of the series of plays put on in the hall of Trinity College for King James and Prince Charles when they visited the university in March 1615. (Charles had paid a previous visit, with the Elector Palatine, in 1613; on that occasion the Elector Palatine slept through a play by Donne's friend Samuel Brooke called *Adelphe* – it lasted seven hours – and both princes complained, when they got back to Newmarket, of its length and stupidity.) For this second visit, Herrick's fellow students at St John's put on a comedy called *Aemilia*, by one Cecil, Fellow of the college; a Latin pastoral by Brooke and an English comedy by another Trinity playwright were performed on subsequent nights. But the great event of the visit was the performance on the second night by the students of Clare of the satirical Latin comedy *Ignoramus* by George Ruggle (1575–1622), Fellow of Clare. Once again, the play made fun of lawyers like the much-vilified Francis Brackyn, and though this play too lasted a gruelling five hours, the king enjoyed it so hugely that he came back in May expressly to see it again.

By now, with their satire, their hobby horses, and their clowns, college plays were becoming public entertainments rather than the academic exercises they were originally intended to be, and incurred increasing censure from the Puritans. In 1623, the king was so pleased by a comedy put on by the students of Queens', *Fucus Historiomastix* by R. Ward, that he persuaded them to give a repeat performance at Newmarket. This occasioned a sarcastic ballad from Henry Molle of King's (later Public Orator):

> The Queenes Colledge Play, from Cambridge away
>   The king to the Court did call,
> Because it was pitty, that a thinge so witty
>   Should dye in a private Hall.
>
>   . . . . . .

---

[3] Herrick is the chief character in Rose Macaulay's novel *They Were Defeated* (1932), set in pre-Civil War Cambridge. Cleveland, Cowley, Crashaw, Milton, and Marvell also appear.

> Three coaches came empty to carry some twenty
>   With bagge and baggage to boote,
> And when they had done, 'twas twenty to one
>   They had not come home on foote.
> Sure they were not wise that did them advise
>   To appeare in so publike a place,
> But things that are vicious will still bee ambitious
>   To runne into farther disgrace.

Molle was particularly annoyed by the caricature of a Puritan in the play, performed by an actor in holy orders. Although there were many, like Herbert and Herrick, who combined clerical vocations with worldly recreations, others, like Molle or Milton, took a poor view of the trend in student dramatics.

A play about fishing by Phineas Fletcher (1582–1650), one of Giles Fletcher the Elder's two literary sons, was prepared for the king's 1615 visit but performed after his departure. Phineas Fletcher, who had followed his father to King's, later produced the extremely baroque poem *The Purple Island*, an unlikely allegory of the human body, again with fishy sequences. The river Cam features like a leitmotiv in Fletcher's poems, in several of which he laments his unrequited love for a local girl called Fusca, whom he met in 'the field that looks towards the Plough, and whose name springs from the filthy bear' – probably near the bear-baiting pits at Chesterton. The poet sighs over Fusca as he sits

> Where lovelie Came doeth lose his erring waye
> While with his bankes the wanton waters playe
> Which still doe staye behind, yet still doe slippe away.

Despondent when he had to leave Cambridge, probably after forfeiting his fellowship on getting married, Fletcher called down a mock curse in typical imagery:

> But thou, proud Chame, which thus hast wrought me spite,
> Some greater river drown thy hatefull name!
> Let never myrtle on thy banks delight,
> But willows pale, the badge of spite and blame,
> Crown thy ungratefull shores with scorn and shame!
> Let dirt and mud thy lazie waters seize,
> Thy weeds still grow, thy waters still decrease;
> Nor let thy wretched love to Gripus ever cease!

Phineas's younger brother Giles Fletcher the Younger (1588–1623) was at Trinity, where he was elected a Fellow in 1606 and was probably a friend of Herbert's. While at Trinity he wrote his most substantial poem, *Christ's Victory*, dedicating it to the great Dr Nevile, the Master, who did so much to transform the college.

One of Phineas Fletcher's closest friends at Cambridge was the moralist–poet Francis Quarles (1592–1644), who studied at Christ's from 1605 to 1609, and whose *Emblems* and *Hieroglyphikes* were the seventeenth century's best-selling books of verse. (As Horace Walpole lamented, 'Milton was forced to wait till the world had done admiring Quarles.') After leaving Cambridge, Quarles was for a while cup-bearer to Elizabeth of Bohemia, daughter of James I. In 1644 he went to Oxford to support King Charles, but at the king's defeat he was himself ruined and died of grief. Quarles was one of several leading Caroline poets to study at Cambridge. James Shirley (1596–1666), author of the *Maid's Revenge* and other tragedies, migrated from Oxford to St Catharine's in 1615 and took his degree in 1617.[4] Edmund Waller (1606–87), who studied at King's between 1620 and 1622, left without a degree, as did the flamboyant and aristocratic Sir John Suckling (1609–42), who came up to Trinity in 1623. In March 1628 Suckling acted the Prologue in a play performed before King Charles, stroking a snail held in the palm of his hand as an image of the students' frail comedy.

In 1622 Michael Drayton (1563–1631) published his major work, *Poly-Olbion*, a colossal survey of the whole of England in thirty 'songs', recounting its topographical beauties and legends, with special emphasis on rivers and streams. Song XXI focusses on Cambridge and Ely, and, though there is no evidence that Drayton ever lived in Cambridge, he shows close familiarity with the area. After discussing the Devil's Dyke (the ancient earthwork that crosses Newmarket Heath), Drayton recounts a legend of his own of

> Old Gogmagog, a Hill of long and great renowne,
> Which near to *Cambridge* set, o'erlooks that learned Towne.

In Drayton's version, Gogmagog is a comic giant who falls in love with 'most delicious Grant', the nearby river; in his attempt to woo her, he promises all manner of uncouth gifts. Drayton goes on to describe the beauties of the river above Cambridge:

> Wherefore to shew herself er'e she to *Cambridge* came,
> Most worthy of that Towne to which she gives the name,
> Takes in her second head, from *Linton* comming in,
> By Shelford having slid, which straightway she doth win:
> Then which, a purer Streame, a delicater Brooke,
> Bright *Phoebus* in his course doth scarcely overlooke.
> Thus furnishing her bankes, as sweetly she doth glide
> Towards *Cambridge*, with rich Meads layd forth on either side.

Finally Drayton invokes the Muses to patronise Cambridge, concluding with a reference to the university's official device (used on the title pages of its books):

---

[4] According to Wood's *Athenae Oxonienses*, the reason for Shirley's transfer was that he had an excessively large mole on his cheek, which the Master of his college, William Laud, said disqualified him from holy orders. Cambridge apparently did not object to the mole.

> O noble *Cambridge* then, my most beloved Towne,
> In glory flourish still, to heighten thy renowne:
> In woman's perfect shape, still be thy Embleme right,
> Whose one hand holds a Cup, the other beares a Light.

In 1624 a youth who was destined to be the century's leading Cambridge wit came up with a scholarship from Westminster to Trinity. Within two years, Thomas Randolph (1605–35) had already established a brilliant reputation among the students, and his verses were circulating widely in manuscript. He was also (like a later wit, C. S. Calverley) no mean scholar, and a year after he had taken his BA the Master of his college, Bishop Mawe, wrote to the Chancellor of the University recommending him as 'one of extraordinary parts of wit and learning, and so approved by the whole University that scarce an age brings forth a better or the like'. A month later, in September 1629, as a result of this letter, Randolph was appointed to a minor fellowship by royal mandate.

When one of the perennial town/gown altercations broke out, this time over the price of candles, and the town authorities referred the matter to the king, Randolph produced a skit, 'The Townsmen's Petition of Cambridge', to satirise their hopes:

> But wot ye what the King did think,
>   And what his meaning was;
> I vow unto you by this drink,
>   A rare device he has:
> His Majesty hath penn'd it,
>   That they'll be ne'er the better;
> And so he means to send it,
>   All in a Latin letter,
> Which when it comes for to be read,
>   It plainly will appear,
> The townsmen they must hang the head,
>   And the Scholars must domineer.[5]

In 'On Six Maids Bathing in the River Cam', the poet, taking the evening air along the Backs by Queens', encounters a sight to gladden any scholar's eye in those days when Fellows of colleges were forbidden to marry, when female company was practically unobtainable at Cambridge, and when even college bedmakers were selected for their ugliness.

> When bashful daylight now was gone,
> And night, that hides a blush, came on,
> Six pretty nymphs, to wash away

---

[5] Professor G. C. Moore Smith, however, doubted Randolph's authorship of this poem, which he dated c. 1604.

> The sweating of a summer's day,
> In Cam's fair stream did gently swim,
> And naked bathe each curious limb.

When the university was forced to close down by the plague of 1630, Randolph went to London, becoming a disciple of Ben Jonson and contributing plays to the King's Revels. But he was back in 1631 to take his MA. He was a prolific writer of comedies, several of which – two 'shows', *The Conceited Peddler* and *Aristippus or the Jovial Philosopher*; two five-act plays, *The Muses' Looking-Glass* and *Hey for Honesty*; and a pastoral called *Amyntas* – were probably put on in Trinity's Comedy Room. Most of them abound with local references, particularly to Cambridge taverns. Messrs Hamon, Wolfe, and Farlowe, land-lords of the Dolphin, Rose, and Mitre respectively, are called 'the three best tutors in the universities', and in similar vein the Prologue of *The Conceited Peddler*, enlarging on his own learning, brags:

> Generous gentlemen, such is my affection to Phoebus and the ninety-nine Muses, that for the benefit of this royal university, I have strodled over three of the terrestrial globes with my geometrical rambling, viz., the Asia of the Dolphin, the Afrique of the Rose, the America of the Mitre, besides the *terra incognita* of many an alehouse.

In *Aristippus* there are erudite disputations on the merits of sack over ale, and a parody of a matriculation ceremony in which a scholar is inaugurated into the ways of true learning, drinking solemn vows to 'defend the honour of Aristippus, to the disgrace of brewers, alewives, and tapsters', to keep the ordinances instituted by King Sigebert 'for the establishing of good government in the ancient foundation of Mitre College', to 'keep all acts and meetings in the Dolphin Schools', and generally to 'show yourself so diligent in drinking, that the proctor may have no just cause to suspend you for negligence'. When Aristippus is knocked down for his support of sack by two Cambridge brewers, Dick Lichfield (the same barber of Trinity celebrated by Nashe) carries him away and miraculously restores him with one of his potions.

In 1633, to the dismay of all scholars of sack, 'Mitre College', as Randolph's followers called the inn standing at the south end of the site now occupied by the screen of King's, was burnt down. Randolph naturally called for a speedy rebuilding:

> Lament, lament, ye scholars all,
> Each wear his blackest gown,
> The Mitre, that held up your wits,
> Is now itself fall'n down.

> The dismal fire on London Bridge
> Can move no heart of mine:
> For that but o'er the water stood,
> But this stood o'er the wine.

It needs must melt each Christian heart
　　That this sad news but hears,
To think how the good hogsheads wept
　　Good sack and claret tears.

The zealous students of the place
　　Change of religion fear,
That this mischance may soon bring in
　　A heresy of beer.

The high point of Randolph's career came in March 1632, when King Charles and his queen visited Cambridge and the usual entertainments were prepared. The Master of Trinity requested Randolph to write a play for the occasion, but the Vice-Chancellor, Dr Butts of Corpus Christi, supported a rival dramatist, Peter Hausted of Queens'. In the event, both wrote plays, Randolph *The Jealous Lovers* and Hausted *The Rival Friends*, and both were put on amid great controversy, the entire university taking sides. Hausted's play – rather tactlessly a satire on simony and ecclesiastical patronage – proved a flop with the king and his court and with a biassed *claqueur* audience, but Randolph's more lightweight but defter comedy was a sensational hit. Hausted later complained that his play had been 'cried down by boys, faction, envy, and confident ignorance' but the Lord Chancellor is said to have personally reprimanded Dr Butts for allowing it to be performed at all. Butts, a sensitive scholar who had courageously endured harrowing experiences during the plague, hanged himself ten days later in his college room.[6]

Randolph was appointed to act as Praevaricator, or licensed jester, at the Commencement ceremony that July, when Milton, among others, received his MA. He afterwards left Cambridge, perhaps to enlarge his dramatic success in London, but the dissolute lifestyle he had acquired from attendance at Mitre College and the Dolphin Schools led to an early death in 1635. The inscription on his tomb was composed by Hausted.

Jeremy Taylor (1613–67), the devotional writer, was the first writer of note to be born in Cambridge. His father was a barber in Market Street and church-warden of Holy Trinity Church. Taylor was one of the first scholars at the Perse School (founded by Stephen Perse in 1615) and at the age of thirteen proceeded as a Perse Scholar to its founder's old college, Caius. Precociously scholarly, he was elected a Fellow at the age of twenty, and took as pupils a number of other old Perseans. Archbishop Laud, hearing him preach in Cambridge, was so impressed that he obtained for Taylor a fellowship at All Souls College, Oxford.

A churchman of a different stamp was Thomas Fuller (1608–61), who came up to Queens' in 1621. Although his uncle was President of the college, Fuller failed to get a fellowship there and transferred to Sidney Sussex. From 1630 to 1633

---

[6] It is allegedly his ghost that haunts the college. An attempt to exorcise the ghost is mentioned in Shane Leslie's novel *The Cantab* (1926).

he was the curate of St Bene't's, the oldest church in Cambridge, and became a popular and well-loved figure in the town, on friendly terms with rich and poor, scholar and townsman alike. A large and genial man of invariable good humour, with a humanity that always allowed him to see the best in others, Fuller was one of the most entertaining historians of the age, eminently readable if not always strictly accurate. His works include the first *History of the University of Cambridge* to be written in English and the monumental *Worthies of England*.

It was Fuller who delivered the funeral sermon at St Bene't's for one of its most celebrated parishioners, Thomas Hobson (1544–1631), the university carrier. Hobson had built up his business through three reigns as the official carrier of post, packages, and people between Cambridge and London, becoming one of the wealthiest and most famous of Cambridge citizens. Even in his eighties he still insisted on driving his eight-horse wain in person over the difficult three-day journey, and it was said that his death on 1 January 1631 was the result of his enforced idleness when communication with the capital was banned during the plague. Hobson was also the first person to hire out horses, and to his contemporaries his name was a byword for thrift. It was Hobson's insistence that his horses be hired out in strict rotation, rather than according to the customer's preference, that gave rise to the popular expression 'Hobson's choice'.

The demise of this local institution produced a rash of epitaphs (thirteen have survived). In very different vein from the lachrymary productions on the deaths of the great, these are full of punning references to wains and letters:

> Hobson (what's out of sight is out of mind!)
> Is gone, and left his letters here behind;
> He that with so much paper used to meet
> Is now, alas, content to take one sheet.

and

> Then I conjecture Charles the northern swain
> Whistled up Hobson for to drive his wain.
> He is not dead, but left his mansion here;
> He has left the Bull and flitted to the Bear.

and

> Here Hobson lies, amongst his many betters,
> A man not learned, yet a man of letters.
> The scholars well can testify as much
> Who have received them from his pregnant pouch.

and (by Randolph)

> Charon, take Hobson's ghost and let it pass
> By the land the same that it by water was.
> Thy cousin ghost, a sprite to poets dear,

> To Elysian waft, a jocund mariner.
> He'll pay the royal fare. Deny this pain
> And he shall ride to heav'n in his own wain.

But the 'supreme waggoner's' most famous epitaph was to come from what might seem the unlikeliest pen – Milton's.

5

'The Lady of Christ's'

Though third among the colleges in number of students, Christ's still possessed only the one crowded court when John Milton (1608–74) came into residence as a pensioner in the summer term of 1625. Tradition has assigned to him choice rooms on the first floor just to the left of the entrance gate (M3; they were later occupied by C. P. Snow), but if he ever occupied these (the first floor was usually reserved for Fellows, and it may be that later porters, weary of requests to be shown 'Milton's rooms', picked a set close to their lodge) it must have been towards the end of his stay; even then he would have had to share them. According to the antiquary William Stukeley, who made enquiries in 1740, the sixteen-year-old freshman more probably lodged in 'Rat's Hall', a 'temporary' wooden structure (it lasted from 1613 to 1731) beyond the kitchens in what is now the second court.

Rat's Hall must have come as an unpleasant surprise to Milton, with his long hair, pale, girlish features, precise, careful speech, and weak, watchful eyes. His boyhood had been spent in quiet study, partly at St Paul's School, partly with private tutors at his parents' home near Cheapside. 'From the twelfth year of my age I scarcely ever went from my lessons to bed before midnight. Then, when I had acquired various tongues and also some not insignificant taste for the sweetness of philosophy, [my father] sent me to Cambridge.' At Christ's, his fellow students – more studious, many of them, to cheat the regulations and have a good time than to acquire learning – soon produced a nickname for him: *Domina*, the Lady.

Despite his long-standing bookishness, Milton thought of himself as a slow developer: 'I do notice a certain belatedness in me', he confessed. Though he was somewhat older than his school friend Charles Diodati, the latter had already been at Oxford two years before Milton came to Cambridge. Thomas Fuller, his exact contemporary, had been at Queens' five years when Milton arrived at Christ's. Milton was not awarded one of the scholarships from St Paul's.

The student's life had not changed much since Marlowe's day. For all the intellectual fervour of the Renaissance, the curriculum remained conservatively medieval, with the emphasis still on chop-logic disputations and stylised Latin declamations. Milton made no secret of his hatred of it. In an academic exercise, probably done towards the end of his Cambridge career, he expressed the opinion: 'these studies neither delight nor instruct nor promote any common good'; Hercules, he says, derived more joy from cleaning out the Augean stables than university students do from reading scholastic philosophers, whose teaching leads merely to endless trivial quibbling, not to broadened knowledge and understanding. Francis Bacon, who had left Trinity with similar opinions, had attacked the outmoded Aristotelian teaching in his *Advancement of Learning*, calling for a much wider syllabus. (Bacon had intended to found a lectureship in history at Cambridge, but when he died in 1626 left no money for it. Fulke Greville did found one the following year, but it ran immediately into disfavour with the authorities.) Milton was a staunch admirer of Bacon, calling him one of the 'greatest and sublimest wits in sundry ages'. Nevertheless, despite his misgivings, Milton stayed the course for the full seven years and took his MA; and the lasting effect of his Cambridge training, especially the requirement to stand up and support one side or the other of a philosophical proposition, can be seen in the vigour of his later polemical pamphlets, or in the twin poems 'L'Allegro' and 'Il Penseroso' (probably written soon after leaving Cambridge), which closely resemble the two sides of a disputation.

For another reason, too, Milton felt out of tune with official attitudes at Cambridge, for he was a Puritan and an anti-royalist at a time when the schism between crown and parliament was widening irreparably. Milton arrived at Cambridge almost simultaneously with the accession of Charles I, and his first awareness of Charles's autocratic behaviour may have been when the university was coerced into electing his favourite, George Villiers, Duke of Buckingham, as its Chancellor. In fact, the king turned out to be a great patron of the universities, and Buckingham, among other benefactions, bequeathed a priceless collection of oriental manuscripts to the University Library; but that will not have altered Milton's feelings. Although, in the convention of the time, he composed numerous epitaphs and verses on members of the university and other worthies, he never penned a single line in honour of royalty, nor contributed to the commemorative volumes.

The Fellows of his college, however, were themselves far from united on political matters, and three among the tutors were later to be punningly differentiated: the students of William Power, considered liberal, were nicknamed Poweritans; those of William Chappell, considered rather strict, Puritans; and those of moderate Joseph Mede, Medians. Mede, with his noble personality and progressive ideas, would have made an ideal tutor for Milton, but instead he was put under Chappell, a brilliant disputant who worked his pupils hard and got good academic results but was possibly rather impatient of too much idiosyncrasy of mind. Chappell was a supporter of Laud, Charles's royalist archbishop, who later made him an Irish bishop; and probably he and Milton were both temperamentally and ideologically unsuited. At any rate, according to the biographical notes compiled by John Aubrey, who obtained the information from Milton's younger brother Christopher, they soon fell out. 'His first tutor there was Mr Chappell, from whom receiving some unkindness he was afterwards (though it seemed opposite to the rules of the college) transferred to the tuition of one Mr Tovey.' Between the lines of his manuscript, by the word 'unkindness', Aubrey pencilled the gloss 'whipped him'.

'I am ashamed to relate what I fear is true,' wrote Dr Johnson in his *Life of Milton*, 'that Milton was one of the last students in either university that suffered the public indignity of corporal correction.' (In fact corporal punishment was not unknown even in Johnson's day at Oxford.) Whether Milton was actually whipped remains very doubtful. Students under the age of eighteen certainly could be punished in this way, though by the dean rather than their tutor. Possibly his Baconian prejudices, untactfully and prematurely expressed, angered Chappell, intemperate words were exchanged, and punishment was inevitable. Whipped or not, Milton certainly seems to have been rusticated, probably in March 1626.

In a Latin verse letter (his *Elegia Prima*) written from home to Diodati at Oxford, Milton pretended to be unbothered by his punishment.

> I cannot say I am eager at the moment to go back to the reedy Cam, I am not exactly prostrate with nostalgia for that forbidden abode. With its unpleasing bare fields devoid of soft shade, how uncongenial that place is to devotees of Apollo! Nor am I inclined to endure the threats of an unsympathetic tutor and other such indignities which my spirit will not bear. If this is exile, to be back in the parental home again and, free from torments, to enjoy pleasant diversions, then I willingly accept the name and fate of outlaw and rejoice to be banished.

The 'pleasant diversions' apparently include theatres and girls, though on closer reading the former turn out to comprise Latin authors rather than live entertainment, the latter to have been admired from a distance.[1] He keeps up the insouciance until the end of the letter, then confesses: 'By the way, it has been decided that I must go back to the Cam's sedgy fens, back to the classroom's hoarse murmur.' His new tutor, Nathaniel Tovey, aged twenty-seven, son of a friend of the Diodatis, was perhaps young and perceptive enough to realise that Milton needed rational, two-way argument, not force-feeding with dogma. Christopher Milton, who entered Christ's in 1631, was also put under Tovey.

If Milton's relationship with his tutor had been resolved, that with his fellow students – 'the classroom's hoarse murmur' – continued to be tricky. Brought up in a puritan ethic and only too aware of his own specialness, he must have looked

---

[1] According to romance, Milton, walking one day near Cambridge, fell asleep under a tree; an Italian lady, passing in a carriage, was so struck by his beauty that she stopped to admire him, and, writing some lines on a piece of paper, placed it in his hand. When he awoke and read the paper, he conceived such a passion for his unknown admirer that he later went to Italy in quest of her. Exactly the same story, however, has been told of other poets elsewhere. (Bulwer-Lytton used the legend as basis for his poem 'Milton', written when he was himself an undergraduate.)

with distaste on the attitudes of some of them. Destined, without vocation, for the church, the only ambition of many of them was to scrape through their exams into safe country livings. Yet he, with a unique vocation to explain the ways of God to man, was already doubting his suitability for the ministry, or its for him.

He felt especial contempt for the participation of future clerics in college dramatics. Many of the actors in the 1615 performances of *Ignoramus* went on to become divines – a contemporary called them 'a perfect diocese of actors' – and the same could probably be said of the rival plays by Randolph and Hausted put on for Charles's visit of 1632, at which Milton was apparently present. In one of his later pamphlets, *An Apology for Smectymnuus* (1642), Milton recalled the occasion with displeasure:

> In the Colleges so many of the young Divines, and those in next aptitude to Divinity have bin seene so oft upon the Stage writhing and unboning their Clergie limmes to all the antick and dishonest gestures of Trinculo's, Buffons, and Bawds; prostituting the shame of that ministery which either they had, or were nigh having, to the eyes of Courtiers and Court-Ladies, with their Groomes and *Madamoisellaes*. There while they acted, and overacted, among other young scholars, I was a spectator; they thought themselves gallant men, and I thought them fools, they made sport, and I laught, they mispronounc't, and I mislik't, and, to make up the *atticisme*, they were out, and I hist.

Though Puritans were not always the killjoys they were subsequently made out to be (Milton enjoyed music and theatre and took up fencing at Cambridge), there is a pejoratively puritanical tone to this passage.

That Milton did not disapprove of legitimate vacation entertainments, however, may be inferred from his election as 'Father', or master, of revels for the Long Vacation festivities at Christ's in 1628. The revels were supposed to be conducted wholly in Latin, and the traditional high point was a witty speech from the Father full of topical allusions; so the choice of Milton is a tribute to his reputation as a Latinist, but may also reflect the students' growing realisation that the 'Lady of Christ's' possessed inner authority. Indeed, in his speech he took advantage of his temporary status to rebuff once and for all the suggestion of effeminacy:

> By some of you I have recently been called Lady. Why do I seem to them too little of a man? Is it because I have never been able lustily to quaff great tankards, or because I have not calloused my hands holding a plough, or because I have never lain down and snored at midday like a seven years' herdsman; or perhaps, indeed, because I have never proved my manhood in the same way as those debauched ruffians? Would they could as easily put off their asshood as I my supposed ladyhood.

Rather straining with desire to be a success, Milton turns puns on the names of his colleagues – Rivers, Bird, Goose, Sparks the porter – and is breezy with self-analysis and forced humour. Then suddenly (and contrary to the rules) he breaks into English – 'Hail, native language' – and, dropping the undergraduate humour, tries his poetic wings in impressively soaring imagery, ending with the announcement that he already has an ambition for epic subjects:

> Yet I had rather, if I were to choose,
> Thy service in some graver subject use.

In 1628 Milton proudly sent a friend at Oxford, Alexander Gill (son of the headmaster of St Paul's), his very first production to appear in print. Apparently, a Fellow of Christ's, presenting for a degree in philosophy, had not felt up to the task of composing the required disputation, and had got the obliging young Latinist to do it for him. As was normal practice, copies were printed for the audience. In an accompanying letter, Milton again complains of the lack of serious scholarship at Cambridge, of verbal cleverness passing for true knowledge. 'For myself, finding almost no real companions in study here, I should certainly be looking straight back to London, were I not meditating a retirement during this summer vacation into a deeply literary leisure.'

Only weeks later, Buckingham was assassinated, and Gill recklessly drank a toast to the assassin in his Oxford college bar. When his papers were seized, they were found to contain sentiments such as that the king was 'fitter to stand in a Cheapside shop with an apron before him . . . than to govern a kingdom'. He was hauled before the Star Chamber, stripped of his degrees, fined £2000, and sentenced to lose both ears. The last punishment was later remitted; but the affair can only have deepened Milton's growing passion over the issues of the day.

The same year that he broke into English in his vacation speech, Milton produced another poem in English, on the death of his sister's first child; but 'On the Death of a Fair Infant Dying of a Cough' is as emotionally cold as his Latin elegies for university personages. Yet only a year later, waking early on Christmas day, 1629 – at Cambridge or London is not known – he sat down and wrote his magnificent ode 'On the Morning of Christ's Nativity', a poem that at one stroke revealed him as a consummate and original poet.

His first English poem to see print, however – his lines on Shakespeare in the 1632 edition of Shakespeare's works (the Second Folio) – was less inspired. Ben Jonson prepared the edition. The Mermaid tavern was only just along the street from Milton's home; could the earnest young Cambridge scholar and the roistering old dramatist have met?

Spring 1630 saw Cambridge emptied by the plague. Joseph Mede wrote from Christ's that 'our university is in a manner wholly dissolved; all meetings and exercises ceasing. In many colleges almost none left.' Milton's movements during this year are unknown. Possibly he went over to Stowmarket in Suffolk to visit his friend Thomas Young, his boyhood private tutor, who had recently been appointed vicar there. (He later became Master of Jesus College.) It was as an indirect result of this plague that Hobson the carrier died, and when the university reassembled, Milton, who had doubtless travelled in Hobson's wain to London or back and received his mail from Hobson's hand, joined in the student versifying. His two Hobson poems display an undergraduate humour similar to his vacation speech, but touch on death more sympathetically than his previous elegies.

> Here lies old Hobson: Death has broke his girt,
> And here, alas, hath laid him in the dirt;
> Or else, the ways being foul, twenty to one
> He's here stuck in a slough, and overthrown.
> 'Twas such a shifter that, if truth were known,
> Death was half glad when he had got him down;
> For he had any time this ten years full
> Dodged with him betwixt Cambridge and the Bull.[2]
> And surely Death could never have prevailed,
> Had not his weekly course of carriage failed;
> But lately, finding him so long at home,
> And thinking now his journey's end was come,
> And that he had ta'en up his latest inn,
> In the kind office of a chamberlin
> Showed him his room where he must lodge that night,
> Pulled off his boots, and took away the light.
> If any ask for him, it shall be said,
> Hobson has supped, and's newly gone to bed.

The second poem, slightly longer and fuller of puns, is less effective.

Milton's anti-royalist sentiments cannot have been softened by a turn of events in 1630 which some biographers have interpreted as another brush with the college authorities. A fellowship fell vacant at Christ's and the king ordered the college, 'notwithstanding any statute, ordinance, or constitution to the contrary', to appoint Edward King, son of his Secretary for Ireland. King was three years younger than Milton, had only just taken his BA, and was a pupil of Chappell's. There is no evidence, however, that Milton expected the fellowship for himself; indeed, he would have been debarred by the rule that there could be only one Fellow from each county, his county being already 'filled'. Another election followed in 1631, and again a youthful candidate was appointed, though the Master, Dr Bainbridge, opposed him on the ground that 'another holds so strong'. Again, there is no evidence that 'the other' was Milton.

Whether or not Edward King had taken Milton's fellowship, he was instrumental a few years later in inspiring Milton to another of his early masterpieces. It is not known how friendly they were, but when in 1637 King was drowned in a shipwreck on his way to Ireland and his Cambridge friends decided to collect

---

[2] The Bull Inn, Bishopsgate, was Hobson's stopping place in London.

a memorial anthology, Milton, then living in seclusion outside London, was invited to contribute. The volume, *Justa Edovardo King, Naufrago, ab Amicis Moerentibus*, printed by Thomas Buck in 1638, contained the usual curious and mediocre verses in Latin, Greek, and English, but concluded with something that not only dwarfed the rest but put in the shade the whole lifeless tradition of university memorials. 'Lycidas' was modestly signed 'J.M.'[3]

Meditating on premature death, Milton laments that King, so well fitted for the ministry, could be taken, while others, lacking true vocation, succeed to undeserved livings. Milton takes the opportunity to attack the clergy who fail in their duties – 'the hungry sheep look up, and are not fed' – and refers to his student days at Christ's with King:

> For we were nursed upon the self-same hill,
> Fed the same flock, by fountain, shade, and rill . . .

They were poets both:

> Meanwhile the rural ditties were not mute;
> Tempered to th'oaten flute.
> Rough satyrs danced, and fauns with cloven heel
> From the glad sound would not be absent long,
> And old Damoetas loved to hear our song.

The pastoral imagery is not meant to stand for anything precise, but the 'rough satyrs' and 'fauns with cloven heel' may vaguely represent their fellow undergraduates, 'old Damoetas' perhaps Mede or another of the tutors (a tutor called Dametas is referred to in the first *Return from Parnassus*, so conceivably it was a traditional name for an elderly don).

Milton was admitted MA in July 1632, and left Cambridge after seven years of residence. By this time he had abandoned all idea of a clerical or professional career and committed himself to poetry; yet he still lacked a higher motivation and, aware as ever of his tardiness of development, summed up his feelings soon afterwards in a sonnet:

> How soon hath time, the subtle thief of youth,
> Stol'n on his wing my three and twentieth year!
> My hasting days fly on with full career,
> But my late spring no bud or blossom shew'th.

He was to spend the next six years immersed in private study – modern languages and literature, history, music – of the sort that Aristotelian Cambridge had not encouraged; then to plunge into twenty years of political involvement, culminating in his appointment as Cromwell's Latin Secretary. It was only with the onset of blindness and his withdrawal from politics at the Restoration that he at

---

[3] Trinity College possesses the original manuscript of 'Lycidas'; the University Library has a copy of the *Justa* with Milton's marginal corrections.

last dedicated himself to the principal work of his life, the writing of *Paradise Lost.*

A bust of Milton done at the age of forty-six is preserved in the Combination Room at Christ's. The tree in the Fellows' Garden traditionally known as 'Milton's Mulberry' was probably in fact planted in the year of his birth as one of a consignment of three hundred mulberries which the college bought to humour King James in a scheme for introducing a silk industry to England (in the event they turned out to be the wrong sort of mulberries for silkworms). There is no evidence that Milton planted the tree or sat under it or had any other connection with it, though, curiously, a separate tradition does have him planting mulberry trees at Stowmarket during one of his visits to Young (the last survived until 1939). Could these have been cuttings from one of the Christ's plants?[4]

Referring in *An Apology for Smectymnuus* to his Cambridge days, and refuting an aspersion that the university had expelled him – 'vomited him out' – Milton thanked his attacker for this lie:

> for it hath given me an apt occasion to acknowledge publickly with all gratefull minde, that more than ordinary favour and respect which I found above any of my equals at the hands of those courteous and learned men, the Fellowes of that Colledge wherein I spent some yeares: who at my parting, after I had taken two degrees, as the manner is, signifi'd many wayes, how much better it would content them that I would stay; as by many Letters full of kindnesse and loving respect both before that time, and long after, I was assur'd of their singular good affection towards me.

There are lines in 'Il Penseroso' that sound like an evocation of King's College Chapel:

> But let my due feet never fail
> To walk the studious cloister's pale,
> And love the high embowèd roof,
> With antique pillars massy proof,
> And storied windows richly dight,
> Casting a dim religious light . . .

Nevertheless, his true feelings about his time at Christ's – as, no doubt, the college's about him – must have been mixed. A Roundhead with long hair, a creditable disputant who sneered at disputations, a Puritan who fell out with his 'Puritan' tutor, a model scholar passed over for fellowships, a soft face and a sharp tongue, L'Allegro and Il Penseroso together – the subtle complexities of Milton's character were already more than evident at Cambridge.

---

[4] Pembroke until recently outbid Christ's with a mulberry supposedly planted by Spenser. Sidney Sussex once boasted a pear tree planted by Oliver Cromwell. There is another mulberry, coeval with that at Christ's but not planted by a celebrity, in the Fellows' Garden at Jesus.

6

'Time to leave the books in dust'

Pre-Civil War Cambridge nursed all shades of political and religious opinion. The university of Milton and Cromwell was equally that of such royalists and High Church believers as Quarles, Cleveland, Crashaw, and Cowley; it had also its very own brand of philosophico-religious belief in the group known as the Cambridge Platonists, of whom the chief members were Henry More (1614–87), Ralph Cudworth (1617–88), and Nathanael Culverwel (c. 1619–c. 1651), and who tried to combine puritan morality with Renaissance humanism. Poetry was very much in the air; like Henry More, many without great poetic talent nevertheless used verse for the expression of their ideas.

More, who entered Christ's while Milton was still there, was a fellow contributor to the Edward King memorial volume; another was John Cleveland (1613–58), a satirical poet of crudely metaphysical style, who was Father of the college revels the year after Milton. Cleveland transferred in 1634 to a fellowship at St John's, a more avowedly royalist college than Christ's, and altogether spent fifteen years at Cambridge. Many of his poems are aimed at a university audience.

By comparison with the subtle music of 'Lycidas', Cleveland's two elegies on King seem coarsely hyperbolic:

> We of the Gown our libraries must tosse,
> To understand the greatnesse of our losse,
> Be pupills to our grief, and so much grow
> In learning, as our sorrows overflow.
> When we have fill'd the rundlets of our eyes,
> We'll issue't forth, and vent such elegies,
> As that our tears shall seem the Irish seas,
> We floating Islands, living Hebrides.

Many of his other poems satirise local politics. The girl in 'Square-Cap' is determined what sort of headgear she wants on her lover – not the soldier's Monmouth cap nor the cleric's satin, but the graduate's traditional square cap, recently abolished by the Puritans as 'an invention which contravened the natural shape of the head':

A Cambridge-Lasse, *Venus*-like, borne of the froth
Of an old half-fill'd Jug of Barley broth,
    She, she is my Mistris, her Suitors are many,
    But shee'l have a *Square-cap*, if ere she have any.

Another poem, 'How the Commencement Grows New', got Cleveland into trouble, perhaps because it made fun of a serious subject – the cancellation of the Commencement ceremony of 1636 because of the plague.

When Cromwell was elected MP for the town in 1640 with a majority of one, Cleveland exclaimed that 'that single vote had ruined both Church and Kingdom'. In March 1642, when the king passed through Cambridge on his way north to gather his forces for the stand against parliament, Cleveland delivered a loyal oration at St John's that outshone even those of the Master of Trinity and the Public Orator (Henry Molle): Charles let him kiss his hand and commanded a copy to be sent after him. But when Cromwell's forces took control of the town in 1644, Cleveland prudently took to his heels, abandoning his furniture, and joined the king at Oxford. With the royal defeat in 1646 he disappeared into twilit obscurity, shifting from place to place, unable to return to Cambridge, finally dying in London 'of the scurvy'. Though his poems had great topical popularity, Dryden later judged that 'we cannot read a verse of Cleveland's without making a face at it, as if every word were a pill to swallow'.

A fate somewhat similar to Cleveland's awaited Richard Crashaw (1612–49), who came up to Pembroke from Charterhouse School in 1631 already with something of a literary reputation. Within a year he was contributing the usual elegies, including one on Samuel Brooke, Master of Trinity, and no fewer than five on William Herries, a young but brilliant Fellow of Pembroke who had been Milton's contemporary at Christ's.

Crashaw graduated in 1634, and in the same year his first book, a volume of Latin epigrams, was brought out by Thomas Buck. It had dedications to the Master of his college, a noted anti-Puritan whom Crashaw praised for his embellishment of the chapel, and to his tutor, Tournay, another High Church-man. The following year Crashaw was elected to a fellowship across the street at Peterhouse, a college which, under Matthew Wren and John Cosin, had become the leading centre of High Church practices in Cambridge. Here he actively participated in the beautifying of the new chapel, and two Latin poems of this date appealed for funds for other college buildings.

Peterhouse had hitherto used the next-door church of Little St Mary's for its worship, and it seems that Crashaw also took up some sort of official duty there. The preface to his principal work, *Steps to the Temple* (1646), says,

> Reader, we style his sacred poems *Steps to the Temple*, and aptly, for in the temple of God, under his wing, he led his life in St Mary's Church near St Peter's College. There he lodged under Tertullian's roof of angels; there he made his nest more gladly than David's swallow near the house of God; where like a primitive

saint, he offered more prayers in the night than others usually offer in the day;
there, he penned these poems, *Steps* for happy souls to climb heaven by.

One of Crashaw's pupils at Peterhouse was Ferrar Collet, nephew of Nicholas
Ferrar, and through him Crashaw was brought into the Little Gidding circle,
whose community must have suited his temperament perfectly, being High,
devout, monastic. He made frequent journeys to Little Gidding to join in their
vigils.

Crashaw made no more secret of his royalist feelings than did Cleveland, and
in 1642 clubbed together with other Peterhouse Fellows to guarantee Charles a
loan. Later he too judged it safer to flee the town. Soon after his departure, in
December 1643, William Dowsing, appointed to enforce parliament's ordinance
for the removal of statues, pictures, altars, and crucifixes from places of worship,
visited Peterhouse and Little St Mary's and destroyed all the embellishments that
Crashaw had so loved and added to. Cosin was expelled from his mastership,
Crashaw and four others (including his fellow poet Joseph Beaumont) from their
fellowships. So ended what Crashaw termed 'the little contentful kingdom' of his
years at Cambridge. Like Cleveland, Crashaw disappeared into obscurity. He was
at Oxford, then in Holland and Paris; finally, having gone over completely to
Roman Catholicism, he died in penurious exile in Italy.

Six years younger than Crashaw, his friend Abraham Cowley (1618–67) had
already published a volume of poems and written a comedy in the style of
Randolph by the time he came up to Trinity from Westminster School in 1636,
and he soon attracted further attention by writing a Latin comedy, *Naufragium
Joculare*, for his fellow students to perform. Cowley's dramatic ability was
recognised, and in March 1642, when the eleven-year-old Prince of Wales visited
the university (two days before the visit by the king at which Cleveland made his
oration), Cowley was commissioned at a week's notice to write a play for the
occasion. *The Guardian*, a slick Jonsonesque comedy full of stock satirical
characters, served the purpose well, and the prince 'commended the performance
and gave all signs of great acceptance which he could, and more than the
University dared expect'. Almost immediately afterwards, however, parliament
put a total ban on stage plays, thus frustrating the careers of aspiring play-
wrights like Cowley and virtually killing off the tradition of college plays.
After the Restoration Cowley revised his student composition and, under
the new title of *The Cutter of Coleman Street*, it achieved a wider London
acclaim.

Cowley had a gift for friendship. In Paris he later came to the rescue of the
destitute Crashaw, and he wrote an elegy on Crashaw's death. But more poignant
is his elegy 'On the Death of Mr William Hervey', which records another
Cambridge friendship which ended tragically. Little is known about Hervey
except that he entered Pembroke in 1636, became Cowley's intimate friend, and
died at Cambridge in May 1642. Cowley calls him 'the truest *Friend* on earth'

and says: 'A strong and mighty *Influence* joyn'd our *Birth*.' Possibly this was another instance of Cambridge *amor platonicus*.

> Ye fields of *Cambridge*, our dear *Cambridge*, say,
> Have ye not seen us walking every day?
> Was there a *Tree* about which did not know
>   The *Love* betwixt us two?
> Henceforth, ye gentle *Trees*, for ever fade;
>   Or your sad branches thicker joyn,
>   And into darksome shades combine,
> *Dark* as the *Grave* wherein my *Friend* is laid.

Elected a Minor Fellow of Trinity in 1640, Cowley seemed in line for a full fellowship in 1643, but the political situation destroyed his Cambridge career too. Like the others, he fled to Oxford, where he entered himself at St John's College. In 1644, like Crashaw, he was expelled from his Cambridge fellowship, which he did not recover until after the Restoration. In the Latin 'Elegia Dedicatoria' prefaced to his *Poems* of 1656, Cowley laments his enforced absence from Cambridge, that place of poetry and tranquillity where, he says, he used to sit by the Cam singing his boyish melodies.[1]

Andrew Marvell (1621–78), though three years younger again than Cowley, came up to Trinity as a sizar four years before Cowley, in 1633, at the extremely tender age of twelve. The Marvells were a Cambridgeshire family of yeoman stock, who can be traced in the villages of Shepreth and Meldreth as far back as 1279. The poet's father was probably born in the house in Meldreth that remained known as The Marvells until the nineteenth century; he was himself educated at Emmanuel College, took holy orders, and moved to Yorkshire, where the poet was born and brought up.

Little is known about Marvell's Cambridge career, and he wrote no poetry of significance during it. In 1637, still only sixteen, he contributed Greek and Latin verses to a commemorative volume on the birth of a royal child (Crashaw, Cowley, and Beaumont were also contributors). The following year he was appointed to a scholarship worth 13s 4d a year, plus a shilling a week for food.

A curious tradition relates that Marvell's undergraduate studies were interrupted at some stage when 'some Jesuits with whom he was then conversant, seeing in him a genius beyond his years . . . used all the arguments they could to seduce him away, which at last they did'. His father came from Hull to search for the truant, tracked him down in a bookseller's shop in London, and 'prevailed with him to return to the college'. If authentic, the story seems to indicate a streak

---

[1] The ejected Cowley's line 'O Camus! Phoebo nullus quo gratior amnis!' ('no stream is more attractive to Apollo') contrasts with the rusticated Milton's line 'Quam male Phoebicolis convenit ille locus!' ('nowhere is more uncongenial to Apollo').

of rebelliousness and a malleability in his religious outlook (it was to be several years before he committed himself to the Puritan cause). His name is absent from the next volume of royal commemorations when the other three poets again vented their loyal feelings.

Marvell took his BA in 1639 and had probably intended to continue for his MA, but his father was drowned in the Humber in 1641, and he abandoned his studies and left Cambridge. Inheriting family property at Meldreth, he was able to spend the next years travelling in Europe. More than likely he had become friendly at Trinity with one of the leading Cavalier poets, Richard Lovelace (1618–58), who studied there briefly after graduating from Oxford: in 1648 Marvell's poems show that his sympathies were, if anything, still with the Cavaliers.

Though Marvell himself spent much of the Civil War period abroad, the opening lines of his 'Horatian Ode' (1650) sum up this turbulent epoch when force of arms defeated strength of reason, when soldiers ousted scholars:

> The forward youth that would appear
> Must now forsake the Muses dear,
> > Nor in the shadows sing
> > His numbers languishing.
> 'Tis time to leave the books in dust,
> And oil th'unused armour's rust,
> > Removing from the wall
> > The corslet of the hall.

The particular tribulations endured by Cambridge during the war are narrated in a propagandist work, the *Querela Cantabrigiensis* (1646), based on material collected by an expelled royalist, John Barwick of St John's, and published from Oxford. This relates how masters of colleges were evicted and imprisoned, students' rooms turned into billets, college groves cut down, King's College Chapel used as a drill hall, the Prayer Book torn up in Great St Mary's, sacred monuments destroyed, and 'sanctuaries of learning and piety' turned generally into 'mere spittals and bawdy-houses for sick and debauched soldiers, being filled with queans, drabbs, fiddlers, and revels, night and day'. When the Barebones Parliament of 1653 seriously debated abolishing schools and universities altogether, Quarles's prescient earlier verses satirising the Puritans' excesses became urgently relevant:

> We'll down with all the Varsities
> > Where learning is profest,
> Because they practise and maintain
> > The language of the Beast;
> We'll drive the Doctors out of doors,
> > And all that learned be;
> We'll cry all arts and learning down –
> > And hey! then up go we.

Cromwell's commonwealth was in full swing when John Dryden (1631–1700) came up to Trinity as a pensioner in 1650. He had already, as a Westminster schoolboy, had an elegy printed commemorating the death of a nobleman's son (Marvell wrote a poem for the same collection), but, like Marvell, he seems to have written nothing of significance while at Cambridge. His university career, in fact, is as obscure as Marvell's, with which it shares some traits – an unexplained contretemps, departure hastened by family death, and a later unfounded slur of expulsion. Apart from a letter from Dryden at Cambridge to his cousin Honor, written in 1653, and the facts that he was elected to a scholarship in October 1650 and that his tutor's name was John Templer, virtually the only record of his student days is of a disciplinary nature. An entry in the Conclusion Book (minute book of college meetings) for July 1652 reads:

> Agreed then that Dreyden be put out of Commons for a forthnight at least, & that he goe not out of the Colledg during the time aforesaid excepting to sermons without express leave fro the Master or Vicemaster. & that at the end of the forthnight he read a confession of his crime in the hall at Dinner time; at the three fellowes table. His crime was his disobedience to the Vicemaster & his contumacy in taking of his punishment inflicted by him.

The precise nature of the original offence is not known.

Dryden took his BA in March 1654 and no doubt would have stayed on, but when his father died three months later he returned to the family estates in Northamptonshire to take up his responsibilities as head of the family and never returned to Cambridge. Trinity kept his place open for him until April 1655.

Not only did Dryden never return, in his later years he keenly patronised Oxford. Converted to Roman Catholicism in 1687, he became a staunch supporter of James II, and when the king was busy putting Catholics illegally into Oxford fellowships rumours floated that Dryden had put his name forward for the position of either President of Magdalen or Warden of All Souls. Nothing came of it, though his son was squeezed into a fellowship at Magdalen. That Dryden was something of a turncoat (his first major publication had been 'Heroique Stanzas to the Glorious Memory of Cromwell' and he had worked for Cromwell with Milton and Marvell) cannot be denied; but his often quoted lines

> Oxford to him a dearer name shall be
> Than his own mother university.
> Thebes did his green, unknowing youth engage,
> He chooses Athens in his riper age.

were in fact written in 1676 as part of one of several 'Prologues to the University of Oxford' which he wrote to precede performances given by the London stage companies on their summer tours to Oxford. They are little more than a humorously flattering witticism to get a student audience warmed up. (He once remarked: 'How easy 'tis to pass anything upon an university, and how gross flattery the learned will endure.') Dryden's funeral oration in Westminster

Abbey was delivered by Sir Samuel Garth, physician, orator, poet, and fellow Cantabrigian, so in a sense Cambridge can claim to have had the last word.

One of Dryden's contemporaries, however, was very little inclined to praise him. Thomas Shadwell (1640–92), who entered Caius in 1656 but does not seem to have taken a degree, went on to become a successful dramatist. His virulent hatred of Dryden has never been satisfactorily explained; but in 1682 he lampooned Dryden, now the first official Poet Laureate, in *The Medal of John Bayes*, claiming among other things that

> At Cambridge first your scurrilous vein began,
> Where saucily you traduced a nobleman;
> Who for that crime rebuked you on the head,
> And you had been expell'd had you not fled.

Dryden retaliated with *Mac Flecknoe* ('The rest to some faint meaning make pretence, / But Shadwell never deviates into sense'). When Dryden was deprived of his offices in 1688, it was the 'True-Blue Protestant' Shadwell who took over as Poet Laureate.

7

'And so . . . to Cambridge'

Like the Marvells, the Pepyses had been established in Cambridgeshire for
centuries, particularly in the village of Cottenham, six miles north of Cambridge,
where in medieval times they had worked as reeves and bailiffs in the service of
Crowland Abbey's manor there. In the reign of Elizabeth (so Pepys records in his
diary on 12 June 1667) there were twenty-six men of the name in Cottenham
alone.

The first Pepys to rise in the world was the diarist's great-grandfather, John
Pepys of Cottenham, who married an heiress in 1579 and so acquired the manor
of Impington, three miles north of Cambridge, where he built himself an
imposing manor house (demolished in 1953). His youngest son, Talbot Pepys,
who inherited the estate, became MP and Recorder (in succession to Francis
Brackyn) for Cambridge, as in his turn did Talbot's eldest son Roger. Another
son, Dr John Pepys, Fellow of Trinity Hall, was also a lawyer. Talbot, Roger,
John, and other local relations feature in the pages of Pepys's diary.

Pepys's father was born in Impington but migrated to London to try his fortune
as a tailor; Samuel Pepys (1633–1703) was his eldest surviving child. During the
Civil War young Pepys was sent to stay with his father's eldest brother Robert,
who had himself migrated from Impington to Brampton, near Huntingdon; and
for a while Pepys attended the Huntingdon Free School. Just up the road was
the great house of Hinchingbrooke, home of the Mountagus, one of the most
influential families in the land: Talbot Pepys's sister Paulina (Pepys's great-aunt)
had married Sir Sidney Mountagu and it was probably at this time that Pepys first
met their son Edward, later to be the first Earl of Sandwich and Pepys's patron
and first employer.

Back in London, Pepys was sent to St Paul's School, from which he won a
leaving exhibition to help him to go to university. Cambridge was the obvious
choice and Trinity Hall the college with family connections, and in 1650 he
was entered there as a sizar; but he transferred his name almost at once to
Magdalene, no doubt fishing for a scholarship. (The Master of Magdalene had
a house near the Pepyses in Salisbury Court; Pepys's tutor at Magdalene,

Samuel Morland, knew the Mountagus – possible reasons for the choice of college.)

The college Register records that Pepys was admitted in October 1650, but a note in the diary (31 December 1664) testifies to Pepys's actual date of arrival: 'Went to reside in Magd. Coll. Camb., and did put on my gown first March 5 1651.' A month later Pepys obtained a Spendluffe Scholarship; in October 1653 he was preferred to the more recent Smith Scholarship – evidence that he was considered a bright and deserving student. But perhaps he over-celebrated his good fortune, for only a week or two later there is a further entry in the college register (21 October 1653): 'Peapys and Hind were solemnly admonished by myself and Mr Hill for having been scandalously overseen in drink the night before. This was done in the presence of the Fellows then resident, in Mr Hill's chamber.' Poetic justice was done six years later when he was entertained to a 'very handsome supper' with the Fellows in the very same chamber.

Pepys's tutor Morland was an absent-minded scientist, inventor of the ear trumpet and of a primitive computer, an early experimenter with steam, equally at home among diplomacy and hydrostatics, ciphers and Latin. He was later awarded a baronetcy for his undercover services to the king during the Common-wealth, but was improvident with money, and Pepys did not retain a high opinion of him ('is believed to be a beggar. And so I ever thought he would be' – 25 November 1664).

Scraps of information about Pepys's college days are scattered about the pages of his diary. His chamber fellow at Magdalene was Robert Sawyer, later Attorney-General; he played music with one Nicholson; knew Sir John Skeffington – 'one with whom I had no great acquaintance, he being then (God knows) much above me' – and even Dryden. Another contemporary at both St Paul's and Magdalene was Richard Cumberland, later Bishop of Peterborough, at one stage a prospective husband for Pepys's sister. Pepys enjoyed keeping up old college contacts in later life: on 10 February 1667 he bumped into one Carter, and 'had much talk of all our old acquaintance of the College, concerning their various fortunes; wherein, to my joy, I met not with any that have sped better than myself'.

As well as cultivating his musical interests, Pepys once tried his hand at writing a romance, *Love a Cheat*, which he found again among old papers in 1664 and 'reading it over tonight, I liked it very well and wondered a little at myself at my vein at that time when I wrote it'. One of his Cottenham cousins introduced him to a convivial bawd, Mrs Aynsworth, 'the woman that, among other things . . . did teach me *Full forty times over*, a very lewd song'. Subsequently banished from Cambridge by the proctors, she transferred her activities to the Reindeer Inn at Bishop's Stortford; Pepys lodged there on 7 October 1667 on one of his trips to Cambridge, 'but there was so much tearing company in the house, that . . . I had no opportunity of renewing my old acquaintance with her' – perhaps just as well, since he had his wife with him.

Pepys often walked with friends in the environs of Cambridge, and on a summer day in 1653 drank gratefully and copiously from a conduit head known as Aristotle's Well (probably the one off Madingley Road that supplies the fountain in Trinity Great Court) and was in agonies of pain for days as a result. Like Erasmus, Pepys suffered from the stone, and the draughts of cold spring water carried the stone from his kidneys into his bladder. Unlike Erasmus, however, Pepys had no complaint with the college beer (in which, presumably, he was 'overseen' a few months later and which on a visit in 1668 he praised as 'the best I ever drank').

It was probably while at Magdalene that Pepys learnt the system of shorthand which he later used in the diary. Thomas Shelton's *Tachygraphy*, which had already gone through three editions at the University Press, must have been as much a boon to the student dependent on accurate lecture notes (at a time when few could afford books of their own) as it was to the busy Naval Office bureaucrat that Pepys later became.

Pepys took his degree in 1654 and returned to London. It is not known if he revisited Cambridge before the opening of the diary on 1 January 1660; but in the eight and a half years covered by the diary there are several descriptions of trips to Cambridge. The first of these, on 25–7 February 1660, records a weekend visit to see his youngest brother John installed in his turn as an undergraduate. Again there was an initial switching of colleges with an eye to a scholarship – this time from Magdalene to Christ's.

Setting out early from London, where the talk was all of the impending Restoration, Pepys got only as far as Fowlmere, six miles short of Cambridge, by nightfall, putting up at the Chequers (still in existence). By eight next morning he was at the Falcon in Petty Cury, where his father and brother were staying. After seeing John admitted at Christ's, Pepys made a courtesy call on the Fellows of Magdalene. In the afternoon he visited his Angier cousins (John Angier was a local tailor; his brother Percival had married a Pepys), bought a defence of Charles I in Morden's bookshop (monarchy being back in vogue), and gravitated with friends

> to the Three Tuns,[1] where we drank pretty hard and many healths to the King &c till it began to be darkish; then we broke up and I and Mr Zanchy went to Magdalen College, where a very handsome supper at Mr Hills chamber, I suppose upon a club among them; where in their discourse I could find that there was nothing at all left of the old preciseness in their discourse, especially on Saturday nights.

– a comment on the academic deterioration after a decade of Puritan rule. On Sunday morning he strolled about King's and attended service in St Botolph's, before dining with John's tutor. Returning to Magdalene, he fell in again with Clement Sankey and John Peachell (later Master of the college), with whom he

---

[1] On the corner of Market Hill and St Edward's Passage. The site was redeveloped by King's in 1961.

adjourned this time to the Rose,[2] where they 'sat drinking the King's and his whole family's health till it began to be dark'. When they left, Pepys searched out his family and returned to the Rose for a second bout, 'not telling them that we had been there before'. Then to his Angier cousins for supper, with 'a quart or two of wine' sent on at Pepys's expense from the tavern. After supper, his friend Fairbrother of King's took him aside and showed him some 'pitiful' verses he had written on the puritan pamphleteer William Prynne, hoping that Pepys would use his influence to get him some position for them,

> which I said I would do, but did laugh in my sleeve to think of his folly, though indeed a man that hath always expressed great civility to me . . . I took leave of all my friends and so to my Inn. Where . . . I bade good-night to my father; and John went to bed but I stayed up a little while, playing the fool with the lass of the house at the door of the chamber; and so to bed.

Next day, on his way back to London, he stopped at Audley End, where he drank further healths to the king and played his flageolet in the cellars of the great house, admiring the echo.

On 6 July 1661, Pepys was woken by news that Uncle Robert of Brampton had died. He rose in excitement and high expectation, and posted at once to Brampton, covering the distance in one day, 'greedy to see the Will'. It turned out that his uncle had left his affairs in disorder, and Pepys's inheritance proved in many ways a nuisance and the cause of many subsequent trips to the area. On this occasion he spent two weeks away from London. On 15 July, seeking family documents at Impington, he rode over to Cambridge:

> Up by 3 a-clock this morning and rode to Cambrige, and was there by 7 a-clock. Where after I was trimmed, I went to Christ College and find my brother John at 8 a-clock in bed, which vexed me. Then to Kings College chappell, where I find the scholers in their surplices at the service with the organs – which is a strange sight to what it used in my time to be here.

Surplices, organs – the puritan austerities were fast vanishing. Once again the same names briefly recur in the diary – Sankey, Fairbrother, Cousin Angier, the Rose – before Pepys rides on to Impington, where he finds Great-uncle Talbot sitting all alone, 'like a man out of the world. He can hardly see; but all things else he doth pretty livelyly.' A fortnight later, Pepys was back again to consult with Roger Pepys over the legal problems of his inheritance; they met at Shire Hall, where Roger was attending the Assizes as Recorder of Cambridge, and dined with Dr John of Trinity Hall. Afterwards Pepys once more made merry with his Magdalene friends at the Rose. He spent the weekend at Impington, having the best chamber and picking fruit in the orchard on Sunday. Then he rode back to Brampton and his father, 'who could decerne that I had been drinking, which

---

2 For many years one of the town's leading inns; Rose Crescent marks the site of its yard.

he did never see or hear of before' – was the father or the son the victim of self-deception?

When he returned in September to attend a court hearing at Graveley, he brought his wife along to show her his Cambridge haunts. She especially wanted to see Sturbridge Fair, 'but the fair was almost done, so we did not light there at all, but went back to Cambridge and there at the beare[3] had some herings, we and my brother'.

In October 1662, when Pepys again came to seek Roger's advice and once more put up at the Bear, he was excited to learn that a Congregation was to be held for the election of university officers. Supplied with gown, cap, and hood by the obliging Fairbrother, he entered the Regent House and duly voted as a fully fledged MA,[4] 'being much pleased of doing this jobb of work, which I have long wished for and could never have had such a time as now to do it with so much ease'. After visits to Impington and Brampton, Pepys returned via Cambridge in order to show its sights to a friend,

> and so by Moonelight most bravely all the way to Cambrige with great pleasure; whither we came at about 9 a-clock and took up at the beare, but the house being full of guests, we had very ill lodging, which troubled me. But had a supper and my mind at good ease, and so to bed.

Next morning he was summoned from his slumbers by a string band, and breakfasted in the room where Cromwell's Eastern Association had met 'to plot and act their mischiefs in those counties'.

The Pepys who next visits Cambridge, on 8 October 1667, is a Pepys gone up grandly in the world. He has survived the Plague and the Fire, and is in a couple of weeks to deliver his celebrated defence of the Navy Office at the Bar of the House of Commons. Travelling in a hired coach-and-four with his wife and the delectable new maid Deborah Willet, with his servant Will Hewer and another naval clerk in horseback attendance, he puts up at the Rose so that the ladies can meet the original of a character in a comedy by Dryden they have recently seen.

> . . . away to Cambrige, it being foul, rainy weather; and there did take up at the Rose, for the sake of Mrs Dorothy Drawwater, the vintener's daughter, which is mentioned in the play of *Sir Martin Marr-all*. Here we had a good chamber and bespoke a good supper; and then I took my wife and W. Hewer and Willett (it holding up a little) and showed them Trinity College and St Johns Library, and went to King's College chapel to see the outside of it only, and so to our Inne; and with much pleasure did this, they walking in their pretty morning gowns, very handsome, and I proud to find myself in condition to do this; and so home to our

---

[3] Market Passage marks the site of the Black Bear's yard.
[4] He had taken the degree *in absentia* in 1660 with Fairbrother's assistance, at a cost of £9 16s 0d – an indication of how the academic requirements had been relaxed in the thirty years since Milton's time.

lodging, and there by and by to supper with much good sport, talking with the drawers concerning matters of the town and persons whom I remember; and so after supper to cards and then to bed, lying, I in one bed and my wife and girl in another in the same room; and very merry talking together and mightily pleased both of us with the girl.

With the town waits in attendance next morning and beggars at the coach door, he can justifiably feel he has 'made good':

Up, and got ready and eat our breakfast and then took coach; and the poor, as they did yesterday, did stand at the coach to have something given them, as they do to all great persons, and I did give them something; and the town musique did also come and play; but Lord, what sad music they made . . .

The main object of this trip was to recover his gold from the garden at Brampton, where he had buried it during the recent invasion scare.

On 23 May 1668, the last full year of the diary, Pepys arrived by public coach in torrential rain, again on his way to Brampton. His father, who had retired to the house there, sent a man with a horse to meet him but Pepys put up overnight at the Rose because of the floods. As well as being one of the town's principal inns, the Rose was a popular student lodging house (the 'Wolf's College' of Randolph's day), as Pepys had cause to regret: 'after supper to bed and lay very ill by reason of some drunken scholars making a noise all night'. Two days later, on his return journey, he wandered in sentimental mood about his old student haunts before catching the London coach:

I took my boy and two brothers and walked to Magdalen College; and there into the Butterys as a stranger and there drank my bellyfull of their beer, which pleased me as the best I ever drank; and hear by the butler's man, who was son to Goody Mulliner over against the College that we used to buy stewed prunes of, concerning the College and persons in it; and find very few, only Mr Hollins and Peachell I think, that were of my time. But I was mightily pleased to come in this condition to see and ask; and thence, giving the fellow something, away; walked to Chesterton to see our old walk; and there into the church, the bells ringing, and saw the place I used to sit in; and so to the ferry, and ferried over to the other side and walked with great pleasure, the river being mighty high by Barnwell Abbey; and so by Jesus College to the town, and so to our quarters and to supper; and then to bed, being very weary and sleepy, and mightily pleased with this night's walk.

Though Pepys enjoyed his Cambridge trips, they were no more than brief diversions from the London spheres where his real interests and ambitions lay. But in 1681 he may have been tempted to return to Cambridge in earnest. Expelled from his post as Secretary to the Admiralty, imprisoned for some months in the Tower, and now out of office and idle, he toyed with the idea of retreating into some congenial academic niche to devote himself to such long-neglected literary projects as his planned history of the navy. He made overtures, sounded out his old university contacts, and on 8 August 1681, when Provost Page of King's College fell down dead 'in the act of rebuking an irregular scholar', a special messenger was dispatched to Pepys with the news: 'The preferment is £700 per annum and I am sure you would be as acceptable a man as the King could present unto it so that if no time be lost I should with all joy imaginable salute you Provost.' Pepys hesitated, tempted by this plum position. A wealthy man now, he was even willing to donate his first year's salary to the college. But he scrupled that he was not academically qualified for the position; moreover, running over in his mind that Cambridge fraternity he had known – improvident Morland, inebriate Peachell, Sankey who 'in his talk is but a mean man', Fairbrother at whom once 'I did laugh in my sleeve', and latterly Dr Vincent of Clare, dabbler in invisible inks and luminous watches – he probably decided that London, for all its merciless reversals of fortune, was his true environment. Three years later he was reappointed to his Admiralty post and elected President of the Royal Society. The naval history was never written.

Throughout his life, but especially in his later years, Pepys expended much money and loving care on his private library. When he died childless in 1703 he willed the library to John Jackson, his sister's younger son, with instructions that after Jackson's death it should go, intact and exactly as he had arranged it, to a university college, preferably Magdalene. Jackson, himself a Magdalene man, made the appropriate arrangements, choosing for its new home rooms in the New Building to which Pepys had himself subscribed. The Bibliotheca Pepysiana arrived at Magdalene after Jackson's death in 1724.

Pepys limited the library to exactly three thousand volumes, arranged by order of height rather than subject in twelve oak 'presses' specially built by a naval master joiner, the earliest bookcases to have glass doors. All the books, whose choice exemplifies the exceptional breadth of Pepys's interests, are beautifully bound, with his name and personal crest and arms on the covers. Among the many treasures are medieval manuscripts, twenty-five incunabula (including seven Caxtons), vast quantities of naval material gathered preparatory to his history, and collections of engravings, ballads, maps, chapbooks, and music.

But the library's most celebrated possession must be the six manuscript volumes of the diary itself, written in shorthand, to which, for a century after Pepys's death, no one seems to have paid more than cursory attention. In fact it was not until 1819, after the successful publication of Evelyn's diary, that Lord Braybrooke, brother of the Master of Magdalene, employed an impecunious undergraduate of St John's, John Smith, to transcribe the diary for him. Smith devoted three years to the task for a not excessive payment (£200; Sir Walter Scott received £100 for reviewing the work when it was published), apparently unaware that the key to the shorthand, Shelton's *Tachygraphy*, was itself in the library. Braybrooke, whom Smith never met, somewhat cavalierly edited and condensed the result and published it in 1825 as *Memoirs of Samuel Pepys*. The book's success was immediate and it went through numerous subsequent editions; but not until the 1970s, under the editorship of Robert Latham, Pepys Librarian, and William Matthews, did a complete and unbowdlerised edition of one of the best-known and best-loved works in the language finally appear.[5]

---

[5] Other Cambridge diarists include Samuel Newton (1629–1718), alderman and later Mayor, whose diary, published in 1890, covers the years 1664–1717; Isaac Reed (1742–1807), Fellow of Emmanuel, whose diary for 1762–1804 was published in 1946; Joseph Romilly (1791–1864), Fellow of Trinity and University Registrary, whose diary for 1832–47 was published in 1967 and 1994; Josiah Chater (1828–1908), a woollen draper, whose diary for 1844–84 was published in 1975; and A. C. Benson, Master of Magdalene (see chapter 18 below). *The Diary of Samuel Pepys Esq., While an Undergraduate at Cambridge* (1864) is, needless to say, a spoof.

8

'Ignorance in stilts'

There was no rollicking at the Rose when John Evelyn (1620–1706), Pepys's Royal Society friend and fellow diarist, visited Cambridge in August 1654. An Oxford man who lacked Pepys's garrulity and human inquisitiveness, Evelyn confided dry comments to his journal. 'The whole town is situate in a low dirty unpleasant place, the streets ill-paved, the air thick and infected by the fens', he wrote. At St John's College Library he observed 'trifles . . . of no great value' apart from a portrait of John Williams, Archbishop of York, 'my kinsman, and their great benefactor'. Trinity Great Court, reputed to be the finest university quadrangle in Europe, 'in truth is far inferior to that of Christ Church in Oxford'. The Schools 'are very despicable, and Public Library but mean'. Evelyn admired the new Fellows' Building at Christ's, the unfinished new court at Clare, and 'old Hobson the pleasant carrier's beneficence of a fountain'; but the only sight to carry him away was King's College Chapel, from the roof of which 'we could descry Ely, and the encampment of Sturbridge Fair now beginning to set up their tents and booths'.

Equally primly discriminating was the diarist Celia Fiennes (1662–1741), who travelled the length of England sidesaddle, disparaging ancient monuments and applauding fashionable improvements, and who visited Cambridge in 1697. She heartily approved the recent landscaping of the Backs – 'the river runs at the back side of most of the colleges; they have fine stone bridges over it and gates that lead to fine walks' – and such new buildings as the Wren Library at Trinity – 'the room spacious and lofty, paved with black and white marble . . . and the finest carving in wood in flowers, birds, leaves, figures of all sorts as I ever saw'. She too climbed to the top of King's Chapel – 'the finest building I have heard of' – but at St John's, where Evelyn had sniffed about the library, she took the air in the garden, with its 'close shady walks and open rows of trees and quickset hedges'.

Two late seventeenth-century Cambridge writers were launched on their careers by noble patronage. Nathaniel Lee (c. 1650–92) was a Fellow of Trinity when his poetic effusions were brought to the notice of the Duke of Buckingham, in Cambridge in 1671 to be installed as Chancellor. Buckingham was so impressed that he carried Lee back to London with him, but there promptly forgot about his protégé, who, after failing as an actor, eventually achieved fame as a dramatist.

Matthew Prior (1664–1721) must have been London's most scholarly pot-boy when discovered by the Earl of Dorset in a tavern and dispatched at his expense to Cambridge. He entered St John's in 1682, was elected to a fellowship in 1688, and while there wrote his first poetry. In 1690 Prior joined the diplomatic service, rising to the rank of ambassador, but prudently retained his fellowship, which, when he fell into disgrace in 1715, provided his only income. Later he found fresh patrons in the Harleys of Wimpole Hall (eight miles south-west of Cambridge), who amassed the great library later acquired by the British Museum and were friends of Pope and Swift. Some lines of Prior's, declaimed in 1719 in the library of St John's when the Harleys were visiting from Wimpole, fulsomely compare Lady Harley with the college's foundress, Lady Margaret Beaufort. Prior, who died at Wimpole, left some sumptuously bound books to his old college, together with his portrait in ambassador's costume. A wit equally at home among lords or ale-house wives, Prior could turn his hand to flattery or debunking at a moment's notice. Kept standing once, despite his ambassador's rank, during an interview with the Master of St John's (who apparently hoped for ecclesiastical preferment), he wrought a satirical epigram on the subject while walking back from the college to the Rose where he was dining:

> I stood, sir, patient at your feet,
>   Before your elbow-chair;
> But make a bishop's throne your seat,
>   I'll *kneel* before you there.
> One only thing can keep you down
>   For your great soul too mean:
> You'd not, to mount a *bishop's* throne,
>   Pay homage to the *queen*.

A contemporary student of Prior's was the great classical scholar and tyrannical Master of Trinity, Richard Bentley (1662–1742). Beginning as a Johnian sizar, Bentley went on to become the King's Librarian in London at an early age, and soon acquired both fame for his scholarship and notoriety for his literary warfare. Both qualities were manifest in his first great work, the *Dissertation on Phalaris* (1699), which devastatingly exploded the misinformed views on ancient authors of such writers as the aging Sir William Temple (formerly of Emmanuel). Jonathan Swift, then acting as Temple's secretary, celebrated the protracted fracas that ensued in one of his first satires, *The Battle of the Books*.

More embittered battling – in print and in the courts – followed Bentley's arrival in 1700 as Master of Trinity. Although his long-running feud with the Fellows culminated in his legal ejection from the mastership in 1734, in fact he continued blithely to occupy the Lodge until his death eight years later at the age of eighty. Despite his despotic methods, Bentley modernised the college in a manner Celia Fiennes would have commended, and so restored the University Press as to earn the title of its 'second founder'. But only Bentley could have mustered the energy, arrogance, and scholarship to bring out an 'improved' edition of Milton's *Paradise Lost*. Affecting to believe that the blind poet's true intentions had been perverted by careless amanuenses and meddling editors, Bentley resolutely attacked the text with his blue pencil, turning Miltonisms into Bentleyisms and removing passages of which he disapproved with such comments as 'a silly interruption of the story'. For all its presumptions, however, Bentley's *Paradise Lost* constituted the first scholarly textual edition in English literature.[1]

A person of Bentley's controversial stature was naturally the subject of innumerable pamphlets, satires, squibs, and lampoons. Alexander Pope included him among the university Dunces in Book IV of *The Dunciad*, published in 1742 just before Bentley's death. Pope dubs Bentley the 'Aristarch' after a celebrated Greek 'corrector' of Homer, and makes a pun on Bentley's favourite drink.

> As many quit the streams that murmuring fall
> To lull the sons of Margaret and Clare Hall,
> Where Bentley late tempestuous wont to sport
> In troubled waters, but now sleeps in port.
> Before them marched that awful Aristarch;
> Ploughed was his front with many a deep remark:
> His hat, which never vailed to human pride,
> Walker with reverence took, and laid aside.

Although in Pope's version 'Frog' Walker, Bentley's appointee as Vice-Master, is used like a servant, he was in fact fondly attached to Bentley. Bentley's grandson, Richard Cumberland (1732–1811), an author of sentimental comedies who was born in the Master's Lodge, defended Walker in his *Memoirs*: 'As for the hat, I must acknowledge it was of formidable dimensions, yet . . . Pope found an office for Walker that I can well believe he was never commissioned to in his life.'[2]

Another target for Pope was Laurence Eusden (1688–1730), also of Trinity, one of the least distinguished of all Poets Laureate:

> Know Eusden thirsts no more for sack or praise;
> He sleeps among the dull of ancient days.

---

1 Milton received five pounds for *Paradise Lost*. For his 'improved' version, Bentley received a hundred guineas.
2 Among later writers, Lord Macaulay described the Battle of the Books in his essay on Sir William Temple (1838); Virginia Woolf sketched a portrait of Bentley (in *The Common Reader*, 1925); and Lytton Strachey depicted Bentley's war with the Fellows of Trinity through the eyes of his principal adversary in 'The Sad Story of Dr Colbatch' (*Portraits in Miniature*, 1923).

A Yorkshireman like Bentley, Eusden entered Trinity in 1705 and was elected to a fellowship in 1712. In 1714 he followed in Cleveland's steps by incurring wrath with some satirical *Verses at the Last Publick Commencement at Cambridge*. These were declaimed in Great St Mary's on one of the university's grandest occasions, the so-called Public Commencement (a glorified version, held to celebrate some national event such as a new monarch, of the annual Commencement ceremony held in June), satire being so customary to the eighteenth century that it was even incorporated into occasions like this.[3] At the 1714 ceremony, the main verse 'Music Speech' was delivered by Roger Long (later Master of Pembroke), who made sport of the fact that the ladies, after straitlacing themselves for months in order to 'look fuller in the chest, and more slender in the waist' for the occasion, had that year been hidden away in the chancel pews instead of adorning their usual galleries. Eusden's speech, delivered to the same distinguished congregation, satirised in like vein the latest fashion of hoop-petticoats, suggesting how classical mythology would have had to be rewritten if goddesses had worn such 'machines', and contrasting the promiscuous present age with previous centuries:

> Then Barnwell virgins might securely rove,
> Unharmed, though rifled in the neighbouring grove;
> No Proctor's staff yet walked its awful round,
> Nor midnight purple startled at the sound;
> Ere Sunday nymphs on Clare Hall Piece were seen,
> Or coffee booths aspired on Jesus Green;
> Ere Covent Garden mistresses came down,
> And taught the youths to tympanize the town;
> Ere Sophs had learnt with hums the pit to fill,
> Or Beaux to flutter round the Market Hill.

Though Victorian editors thought Eusden's poem 'unfit for modern print', its chief offence against morality was its having been recited by a reverend academic in a university church. Eusden's later poetry was duller. Changing his tune from satire to sycophancy, he eased himself into the laureateship in 1718; but his tenure was chiefly remembered for his drinking. As Gray summed up, 'Eusden was a person of great hopes in his youth, though at last he turned out a drunken parson.'

William Stukeley (1687–1765), co-founder of the Society of Antiquaries and author of an influential book on Stonehenge, conceived his love of antiquities

---

[3] At ordinary Commencements, an official known as the 'Praevaricator' (Randolph held the post in 1632) traditionally sent up well-known university figures and recent events (the Oxford equivalent was known as 'Terrae Filius'). Another such figure was 'Mr Tripos', originally the official who sat on a three-legged stool in medieval times and disputed with degree candidates but by the end of the seventeenth century the licensed jester of the graduation ceremony. During the eighteenth century Mr Tripos was suppressed, though humorous Latin 'Tripos Verses' continued to be printed on the backs of the lists of successful candidates. (Gray wrote Tripos Verses in 1736, Smart in 1740–2.)

while at Corpus Christi in 1703–9. 'I frequently took a walk to sigh over the ruins of Barnwell Abbey', he recalled, 'and made a draught of it, and used to cut pieces of the yew trees there into tobacco stoppers, lamenting the destruction of so noble monuments of the piety and magnificence of our ancestors'. Similarly he used to 'sit an hour or two together in the antechapel of King's College, viewing and contemplating the building'.

In the Long Vacation of 1710, a journal-keeping, library-trotting German breezed incredulously through Cambridge. Zacharias Conrad von Uffenbach (1683–1734) considered Cambridge town 'no better than a village'. The inns were ill-appointed, no one could speak German, there was endless trouble getting libraries opened up, and he was 'amazed to find . . . that the professors only lecture in the winter, and then . . . to bare walls, for no one comes to hear them'. Uffenbach's German contempt surpassed Evelyn's merely Oxonian belittlement. The libraries especially outraged him. At Caius, the manuscripts were kept in 'a miserable garret under the roof, which could have been very little or not at all visited, for the top step was buried in pigeons' dung and the manuscripts lay thick with dust on the floor'. At Peterhouse he had to wrap himself in a towel to protect his clothes. In Magdalene College Library 'all the books, with hardly one exception, are entirely overgrown with mould'. At the University Library the attendant, noting his interest in a codex of Josephus, happily tore him out a page.

Uffenbach visited Greek's coffee house where, 'particularly in the morning, and after three o'clock in the afternoon, you meet the chief professors and doctors, who read the papers over a cup of coffee and a pipe of tobacco, and converse on all subjects'. Calling on Bentley in his expensively rebuilt Lodge, Uffenbach found him 'as well lodged as the Queen at St James's, or better'. Bentley, 'rather tall and spare and red in the face', spoke 'tolerably intelligible Latin' for an Englishman, and 'talked very big' of his forthcoming edition of Horace, 'scorning all other editions'. While in Cambridge, Uffenbach made enquiry about the Wandering Jew, the mythical figure popular in German literature who was said to have been condemned by Christ to wander the earth until the Second Coming. A German author, Wilhelm Tentzel, had reported him as having been sighted in Cambridge, where the professors had been amazed at his knowledge of languages and his fund of tales; but Uffenbach could not find anyone to verify the story.

John Byrom (1691–1763) was on good terms with all the Bentley family, especially the beautiful daughter 'Jug' (who has been identified with the 'Phoebe' in his amusing 'Ballad'). Author of the hymn 'Christians awake', poet, and diarist, Byrom was at Trinity from 1708 to 1717, but his Jacobite sympathies obliged him to resign his fellowship and he spent the rest of his life as a peripatetic teacher of shorthand. Intriguingly, the first known mention of Pepys's diary occurs in a letter written to Byrom in 1728 by a fellow shorthand enthusiast who had visited the Pepys Library and found the diary volumes by chance. But Byrom, admirably qualified to be the first to decipher the work, does not appear to have followed up the hint.

Byrom's Jacobite sympathies and mystical leanings were shared by his friend and Emmanuel contemporary William Law (1686–1761), author of *A Serious Call to a Devout and Holy Life*. Law was elected a Fellow of Emmanuel in 1713 but fell out with the college and lost his degrees over a speech condemning the government. He later became private tutor to Edward Gibbon, father of the historian, and accompanied him back to Emmanuel in 1727. The *Serious Call* was partly written at Cambridge during this stay.

Statesman, diplomatist, slighting and immortally slighted patron of Dr Johnson, author of pragmatic letters to his bastard son, Lord Chesterfield (1694–1773) graced Trinity Hall with his presence in 1712–13. A letter written from Cambridge already crackles with worldly irony:

> I find the college where I am infinitely the best in the university; for it is the smallest, and it is filled with lawyers, who have lived in the world, and know how to behave. Whatever may be said to the contrary, there is certainly very little debauchery in this university, especially amongst people of fashion, for a man must have the inclinations of a porter to endure it here.

Jacobite disturbances at Oxford in 1715 prompted the new king, George I, to dispatch the cavalry; Whig Cambridge's loyal address on his accession was rewarded by his gift of the magnificent library of the late Bishop of Ely. The twin events inspired an exchange of epigrams. Dr Trapp of Oxford led off:

> King George, observing with judicious eyes
> The state of both his universities,
> To Oxford sent a troop of horse; and why?
> That learned body wanted loyalty.
> To Cambridge books he sent, as well discerning
> How much that loyal body wanted learning.

Hearing Dr Johnson reciting this years later, Sir William Browne (1692–1774), Fellow of Peterhouse, instantly riposted for Cambridge:

> The king to Oxford sent a troop of horse,
> For Tories own no argument but force;
> With equal skill to Cambridge books he sent,
> For Whigs admit no force but argument.

Appropriately, Browne later founded the university gold medals for Greek odes and epigrams; but Trapp's censure was partly justified by the way the University Library left the 30,000 books sent by the king lying about for years in heaps; 'cartloads' are said to have been pillaged before proper accommodation was provided for them.

Unlike Uffenbach's, the eye of Daniel Defoe (c. 1659–1731), who passed through Cambridge in September 1722, lit not on libraries but on men and markets. His *Tour through the Whole Island of Great Britain* skimps scenic or antiquarian description, focussing instead on everyday life. Looking down on murky Cambridge from the Gog Magog Hills, Defoe was moved to compassion for 'the many thousands of families that were bound to or confined in those fogs, and had no breath to draw than what must be mixed with those vapours, and that steam which so universally overspread the country'. What Defoe had come to see was Sturbridge Fair – 'not only the greatest in the whole nation, but in the world' – which John Bunyan had probably taken as the model for Vanity Fair in his *Pilgrim's Progress* (1678) and which was by now at the height of its size and celebrity.

Defoe found the fair arranged in streets like a town, with its own 'coffee-houses, taverns, brandy-shops, and eating-houses, innumerable, and all in tents', counted as many as fifty hackney coaches from London, and even found wherries brought down on waggons to ply on the Cam. Wandering its vast encampment, he noted down the various commodities on sale and enquired into customs and regulations. When at last he turns his unwilling attention to Cambridge itself, it is to mention only one college by name, Magdalene, and that for its insalubrious location (it was surrounded by brewhouses and brothels). Padding a paragraph on the interdependence of university and town, he moves quickly on. There is no mention in Defoe of the landscaping and building applauded by Fiennes – nor of the accompanying degeneracy of morals and learning.

Edward Ward (1667–1731), London tavern-keeper and author of the scurrilous *London Spy*, made no such error of omission in his pamphlet *A Step to Stir-Bitch Fair: With Remarks upon the University of Cambridge* (1700). His objective too was to see the great fair where 'vice, merchandise and diversion draw the Cambridge youth, London traders, Lynn whores, and abundance of ubiquitarian strollers into a promiscuous assembly', though his particular interest was more with the vice and diversion than the merchandise. After travelling down from London in a packed coach, enjoying salacious anecdotes on the way, Ward put up 'by the sign of the Devil's Lap-Dog in Petty Cury', which had a 'plump, young, brisk, black, beautiful, good landlady' on whose account the scholars 'crept in as fast and as slily, for either a kiss, a kind look, or a cup of comfort, as hogs into an orchard after a high wind'. Of the gownsmen to be seen in the streets, some looked 'with as meagre countenances as if in search of the philosopher's stone they had studied themselves into a hypochondriac melancholy', while others were as 'plump and as jolly as a painted Bacchus bestriding a canary butt'. The town itself was abominably dirty and most of its streets 'so very narrow, that should two wheelbarrows meet in the largest . . . they are enough to make a stop for half an hour'.

Next day Ward strolled to the fair, eschewing the hackney coaches – in which 'for eighteen pence a scholar and his mistress may have a running bawdy-house to themselves, draw up their tin-sashes, pinked like the bottom of a cullender, and hug one another as private as they please' – passing on his way through 'Bawdy Barnwell, so called from the numerous brothel-houses it contains for the health, ease and pleasure of the learned vicinity'. The fair itself teemed with 'such a multitude of gentry, scholars, tradesmen, whores, hawkers, pedlers and pickpockets, that it seemed to me . . . to show the world in epitomy'. In Cooks' Row – 'more properly Cuckolds' Row' – where the booksellers congregate, he observes students pilfering books they cannot afford in the long sleeves of their gowns, and listens to the facetious patter of one of the London auctioneers.[4]

William Pattison (1706–27), practically the only poet ever to emerge from Sidney Sussex College, depicted Cambridge in more romantic guise in his verse epistle to a school friend, 'The College Life' (1725). With its beautiful riverside and a string of poets already to its credit, Cambridge seemed to the freshman to possess the appearance and glamour of a cradle of the Muses:

> Then, lost in thought, where aged Cam divides
> Those verdant groves that paint his azure tides,
> With musing pleasure I reflect around,
> And stand enchanted in poetic ground.
> Straight to my glancing thought those bards appear
> That filled the world with fame, and charmed us here.
> Here Spenser, Cowley, and that awful name
> Of mighty Milton, flourished into fame;
> From these amusing groves, his copious mind
> The blooming shades of Paradise designed.
> In these retirements Dryden fanned his fire,
> And gentle Waller tuned his tender lyre.

But first appearances deceived, and Pattison soon found Cambridge to be less congenial to budding poets than he thought. Quarrelling with his tutor and threatened with expulsion, he absconded to London, leaving these verses, according to legend, pinned to his abandoned gown:

> 'Tired with the senseless jargon of the Gown,
> My master left the college for the Town;
> Where, from pedantic drudgery secured,
> He laughs at follies which he once endured;
> And scorns his precious minutes to regale
> With wretched college wit, and college ale . . . '

Pattison's hopes for literary success in London were to be cruelly dispelled. Despite encouragement from Eusden and Pope, he was soon reduced to sleeping on park benches, and died in abject poverty aged twenty-one.

---

[4] It was in Cooks' Row in 1662 that Isaac Newton, then a freshman at Trinity, bought his first book on astrology. In 1666 he bought at Sturbridge Fair the prism with which he investigated the nature of light, and which he is seen holding in Roubiliac's statue of him in Trinity antechapel.

Laurence Sterne (1713–68), who entered Jesus College in 1733 as a fatherless sizar, came from a family closely associated with the college. His great-grandfather, Richard Sterne, had been Master of the college until ejected and imprisoned by Cromwell; translated at the Restoration to the Archbishopric of York, he had founded some scholarships at Jesus, to one of which Sterne soon succeeded.

The author of *Tristram Shandy* entered Jesus in appropriately Shandean fashion, with his name incorrectly inscribed in the register as Henry – an act of carelessness echoed by Tristram's christening in the novel. Very poor, even with the scholarship, he was obliged to run up debts which took years to pay off, but made a lifelong friend in John Hall (1718–85), a wealthy young squire four years his junior who arrived as a fellow-commoner in 1735. Despite their different social circumstances, they became inseparable companions, calling one another 'cousin' and, according to tradition, sitting reading together beneath the great walnut tree that filled the college court. (Uffenbach on his visit to the college had ordered his servant to measure the tree's spread: ninety-six feet.) Sterne, facetious, sentimental, but the more scholarly, was able to help Hall with his studies; Hall, gregarious, light-hearted, impressionable, probably helped Sterne with money but also introduced him to fast and doubtless expensive circles.

Hall, who later double-barrelled himself into Hall-Stevenson, was the author of *Crazy Tales*, ribald imitations of French verse tales, and presided over a club of 'Demoniacs', of which Sterne was a member, at his Yorkshire seat, Crazy Castle. There is a memory of his college days in *Crazy Tales*:

> At Cambridge many years ago,
>   In Jesus, was a walnut tree –
> The only thing it had to show,
>   The only thing folks went to see.
> Being of such a size and mass,
>   And growing in so wise a college,
> I wonder how it came to pass
>   It was not called the Tree of Knowledge.

When Sterne graduated in 1737 he accepted the lowly position of assistant curate at St Ives, twelve miles from Cambridge. But in 1741 he became a prebendary of York, where he was to be celebrated for his preaching. The tuberculosis that eventually killed him had first announced itself at Cambridge, where he experienced a haemorrhage of the lung. A gruesome tradition recounts that after his death in London his remains were dug up by body-snatchers, smuggled to Cambridge, and sold to the School of Anatomy for dissection. One of the students, an old acquaintance of Sterne's, happened to lift the covering after dissection to look at the face, recognised the features, and fainted. A further embellishment claims that the skull of 'Yorick', as Sterne signed himself, was afterwards preserved in the Anatomy Museum. Sterne, who had a taste for the macabre (a caricature portrait at Jesus by Thomas Patch shows him raising his hat to Death), would have enjoyed the story.

Francis Coventry (1725–54), who studied at Magdalene and graduated as Second Wrangler[5] in 1749, wrote a single bestselling novel before his early death. *The History of Pompey the Little*, which he began writing while a student and which is probably the earliest novel with scenes set in Cambridge, was the literary rage of 1751. It relates the episodic adventures of a lapdog who, passing from one owner to another through all classes of society, witnesses the range of contemporary baseness and corruption.

At one point Pompey falls into the hands of a fellow-commoner named Qualmsick, who carries him off to Cambridge. Qualmsick is allowed great indulgence by his college, 'for as tutors and governors of colleges have usually pretty sagacious noses after preferment, they think it impolitic to cross the inclinations of young gentlemen, who are heirs to great estates, and from whom they expect benefices and dignities hereafter'. Qualmsick plays a prank, of the sort familiar from the cartoons of Rowlandson, on a don called Williams. A college bedmaker having been 'brought to bed, without having any husband to father the child', Qualmsick leaves a wicker basket at Williams's door with the note:

> Honourable Sir,
> Am surprised should use me in such a manner; have never seen one farthing of your money, since was brought to bed, which is a shame and a wicked sin. Wherefore have sent you your own bastard to provide for, and am your dutiful servant to command till death –
>
> > Betty Trollop

Williams is called upon to explain himself before the Master and Fellows; but the basket turns out to contain only Pompey, who thus passes into the ownership of Williams, a model of the idle, ignorant, sybaritic don of the time:

> Mr Williams was, in the first place, a man of the most punctilious neatness; his shoes were always blacked in the nicest manner, his wigs were powdered with the exactest delicacy, and he would scold his laundress for a whole morning together, if he discovered a wry plait in the sleeve of his shirt . . . He rose constantly to chapel, and proceeded afterwards with great importance to breakfast, which, moderately speaking, took up two hours of his morning. When this was over, he amused himself either in paring his nails, or watering two or three orange-trees, which he kept in his chamber . . . or in changing the situation of the few books in his study. The *Spectators* were removed into the place of the *Tatlers*, and the *Tatlers* into the place of the *Spectators*.

Dons are similarly lampooned by John Duncombe (1730–86), himself a Fellow of Corpus Christi, in a parody of Gray's 'Elegy' entitled 'An Evening Contemplation in a College' (1753):

---

[5] I.e. second in the tripos list. 'Wranglers' were those who took first-class degrees.

Now shine the spires beneath the paly moon,
And through the cloister peace and silence reign,
Save where some fiddler scrapes a drowsy tune,
Or copious bowls inspire a jovial strain.

Save that in yonder cobweb-mantled room,
Where lies a student in profound repose
Oppressed with ale, wide echoes through the gloom
The droning music of his vocal nose.

Within those walls, where through the glimmering shade
Appear the pamphlets in a mouldering heap,
Each in his narrow bed till morning laid,
The peaceful fellows of the college sleep.

. . . .

Oft have they basked along the sunny walls,
Oft have the benches bowed beneath their weight;
How jocund are their looks when dinner calls!
How smoke the cutlets on their crowded plate!

Students who imitated the idle ways of their elders were known in the jargon of the day as Loungers. The first issue of *The Student: or The Oxford and Cambridge Monthly Miscellany* (1750–1), the very first student magazine (partly edited by Christopher Smart), warns prospective freshmen that 'in every college there is a set of idle people called Loungers, whose whole business is to fly from the painful task of thinking'. A poem in a later issue outlines the Lounger's day:

I rise about nine, get to breakfast by ten,
Blow a tune on my flute, or perhaps make a pen;
Read a play till eleven, or cock my laced hat;
Then step to my neighbour's, till dinner, to chat.
Dinner over, to Tom's or to Clapham's I go,
The news of the town so impatient to know . . .
From the coffee-house then I to tennis away,
And at six I post back to my college to pray.
I sup before eight, and, secure from all duns,
Undauntedly march to the Mitre or Tuns.

When the Duke of Newcastle, the new Chancellor, introduced draconian regulations in 1750 to tighten up university discipline, there was an outburst of resentment, including a poem entitled *The Capitade*, attributed to Thomas Nevile of Jesus, which satirised the university authorities, and an eschatological pamphlet entitled *David's Prophecy*, which compared Cambridge to Sodom and Gomorrah and resulted in its author, William Waller of Trinity, being expelled for blasphemy. Another poem in *The Student*, however, advised the undergraduate with sufficient 'cheek' simply to take no notice of the regulations:

> Whoe'er with frontless phiz is blest,
> Still in a blue or scarlet vest
>   May saunter through the town,
> Or strut regardless of the rules,
> Even to St Mary's or the Schools,
>   In hat or poplin gown.
>
> A dog he unconcerned maintains,
> And seeks with gun the sportful plains
>   Which ancient Cam divides;
> Or to the Hills on horseback strays
> (Unasked his tutor), or his chaise
>   To famed Newmarket guides.

If satire was endemic to the age, so was its corollary, sycophancy. Visits of the Chancellor evoked flurries of odes in his honour and the commemorative volumes on royal occasions became increasingly sumptuous folio affairs, with no expense spared over print, paper, or binding, their pages filled with polyglot perfervidities by poets jostling for notice. The 1748 volume on the Peace of Aix-la-Chapelle, for instance, contained panegyrics on the king by Christopher Anstey, John Duncombe, James Marriott, William Mason, Thomas Nevile, Christopher Smart, and William Whitehead, among many others, of which these lines of Smart's are above the general level:

> Of Camus oft the solitary strand
>   Poetically pensive will I haunt:
> And, as I view th'innumerable sand,
>   Think on thy bounties; and with transport chaunt,
> That now no more Bellona's brazen car
>   Affrights Urania in her blissful seat;
> Nor stratagem, the subtlest snake of war,
>   Plots to entangle every pilgrim's feet:
> That now no lures our vagrant steps mislead;
> Except the harmless Syrens of the mead,
>   Deftly secrete in hawthorn ambuscade,
> Charm the romantic rover to the upland glade.

The collection celebrating the Peace of Fontainebleau in 1763, however, was the last to appear from either university – an abrupt demise of a tradition that seemed to have life, if never much vitality, still in it.

On the evening of 16 February 1765, the Honourable Topham Beauclerk, a literary young man from London, drew up in his phaeton at the Rose. Beside him sat the bulky form of Dr Samuel Johnson (1709–84), paying, rather on the spur of the moment, his one and only visit to Cambridge. Currently at the height of his fame, Dr Johnson stayed at the Rose from Saturday until Tuesday. His main purpose, it seems, was to meet his long-standing correspondent the Shakespearean scholar Dr Richard Farmer (1735–97), Fellow (later Master) of Emmanuel.

Otherwise, he associated only with a select circle of young friends, and 'seemed studious to preserve a strict incognito'.

At Trinity Library on the Sunday, Johnson picked up a seventeenth-century folio near the door, the *Polyhistor* of Morhof, with the words: 'Here is the book upon which all my fame was originally founded; when I had read this book I could teach my tutors!' After supper at Sidney Sussex, he 'drank sixteen dishes of tea' and dissertated gloriously until dawn on a variety of subjects. On the Monday, he 'rolled or waddled' through the other colleges, looked in at a chemistry experiment being conducted by Professor Richard Watson,[6] and was finally introduced to Farmer. After supper with a friend of Beauclerk's in Nevile's Court, Trinity, Johnson took a candle and disappeared alone into the library for a couple of hours; but about twelve, just when everyone was about to leave, he returned and 'began to be very great'.

According to one of those present, Baptist Noel Turner of Emmanuel, minority politics being discussed, Johnson, who had a pain, bent his face to the fire with the words: 'This minority cheek of mine is warring against the general constitution.'

> 'Nay, Doctor,' said Beauclerk, who well knew how to manage him, 'you mustn't talk against the minority, for they tell you, you know, that they are your friends, and wish to support your *liberties*, and save you from oppression.' Johnson: 'Why yes, Sir, just as wisely, and just as necessarily as if they were to build up the interstices of the cloisters at the bottom of this court, for fear the library should fall upon our heads, Sir.'

When someone mentioned Christopher Smart, late of Pembroke, Johnson surprised the company by reciting Smart's Latin Tripos Verses; but said Smart was mad. Beauclerk: 'What do you mean by mad, Doctor?' Johnson: 'Why, Sir, he cannot walk the streets without the boys running after him.' (Yet the boys had run after Johnson himself only that morning.) Suddenly Johnson exclaimed:

> 'Come now, I'll give you a test, now I'll try who is a true antiquary amongst you. Has any of this company ever met with the history of *Grobianus and Grobiana*?' Farmer, drawing the pipe out of his mouth, followed by a cloud of smoke, instantly said, 'I've got the book.' 'Gi'me your hand, gi'me your hand,' said Johnson, 'you are the man after my own heart.' And the shaking of two such hands, with two such happy faces attached to them, could hardly, I think, be matched in the whole annals of literature.

Johnson promised to stay at Emmanuel that summer – 'it must be in no term, for his hours are not very academic and I have been obliged to work double tides

---

[6] Johnson was apparently satisfied by the experiment, though Watson later confessed that before his appointment as Professor of Chemistry the previous year he had 'never read a single syllable on the subject nor seen a single experiment'. Seven years later, similar qualifications brought him the Regius Professorship of Divinity.

ever since', as Farmer told Thomas Percy – but in the event never took up the invitation.

A few months later, on 17 June 1765, the poet William Cowper (1731–1800) was discharged from Dr Cotton's House for Madmen at St Albans and took the coach for Cambridge, where his younger brother John was a Fellow of Corpus Christi. A tormented sufferer from the twin eighteenth-century malaises of melancholy and religious mania, Cowper had recovered sufficiently from a suicidal attack to embark on a new life in the country. His brother agreed to have him near him, though curiously the nearest lodgings he could find were in Huntingdon. After a few days of rapt evangelical talk in Cambridge, Cowper moved into the lodgings, from which he rode over each week to see John.

Failing to convert John to his new faith, however, and eventually moving away from Huntingdon to Olney in Buckinghamshire, Cowper did not see much more of his brother until news came in 1769 that he was seriously ill. Visiting him on his deathbed, he was appalled to find John frittering away his last moments reading plays and again set to, this time, according to tradition, effecting a last-minute conversion.

What Cowper saw of Cambridge on these visits led him later, in Book II of *The Task* (1785), to berate the state of the universities, where

> The schools became a scene
> Of solemn farce, where Ignorance in stilts,
> His cap well lined with logic not his own,
> With parrot tongue performed the scholar's part,
> Proceeding soon a graduated dunce.

Newcastle's attempts to instil discipline had clearly failed, rich heirs continuing to treat the place as a playground:

> The curbs, invented for the mulish mouth
> Of headstrong youth, were broken; bars and bolts
> Grew rusty by disuse; and massy gates
> Forgot their office, opening with a touch;
> Till gowns at length are found mere masquerade;
> The tasselled cap and the spruce band a jest,
> A mockery of the world! What need of these
> For gamesters, jockeys, brothellers impure,
> Spendthrifts, and booted sportsmen, oftener seen
> With belted waist and pointers at their heels
> Than in the bounds of duty?

There were, nevertheless, exceptions:

> All are not such. I had a brother once –
> Peace to the memory of a man of worth,
> A man of letters, and of manners too!
>
> . . .

> He graced a college, in which order yet
> Was sacred; and was honoured, loved, and wept.

Cowper's biography was written by his friend William Hayley (1745–1820), educated at Trinity Hall in 1763–7, a leisurely, slightly eccentric man of letters from Chichester who also befriended William Blake.

Thomas Chatterton (1752–70), the Bristol boy poet and medieval pasticheur, never visited Cambridge himself; but after his death, when the authenticity of his 'Thomas Rowley' productions was hotly debated, their most enthusiastic believer was Dr Robert Glynn, Fellow of King's and celebrated Cambridge physician (he attended John Cowper and Thomas Gray on their death-beds). Glynn acquired over two hundred Chatterton manuscripts and in his turn bequeathed them to the British Museum. The King's College accounts for 1778 record: 'Given to the mother of the poet Chatterton by order of the congregation, £2 2s'; she was also sent money out of the chapel offertory at Emmanuel (where Dr Farmer was Master). An early edition of the Rowley poems was published at Cambridge in 1794 (see p. 116). Thomas Mathias in his *Pursuits of Literature* commented that while Isis had 'turned her current in disdain' on Chatterton's claim, Cam had 'received the Bard with all his train'.

Solemn Evelyn, progressive Fiennes, bibliomaniacal Uffenbach, mercantile Defoe, ribald Ned Ward, portentous Dr Johnson, disturbed and denunciatory Cowper: a notable cross-section of literary tourists had visited Cambridge since the mid-seventeenth century; yet Cambridge had given little back to literature in this time. In prose, Sterne alone stands out as an innovator; among poets, the period between Dryden and Wordsworth would be desolate of greatness but for the names of Smart and Gray.

9

'Far from the madding crowd'

At Eton they had been the 'Quadruple Alliance': illustrious Horace Walpole (1717–97), Prime Minister's son; sensitive Richard West; ambitious Thomas Ashton; melancholy Thomas Gray (1716–71). Gray, the only survivor of twelve infants, son of a drunken, half insane London scrivener, never forgot the brief sunlight of those days at Eton, 'Where once my careless childhood strayed, / A stranger yet to pain'. There the four friends had strolled arm in arm, quoted classics and poetry back and forth, called each other by exotic nicknames – Celadon, Favonius, Almanzor, Orozmades – and written gay, elegant letters when separated.

Separated they were increasingly to be. West went off to repine, lonely and consumptive, at Oxford. The other three came to Cambridge – but Walpole, though officially in residence at King's, found London society more to his fancy, and Ashton, also at King's, while continuing to cultivate Walpole, began to drop Gray.

King's was the traditional college for Etonians, but Gray for some reason went instead to Peterhouse, where he knew no one, made few friends, and had rooms overlooking the gloomy churchyard of Little St Mary's. His first impressions of Cambridge on arrival in October 1734, as conveyed to the absent Walpole, were hardly flattering:

> it is a great old Town, shaped like a Spider, with a nasty lump in the middle of it, and half a dozen scambling long legs . . . The Masters of Colledges are twelve grey-hair'd Gentlefolks, who are all mad with Pride; the Fellows are sleepy, drunken, dull, illiterate Things; the Fellow-Commoners are imitatours of the Fellows, or else Beaux, or else nothing: the Pensioners grave, formal Sots, who would be thought old; or else drink Ale, and sing Songs against ye Excise. The Sizers are Graziers Eldest Sons, who come to get good Learning, that they may all be Archbishops of Canterbury.

Ashton invited Gray to the Mitre, next to King's, where Etonian wits forgathered, but Gray was perhaps too shy to go. Yet a fortnight later the amazed freshman found himself at a rowdy tobacco party:

> . . . do but imagine me pent up in a room hired for the purpose, and none of the
> largest, from 7 a-clock at night, till 4 in the morning! 'midst hogsheads of Liquor
> and quantities of Tobacco, surrounded by 30 of these creatures, infinitely below
> the meanest People you could even form an Idea off, toasting bawdy healths
> and deafned with their unmeaning Roar; Jesus! . . . you'll think it a strange
> compliment, when I tell you how often I thought of you, all the while.

Orozmades thought of Celadon, but Celadon still did not come to join him.
Orozmades grew morbid, shut in his large friendless room with the gravestones
below.

> . . . at midnight, being a hard frost; I had wrapt myself up in my Shroud very
> snugg and warm; when in comes your Letter, which . . . made me stretch my
> Skeleton-jaws in such a horse-laugh, that all the dead pop'd up their heads and
> stared: but to see the frowzy Countenances of the Creatures especially one old
> Lady-Carcase, that made most hideous Grimaces, and would needs tell me, that
> I was a very uncivil Person to disturb a Woman of her Quality, that did me the
> honour to lie so near me.

Gray's second term came, and he began to settle down. 'In Cambridge there is
nothing so troublesome, as that one has nothing to trouble one,' he informed
Walpole. 'Every thing is so tediously regular, so samish, that I expire for want
of a little variety.' Little could he have guessed that on one side or other of
Trumpington Street, apart from occasional scenic expeditions to obtain 'a little
variety', he would reside for the rest of his life.

Gray soon won a couple of scholarships – money he badly needed. But the
curriculum oppressed him with its obsessive emphasis on mathematics, and he
considered his tutor, Birkett, an ignorant drunkard. Poetry and the classics
were totally neglected. Ashton, writing to West, wrily depicted the fate of a
Cambridge poet: 'I fancy I have told you that a wild young Poet of Trinity
College has taken a mad flight out of a garret Window: but finding no Castle in
the air to rest at, his wings failed him and so he dropt. His Life is not despaird of.'
Walpole, making his appearance at last, grandly took lessons from the blind
mathematics professor, Saunderson, only to be mortified to be told: 'Young man,
it would be cheating you to take your money, for you can never learn what I am
trying to teach you.' He took up Italian and drawing instead, with shorthand
lessons from John Byrom. He too lamented that 'We have not the least poetry
stirring here; for I can't call verses on the 5th of November and 30th of January
by that name.' Making the most of what call there was for their talents, Gray,
Walpole, and Ashton all contributed Latin poems to the 1736 collection on the
marriage of the Prince of Wales. West, who contributed to the corresponding
Oxford *Gratulatio*, thought Gray's the best from Cambridge, though that was
'no great compliment' considering what 'soft unmeaning stuff' the general run
comprised. Gray's poem must have impressed the authorities, for he was
appointed to write some of that year's Tripos Verses too. But Gray undoubtedly

expressed the feelings of all three of them when he wrote to West in December
1736:

> Surely it was of this place, now Cambridge, but formerly known by the name of
> Babylon, that the prophet spoke when he said, 'the wild beasts of the desert shall
> dwell there, and their houses shall be full of doleful creatures, and owls shall build
> there, and satyrs shall dance there; their forts and towers shall be a den for ever,
> a joy of wild asses . . . '

In the same letter Gray informed West that he had got out of studying
mathematics and the other uncongenial BA subjects by taking up law instead:
'I do not take degrees, and, after this term, shall have nothing more of college
impertinencies to undergo.' In practice he appears to have been allowed to go his
own way, studying the classics and whatever else appealed to him. But the routine
remained 'samish'. In 1737 he described his life as 'oscillatory', swinging 'from
Chapell or Hall home, and from home to chapell or hall'. He seems to have made
no friends in his college, though he did manage to meet two men from across the
way at Pembroke who were later among his closest friends – Thomas Wharton, a
medical student from Durham, and James Brown, already a Fellow, who spotted
and encouraged Gray's literary talent.

Despite his distaste for certain aspects of Cambridge life, when his undergraduate days came to an end in 1738 Gray wrote to Walpole:

> I have a sort of reluctance to leave this place, unamiable as it may seem; 'tis true
> Cambridge is very ugly, she is very dirty, and very dull; but I'm like a cabbage,
> where I'm stuck, I love to grow; you should pull me up sooner, than any one, but
> I shall be ne'er the better for transplanting.

Walpole in fact 'pulled Gray up' by inviting him to accompany him on an
expenses-paid Continental tour. They were away for two years, but the tour
ended bitterly when the introverted, scholarly Gray fell out at last with the
extrovert, socialising Walpole. His deepest friendship was never really repaired.

While Gray rhapsodised over alpine scenery, sat in the corner at Florentine
parties, and pored over effaced Roman inscriptions, a poet as temperamentally
different as possible arrived at Cambridge. Christopher Smart (1722–71) came up
to Pembroke from Durham in October 1739. A neighbour of his, the Duchess of
Cleveland, had granted the fatherless but bright and cheerful boy forty pounds a
year for as long as he stayed at the university; for the rest, Smart paid for his
tuition by fulfilling a sizar's usual menial duties. While Gray from the cradle to
the grave never set his hand to any domestic chore, Smart washed up and mopped
out with a will. Moreover, Smart was self-evidently what Gray (who had still
composed practically nothing) could not yet be suspected of being – a poet. He
was a compulsive versifier, whose brilliant facility was quickly recognised by the
university. He was assigned to compose the Tripos Verses not once but regularly,
and in 1742 won the coveted Craven Scholarship with a Latin translation of

Pope's *Ode on St Cecilia's Day*. (Bentley was the adjudicator; it was his last public deed.) The award was worth twenty pounds a year, and brought Smart the congratulations of Pope himself.

Where Gray stood apart, Smart immersed himself. In the college courts and hall, in hostelries and shops, he was greeted by all as a charming, versatile young man who could mint an epigram in a twinkling and entertain any company. Appalled like Gray at the low state of classical studies, he did something more than complain, he made poetry out of it. He took as his image something else that appalled him, a miserable clipped eagle chained up in a court at Trinity:

> Oh cruel fate! what barbarous hand,
>   What more than Gothic ire,
> At some fierce tyrant's dread command,
>   To check thy daring fire,
> Has placed thee in this servile cell,
> Where Discipline and Dulness dwell?

and drew the comparison:

> Type of the fall of Greece and Rome,
> While more than mathematic gloom
>   Envelopes all around!

In different mood, he celebrated an evening frittered away at the Mitre in a time-evaporating reverie of the sort known to students from time immemorial – the rapt contemplation of a barmaid's person.

> No handkerchief her bosom hid,
>   No tippet from our sight debars
> Her heaving breasts, with moles o'erspread,
>   Marked, little hemispheres, with stars;
> While on them all our eyes we move,
> Our eyes that meant immoderate love.
>
>   . . . .
>
> 'But hark,' she cries, 'my mamma calls,'
>   And straight she's vanished from our sight;
> 'Twas then we saw the empty bowls.
>   'Twas then we first perceived it night;
> While all, sad synod, silent moan,
> Both that she went – and went alone.

With similar facility, Smart turned the proud occasion when he took his BA in 1743 into mock-Horatian verse:

> 'Tis done: I tower to that degree,
>   And catch such heavenly fire,
> That Horace ne'er could rant like me.
>   Nor is King's Chapel higher.

> My name, in sure recording page,
>   Shall time itself o'erpower;
> If no rude mice, with envious rage,
>   The buttery books devour.

Meanwhile, in 1742, Gray had crept back to Peterhouse. His four years away had brought the two most traumatic events of his life – the rupture with Walpole and, soon afterwards, the death of West. Gray could not help regretting that he had not seen more of West – who had been shy and literary like himself and equally at a loss what to do in the world, but whose friendship he had neglected while Walpole whirled him through the salons of Europe. Now suddenly West was gone. More than ever, 'melancholy marked him for her own'.

Gray's widowed mother had retired to Stoke Poges in Buckinghamshire, and it was while staying there that he began to compose some of his best and most famous poems. First came a moving sonnet on West's death; then, revising the scenes of their boyhood happiness and meditating over a fresh generation of 'little victims' at play, the 'Ode on a Distant Prospect of Eton College'. Finally, musing in Stoke Poges churchyard, he conceived the idea for his 'Elegy Written in a Country Churchyard' which, slow worker that he was, he would spend several years, mainly at Cambridge, fastidiously polishing.

Still undecided about a profession, Gray returned to Peterhouse to complete his degree in law, greeting his alma mater, in a 'Hymn to Ignorance', with customary irony:

> Hail, horrors, hail! ye ever gloomy bowers,
> Ye gothic fanes, and antiquated towers,
> Where rushy Camus' slowly-winding flood
> Perpetual draws his humid train of mud:
> Glad I revisit thy neglected reign,
> Oh take me to thy peaceful shade again.
> But chiefly thee, whose influence breathed from high
> Augments the native darkness of the sky –
> Ah, Ignorance! soft salutary power!
> Prostrate with filial reverence I adore . . .

With the aid of inheritances, Gray was able this time to reside as a fellow-commoner, with the privilege of dining on high table in his blue and silver gown and socialising with the Fellows in their Combination Room. During his absence the building where he had formerly lodged had been demolished and replaced by Sir James Burrough's classical Fellows' Building, in which he was allotted top front rooms, probably as their first occupant. His sitting-room looked out along Trumpington Street towards open country, his bedroom across the churchyard towards the distant bulk of King's Chapel. These rooms Gray brightened in time with books and prints, a harpsichord, Japanese vases, window-boxes, and bouquets of flowers. He assiduously studied his chosen subject for a year, and actually took the degree of Bachelor of Civil Law (the only degree he ever took) the same year that Smart took his BA. There the pretence for a vocation for the law ended. Though he never became a Fellow of any college, nor undertook any duties, he continued placidly to reside. Dull, unamiable Cambridge had claimed him for her own.

Though dining and lodging at Peterhouse, Gray spent increasing amounts of time across the street at Pembroke. His letters to Dr Wharton, now returned to Durham, are full of the interminable college politics that he both laughed at and loved. Pembroke was then under the domination of the octogenarian Roger Long, who had set up a hollow revolving planetarium (the 'Zodiac Room') in the grounds, paddled a water-velocipede about the lake, and obstreperously vetoed the election of new Fellows. When Pembroke celebrated its four hundredth anniversary in 1743, Gray mocked: 'Won't You come to the Jubilee? Dr Long is to dance a Saraband and Hornpipe of his own Invention without lifting either Foot once from the Ground.'

It may have been the 'jubilee' that first brought Smart to Gray's attention, for Smart's talents were naturally in demand for such an occasion and he composed an ode invoking the spirits of the college's foundress, Mary de Valence, and such past members as Spenser. The two poets did not take to each other. Gray was normally at his best with younger men – provided they looked up to him with appropriate respect. Smart did not. Indeed, he seems to have had nothing but contempt for Gray, whom he portrayed in a vivid if cruel snapshot – 'Gray *walks* as if he had fouled his small-clothes, and *looks* as if he smelt it' – which evokes the mincing step, gown clutched behind, and supercilious face familiar from other descriptions. Again, an 'Epigram Extempore on a Cold Poet', published in *The Student*, which Smart edited after leaving Cambridge, sounds like a Parthian shot at costive, pyrophobic Gray:

> Frigidio's muse, from ardour free,
>   Whene'er he tunes his lyre,
> Gives him a leaden policy
>   T'insure his works from fire.

Gray in return retreated before Smart's academic success and social ease into patronising pity for the crazy young fool who, exactly as Gray foretold, would fritter his advantages insanely away. Writing to Wharton in 1747, Gray paints a facetious but prescient picture of Smart, who, a Fellow of his college since 1745 and a Praelector in Philosophy and Rhetoric, was nevertheless, with drinking excesses and debts, getting out of control.

> and as to Smart, he must necessarily by abîmé, in a very short Time. His Debts daily increase . . . In the mean time he is amuseing himself with a Comedy of his own Writing, which he makes all the Boys of his Acquaintance act, and intends to borrow the Zodiack Room, and have it performed publickly. Our Friend Lawman, the mad Attorney, is his Copyist; and truly the Author himself is to the

full as mad as he. His Piece (he says) is inimitable, true Sterling Wit, and Humour by God; and he can't hear the Prologue without being ready to die with Laughter. He acts five Parts himself, and is only sorry, he can't do all the rest. He has also advertised a Collection of Odes; and for his Vanity and Faculty of Lyeing, they are come to their full Maturity. All this, you see, must come to a Jayl, or Bedlam, and that without any help, almost without Pity.

Smart's comedy, *A Trip to Cambridge: or The Ungrateful Fair*, probably the very last college play, has not survived. Apparently full of hilarity, it featured a wealthy baronet and his niece visiting his nephew, a fellow-commoner at Trinity, and a poor sizar from Emmanuel who tricks the old man into bestowing both niece and fortune upon him. It was acted in the college hall (Gray's reference to the Zodiac Room was a typical piece of belittlement) with a distinguished cast, Smart himself playing the baronet.

But Smart's extravagances were getting out of hand. He occupied an expensive set of rooms, wore fancy embroidered waistcoats, drank prodigiously. When in November he was arrested for debt, Gray was prompt to regale Wharton with details, describing how, to prevent Smart from being thrown into prison, the Fellows had lent him the money, keeping him confined to his room lest other creditors 'should snap him'. When it was found that his debts in Cambridge totalled over £350, Smart was advised 'to go off in the night and lie hid somewhere or other' until something had been arranged. Gray advised Wharton, living in Smart's home town, not to spread the news. Smart now desperately needed the forty pounds a year which his patron still afforded him.

Though Gray could summon little pity for Smart, events both now and later proved that Smart had many friends in Pembroke. Somehow the dunning trades-men were bought off, and Smart returned to college, where he continued to reside more moderately for another couple of years. But he could not subdue his own recklessness. To live within his means, observing his duties and fulfilling his obligations, became irksome. Suddenly, in 1749, he threw up everything and disappeared to London with the intention of making a living by his pen. Even then, his college continued to vote him money 'in lieu of commons', and he was not deprived of his fellowship until 1753 when they discovered he had married his publisher's step-daughter. (Until the nineteenth century, Fellows were supposed to remain celibate.) Even then, his name was retained on the college books to enable him to continue to compete for the university Seatonian Prize. This prize, bequeathed in 1750 by Thomas Seaton, Fellow of Clare, and worth thirty pounds, was for the best poem in English by a Master of Arts on the subject of one of the attributes or perfections of the Supreme Being (a requirement soon dropped: the set subject for 1774 was 'Duelling'). It was the first prize at Oxford or Cambridge for English poetry, and Smart was its first winner – indeed, he carried it off five times in the first six years, turning out without trouble hundreds of blank-verse lines on God's Eternity, Immensity, Omniscience, Power, and

Goodness. (Apart from W. M. Praed in 1830, he is the only famous poet ever to have won this prize.)

Seaton himself, who had founded the prize that God might be everlastingly praised, would have been taken aback by the enthusiasm soon displayed by his prize's winner. By 1756, as Gray had predicted, Smart was insane, consumed with a religious mania that obliged him to fall to his knees in the street to invoke God's name. While shut away in Bedlam, he wrote his wildly magnificent *Jubilate Agno* and *A Song to David*, the former scintillating with illogical juxtapositions:

> For the two universities are the eyes of England.
> For Cambridge is the right and the brightest.
> For Pembroke Hall was founded more in the Lord than any College in Cambridge.
> For mustard is the proper food of birds and men are bound to cultivate it for their use.

On his release in 1763, friends again rallied round, subscribing generously to his translation of the Psalms, though no one seems to have appreciated the originality of the poetry now coming from his pen. Gray's close friend and fellow poet William Mason (1724–97), another Fellow of Pembroke, who collected the subscriptions ('Let Mason, house of Mason rejoice with Suberies the capitol cork tree. Lord be merciful to William Mason'), mentioned, 'I have seen his *Song to David* and from thence conclude him as mad as ever.' Smart died on 21 May 1771, abandoned, diseased, praising God, in the Marshalsea debtors' prison.

Gray, meanwhile, had met with troubles of his own. He cultivated anxieties: about his health, about people's opinions of him, about the possibility of theft or attack by dogs, above all about fire. He had good reason to fear fire: in 1748 his family home had been burnt to the ground. Moreover, he was often terrified by the rowdier aspects of Cambridge, where the Bucks, as he once wrote, 'set women upon their heads in the streets at noonday, break open shops, game in the coffee-houses on Sundays'. He began to conceive an anxiety lest George Forester, a particularly riotous Buck who had the rooms opposite, or Bennet Williams, another fellow-commoner on the ground floor, would set the place ablaze in their nightly revels. As he huddled over his books or lay sleepless listening to their drunken uproar, it was easy for his tortured imagination to picture an upset candle sending flames leaping up the high wooden staircase, his only means of escape. In January 1756 he wrote urgently to Wharton, then in London:

> I beg you to bespeak me a Rope-Ladder (for my Neighbours every day make a great progress in drunkenness, which gives me reason to look about me). It must be full 36 foot long, or a little more, but as light and manageable as may be, easy to unroll, and not likely to entangle. I never saw one, but I suppose it must have strong hooks, or something equivalent, a-top, to throw over an iron bar to be fix'd withinside of my window. However you will chuse the properest form, and instruct me in the use of it.

The rope ladder – 'soft as the silky cords by which Romeo ascended to his Juliet' in a contemporary description – was delivered; the iron bar installed (in the event on the outside of the bedroom window, where it remains in position to this day); and the inevitable result was that Forester and Williams, rising early one morning to go hunting with their friend Viscount Perceval of King's and others, raising their eyes to the 'iron machine' at Gray's window, hit on the wheeze of testing the poet's emergency preparedness as an aperitif to their day's sport. Dispatching Perceval's servant, Joe Draper, to roar out 'Fire!' at the top of his voice outside Gray's door, they waited below to see the author of the 'Elegy' descend in his nightcap into the dark churchyard, there, with luck, to 'whip the butterfly up again'. Gray indeed, woken and greatly agitated, protruded his head from the window but must have spotted his tormentors in the dim light and understood their game. He withdrew in anger and they no doubt mounted their horses with laughter enough.[1]

For Gray, however, the young men's practical joke was to constitute 'a sort of Aera in a life so barren of events as mine'. Deeply mortified, he made formal complaint to the Master and Fellows, but they (observing perhaps Pompey the Little's reflections on rich heirs as a source of preferments) laughed the matter aside as a 'boyish frolic'. For once in his life Gray, recorded in the buttery books as having dined with his persecutors on high table during the week ending 5 March, acted fast. Though his name was already down on the list for the following week, the butler was obliged to cross it out, for Gray, taking with him his 'rope-ladder and firebags', had already gone. Nor far, admittedly: only across the road into the college where for so long he had felt so much more at home. On 6 March 1756 he was admitted at Pembroke.

Gray skated delicately over the reasons for his removal in his first letter to Wharton from his new home.

> I left my lodgings, because the rooms were noisy, and the People of the house dirty. This is all I would chuse to have said about it . . . all, I shall say more, is, that I am for the present extremely well lodged here, and as quiet as in the Grande Chartreuse; and that everybody (even the Dr Longs and Dr Mays) are as civil, as they could be to Mary de Valence in person.

A year later he moved into even better rooms, in the Hitcham Building in the second court; here his front room (now preserved as the Gray Room) looked out into the court, while his bedroom overlooked the Master's Garden and a third

---

[1] Later embellishments, accepted with incredible credulity by Edmund Gosse and after him by Leslie Stephen in the *Dictionary of National Biography*, are mere invention: 'The ruse succeeded only too well: Gray, without staying to put on his clothes, hooked his rope-ladder to the iron bar, and descended nimbly into the tub of water, from which he was rescued with shouts of laughter by the unmannerly youths. But the jest might easily have proved fatal; as it was, he shivered in the February air so excessively that he had to be wrapped in the coat of a passing watchman' (Gosse, *Gray*, 1882). Gosse derived the watchman's coat from a writer with no connection with Cambridge, Archibald Campbell in *The Sale of Authors* (1767); the tub of water occurs in Robert Southey's *Letters from England* (1807), R. Gooch's *Facetiae Cantabrigienses* (1825), and J. M. F. Wright's *Alma Mater: or Seven Years at the University of Cambridge* (1827).

room housed his overflow of books. (In 1768 he was again woken in the night by an alarm of fire – this time no prank. 'I assure you it is not amusing to be waked between 2 and 3 in the morning and to hear, Don't be frighted, Sir! but the college is all of a fire.' But the blaze was in the opposite building and speedily extinguished.) In these rooms – for which he paid an annual rental of eight pounds – Gray lived for the rest of his life.

Gray's 'Elegy', published at last in 1751, had been an instant success, and was followed up in 1753 by a sumptuous edition, masterminded by Walpole, of six poems with elaborate illustrations by Richard Bentley, son of the Master of Trinity. Fame suddenly descended on Gray – much to his horror. In 1757, when the Poet Laureateship became vacant, he was offered the post, but shied from the limelight, making ungrateful remarks on the position and its past incumbents. The post went instead to William Whitehead (1715–85), the only Laureate born in Cambridge. Whitehead's father had been Pembroke's local baker (though better known as the owner of some property at Grantchester nicknamed 'Whitehead's Folly'). Baptised in St Botolph's, Whitehead had gone to Winchester and then, after his father's death, to Clare College, where he obtained an unusual scholarship endowed expressly for the orphaned sons of bakers. He became a Fellow of Clare in 1742 and his first poetic efforts were published at Cambridge. Genial and inoffensive, he later came in for the customary attacks on the worthlessness of his poetry: Charles Churchill (1731–64), whose own brief studies at St John's had terminated when his 'Fleet' marriage was discovered, in particular called Whitehead 'Dulness and Method's darling son', to which Whitehead replied with self-deprecating amiability.

While Walpole and his Strawberry Hill press had been largely responsible for establishing Gray's reputation, Gray in return supplied Walpole with scholarly material for his historical researches. Walpole had only to ask about the circumstances of Henry VI's marriage or the contents of Perkin Warbeck's proclamation to get back pages of closely written information. Shut up in his Cambridge retreat, Gray had quietly become one of the most erudite men alive. Employing the pursuit of knowledge as an antidote to the sorrows of reality, he had tackled subject after subject with the same patient, exhaustive enquiry. He kept massive notebooks crammed with facts and quotations, noting down everything from ancient Greek diets and the treatment for a viper's bite to the temperature in his room and which birds were singing. Yet, for all his learning, he never found the occasion to work his knowledge up into a book so that others might share it. The nearest he came was some notes towards a history of English poetry.

Around Gray gathered a select circle of friends. William ('Scroddles') Mason was one, ambitious but 'a good and well-meaning creature', eventually to be Gray's literary executor and biographer. Author among much else of a lifeless *Ode on the Installation of the Duke of Newcastle* (1749) and the leaden blank-verse *Mirth* (1774), Mason for long harboured unfulfilled hopes of himself obtaining the Laureateship. Norton Nicholls of Trinity Hall, who met Gray at a tea party and thought him 'one of the greatest men who ever existed in the world', was another favourite. The antiquary William Cole (1714–82), who had known Gray and Walpole at Eton, went to Clare and King's and became curate of nearby Waterbeach and Milton. An indefatigable local historian, he bequeathed a hundred folio volumes of information he had collected to the British Museum. Christopher Anstey (1724–1805), like Cole a Cambridgeshire man (Cole was born at Little Abington, Anstey at Brinkley), was also at Eton and King's, where he became a Fellow. Resenting, as an infringement of the special privileges of his college, a requirement to perform a public declamation in order to qualify for his MA, Anstey exhibited his individuality and wit by going into 'a rhapsody of adverbs' which turned the proceedings to farce. He was refused his degree, but continued to reside until 1754 when he inherited estates at Trumpington. Moving into Anstey Hall, he became an extrovert, fox-hunting squire, shunning politics and the public life, enjoying literary ease, and writing popular light verse. His satire of fashionable spa society, *The New Bath Guide*, was published in Cambridge in 1766, and brought Anstey overnight fame, Walpole writing of it that it 'will make you bepiss your cheeks with laughter – so much wit, so much humour, fun, poetry, so much originality, never met together before'. Anstey translated Gray's 'Elegy' into Latin.

If Gray had favourites, he also cultivated his antipathies. Dr Long was one; Dr Chapman, Master of Magdalene, another. As Gray wrote to a friend during the Long Vacation of 1760,

> Cambridge is a delight of a place, now there is nobody in it. I do believe you would like it, if you knew what it was without inhabitants. It is they, I assure you, that get it an ill name and spoil all. Our friend Dr Chapman (one of its nuisances) is not expected here again in a hurry. He is gone to his grave with five fine mackerel (large and full of roe) in his belly. He ate them all at one dinner; but his fate was a turbot on Trinity Sunday, of which he left little for the company besides bones. He had not been hearty all the week; but after this sixth fish he never held up his head more, and a violent looseness carried him off. They say he made a very good end.

Gray set his face even more implacably against the illustrious Duke of Newcastle, with his patronage and banquetings, and against the profligate fourth Earl of Sandwich whom he attacked as 'Jemmy Twitcher' in a virulent satire, *The Candidate* (1764), when this member of the notorious 'Hell-Fire Club' sought appointment as High Steward of the university. (Churchill also weighed in with a piece on the same subject and with the same title.)

One nobleman Gray did defer to was Newcastle's successor as Chancellor, the Duke of Grafton, who had been a contemporary fellow-commoner at Peterhouse. One of the most desirable positions at Cambridge was the Regius Professorship of Modern History, worth £400 a year; and in 1762, with uncharacteristic boldness,

Gray put in for the post (the only time he ever applied for a job). On this occasion he was passed over in favour of a worthless drunkard, Laurence Brockett; but in 1768, when Brockett fell from his horse while returning from a carouse with Lord Sandwich at Hinchingbrooke and broke his neck, Gray again allowed his name to go forward. Grafton, then virtually Prime Minister, supported his candidature to the king, and Gray was awarded the professorship.

In return for this favour, Gray felt obliged to undertake the *Ode for Music* for Grafton's installation. But composing to order was an agonising matter and for long no progress was made. Then one day, with time running short, Nicholls, calling on Gray, was astounded by his friend's flinging open the door and roaring: 'Hence, avaunt! 'Tis holy ground!' Gray was not deranged, but had at last produced the opening line. Full of sonorous references to college founders, and better at least than Mason's effort of twenty years before, Gray's ode was performed in the Senate House to music by Professor Randall on 1 July 1769. It contains the lines, put into the mouth of Milton:

> Ye brown o'erarching groves,
>   That contemplation loves,
> Where willowy Camus lingers with delight!
>   Oft at the blush of dawn
>   I trod your level lawn,
> Oft wooed the gleam of Cynthia silver-bright
> In cloisters dim, far from the haunts of Folly,
> With Freedom by my side, and soft-eyed Melancholy.

Having criticised previous incumbents for not doing anything, Gray next set about preparing his inaugural lecture. To be delivered in Latin, it would deal with the study not only of history, but also of historical sources; indeed, he decided, it ought to include the study of other subjects, such as languages, necessary for the understanding of historical sources. It would be masterly, weighty, definitive. On no account must its content or delivery or the quality of the Latin invite ridicule. Unsurprisingly, though Gray worked on the project for his remaining two years, the lecture was never given.

Right at the end of Gray's life, a wholly unforeseen event occurred. While staying in Bath, Nicholls bumped (literally) into a twenty-one-year-old Swiss aristocrat, Charles Victor de Bonstetten, and brought him to meet Gray. Gray was more than merely charmed. The lifeless habits and mental routines of a lifetime were suddenly swept into confusion. Bonstetten stayed in Cambridge for several weeks in the spring of 1770, meeting everyone, dining everywhere, studying everything – but above all waiting on Gray. Gray and he read through Shakespeare and Milton together, Bonstetten in awe of his teacher, Gray intoxicated by his pupil. Bonstetten wrote: 'I eat every day in his rooms; he lives in great retirement, and is so kind as to show pleasure in seeing me. I call on him at any hour, he reads with me what I wish, I work in his room.' Gray wrote: 'I never saw such a boy . . . He is busy from morn to night, has no other amusement than that of changing one study for another, likes nobody, that he sees here, and yet wishes to stay longer.'

Too soon, this last shaft of sunlight was dispersed. The weeks fled, Bonstetten was recalled to Europe, Gray realised too late the folly of abandoning, even for a moment, his iron-hooped emotional detachment. Gray could not bear to see Bonstetten packing his cases. 'He gives me too much pleasure, and at least *an equal share* of inquietude,' he confided to Nicholls. 'I have never met with so extraordinary a Person. God bless him! I am unable to talk to you about any thing else, I think.' Gray went with Bonstetten to London and 'pack'd him up with my own hands in the Dover-machine'. Then, back in Cambridge, he succumbed to a massive melancholic reaction. The mere sight of his rooms was unbearable. '*Was never such a gracious Creature born!* Burn my letter that I wrote you . . . You will think, I have caught madness from him . . . I am destitute of all things. This place never appear'd so horrible to me, as it does now.'

On 12 April 1770, Gray wrote to Bonstetten: 'I am grown old in the compass of less than three weeks, like the Sultan in the Turkish Tales, that did but plunge his head into a vessel of water and take it out again . . . and found he had passed many years in captivity . . . I did not conceive . . . the solitude and insipidity of my own condition, before I possess'd the happiness of your friendship.' A week later: 'The known sound of your voice still rings in my ears. There, on the corner of the fender, you are standing, or tinkling on the Pianoforte, or stretch'd at length on the sofa.'

Illness set in. The gout confined Gray to his rooms for a month, then he caught a dangerous chill while walking on the Gogs. The only good news was his friend Brown's election as Master in place of the unlamented Dr Long. Slowly the image of Bonstetten receded – only to be revived the following summer when Gray and Nicholls were invited to Switzerland. It might have done Gray good: the change of air, the mountain scenery, the effervescent Bonstetten – it was almost a doctor's prescription for Gray's condition. But it came too late.

Gray got as far as London that July, but had to return to Cambridge ill and feverish. On 24 July 1771, while dining in hall, he was overcome with nausea and put to bed. Some cousins who lived in the town came to look after him, but he died on 30 July, just two months after Smart. He was buried beside his mother at Stoke Poges. On 17 August, Brown wrote to Wharton: 'Everything is now dark and melancholy in Mr Gray's room, not a trace of him remains there; it looks as if it had been for some time uninhabited, and the room bespoke for another inhabitant.'

Gray and Smart – Cambridge contemporaries, poets of comparable stature – could not have been more different: Gray withdrawn, snide, careful; Smart familiar, fanatical, profligate. While Smart could scribble on any subject, sacred or profane, that circumstance or the organisers of poetry prizes threw up, for Gray writing was the extraction of blood from stone. Gray lived in comfort and complained; Smart was driven from garret to madhouse rejoicing in the Lord every step of the way ('For I bless the Lord Jesus from the bottom of Royston Cave to the top of King's Chapel'). Gray reined his talents, writing 'what was oft said, but ne'er so well expressed'; Smart dissipated his talents, was incomprehensibly original. Gray was melancholy, but sane to the point of dullness; Smart flamboyant to the point of insanity.

Gray chose to escape life's threats by imitating the village forefathers of his 'Elegy':

> Far from the madding crowd's ignoble strife,
>   Their sober wishes never learned to stray;
> Along the cool sequestered vale of life
>   They kept the noiseless tenour of their way.

He avoided its threats, but also its challenges and rewards. 'Gray n'avait jamais aimé', Bonstetten judged, but it was the courage, not the ability, to love that Gray lacked. Smart never lacked courage. His reckless abandonment of Cambridge, often seen as a failure of will, was a courageous gamble. In Cambridge he would have gone on being everyone's favourite drinking companion and a feted winner of prizes, for ever drawing on the Clevelands' patronage and running up debts which his college would bail him out of – and able to portray the plight of a caged eagle as no more than a symbol of contemporary university studies. In London, penury and madness awaited him, but also heights of simple and undeflected compassion for all things:

> Know when the frosty weather comes,
>   'Tis charity to deal
> To wren and redbreast all thy crumbs,
>   The remnant of thy meal.

While Smart in his destitution spared thought for the wren and the redbreast, Gray in his elegant Cambridge rooms entered up lists of ornithological names in his interleaved Linnaeus. The contrast is profound.

10

'I was not for that hour,
nor for that place'

Gray, one of the first poets to develop a romantic taste for wild landscape (as against the Augustan taste for artificially pastoralised landscape), had passed through the Lake District in 1769 on one of his summer excursions. In 1779, William Wilberforce, in his last vacation as a student at St John's, had made a similar tour, calling in the course of it on one of the Fellows of his college, the Reverend William Cookson.[1] On 30 October 1787, the same William Cookson sped southwards in his chaise across the Huntingdon plain, bearing with him two young nephews from Lakeland, John Myers and William Wordsworth (1770–1850), to be entered in their turn at St John's. Wordsworth, venturing for the first time away from his native mountains and torrents, peered ahead, as he later recounted in Book III of his great autobiographical poem, *The Prelude* (published 1850), at the flat country within which lay the hope of his adolescent dreams.

> It was a dreary morning when the wheels
> Rolled over a wide plain o'erhung with clouds,
> And nothing cheered our way till first we saw
> The long-roofed chapel of King's College lift
> Turrets and pinnacles in answering files,
> Extended high above a dusky grove.
>
> Advancing, we espied upon the road
> A student clothed in gown and tasselled cap,
> Striding along as if o'ertasked by Time,
> Or covetous of exercise and air;
> He passed – nor was I master of my eyes
> Till he was left an arrow's flight behind.
> As near and nearer to the spot we drew,
> It seemed to suck us in with an eddy's force.
> Onward we drove beneath the Castle; caught,

[1] Wilberforce's journal of his tour was published in 1983.

While crossing Magdalene Bridge, a glimpse of Cam;
And at the *Hoop* alighted, famous Inn.

(III, 1-17)

As they stepped down in the yard of the great coaching inn in Bridge Street, Wordsworth's excitement must have mounted at the sight of flocks of capped and gowned figures, while all around there was the unloading of trunks.

Uncle William, bringing up his nephews fashionably late – other freshmen had been in residence for a fortnight – took them at once to St John's to be admitted as sizars and assigned their rooms. Though the sizars' life was losing much of its former servility (at St John's their last menial duty, serving at table, had been abolished the previous year), they still fed on the leftovers from high table and were given the worst accommodation. Wordsworth was directed to a poky little room above the kitchen on F staircase (then known as Pump Staircase) – a later visitor was to describe it as 'one of the meanest and most dismal apartments, it must be, in the whole university'.[2] Its smallness probably did not distress him that first night. Throwing his valise, containing a new velvet coat for evening wear, a brown leather manuscript book, and his other clothes prepared for him by the loving hand of his sister Dorothy, onto the bed in the windowless bedroom closet, and peeping across the intervening side alley at the great windows of Trinity Chapel, he was not to know that his three years of habitation in that 'unlovely cell' were largely to be ones of profitless disappointment.

> The Evangelist St John my patron was:
> Three Gothic courts[3] are his, and in the first
> Was my abiding-place, a nook obscure;
> Right underneath, the College kitchens made
> A humming sound, less tuneable than bees,
> But hardly less industrious; with shrill notes
> Of sharp command and scolding intermixed.
> Near me hung Trinity's loquacious clock,
> Who never let the quarters, night or day,
> Slip by him unproclaimed, and told the hours
> Twice over with a male and female voice.
> Her pealing organ was my neighbour too;
> And from my pillow, looking forth by light
> Of moon or favouring stars, I could behold
> The antechapel where the statue stood

---

[2] Miss Fenwick, who was shown the room by Wordsworth in 1839. The room was removed in 1893 to add height to the kitchens, but more recently has been reinstated and combined with an adjoining set to form a conference room known as the Wordsworth Room.

[3] 'Gothic courts' in the version published in 1850 (here followed throughout): 'gloomy courts' in the original 1805 version.

Of Newton with his prism and silent face,
The marble index of a mind for ever
Voyaging through strange seas of Thought, alone.

(III, 46–63)

Wordsworth hero-worshipped Newton. His school at Hawkshead had given him an excellent start in mathematics, and there seemed no reason why he should not follow in the steps of many previous Hawkshead boys at Cambridge by taking a good degree and winning a fellowship. His uncle certainly hoped he would. But while Wordsworth enjoyed Newtonian theories and had shone under enlightened tutelage at school, it was not long before the contemporary Cambridge system – with its post-Newtonian over-preoccupation with mathematics, its concomitant neglect of both classical and living literature, and its viciously competitive examination course – killed all desire in him for academic distinction.

Of College labours, of the Lecturer's room
All studded round, as thick as chairs could stand,
With loyal students faithful to their books,
Half-and-half idlers, hardy recusants,
And honest dunces – of important days,
Examinations, when the man was weighed
As in a balance! Of excessive hopes,
Tremblings withal and commendable fears,
Small jealousies, and triumphs good or bad,
Let others that know more speak as they know.
Such glory was but little sought by me,
And little won.

(III, 64–75)

His tutor, Edward Frewen, a friend of Uncle William's, procured a Foundress's Scholarship for him, and at first, knowing as he already did more Euclid than a dozen public-school freshmen, Wordsworth could afford to treat his studies leisurely – 'and this was for me unlucky, because I had a full twelve-month's start of the freshmen of my year, and accordingly got into rather an idle way', as he lamented in old age. At the end of his first term he was placed in the first class in his college examinations; by the end of the year he had dropped to the second; thereafter he was unplaced, not bothering to sit all the papers. To his uncle's disquiet, he had become a 'non-reading man' – that is, one who did not intend to try for an honours degree.

There remained plenty, however, to occupy him at Cambridge. To start with, there was the freshman's usual access of freedom and self-importance to be savoured. Dressed in the dandyish undergraduate attire of the time (at St John's students who wore trousers instead of hose to hall were marked absent), he roved among old school friends and new acquaintances.

> I was the Dreamer, they the Dream; I roamed
> Delighted through the motley spectacle;
> Gowns grave, or gaudy, doctors, students, streets,
> Courts, cloisters, flocks of churches, gateways, towers:
> Migration strange for a stripling of the hills,
> A northern villager.
>   As if the change
> Had waited on some Fairy's wand, at once
> Behold me rich in monies, and attired
> In splendid garb, with hose of silk, and hair
> Powdered like rimy trees, when frost is keen.
> My lordly dressing-gown, I pass it by,
> With other signs of manhood that supplied
> The lack of beard. – The weeks went roundly on,
> With invitations, suppers, wine and fruit,
> Smooth housekeeping within, and all without
> Liberal, and suiting gentleman's array.
>
>   (III, 30–45)

Though he never found the noble minds he had looked for, he could not fail to be carried away by

> So many happy youths, so wide and fair
> A congregation in its budding-time
> Of health, and hope, and beauty, all at once
> So many divers samples from the growth
> Of life's sweet season.
>
>   (III, 218–22)

There were plenty of alternatives to 'College labours':

> Companionships,
> Friendships, acquaintances, were welcome all.
> We sauntered, played, or rioted; we talked
> Unprofitable talk at morning hours;
> Drifted about along the streets and walks,
> Read lazily in trivial books,[4] went forth
> To gallop through the country in blind zeal
> Of senseless horsemanship, or on the breast
> Of Cam sailed boisterously, and let the stars
> Come forth, perhaps, without one quiet thought.
>
>   (III, 246–55)

---

[4] A plentiful stock of 'lounge books', among much else, was kept by the principal bookseller of the time, John Nicholson (1730–96), at his shop next to King's. He was popularly known as 'Maps' from his habit of touring the colleges crying 'Maps, sir!'; his portrait in pursuit of trade still adorns the entrance hall of the University Library.

But Wordsworth's reading was not all trivial. Although it was unheard of for a sizar to take lessons in languages (more appropriate for fellow-commoners like Horace Walpole, as preparation for their Grand Tours), Wordsworth took Italian lessons from Agostino Isola, a Milanese émigré appointed as a university teacher by Gray. As a translator of the Italian poets, Isola was an ideal instructor for him. Wordsworth also apparently taught himself French and Spanish, for Dorothy wrote in 1791 that 'he reads Italian, Spanish, French, Greek and Latin, and English, but never opens a mathematical book'.

His readings in the English poets were made more meaningful for him by the fact that so many of them had lived, walked and written among those same courts and streets.

> I could not print
> Ground where the grass had yielded to the steps
> Of generations of illustrious men,
> Unmoved. I could not always lightly pass
> Through the same gateways, sleep where they had slept,
> Wake where they waked, range that inclosure old,
> That garden of great intellects, undisturbed.
>
>   . . . .
>
>   Beside the pleasant Mill of Trompington
> I laughed with Chaucer; in the hawthorn shade
> Heard him, while birds were warbling, tell his tales
> Of amorous passion. And that gentle Bard,
> Chosen by the Muses for their Page of State –
> Sweet Spenser, moving through his clouded heaven
> With the moon's beauty and the moon's soft pace,
> I called him Brother, Englishman, and Friend!
> Yea, our blind Poet, who, in his later day,
> Stood almost single; uttering odious truth –
> Darkness before, and danger's voice behind,
> Soul awful – if the earth has ever lodged
> An awful soul – I seemed to see him here
> Familiarly, and in his scholar's dress
> Bounding before me, yet a stripling youth –
> A boy, no better, with his rosy cheeks
> Angelical, keen eye, courageous look,
> And conscious step of purity and pride.
> (III, 258–64, 275–92)

Attending a wine party one day in the rooms of a Hawkshead friend, Edward Birkett of Christ's, and being told that the rooms had formerly been Milton's, Wordsworth's heart almost burst at the thought. (One cannot resist a suspicion that the abstemious Wordsworth, diffident among lively drinking men, was told the story as a device to encourage him to wet his lips.)

> Among the band of my compeers was one
> Whom chance had stationed in the very room
> Honoured by Milton's name. O temperate Bard!
> Be it confest that, for the first time, seated
> Within thy innocent lodge and oratory,
> One of a festive circle, I poured out
> Libations, to thy memory drank, till pride
> And gratitude grew dizzy in a brain
> Never excited by the fumes of wine
> Before that hour, or since. Then, forth I ran
> From the assembly; through a length of streets,
> Ran, ostrich-like, to reach our chapel door
> In not a desperate or opprobrious time,
> Albeit long after the importunate bell
> Had stopped, with wearisome Cassandra voice
> No longer haunting the dark winter night.
>
> (III, 293–208)

How he hated the twice-daily chapel services which that bell summoned him to. He, who had worshipped his Creator spontaneously among peaks and valleys, found the forced ritual of surplices and head-counting a charade worse even than that of the lecture-room:

> Let them parade among the Schools at will,
> But spare the House of God. Was ever known
> The witless shepherd who persists to drive
> A flock that thirsts not to a pool disliked?
> A weight must surely hang on days begun
> And ended with such mockery.
>
> (III, 404–9)

But compulsory chapel and the fiercely competitive examinations were not the only aspects of university life that revolted him. His Cambridge was that depicted by Henry Gunning (1768–1854) in his *Reminiscences of Cambridge* (1854). Gunning came up to Christ's just three years before Wordsworth and spent seventy years at Cambridge, rising to become Esquire Bedell. He believed the 1780s 'to have been the very worst part of our history. Drunkenness being the besetting sin of that period, I need scarcely add that many other vices followed in its train.' These included idleness, ignorance, gourmandising, and corruption – 'men of commanding talents and great acquirements scrupled not, as Examiners, for the sake of making money, to assign the highest honours in the power of the University to bestow, not on the most deserving, but upon those who had been fortunate enough to avail themselves of their instruction as Private Tutors!' Gunning's tutor at Christ's used to receive his pupils booted and spurred, ready to take to his horse, and so discouraged him that, like Wordsworth, he became a 'non-reading man'. Wilberforce, as a fellow-commoner at St John's, had been similarly dissuaded by his teachers from bothering himself with books. Little wonder that Wordsworth thought the dons less worthy of respect than the aged rustics of home:

> the grave Elders, men unscoured, grotesque
> In character, tricked out like aged trees
> Which through the lapse of their infirmity
> Give ready place to any random seed
> That chooses to be reared within their trunks.
>
> (III, 542–6)

True knowledge, wisdom and love of beauty were clearly the last things anyone was likely to carry away from Cambridge; instead, the student encountered

> Honour misplaced, and Dignity astray;
> Feuds, factions, flatteries, enmity, and guile,
> Murmuring submission, and bald government,
> (The idol weak as the idolator),
> And Decency and Custom starving Truth,
> And blind Authority beating with his staff
> The child that might have led him; Emptiness
> Followed as of good omen, and meek Worth
> Left to herself unheard of and unknown.
>
> (III, 600–8)

'Unheard of and unknown': there is an almost total lack of any contemporary account of Wordsworth at Cambridge. He did not belong, he remained throughout 'a lodger in that house of letters', experiencing

> a strangeness in the mind,
> A feeling that I was not for that hour,
> Nor for that place.
>
> (III, 80–2)

Was the fault wholly Cambridge's, or partly his? Looking back in *The Prelude* (which he first drafted between 1799 and 1805), he made various excuses for himself – 'I was ill-tutored for captivity', 'I was a spoiled child . . . rambling like the wind'. But, even if the system had been more congenial, it is doubtful whether he would have made a bigger mark at Cambridge, or whether more academic application would have significantly benefited his poetry.

Though for the most part his 'imagination slept' at Cambridge, he never wholly lost his sense of communion with nature. The Cambridgeshire landscape, with its slack, silent river and damp wastes beneath an engulfing sky, might seem dull enough, but he discovered to his surprise that the same invisible spirit moved among things even here:

> ofttimes did I quit
> My comrades, leave the crowd, buildings and groves,
> And as I paced alone the level fields
> Far from those lovely sights and sounds sublime
> With which I had been conversant, the mind
> Drooped not; but there into herself returning,
> With prompt rebound seemed fresh as heretofore.
>
> (III, 91–7)

The very difference between this landscape and that of home enabled him to expand his understanding to a more universal level. Even here, all 'That I beheld respired with inward meaning'.

Even within Cambridge there were natural objects to commune with. St John's had extensive grounds where he loved to wander on deserted winter evenings, and there too he could find profounder texts than the arid tomes of the reading-men:

> A single tree
> With sinuous trunk, boughs exquisitely wreathed,
> Grew there; an ash which Winter for himself
> Decked as in pride, and with outlandish grace:
> Up from the ground, and almost to the top,
> The trunk and every master branch were green
> With clustering ivy, and the lightsome twigs
> And outer spray profusely tipped with seeds
> That hung in yellow tassels, while the air
> Stirred them, not voiceless. Often have I stood
> Foot-bound uplooking at this lovely tree
> Beneath a frosty moon. The hemisphere
> Of magic fiction, verse of mine perchance
> May never tread; but scarcely Spenser's self
> Could have more tranquil visions in his youth,
> Or could more bright appearances create
> Of human forms with superhuman powers,
> Than I beheld loitering on calm clear nights
> Alone, beneath this fairy work of earth.[5]
>
> (VI, 76–94)

What did his contemporaries think of this sensitive, high-spirited but elusive young man, who was among them yet somehow not of them, who enjoyed conventional pleasures – parties, riding, boating – yet did things they did not do? Catching sight of him loping along lane or dyke, staring at trees and sunsets in unaccountable reveries, they must have thought him more than odd.

---

[5] Dorothy visited the tree in 1810, but its exact location is no longer known. Possibly it stood beside the Bin Brook. See 'Wordsworth's Ash Tree', in *The Eagle*, no. 237 (1950).

> Some called it madness – so indeed it was,
> If child-like fruitfulness in passing joy,
> If steady moods of thoughtfulness matured
> To inspiration, sort with such a name;
> If prophecy be madness; if things viewed
> By poets in old time, and higher up
> By the first men, earth's first inhabitants,
> May in these tutored days no more be seen
> With undisordered sight.
>
> (III, 146–54)

The 'tutored' learning of the scarlet doctors was a false achievement if it brought – as it so clearly did – a blunted sensibility.

Wordsworth had begun work on his first significant poem, 'An Evening Walk', during his first summer vacation at home, completing it the following year, 1789. When his uncle married in the autumn of 1788 and took a college living in Norfolk, he brought Dorothy to live with him there, and they passed through Cambridge on the way. 'The buildings added to the pleasure of seeing my Brother very well and in excellent spirits,' she wrote. 'I could scarcely help imagining myself in a different country when I was walking in the college courts and groves; it looked so odd to see smart, powdered heads with black caps like helmets . . . and gowns.'

Wordsworth again returned north for his second Long Vacation, and in the Christmas vacation of 1789 made a first impressionable visit to London. But in his last Long Vacation, just when he should have been working hard for his final examinations, he set off on a venture with a Welsh college friend, Robert Jones – 'staff in hand, without knapsacks, and carrying each his needments tied up in a pocket handkerchief', as Wordsworth later recalled – for a walking tour of France and Switzerland. Though family and friends must have thought the pair of them insane – gentlemen did not go walking, certainly not on Continental tours; besides, France just then was in the midst of revolutionary turmoil – it was to be a formative spiritual experience. They did not get back to Cambridge until November, in time to complete the statutory residence requirements. On 27 January 1791, Wordsworth, Jones, and John Myers were all admitted to pass degrees without honours, Wordsworth having idled the week before his examination reading Richardson's *Clarissa*.

Uncle William must have been in despair: his nephew had failed to take an honours degree, showed no interest in putting himself forward for the vacant fellowship caused by his marriage,[6] frittered away his vacations on walking tours, and made no impression on the university authorities. He called himself a poet, yet he had missed opportunities to promote himself even in that direction. In

---

6 Only two Fellows were allowed from each county at St John's. Uncle William's Cumberland fellowship remained vacant until 1794.

1789, for instance, when the Master of St John's had died and the coffin had as usual been adorned with verses by members of the college, young Wordsworth had not participated.

> My uncle seemed mortified when upon enquiring he learnt that none of these verses were from my pen, 'because', said he, 'it would have been a fair opportunity for distinguishing yourself'. I did not, however, regret that I had been silent on this occasion, as I felt no interest in the deceased person, with whom I had had no intercourse and whom I had never seen but during his walks in the college grounds.

Such sincerity broke incomprehensibly (to a conventional parson's mind) with the long tradition of elegies by means of which so many Cambridge poets had attracted attention to their talents.

Now, after taking a pass degree, Uncle William's errant nephew spent most of 1791 in aimless wandering. Finally, his guardian tried using the young man's literary predilections as a carrot to lure him back towards conventionality. 'My uncle the clergyman', Wordsworth informed a college friend in November, 'proposed to me a short time ago to begin a course of oriental literature, thinking that that was the best field for a person to distinguish himself in as a man of letters'. Wordsworth dutifully returned to Cambridge to pursue the unlikely study of Arabic and Hebrew, but the plan evaporated almost at once. The exciting scenes he had witnessed in France tempted him to return there; and, at last, giving the ostensible reason that he wanted to perfect his French, he recrossed the Channel. He was to be away for a year.

How much more satisfactory to his guardians must have been the temperament and career of Wordsworth's younger brother Christopher (1774–1846), who went up to Trinity in 1792. He cultivated his mathematics, worked industriously, took a good degree, and proceeded to a series of desirable appointments culminating in 1820 in the Mastership of Trinity. But though he did much to expand his college, he was largely remembered in Cambridge as a strict disciplinarian, particularly notorious for his enforcement of chapel attendance. Christopher's three sons were equally distinguished academically: the youngest, also Christopher, won every prize at Trinity, including the Chancellor's English Medal twice; successively Public Orator, headmaster of Harrow, and Bishop of Lincoln, he was to be his uncle's literary executor and first biographer.

Though Wordsworth had no particular empathy with his younger brother, it was to visit him that he made a number of later returns to Cambridge. In 1820 he, his wife Mary, and his sister Dorothy stayed a fortnight at Trinity, Wordsworth writing to his friend Henry Crabb Robinson that what with 'our stately apartments with all the venerable portraits there that awe one to humility, old friends, new acquaintances, and a thousand familiar remembrances, and freshly conjured up recollections, I enjoyed myself not a little'. Among a group of students invited to meet him one evening was John Moultrie (1799–1874), who wrote his own lengthy autobiographical poem, *The Dream of Life*. He recalled the occasion in 'The Three Minstrels':

> One evening – (one to life's decline
>   Since youth remembered) – 'twas my pride
>   To sit, a listener at his side
> Whom I had deemed almost divine.
>
>   . . . .
>
> His face and form were thin and spare
>   As of ascetic anchorite,
>   Yet with us boys in converse light
> He joined with free and genial air.

Wordsworth reported to Crabb Robinson having written a sonnet at Cambridge – possibly that on the portrait of Henry VIII that then hung in the Lodge (now in the hall), but more probably the first of the sequence of three sonnets (published in 1822) in praise of King's College Chapel. King's Chapel had not been without its eighteenth century detractor – William Gilpin (1724–1804), a Hampshire schoolmaster who rode about England in his holidays compiling *Picturesque Tours*, had censured the interior of the building in 1769:

> Its disproportion disgusts. Such height, and such length, united by such straightened parallels, hurt the eye. You feel immured. Henry the Sixth, we are told, spent twelve hundred pounds in adorning the roof. It is a pity he had not spent it in widening the walls. We should then have had a better form, and should have been relieved from the tedious repetition of roses and portcullises.[7]

Wordsworth, though an admirer of Gilpin's book on the Lakes, may have had this passage in mind when he wrote the first sonnet of the three, unconditionally celebrating the chapel's grandeur:

> Tax not the royal Saint with vain expense,
> With ill-matched aims the Architect who planned –
> Albeit labouring for a scanty band
> Of white-robed Scholars only – this immense
> And glorious Work of fine intelligence!
> Give all thou canst; high Heaven rejects the lore
> Of nicely-calculated less or more;
> So deemed the man who fashioned for the sense
> These lofty pillars, spread that branching roof
> Self-poised, and scooped into ten thousand cells,
> Where light and shade repose, where music dwells

---

[7] *Observations on Several Parts of the Counties of Cambridge, Norfolk, Suffolk and Essex* (1809). Gilpin is inaccurate about Henry VI: the roof decorations were added later by the Tudor monarchs who completed the building.

> Lingering – and wandering on as loth to die;
> Like thoughts whose very sweetness yieldeth proof
> That they were born for immortality.

The second sonnet evokes an atmosphere of solemn beauty unrecognised by Gilpin. One is not to look or judge too closely, Wordsworth says: the multi-coloured twilight, the luxuriating 'mazy' sounds of the music, are meant to

> cast, before the eye
> Of the devout, a veil of ecstasy!

J. M. W. Turner, who painted a watercolour of the exterior of King's College Chapel in 1796, in similar mind subordinated strict representation to the creation of ethereal tenuity; and George Dyer in his *History of Cambridge* (1814) wrote of the view of King's and Clare: 'nor must you say this is not Grasmere or Keswick; there is no scene of the kind throughout all England that can be compared with these' – another slap at Gilpin. That Wordsworth continued to feel the chapel misunderstood is indicated by a curious dream he recounted in a letter to William Whewell, Fellow (later Master) of Trinity, in May 1834. In this dream, the waters of the Cam, thrown out of their bed by an earthquake, attacked the base of the chapel.

> Out came the Provost, Fellows and Students, and to my great astonishment, fell to work most manfully for the destruction of the buttresses: in the meanwhile, a crowd gathered, some of whom assisted in the labour. I myself went up and asked what they were about, and why? Some of the most active said we dislike these old-fashioned deformities, the building would look much better without them, and instead of being of use they encumber and weaken it. Others cried out, 'down with them! we are pulling them down, that the flood may have free way.' I continued to look on, and sure enough they got rid of all the buttresses, but the roof and the walls of the chapel fell in, and they who had been so busy were crushed in the ruins.

However, Wordsworth interpreted his dream to Whewell in terms of the proposed abolition of religious tests at the university.

In 1832 St John's persuaded Wordsworth to sit for a portrait, and he accompanied the finished result, by H. W. Pickersgill, with the inevitable sonnet. In 1835 he was able to write proudly to Robert Jones, his fellow miscreant of long ago:

> I called upon the Master of St John's yesterday, but did not get to see him; he is said to wear well. I had a friend with me who took me through the Lodge and in the Combination Room I saw my own picture . . . It looks well, but is of too large a size for the room, and would be seen to better advantage in the Hall. But had there been room for it there, there is an objection to that place – the charcoal smoke, I am told, is ruinous to pictures, and this which is really well done cost money.

It was recognition in his own time, though the aging Wordsworth who revelled in the respect now paid to him was a different man from the radical enthusiast of his college days. In 1847, near the end of his life and now the merest shadow of the poet he had been, Wordsworth managed, with assistance from his nephew Christopher, to compose an ode for the installation of Prince Albert as Chancellor of the university. It was the last poem he ever wrote, and the sort of verse one expects, though hopes not to get, from Poets Laureate on royal occasions.

The tribulations of
Silas Tomkyn Comberbache

If Wordsworth had arrived full of awe, Samuel Taylor Coleridge (1772–1834) arrived febrile with facetiousness: 'Here I am – videlicet – Jesus College. I had a tolerable Journey – went by a night-coach packed up with five more – one of whom had a long, broad, red, hot face – four feet by three . . . ' But the chatter disguised the charity-boy's chronic insecurity, the child prodigy's sapping self-doubt.

Wordsworth was to lament in *The Prelude* that their Cambridge careers had not coincided (they did not meet until 1795). Coleridge's vivacious originality was precisely what he had lacked, while his own steadier influence at this crucial juncture might have forestalled the seeds of dissolution in the younger poet.

> Not alone,
> Ah! surely not in singleness of heart
> Should I have seen the light of evening fade
> From smooth Cam's silent waters: had we met,
> Even at that early time, needs must I trust
> In the belief, that my maturer age,
> My calmer habits, and more steady voice,
> Would with an influence benign have soothed,
> Or chased away, the airy wretchedness
> That battened on thy youth.

Coleridge's life story is a ravel of such might-have-beens.

Wordsworth took his degree in January 1791; Coleridge arrived in October. Yet despite the proximity of their terms of residence, Coleridge's Cambridge already has a surprisingly different ring from Wordsworth's – partly because of the changed intellectual climate brought about by the French Revolution, partly because St John's had been at a reactionary ebb while Jesus was bustling with progressiveness, partly because of the two poets' different temperaments. Both proved academic failures; but while Wordsworth pined in obscurity, Coleridge was the talk of the university, his career effervescing with controversy, truancy, politics, drugs.

Coleridge's childhood had been lonely and unhappy. The youngest of ten children, he had been sent from Devon to Christ's Hospital in London after his father's death, where he consoled himself with his first great addiction – books. Jesus College was probably chosen for him because of the Rustat Scholarships which it offered to the sons of deceased clergymen: he was awarded one soon after arrival, to add to the leaving exhibition of forty pounds a year that he brought from Christ's Hospital.

The Coleridge who descended on Cambridge in the night coach brought with him a precocious reputation for erudition and eloquence. In addition, he had already begun to write poems (the minor poet William Lisle Bowles was his first influence); he had acquired, during a prolonged illness at school, a taste for laudanum (then administered as a universal panacea); and he was in love with one Mary Evans, sister of a schoolfellow.

Wordsworth had arrived late to find everyone already in residence; Coleridge came dashing up and found the place still deserted. Alighting from the coach early on 16 October, he made his way first to Pembroke to look up the only Cambridge person he knew, Thomas Fanshaw Middleton, who had been at school with him and was now in his third year. A classical scholar who later became Bishop of Calcutta, Middleton gave the freshman breakfast before showing him to his own college. Neither the Master of Jesus nor even the tutors being yet in residence, Coleridge was temporarily assigned an absent student's rooms. Knowing no one at Jesus, this most talkative of young men reported to his elder brother George (who had the task of acting as his guardian) that 'I sit down to dinner in the Hall in silence – except the noise of suction, which accompanies my eating – and rise-up ditto. I then walk off to Pembroke and sit with my friend Middleton.' Already he was complaining about his finances: 'One feels cold and naked and shivering, and gelid, and chilly and such like synonimes – without a little money in one's pocket.' In later life, ever ingeniously discovering fresh causes for his troubles, he once claimed that all his miseries began when, allocated rooms of his own at last, he was asked by a tradesman how he would like them furnished. Supposing the man to be employed by the college, he delightedly replied: 'Just as you please, sir.' The man as delightedly took him at his word, saddling him with exorbitant debts that were to hang round his neck as unshakeably as the Ancient Mariner's albatross.

His rooms, the right-hand set on the ground floor of D staircase, opposite the entrance gate, were not only over-furnished, they were damp. The end of November found him 'nailed to my bed with a fit of the Rheumatism', a life-long complaint. 'Cambridge is a damp place – the very palace of winds: so without very great care one is sure to have a violent cold. I am not however certain, that I do not owe my Rheumatism to the dampness of my rooms.' There follows the first reference in his letters to the drug that was eventually to wreck his life: 'Opium never used to have any disagreeable effects on me – but it has upon many.'

He began his studies assiduously enough, attending the daily mathematical lectures and getting additional coaching from Middleton; punctual for chapel services (there being a fine for absence, 'I am remarkably religious upon an economical plan'); avoiding the perils of wine parties; deep in the classics. 'If I were to read on as I do now – there is not the least doubt that I should be Classical Medallist, and a very high Wrangler: but *Freshmen* always *begin* very *furiously*.' By the end of his first term his talents had impressed the Master, Dr William Pearce, who, himself a former Public Orator famed for his talk, appreciated Coleridge's eloquence and breadth of reading. Pearce gave him encouragement. 'If ever hogs-lard is pleasing, it is, when our *superiors* trowel it on,' Coleridge chortled to his brother. In his second term he won a college prize for a Latin declamation on 'Posthumous Fame'.[1] Everything boded well.

His new literary influence was Gray. Middleton probably took him to see Gray's manuscripts at Pembroke, where he copied out some odes; and his letters, particularly those to the Evans family, show the result (compare the letter by Gray quoted on p. 89):

> The quiet ugliness of Cambridge supplies me with very few communicables in the news way. The most important is, that Mr Tim. Grubskin, of this town Citizen, is dead. Poor man! he loved fish too well. A violent commotion in his bowells carried him off. They say, he made a very good end . . .
>
> The Mutton and winter cabbage are confoundedly tough here, tho' very venerable for their old age . . . The River Cam is a handsome stream of a muddy complexion, somewhat like Miss Yates, to whom you will present my Love . . . In Cambridge there are 16 Colleges, that look like work-houses, and 14 Churches, that look like little houses. The town is very fertile in alleys, and mud, and cats, and dogs, besides men, women, ravens, clergy, proctors, Tutors, Owls, and other two-legged cattle.

In his rooms one night, so he assured Mary Evans, the ghost of Gray appeared and commanded him to send her a copy of his poems, which he duly did. A poem sent to George a little later, 'Fragment Found in a Lecture Room', imitates Gray's 'Hymn to Ignorance':

> Where deep in mud Cam rolls his slumbrous stream,
> And Bog and Desolation reign supreme,
> Where all Boeotia clouds the misty brain,
> The owl Mathesis[2] pipes her loathsome strain.
> Far far aloof the frighted Muses fly,
> Indignant Genius scowls and passes by . . .

Coleridge's notions of natural beauty at this date seem ingenuously cockney. He informed Mary in February 1792:

---

[1] A manuscript of this, supposedly in Coleridge's hand, is preserved in the college library. It is described in *The Chanticlere*, no. 2, Lent Term 1886.

[2] I.e. mathematics.

The clear rivulet that runs through the grove adjacent to our College, and the numberless little birds (particularly Robins) that are singing away, – and above all – the little Lambs, each by the side of its Mother – recall the most pleasing ideas of pastoral simplicity.

Wordsworth found Cambridgeshire tame after Lakeland; Coleridge managed to find it excitingly wild. He and Middleton walked out seven miles one Sunday and took tea at a farmhouse – 'the rusticity of the habitation and the inhabitants was charming'. Describing the return journey, when they were overtaken by dark and lost their way, he thrills with fashionable Gothic terrors as he relates their dread of ghosts, their near escape from a quagmire, and their encounter with a local who told stories of Jack o'lanthorns that lure travellers to their deaths, and 'entertained us with many a dreadful tale'.

Another poem ostensibly inspired by his college surroundings, and dispatched to Mary Evans – 'A Wish: Written in Jesus Wood, February 10th 1792' – was in fact a translation of a Greek ode by a former Fellow of Jesus, Dr John Jortin, though he did not tell her so.

> Lo! thro' the dusky silence of the groves,
> Thro' vales irriguous, and thro' green retreats,
> With languid murmur creeps the placid stream
>   And works its secret way!
>
> Awhile meand'ring round its native fields,
> It rolls the playful wave and winds its flight:
> Then downward flowing with awaken'd speed
>   Embosoms in the deep!
>
> Thus thro' its silent tenor may my Life
> Smooth its meek stream, by sordid Wealth unclogg'd,
> Alike unconscious of forensic storms,
>   And Glory's blood-stain'd palm!
>
> And when dark Age shall close Life's little day,
> Satiate of sport, and weary of its toils,
> E'en thus may slumbrous Death my decent limbs
>   Compose with icy hand!

For Mary's sister, Coleridge repeated a story about two drunken scholars who tumble in the water runnel in Trumpington Street: 'We ran to assist one of them – who very generously stuttered out, as he lay sprawling in the mud – Nnnno, nnno! – ssave my ffrfrfriend there – nnever mind me – *I* can swim.'[3] In a letter to George he recounted another familiar freshman tale:

This morning I went for the first time with a party on the River. The clumsy Dog, to whom we had entrusted the sail, was fool enough to fasten it. A Gust of Wind

---

[3] Gunning tells the same story in his *Reminiscences* under the year 1794.

embraced the opportunity of turning over the Boat, and baptizing all that were in it. We swam to shore, and walked dripping home, like so many River Gods. Thank God! I do not feel as if I should be the worse for it.

Though Coleridge must have been the most talked-about freshman of his year, not many *obiter dicta* from this time have survived. When Dr Pearce met him in the street wearing a particularly ragged gown and rebuked him, 'Mr Coleridge, Mr Coleridge, when will you get rid of that shameful gown?' Coleridge is said to have replied, 'Why sir, I think I have got rid of the best part of it already.' On another occasion he described the meat served up in hall: 'We have veal, sir, tottering on the verge of beef!' He later claimed that by his constant recommendation to everyone he met, particularly freshmen, he helped sell complete editions of three books – Simpson's *Euclid*, Hartley's *Observation on Man*, and Bowles's poems.

Coleridge's first year had been something of a balancing act between genuine hard work and an increasing tendency to over-socialise, but it ended with his winning a Browne Gold Medal for a Greek ode on the slave trade (even if, as legend has it, his friends had to lock him in his rooms with pen, ink, and paper to get him to finish it in time). Encouraged by this recognition, he set his sights on winning the Craven Scholarship, which, along with the Chancellor's Classical Medals, counted as the highest award in classics.

By the time he returned for his second year, however, nervous strain was beginning to set in. His first year's debts remained unpaid, and competition for the impending Craven exam was stiff. Possibly he began now to take refuge in opium, for he confessed later that the time he should have spent studying was frittered away in 'soul-enervating Reveries – in building magnificent Edifices of Happiness on some fleeting Shadow of Reality!' He owned to having been 'almost constantly intoxicated' for the entire six weeks preceding the exam. Yet, out of eighteen original candidates, he found himself on a shortlist of four, the others being Christopher Bethell, later Bishop of Bangor, John Keate, later headmaster of Eton, and Samuel Butler, later headmaster of Shrewsbury. With Dr Pearce urging him on and his family impatient to hear good of him, the strain was all the greater for knowing that he was letting slip valuable time in drugged indolence.

The examination was intense. 'I verily believe, we circumnavigated the Encyclopaedia – so very severe an examination was never remembered.' The four being judged of equal merit, the prize was awarded, according to the rules, to the youngest, Butler. Dr Pearce, confessing he thought Coleridge hard done by, awarded him as consolation prize the post of chapel clerk, worth thirty-three pounds a year. With bills mounting up, he was grateful for the money, but a tremendous bitterness with himself set in. In effect, the loss of the Craven marked the end of his hopes for a brilliant academic career. He knew he lacked the mathematical skills to qualify for a Chancellor's Medal. Had not even the acclaimed Middleton, from a similar disability, failed to win one and left without a fellowship? The path that led to the peaks of Fellow, Orator, head of house, was narrow and precipitous; he had stumbled and fallen when scarcely embarked on it.

For a while he was laid low by hopelessness and despair. As usual there were physical symptoms – a nasty abscess of the gum that necessitated further laudanum. He cheered slightly when his mathematical lecturer fell in a pond and was unable to lecture. Distracted by the music practising of his neighbours – 'two of them fiddle-scrapers, the third a flute-tooter' – he acquired a violin and vented his feelings on that. At the end of an even more divagating letter than usual, he joked: 'Are you asleep, my dear Mary? I have administered rather a strong Dose of Opium.'

Then, suddenly throwing aside his academic blues and his mathematical books, he was deep in revolutionary politics. Since his first year he had known William Frend, Fellow and formerly Tutor of Jesus, who had lost his tutorship as a result of a Unitarian pamphlet exhorting the people of Cambridge to 'turn from the false worship of the Three Persons to the worship of the One True God'. Now, in 1793, a further pamphlet, *Peace and Union*, in which Frend outlined relatively mild political improvements, was to result in his total expulsion from college and university.

Frend's cause was turned by the students into a major confrontation with the Tory Establishment which in turn, frightened by events in France, was determined to stamp out any such manifestations of seditious radicalism. Adopting Jacobin modes of dress and behaviour (long loose locks and striped pantaloons were rapidly replacing the powdered hair and silk hose of Wordsworth's day), the students chalked 'Frend for ever!!' on college walls and burnt 'Liberty and Equality' into the lawns of Trinity and St John's with gunpowder.

The Senate House was packed with partisan supporters for Frend's appearance before the Vice-Chancellor's Court in May 1793, and among the crowds in the gallery were both Coleridge and Henry Gunning. According to Gunning's *Reminiscences*, the Senior Proctor, Farish, dispatched to quell the disturbances in the gallery, marked the position of the ringleader and, making his way to the spot, demanded the man's name and college, accusing him of immoderate clapping.

'I wish this was possible,' said the man, and turning round, exhibited an arm so deformed that his hands could not by any possibility be brought together: this exculpation was received with repeated sounds of applause, which continued for some minutes. The name of the young man was Charnock, and his college Clare Hall; the real culprit was S. T. Coleridge, of Jesus College, who having observed that the Proctor had noticed him, and was coming into the gallery, turned round to the person who was standing behind him, and made an offer of changing places, which was gladly accepted by the unsuspecting man. Coleridge immediately retreated, and mixing with the crowd, entirely escaped suspicion. This conduct on the part of Coleridge, was severely censured by the Under-graduates . . .

In fact, the exchange of places had been prearranged with Charnock and, according to another version, Coleridge afterwards gave himself up to the Proctor, who had been perfectly aware of the real culprit's identity.

Himself converted to Unitarianism by Frend, Coleridge was deeply excited by the events, as another picture of him at this time, by his friend Charles Valentine Le Grice (1773–1858), of Christ's Hospital and Trinity, bears witness:

> He was very studious, but his reading was desultory and capricious. He took little exercise merely for the sake of exercise; but he was ready at any time to unbend his mind in conversation, and for the sake of this, his room . . . was a constant rendezvous of conversation-loving friends, – I will not call them loungers, for they did not call to kill time, but to enjoy it. What evenings have I spent in those rooms! What little suppers, or *sizings* as they were called, have I enjoyed; when Aeschylus and Plato and Thucydides were pushed aside, with a pile of lexicons &c., to discuss the pamphlets of the day. Ever and anon a pamphlet issued from the pen of Burke. There was no need of having the book before us. Coleridge had read it in the morning, and in the evening he would repeat whole pages verbatim. Frend's trial was then in progress. Pamphlets swarmed from the press. Coleridge had read them all; and in the evening, with our negus, we had them *viva-voce* gloriously.[4]

At the end of his second year, Coleridge again entered for the Browne Medal, this time with what he considered a better ode than the previous year. But it was 'so *sublime* that nobody could understand it', as he lamented to George, and the prize went to Keate. This fresh disappointment deepened his feeling of inadequacy.

Meanwhile his financial situation had not improved and his second Long Vacation brought a showdown with his family. In the end they agreed to pay his debts and sent him back to Cambridge with what they imagined to be adequate funds; but possibly his debts were worse than he had informed them (he owed his tutor £148) and on his way through London he blew the lot in a mad reckless spree. At the same time, convinced that his love for Miss Evans was hopeless, he was in an emotional turmoil. After a month in Cambridge dissipating himself with harlots, opium, and Chattertonesque notions of suicide, he at last suffered a nervous collapse and, for neither the first nor the last time in his life, bolted. One day he was at Jesus College, the next – vanished into air.

Christopher Wordsworth, who joined a new literary society that Coleridge and Le Grice had formed, recorded in his diary meeting the poet just before he disappeared. At their first encounter, in a coffee-house on 5 November, he, Coleridge, Le Grice, Rough of Trinity, and three others 'got all into a box and (having met with the *Monthly Review* of my brother's poems) entered into a good deal of literary and critical conversation . . . Coleridge spoke of the esteem in which my brother was holden by a society at Exeter'; he also 'talked Greek . . .

---

[4] *Gentleman's Magazine*, December 1834.

and spouted out of Bowles'. Two days later, Coleridge called on Rough with his poems at breakfast and Rough and Wordsworth 'sat in criticism' on them. This was the day that Coleridge first appeared in print, his poem 'To Fortune: On Buying a Ticket in the Irish Lottery' being printed in the *Morning Chronicle* (Wordsworth records reading it next day). On 8 November, the entire society drank wine at Coleridge's. On 13 November, at a meeting of the society in Wordsworth's rooms, Coleridge was to have read a paper but, 'having neglected to write it', declaimed his own poems instead.

Coleridge's account of these weeks is more dramatic:

> When I returned to Cambridge a multitude of petty Embarrassments buzzed round me, like a Nest of Hornets . . . My Agitations were delirium – I formed a Party, dashed to London at eleven o'clock at night, and for three days lived in all the tempest of Pleasure – resolved on my return – but I will not shock your religious feelings – I again returned to Cambridge – staid a week – such a week! Where Vice has not annihilated Sensibility, there is little need of a Hell! On Sunday night I packed up a few things, – went off in the mail – staid about a week in a strange way, still looking forwards with a kind of recklessness to the dernier resort of misery . . .

When the lottery ticket on which he had staked his hopes proved unlucky, he did not commit suicide, however, but instead, spotting a recruiting poster, presented himself on 2 December 1793 for enlistment in the 15th Regiment of Light Dragoons. He gave his name as Silas Tomkyn Comberbache – a suitably clownish *nom-de-guerre* that fitted the initials on his clothes, the surname having been spotted over a shop door somewhere. S. T. Comberbache was posted to Reading for training but turned out to be the most 'indocile equestrian' imaginable. He was constantly falling off his horse or being bolted with, and neglected to groom the animal, maintaining indignantly that 'a horse should rub himself down, and shake himself clean, so to shine in all his native beauty'. Various legends later circulated about his life in the ranks – that he carried Bentley's *Horace* and the works of Casimir in his saddle bag, corrected an officer who had attributed a quotation from Sophocles to Euripides, chalked a Latin tag on the wall where his saddle hung, and entertained his fellow recruits with tales from the classics so vividly narrated that they were convinced he was recounting modern military exploits. Availing themselves of his skills, the troopers agreed to groom his horse if he would write their letters for them.

Meanwhile, Jesus had passed a resolution on 19 December 'that if Coleridge, who has left College without leave, should not return within a month from this day, and pay his debts to his tutor, or give reasonable security that they should be paid, his name be taken off the boards'. This step was apparently not taken, though Coleridge's whereabouts were not unearthed until the beginning of February 1794. Plampin, his long-suffering tutor, agreed to take him back, and there was more clubbing together to bail him out and cover his debts. An obliging officer, to circumvent red tape and expedite his release, discharged Trooper Comberbache as 'insane': a detail his family were soon to be reflecting on.

He was released on 10 April 1794 and returned to Jesus. The college register reads: '1794 Apr: Coleridge admonitus est per magistrum in praesentia sociorum'. On 1 May he wrote more fully to George:

> I have been convened before the fellows – Dr Pearce behaved with great asperity, Mr Plampin with exceeding and most delicate kindness – My Sentence is, a Reprimand . . . a month's confinement to the precincts of the College, and to translate the works of Demetrius Phalareus [*sic*] into English . . . The confinement is nothing – I have the fields and Grove of the college to walk in – and what can I wish more?

Dr Pearce evidently had a motive in setting the Demetrius Phalereus: 'From the Dr's words I suspect that he wishes it to be a publication – as he has more than once sent to know how I go on, and pressed me to exert erudition in some notes – and to write a preface.'

Coleridge got through the summer term without further trouble, dropping his former bad influences, getting up at six to work, and writing for all the prizes. Then when the vacation arrived, he set off on an apparently innocuous pedestrian tour, knapsack on back and pilgrim staff in hand, with Joseph Hucks of Eton and St Catharine's. It was to be a turning point in his life.

Stopping at Oxford on the way to Wales, Coleridge was introduced at Balliol College to an undergraduate called Robert Southey. They began to strike sparks off one another at once, and three weeks vanished in animated discussion of the state of the world and the options for mankind. The French had shown how even the most idealised popular movement could become corrupted and bloodthirsty, and the two young men argued that the civilised world as they knew it was best abandoned altogether. In Southey's Balliol rooms was hatched an ambitious and intoxicating scheme for a group of idealists, complete with womenfolk, to emigrate to America to set up a communistic enclave. Everyone would be equal, all property shared, all work equally distributed. 'When Coleridge and I are sawing down a tree we shall discuss metaphysics,' Southey enthused, 'criticise poetry when hunting buffalo, and write sonnets whilst following the plough'. They called the scheme Pantisocracy.

After walking through Wales preaching Pantisocracy in inns and taverns, Coleridge met up with Southey again in the latter's home town of Bristol. Putting Mary Evans from his mind, he at once gave earnest of his commitment to the enterprise by becoming engaged to Sara Fricker, one of whose sisters was already engaged to Southey, while another was married to a fellow Pantisocrat, Robert Lovell. Money, however, was a more difficult obstacle to surmount than matrimony: £125 each would be needed to set them up on the banks of the Susquehannah (chosen for the name's metrical potential), so they at once communally rattled off a three-act blank-verse drama entitled *The Fall of*

Robespierre, Coleridge writing the first act, Southey the second, Lovell the third, the last two being completed within twenty-four hours (Coleridge, unreliable as ever, took an extra day). Robespierre had been guillotined only a week or two before, and, as Southey later recalled, 'it was written with newspapers before me, as fast as newspapers could be put into blank verse'. Lovell's contribution did not fit the other two, so Southey rewrote it, and Coleridge took the completed manuscript with him back to Cambridge, there to lick it into final shape. He arrived back at Jesus on 17 September, and the following day wrote to his new friend and fellow Pantisocrat (who had decided to abandon Balliol): 'Well, my dear Southey! I am at last arrived at Jesus. My God! how tumultuous are the movements of my Heart – Since I quitted this room what and how important Events have been evolved! America! Southey! Miss Fricker!'

What was to be Coleridge's final term at Cambridge was dispatched in a whirlwind of events. Frenetic and increasingly disputatious letters flew between Jesus College and Bristol (of *course* everyone would be equal, Southey wrote, but couldn't they take just a servant or two?); five hundred copies of *The Fall of Robespierre* were printed by a radical Cambridge printer, Benjamin Flower, with Coleridge's name on the title page ('it would appear ridiculous to put two names to *such* a Work') and a dedication to a fellow Jesus student, Harry Martin, who had considerably put up the cost; and Pantisocracy became the talking point of the university. The authorities, who had not tolerated Frend's pamphlets, were scandalised anew by this latest emission from the press, in which kings were referred to as 'crowned cockatrices, whose foul venom infects all Europe', while bloodthirsty revolutionaries were 'the patriot representatives of France'. Dr Pearce, trying to remain patient, summoned Coleridge and accused him of Jacobinism, to which Coleridge retorted unanswerably that he was neither Jacobin nor Democrat but Pantisocrat. Coleridge's family warned him that if he persisted with Pantisocracy they would have to have him confined to an asylum.

Meanwhile, in an agony of doubt over his commitment to Miss Fricker, and while making desperate last attempts to win over Miss Evans, Coleridge was simultaneously in hot pursuit of Miss Brunton, whose father was actor–manager of the Norwich Company, currently in Cambridge for the Sturbridge Fair. Half the fast set of the university seem to have been serenading her, but Coleridge was looked on with favour, given free tickets for the season, and invited to Norwich. He confessed to being 'bewitched', and gave her a copy of his play, inscribed with suitable effusions.

On 25 September he spent the evening with the Mayor, the notoriously corrupt John Mortlock:

> All last night was I obliged to listen to the damned chatter of Mortlock, our
> Mayor – a fellow, that would certainly be a Pantisocrat, were his head and heart
> as highly illuminated as his Face. At present he is a High Church man and a
> Pittite – and is guilty (with a very large fortune) of so many Rascalities in his
> public Character, that he is obliged to drink three bottles of Claret a day in order

to acquire a stationary rubor and prevent him from the trouble of running back-
wards and forwards for a blush once every five minutes. In the tropical Latitudes
of this fellow's Nose was I obliged to fry.

The following month Dr Edwards of Jesus, 'the great Grecian of Cambridge and
heterodox Divine', invited Coleridge to tea and argued with him over
Pantisocracy for six hours, finally capitulating to Coleridge's oratory. 'I came
home at one o'clock this morning exulting in the honest Consciousness of having
exhibited closer argument in more elegant and appropriate Language, than I had
ever conceived myself capable of.' What the dons thought of him can be judged
from an entry in the diary of Isaac Reed of Emmanuel, who on 8 October learnt
from Dr Pearce that Coleridge

> has imbibed the wild democratic opinion floating about at present concerning
> religion and politicks. He is a disciple of Godwin, the Author of two 4vo Volumes
> on the foundations of religion and politicks, and like him has entertained a
> foolish notion that the Life of man might be protracted to any length. He is an
> enemy to all establishments or religion and conceives there should be no publick
> worship. He is also of opinion that every one should learn some mechanic art
> and has accordingly put himself an apprentice to a Carpenter. He is going to
> America. Dr P[earce] said that [Coleridge] was in town lately and having no
> money to carry him to Cambridge he wrote a poem, an elegy he thought, and sent
> it to Perry, the Editor of the *Morning Chronicle*, offering his correspondence to
> the paper and desiring the return of a guinea which he received. He asserts that
> his play was written in 8 hours. Dr Pearce speaks of him as a very ingenious young
> man, bating these extravagant and foolish notions which he entertains.

Benjamin Flower, the printer of Coleridge's play, was editor of a newly established radical newspaper, *The Cambridge Intelligencer* (1793–1803), in the pages
of which several poems of Coleridge's appeared between 1794 and 1802. On
15 November 1794 the *Intelligencer* announced publication of an edition of
Chatterton's alleged 'Rowley' poems, printed by Flower and edited by a friend
of Coleridge's, Lancelot Sharpe, then still an undergraduate at Pembroke.
Coleridge's long-standing admiration for Chatterton had no doubt been fanned
during his recent visit to Chatterton's home town, Bristol (he and Miss Fricker
were married next year in the very church, St Mary Redcliffe, where Chatterton
had conceived his forgeries), and his enthusiasm probably helped to get the
edition published. Sharpe prefaced the book with Coleridge's own 'Monody on
the Death of Chatterton', written when he was a schoolboy.[5] Other poems by
Coleridge were appearing in the *Morning Chronicle*, including one written on
24 October and originally entitled 'Monologue to a Young Jack Ass in Jesus Piece',
which expresses Coleridge's Pantisocratic sense of equality with all living things:

---

[5] Three weeks later Flower brought out some light verses by Le Grice; in the new year he sold (but
did not print) Hucks's account of his pedestrian tour with Coleridge. Flower published Hucks's
Poems in 1798.

Innocent foal! Thou despised and forlorn!
I hail thee *Brother* – spite of the fool's scorn!
And fain I'd take thee with me to the dell
Where high-souled Pantisocracy shall dwell!

In the pages of *The Cambridge Intelligencer*, and at the end of *The Fall of Robespierre*, Coleridge had advertised for subscriptions for a work he had in hand, *Imitations from the Modern Latin Poets with a Critical and Biographical Essay on the Restoration of Literature*. Subscription would cost fourteen shillings and the work would be published in two volumes 'elegantly printed on superfine paper', shortly after Christmas. It would contain 'a copious selection from the Lyrics of Casimir, and a new translation of the Basia of Secundus', together with other poems which, 'scattered among the heavy collections of Gruter and others, seem to have escaped the notice even of the learned'. It is not known how many ventured to subscribe: like so many of Coleridge's projects, the book never materialised.[6] With less than two months before he could sit for his degree, his emotional crisis reached a new peak. Torn between a hopeless attachment to Mary Evans and his rash engagement to Sara Fricker, he rushed between Cambridge and London, learnt at last that Mary was engaged to someone else, and hurled himself into obscurity and dissipation in London. On 9 December he wrote to Southey that 'they are making a row about me at Jesus'. In fact, his college once again showed tolerance, keeping his name on the books for another term and crediting him with his scholarship stipend, despite his debt to his tutor. But this time he never returned.

Looking back, Coleridge was sometimes tempted to blame Cambridge for many of his life's problems – 'to real Happiness I bade adieu from the moment I received my first Tutor's Bill' – but he was also willing to admit that the fault had been his:

I became a proverb to the University for Idleness – the time, which I should have bestowed on the academic studies, I employed in dreaming out wild Schemes of impossible extrication. It had been better for me if my Imagination had been less vivid . . . My Affairs became more and more involved – I fled to Debauchery – fled from silent and solitary Anguish to all the uproar of senseless Mirth!

In 1818 he looked back 'with what bitter regret, in the conscience of such glorious opportunities', while in his *Biographia Literaria* he bewailed how 'in an inauspicious hour I left the friendly cloisters and happy grove of quiet, ever-honoured Jesus College, Cambridge'. Joseph Hucks, in 'Lines Addressed to S. T. Coleridge' (1798), similarly recalled with nostalgia their friendship and Pantisocratic walking-tour:

---

[6] *The University Magazine* for February 1795, edited by Christopher Wordsworth's circle and printed by Flower, after reprinting the 'Monody on the Death of Chatterton', announced: 'Mr Coleridge of Jesus College will shortly publish some sonnets.' These also did not appear.

> those fair days
> That saw us musing on the willowy banks
> Of Granta's lazy stream; or journeying on,
> Elate with youthful hope, o'er Cambrian wilds;
> Toiling with heavy feet up the steep hill
> Precipitous, o'er many a huge rough rock,
> Or through the lengthening vale or deep-worn glen,
> Dark with impending woods; aye big with schemes
> Air-built, of never-fading happiness:
> Wild dreams of folly in the vacant hour,
> That I once fondly cherished . . .

Coleridge did not revisit Cambridge for forty years; then, at the end of his life, he attended a meeting of the British Association there in June 1833. 'My emotions at revisiting the university were at first overwhelming. I could not speak for an hour; yet my feelings were upon the whole very pleasurable, and I have not passed, of late years at least, three days of such great enjoyment and healthful excitement of mind and body.' His humour had not deserted him: 'The bed on which I slept – and slept soundly too – was, as near as I can describe it, a couple of sacks full of potatoes tied together. I understand the young men think it hardens them. Truly I lay down at night a man, and arose in the morning a bruise.' As ever, there was inspiring talk from him, some of which, delivered in Connop Thirlwall's rooms at Trinity, is purportedly transcribed in Robert Aris Willmott's curious little volume *Conversations at Cambridge* (1836): 'Who that was present will ever forget that evening under the clock at Trinity, which witnessed a symposium from which Plato himself might have carried something away?' Coleridge once again regretted his youthful neglect of his studies, and admitted that he now felt an awe to be walking where the 'feet of Piety and Genius' – especially Newton's feet – had once trodden. 'While passing under the gateway, the form of Newton seemed to rise before me, and I turned round to look at that window where he so often stood, decomposing the rays of morning. There was something inexpressibly delightful in the fancy.'

12

'The happiest, perhaps,
days of my life'

There was to be no 'nook obscure', nor any self-recrimination over examinations or truancy, for George Gordon, sixth Baron Byron (1788–1824), when he came up to Trinity College in October 1805. His first letter from college to his family lawyer and business factotum, John Hanson, set the tone:

> I will be obliged to you to order me down 4 Dozen of Wine, Port – Sherry – Claret, & Madeira, one Dozen of Each; I have got part of my Furniture in, & begin to *admire* a College Life. Yesterday my appearance in the Hall in my State Robes was *Superb*, but uncomfortable to my *Diffidence*.

Club-footed, fat, spoilt, of notorious lineage[1] – Byron felt 'wretched at going to Cambridge instead of Oxford' where his Harrow friends had gone, but where Christ Church, the only college acceptable to him, had not found him acceptable to it. At least he had escaped his impossible mother; and the possession of 'one of the best allowances in college' (which she made possible by impoverishing herself) soon overcame any initial sulks. Within two weeks he was informing his half-sister Augusta:

> As might be supposed I like a College Life extremely, especially as I have escaped the Trammels or rather *Fetters* of my domestic Tyrant Mrs Byron . . . I am now most pleasantly situated in *Super*excellent Rooms, flanked on one side by my Tutor, on the other by an old Fellow, both of whom are rather checks upon my *vivacity*. I am allowed 500 a year, a Servant and Horse, so Feel as independent as a German Prince who coins his own Cash, or a Cherokee Chief who coins no Cash at all, but enjoys what is more precious, Liberty.

---

[1] Many previous Byrons had been at Cambridge, including the first Lord Byron (1599–1652), also at Trinity. An even earlier ancestor, Anthony Byron, son of 'little Sir John Byron with the Great Beard' and heir to Newstead, caused a scandal at Cambridge in 1576 as a fellow-commoner of Queens', by secretly marrying one local young lady while being engaged to another (Cooper, *Annals of Cambridge*, ii. 347–9). He did not inherit, dying young of a fit of laughter at a serving-man's discomfiture.

The exact location of the '*Super*excellent rooms' remains uncertain. The tradition started by J. M. F. Wright in *Alma Mater: or Seven Years at the University of Cambridge. By a Trinity Man* (1827), that Byron resided on κ staircase – 'Mutton-Hole Corner' – of Great Court, can be dismissed. It is more probable that he lived in the more sumptuous Nevile's Court, where 11, on the first floor in the middle of the north side, is thought the most likely set.[2] The expense of furnishing being additional to his allowance, he probably set the upholsterers running in a way to make Coleridge's unfortunate little extravagance at Jesus look trivial; the rooms were papered and painted at Christmas, and a baronial-sized four-poster bed, now preserved at Newstead Abbey, squeezed in.

To Hanson's son, Byron wrote on 12 November:

> College improves in everything but Learning, nobody here seems to look into an author ancient or modern if they can avoid it. The Muses, poor Devils, are totally neglected, except by a few Musty old *Sophs* and *Fellows*, who however agreeable they may be to *Minerva*, are perfect Antidotes to the *Graces*.

To Hanson himself he wrote:

> This place is the *Devil*, or at least his principal residence, they call it the University, but any other appellation would have suited it much better, for Study is the last pursuit of the Society; the Master eats, drinks, and Sleeps, the Fellows *drink*, *dispute* and *pun*, the *employments* of the under Graduates you will probably conjecture without my description. I sit down to write with a head confused with dissipation, which though I hate, I cannot avoid. I have only supped at home 3 times since my arrival, and my table is constantly covered with invitations . . .

He hastily added: 'after all I am the most *steady* man in the college, nor have I got into *many* scrapes, and none of consequence'.

The college contained two supposed wits: the Master, William Lord Mansel (1753–1820), a cracker of donnish epigrams, whose portentous gait Byron one day could not resist mimicking as he followed him out of hall into the Combination Room; and the great classical scholar Richard Porson (1759–1808), whom Byron recalled in later years for his publisher, John Murray, in detestful terms:

> I remember to have seen Porson at Cambridge in the Hall of our College – and in private parties – but not frequently – and I never can recollect him except as drunk or brutal and generally both – I mean in an Evening for in the hall he dined at the Dean's table – & I at the Vice-Master's so that I was not near him . . . but I have seen him in a private party of under-Graduates – many of them freshmen & strangers – take up a poker to one of them – & heard him use language as blackguard as his action[3] . . . of all the disgusting brutes – sulky – abusive – and intolerable – Porson was the most bestial as far as the few times that I saw him went.

---

[2] Robert Robson, 'Lord Byron's Rooms Revisited', *Trinity Review*, Easter 1975. Records of the occupants of rooms at Trinity do not begin until 1824.

[3] According to Hobhouse, it was Byron that Porson threatened.

As a nobleman, Byron dined at the dons' table, and hobbled about the windy courts in a richly embroidered gown with gold-tasselled mortar-board. (On informal occasions the latter was exchanged for a tall black hat; Byron, to be different, wore a white one.) There was no obligation for him to attend lectures, and easy credit could be obtained from local tradesmen. He had with him his grey, Oateater, and his servant, Frank. Each night he had supper with a different gathering, and later he recalled that 'I took my gradations in the vices with great promptitude'. Yet all this meant little to him so long as he could find no object for his sentiments to fix on, and female society fit for a nobleman was scarcely to be found at Cambridge. The Master, it is true, had three marriageable daughters, but otherwise practically the only women to be met with were bedmakers or the denizens of Barnwell and Castle End.

But Byron's proclivities were liberal, and soon a face swam out to engage him. The dull farce of chapel attendance was redeemed by a choirboy's singing. He made the boy's acquaintance – according to a typical legend, by saving him from drowning in the Cam – and focussed his emotions on him. 'His *voice* first attracted my notice, his *countenance* fixed it, & his *manners* attached me to him forever.' John Edleston was two years younger than his noble patron, 'nearly my height, very thin, very fair complexion, dark eyes, & light locks'. Byron later described his crush for the boy as 'a violent, though *pure* love and passion', romantic but not sexual – though the strength of the feelings it aroused forced him, he said, into heterosexual dissipations as a form of repellent sublimation. 'I certainly *love* him more than any human being,' he wrote in July 1807. 'We shall . . . give *Jonathan & David* the "go by" . . . During the whole of my residence at *Cambridge*, we met every day summer & Winter, without passing *one tiresome moment*, & separated *each time* with increasing Reluctance.' (They were actually in residence together for two terms.) In 1811, after Edleston's death, he confessed: 'I believe the only human being, that ever loved me in truth and entirely, was of, or belonging to, Cambridge', and his stanzas 'To Thyrza' were an elegy for this tender and clandestine love:

> Ours too the glance none saw beside;
>   The smile none else might understand;
> The whispered thought of hearts allied,
>   The pressure of the thrilling hand.
>
> The kiss, so guiltless and refined,
>   That Love each warmer wish forebore;
> Those eyes proclaimed so pure a mind,
>   Even Passion blushed to plead for more.

When Edleston gave Byron a cornelian heart, as earnest of reciprocated affection, Byron was sufficiently touched to write some lines on the subject. For his part, gifts and money lavished on Edleston doubtless accounted for some of his first term's reckless expenditure. His bills amounted to £231, and his mother, recognising the profligacy that had enabled his father, Mad Jack Byron, to run through two heiresses' fortunes in his short life, was by January in a state of frantic alarm: 'The bills are coming in thick upon me to double the amount I expected; he went and ordered just what he pleased.' Byron, however, was in no mood for retrenchment. Instead, as soon as he was back in London, he hastened into ruinous arrangements with money-lenders that saddled him with deep and long-standing debts. With his college bills thus settled and 'a few hundreds in ready Cash lying by me', the temptation was to remain in London; and when his second term approached he turned aside all suggestions of a return to Cambridge with excuses and scorn – 'improvement at an English University to a Man of Rank is you know impossible, and the very Idea *ridiculous*,' he told his mother; '. . . having been some Time at Cambridge, the Credit of the University is as much attached to my Name, as if I had pursued my Studies *there* for a Century'. To Hanson he lied that he was 'extremely unwell'. In fact he was busy furthering his 'gradations in the vices' and learning fencing and boxing from Henry Angelo and John 'Gentleman' Jackson.

It was the summer term before Hanson, by threatening to stop his allowance, got Byron back to Cambridge. He returned to Trinity with increased contempt. The only consolation was that his borrowed hundreds made an even bigger splash at Cambridge than in London. He bespoke himself a carriage-and-four with liveried attendants; ordered further improvements to his rooms; threw supper parties and pressed presents on his friends (an extant bill for thirteen pounds from Wilson's, the Cambridge jewellers, is for gold and silver gifts); and donated an ostentatiously large sum to the Pitt memorial fund (he didn't even like Pitt). He invited his London cronies to visit him and flared with anger at the 'insolent and unmerited Conduct of Mr Mortlock' when the Mayor made difficulties about Angelo giving fencing lessons in the town. When his tutor, Thomas Jones, had to chide him for spending so much time among boxers and fencers and others below his rank, Byron drew himself to his height: 'Really, sir, I cannot understand you. With the single exception of yourself, I can assure you that Mr Jackson's manners are infinitely superior to those of the fellows of the college whom I meet at the high table.'

That summer term turned out to be a golden-memoried one for Byron. Edleston was in daily attendance, and there were two new intimates: William Bankes, later an Arabian explorer, in whose rooms he first read Walter Scott's poetry, and Edward Noel Long, a fellow Harrovian whom Byron discovered to be a man after his own heart. Long and he rode together, swam together, lounged together, read Tom Moore's latest poems together. In the evening Long played the flute or cello while Byron listened appreciatively over bottles of soda-water. Long and Edleston 'were the then romance of the most romantic period of my life', Byron recalled in Ravenna in 1821, when a chance reading of some lines of Milton's *Comus* –

> Sabrina fair,
> Listen where thou art sitting
> Under the glassy, cool, translucent wave

– suddenly brought back to him

> I know not how or why – the happiest, perhaps, days of my life . . . when living
> at Cambridge with Edward Noel Long, afterwards of the Guards . . . We were
> rival swimmers – fond of riding – reading – and of conviviality . . . At Cambridge
> – both of Trinity . . . we became very great friends. The description of Sabrina's
> seat reminds me of our rival feats in *diving*. Though Cam's is not a very
> 'translucent wave', it was fourteen feet deep, where we used to dive for, and pick
> up – having thrown them in on purpose – plates, eggs, and even shillings. I
> remember, in particular, there was the stump of a tree (at least ten or twelve feet
> deep) in the bed of the river, in a spot where we bathed most commonly, round
> which I used to cling, and 'wonder how the devil I came there'.

The spot where Byron and Long are supposed to have dived for plates and
shillings had formerly been the mill pool for the Trumpington Mill of Chaucer's
tale; it is now known as Byron's Pool.[4]

After this college idyll, Byron absented himself for an entire year, first at the
seaside with Long, then at Southwell, near his ancestral pile of Newstead Abbey,
where his mother had rented a house. He made strenuous efforts to reduce weight
– playing cricket in seven waistcoats and a greatcoat – and began to put together
his first poems. *Fugitive Pieces* (including one or two rather too racy for
Southwell sensibilities) was privately printed in November 1806, then withdrawn
and reissued in a revised version the following January as *Poems on Various
Occasions*. Finally, the collection was published as *Hours of Idleness* in June.
Among this mixed bag of juvenilia are two satires of Cambridge. In 'Granta: A
Medley', Byron imagines the power to see into the unroofed college rooms at
night. The Fellows are dreaming of bribes and benefices, the fast set are absorbed
in drunkenness and dice, while

> There, in apartments small and damp,
>   The candidate for college prizes
> Sits poring by the midnight lamp;
>   Goes late to bed, yet early rises.

In 'Thoughts Suggested by a College Examination', Byron satirises in *Dunciad*
style the much-dreaded termly viva-voce examinations held in the college hall
with Dr Mansel ('Magnus') presiding in person:

---

4 It was known as Byron's Pool by at least 1851, though the earlier name Old Mills continued
into the 1870s. But an unromantic former vicar of Grantchester used to maintain that the name
was a misnomer and the spot should rightly be 'Brian's Pool'. Indeed, Moss Brian is the hero
of Jack Overhill's novel *The Miller of Trumpington* (1953), set in the eighteenth century.
The footpath to Grantchester, however, was certainly known as 'Lord Byron's Walk' by 1825.

High in the midst, surrounded by his peers,
Magnus his ample front sublime uprears:
Placed on his chair of state, he seems a god,
While Sophs and Freshmen tremble at his nod.
As all around sit wrapt in speechless gloom,
His voice in thunder shakes the sounding dome;
Denouncing dire reproach to luckless fools,
Unskilled to plod in mathematic rules.

Castigating an academic system that sends away its students primed with Euclid and the laws of Sparta but ignorant of Magna Carta, Shakespeare, or Agincourt, Byron holds up for particular ridicule the lifeless approved delivery of candidates for declamation prizes. (Byron fancied himself as an orator and a decade or so later would doubtless have been prominent at the Union.) He had no illusions about academics:

The sons of science these, who, thus repaid,
Linger in ease in Granta's sluggish shade;
Where on Cam's sedgy banks supine they lie,
Unknown, unhonoured live, unwept-for die;
Dull as the pictures which adorn their halls,
They think all learning fixed within their walls:
In manner rude, in foolish forms precise,
All modern arts affecting to despise;
Yet prizing Bentley's, Brunck's, or Porson's note,
More than the verse on which the critic wrote.

In February 1807 Byron's tutor – apparently no condoner of the idle ways of noblemen: he had once proposed the innovation that they should be subjected to the same examinations for degrees as everyone else – wrote requesting an explanation of Byron's continuing absence. The reply he got was a model of adolescent noble hauteur. Cambridge had nothing to teach him, Byron said. Mathematics (Jones's particular subject) might have been of some service, had he been contemplating a military career ('as far as related to Tactics'), but he was not. Nor had he any desire to bewilder himself 'in the mazes of Metaphysics'. Moreover,

I have other Reasons for not residing at Cambridge, I dislike it; I was originally intended for Oxford, my Guardians determined otherwise. I quitted the Society of my earliest associates, who are all '*Alumni*' of the latter, to drag on a weary term, at a place where I had many acquaintances, but few friends. I therefore can never consider *Granta* as my '*Alma Mater*' but rather as a *Nurse* of no very promising appearance, on whom I have been forced, against *her* Inclination, & contrary to mine.

In March he informed Bankes he would be down in the spring to dismantle his rooms and take his farewell. 'The Cam will not be much increased by my tears on the occasion.' In fact it was the end of the summer term before he made his appearance, to settle his debts and 'get rid of Cambridge forever'.

It was a dramatic re-entry. He brought an ink-fresh packet of *Hours of Idleness* to distribute, while his slimming had been so successful (he had shed three stone) that no one recognised him – or so he told a Southwell admirer, Elizabeth Pigot.

> I was obliged to tell every body my *name* . . . Even the *Hero* of my *Cornelian* (Who is now sitting *vis a vis*, reading a volume of my *poetics*) passed me in Trinity walks without recognizing me in the least, & was thunderstruck at the alteration, which had taken place in my Countenance . . . On monday I depart for London, & quit Cambridge forever, with little regret, because our *Set* are *vanished*, & my *musical protegé* above mentioned, has left the Choir, & is to be stationed in a mercantile house of considerable eminence in the Metropolis.

Byron sent Edleston off on 5 July with a farewell dinner for fourteen persons at the Hoop, where twenty-three bottles of wine were consumed and the bill totalled fifteen guineas. With Bankes and Long also departed, and the dons hardly delighted by their portrayal in his poems, Cambridge might seem to have few attractions left; yet so mercurial were Byron's moods that that very night he was scribbling to Miss Pigot:

> Since my last letter I have determined to reside *another year* at *Granta* as my Rooms &c. &c. are furnished in *great Style*, several old friends *come up* again, & many *new* acquaintances made . . . My life here has been one continued *routine* of Dissipation . . . at this moment I write with a *bottle* of *Claret* in my *Head*, & *tears* in my *eyes*, for I have just parted from 'my *Corneilan* [Cornelian]' . . .

Perhaps what induced him to change his mind – apart from the admiration for his stout volume of verse and slim new physique – were two important new friendships. When he went to reclaim his rooms he found that Jones had given them in his absence to another student, Charles Skinner Matthews, with the advice: 'Mr Matthews, I recommend to your attention not to damage any of the moveables, for Lord Byron, Sir, is a young man of *tumultuous passions*.'

> Matthews was delighted with this; and whenever anybody came to visit him, begged them to handle the very door with caution; and used to repeat Jones's admonition in his tone and manner . . . Jones's phrase of '*tumultuous passions*', and the whole scene, had put him into such good humour, that I verily believe that I owed to it a portion of his good graces.

Matthews was a scholar and a wit (and a homosexual), whose hobbies included kicking up a row with his friends outside the Master's Lodge at night, 'and when he appeared at the window foaming with wrath and crying out "I know you, gentlemen, I know you!"' retorting with such punning badinage as 'We beseech thee to hear us, good *Lort*' or 'Good *Lort* deliver us!' John Cam Hobhouse

(1786–1869), Matthews's friend, was more sober. He had taken against Byron in their first year because of Byron's affectations of dress (that white hat), but if he could be prejudiced he could equally, once his affections were won, prove unshakeably loyal. 'Hobby' was to be the steadiest, most faithful friend Byron ever had.

It was the realisation that Byron was a poet that won Hobhouse to his favour. The dons were less impressed. George Pryme, who was in college that month and sat opposite Byron at the Fellows' table, later recalled: 'We entered into conversation about Nottinghamshire, and on other subjects. He was unaffected and agreeable, but we Fellows did not think him possessed of any great talent, insomuch so that when the *English Bards and Scotch Reviewers* appeared without his name, Monk and Rose and I would not believe that *he* was the author.'

Byron kept to his new intention of residing for a degree to the extent of returning punctually in October. It was to be his third and last term of residence. The publication of *Hours of Idleness* had so enheartened him that he was now in the throes of committed authorship. While preparing a second edition, he was also composing a lengthy new *Dunciad*-style satire on the entire literary establishment (originally only *English Bards*, but after the *Edinburgh Review* had pitched into *Hours of Idleness*, extended to include *Scotch Reviewers*). But that was only part of his literary activity, as he informed Miss Pigot on 26 October: 'I have written 214 pages of a novel, one poem of 380 lines, to be published (without my name) in a few weeks, with notes, 560 lines of Bosworth Field, and 250 lines of another poem in rhyme, besides half a dozen smaller pieces.' This did not inhibit him from 'sitting up till four in the morning for these last two days at Hazard ... This place is wretched enough, a villainous chaos of dice and drunkenness, nothing but Hazard and burgundy, hunting, mathematics and Newmarket, riot and racing ... '

Byron did not endear himself to his new tutor, George Tavell (Jones had died) by arriving that term in company with a bear.

> I have got a new friend, the finest in the world, a *tame Bear*, when I brought him here, they asked me what I meant to do with him, and my reply was 'he should *sit* for *a Fellowship*.' – *Sherard* will explain the meaning of the sentence if it is ambiguous. – This answer delighted them not, – We have eternal parties here, and this evening a large assortment of *Jockies*, Gamblers, *Boxers, Authors, parsons*, and *poets*, sup with me. – A precious Mixture, but they go on well together, and for me, I am a *spice* of everything except a Jockey ...

Byron had possibly acquired the bear in London or from one of the travelling menageries (one of the largest, Polito's – 'birds and beasts bought, sold or exchanged' – had exhibited in Cambridge earlier in 1807). He delighted in exotic animals, and this was only one of the first in a growing menagerie of his own that was to include peacocks, mastiffs, monkeys, cats, and geese. He may have attempted to bring it into college more to flout the academic proprieties than with the intention of keeping it there. He had already respected the college regulations by not bringing his favourite Newfoundland dog Boatswain to Cambridge. Whether or not the bear was lodged temporarily in the college, it was soon boarded out at some stables in Ram Yard (near the Round Church), possibly where he kept Oateater and his other horses: a Cambridge tradesman's bill is extant, addressed to 'The Honble Lord Byron', for £1 9s 7d for 'Bread & Milk for the Bear delivd. to Holaday'. Later the bear was forwarded to Newstead Abbey, where it died in May 1810.[5]

But the story of the bear was bait to scurrilous imaginations. Hewson Clarke (1787–1832), a sizar at Emmanuel, who savagely reviewed *Hours of Idleness* that October in the first issue of *The Satirist or Monthly Meteor*, went on to contribute a series of sketches of Cambridge life, in the third of which (June 1808), a lampoon on the aristocratic fast set, he included some verses entitled 'Lord B—n to his Bear':

> Sad Bruin, no longer in woods thou art dancing,
>   With all the enjoyments that Love can afford;
> No longer thy consorts around thee are prancing,
>   Far other thy fate – thou art slave to a Lord!
>
> How oft when fatigued, on my sofa reposing,
>   Thy tricks and thy pranks rob of anguish my breast;
> Have power to arouse me, to keep me from dozing,
>   Or, what's the same thing, they can lull me to rest.
>
> But when with the ardours of Love I am burning,
>   I feel for thy torments, I feel for thy care;
> And weep for thy bondage, so truly discerning,
>   What's felt by a *Lord*, may be felt by a *Bear*!

He appended the information: 'This bear, which is kept in one of his rooms at Trinity, is a great favourite of his Lordship's; and, if report say true, he has been seen to hug it with all the warmth of *fraternal* affection!' Byron was so infuriated that in July he called at Emmanuel in company with Hobhouse and others to challenge the 'skulking scribbler' to a duel. But Clarke was not at home.

Clarke's canard was further elaborated after Byron's death under the fertile pen of J. M. F. Wright in his *Alma Mater*. After recounting how, when he came up to Trinity in 1814 as a penurious sizar, he was allotted gratis a tiny hexagonal cell at the top of 'Mutton-Hole Corner', Wright embroiders on:

---

5 Bears in colleges were not unknown. An entry in the college accounts at Queens' for 1611 reads: 'For taking out the bear and watching it, and scouring the cellar, 2s 6d.' Frank Buckland kept one at Christ Church, Oxford, in the 1840s, and took it to wine parties and boating on the river dressed in cap and gown.

When Lord Byron was at Trinity, he kept in rooms on this staircase, round which you might drive a coach and six, and had, moreover, the use of the small hexagonal one in the tower. His lordship used to parade the streets accompanied by an immense bear, following him like a dog, which bear had the sole use of the apartment in the turret. Poor Bruin peeping out one day from this retreat, bestowed so ardent an embrace upon a 'small college-man', that his lordship was constrained, at the suggestion of the tutor, to 'cut' him. So attached, however, were this singular pair, that the whole power of the tutor was scarcely able to divide them.[6]

The motivation behind both Clarke's and Wright's satire seems to have been resentment at the privileged life of undergraduate noblemen. But apocrypha about the bear continued to be widely enjoyed. Two examples may be given. *The Cambridge Tart* in 1823 printed some lines:

> When Byron was at Trinity,
> Studying classics and divinity,
> He kept a rugged Russian bear,
> Which bear
> Would often scratch and tear
> And dance and roar . . .
> The Master, then a bishop, was so baited,
> He ordered that the beast should quick be sold,
> Or if not sold at least *translated*.
> 'What,' said Lord Byron, '*What* does the Master say?
> Send my friend away?
> No – give my compliments to Doctor Mansel,
> And say, my bear I certainly *can* sell.
> But 'twill be very hard – for tell him, Gyp,
> The poor thing's sitting for a *fellowship!*'

In 1843 *The Illustrated London News* claimed:

> One fine summer's evening, as his lordship and some of his gay companions were sipping their wine and smoking their cigars, with the window of the chief apartment open and the grotesque animal sitting on the window sill with nothing more or less than a cap and gown on him, the dean of the college passed by. Observing the strange and, to him, provoking picture, he immediately sent for Lord Byron and asked him in an angry tone what he meant by such an insult to the college. 'What business, my lord,' said the reverend functionary, 'has a bear in Trinity College?' 'He is reading for a fellowship!' was the instant reply. 'I'd have you know, my lord, that such an insult . . . ' 'Mr Dean, I beg your pardon, not for a Trinity fellowship, but for a Johnian one!' 'Oh, indeed, that alters the case, but pray send him to St John's!' There was at this time a fierce feud between the two colleges.

---

[6] Byron almost certainly did not live on that staircase; no student, however poor, is likely to have been allotted the closet (now a lavatory) at its top; the turret is not hexagonal; and the staircase, far from being wide enough to admit a coach-and-six, is extremely narrow.

More predisposing than the bear was another new friend made in his last term, Scrope Berdmore Davies (1783–1852), a stammering Old Etonian Fellow of King's, whom Byron met through Hobhouse. Davies was an addict of the London gambling tables, where he staked, and sometimes won, ever huger sums. (Byron remembered him fast asleep after one such session with a chamber pot crammed with bank notes beside him.) To Byron, already harassed by usurers, Davies's devil-may-care attitude must have been inspiriting. It was Davies who put up the money for Byron's overseas tour in 1809. Davies was also a keen duellist and a friend of Beau Brummell; like Brummell, after finally ruining himself, he fled abroad, his fellowship being his only income in his last years. When he left London, he deposited in a bank vault a chest of papers, including Byron and Shelley manuscripts, which, when it was opened in 1976, was hailed as the 'literary find of the century'.

Byron forsook Cambridge for good at Christmas 1807. Noblemen normally proceeded straight to the MA degree after two years' residence, but, considering he had kept only three complete terms, the university not unnaturally allowed Byron his degree with some reluctance. He removed the last of his possessions from Trinity in March, and returned for the degree ceremony in July. In contrast to the brain-bending rigours endured by honours candidates, noblemen satisfied the statutes by a two-minute 'huddled' disputation. Tavell took, gladly no doubt, the large fees due from a lord, and Byron doffed his 'tuft' for the last time to his 'unjust nurse'. In *English Bards* he was to call Cambridge 'the dark asylum of a Vandal race'[7] and express an unfilial preference for Oxford. In *Hints from Horace* (1811) he again satirised Cambridge (Fordham was a Cambridge butcher who, in the tradition of Hobson, made a fortune by letting horses to undergraduates):

> Behold him Freshman! forced no more to groan
> O'er Virgil's devilish verses and his own;
> Prayers are too tedious, lectures too abstruse,
> He flies from Tavell's frown to 'Fordham's Mews';
> (Unlucky Tavell! doomed to daily cares
> By pugilistic pupils, and by bears).
> Fines, tutors, tasks, conventions threat in vain,
> Before hounds, hunters, and Newmarket plain.
> Rough with his elders, with his equals rash,
> Civil to sharpers, prodigal of cash;
> Constant to nought, save hazard and a whore,
> Yet cursing both – for both have made him sore;
> Unread (unless, since books beguile disease,

---

7 ' "Into Cambridgeshire the Emperor Probus transported a considerable body of Vandals" – Gibbon's *Decline and Fall*. vol. ii, p. 85. There is no reason to doubt the truth of this assertion; the breed is still in high perfection' (Byron's own note).

The pox becomes his passage to degrees):
Fooled, pillaged, dunned, he wastes his term away,
And unexpelled, perhaps, retires MA.

Byron returned a few times to look up friends. In October 1811, newly back from abroad, he stayed with Scrope Davies at King's, but the occasion was tinged with melancholy, for Matthews (since 1808 a Fellow of Downing) had recently drowned at Paradise Pool in the Cam, entangled in weeds (there is a plaque to him in St Bene't's Church). Long, too, had been drowned, sailing with his regiment to the Peninsular War. Edleston had died of tuberculosis. The river where Matthews and Long and he had swum, the chapel where Edleston had sung, the courts where now-departed friends had strolled – all increased Byron's grief. Scrope got extremely drunk; Byron no doubt did the same.

In November 1814 the now celebrated author of *Childe Harold* came to Cambridge to support his friend William Clark (father of J. W. Clark the Cambridge antiquary) in the election for the professorship of anatomy. He was taken aback by his reception when, as he entered the Senate House to vote, the students in the gallery hurrahed, and distinguished personages, including Bishop Mansel, jostled to escort him. It was a moving moment if, once more, uncomfortable to his diffidence, and Hobhouse afterwards 'found him in the precincts of the Schools sobbing like a child, so completely had the poet been overcome by the rapturous reception he had met with'. For many of his visits Byron came over from Six Mile Bottom, halfway between Cambridge and Newmarket, where his half-sister Augusta (with whom he is reputed to have had an incestuous relationship) lived with her racegoing husband Colonel Leigh at the Lodge (now Swynford Paddocks). It was there that Augusta and Lady Byron first met, not long after the election visit and Byron's ill-fated launch into wedlock, and there Byron wrote parts of *The Corsair*.

After Byron's death in Greece, a full-length statue, originally intended for Westminster Abbey, was executed by the Danish sculptor Bertel Thorwaldsen; but the Abbey scrupled to accept it and it languished for nine years in the Custom House before finally finding a home in 1843 in Trinity College Library. Byron's last mistress, Countess Teresa Guiccioli, may have seen it when, a full thirty years after Byron's death, she made a sentimental pilgrimage to England to visit the places where he had lived. The rooms she was shown on D staircase of Nevile's Court, however, were almost certainly not his.

13

Ciceros and Snobs

While Byron was installing himself in state at Trinity, a poet who came into residence in the same term next door at St John's was climbing to a bare garret (F8 of Third Court) furnished with only a hair mattress. While Byron disputed with Hanson over his allowance, Henry Kirke White (1785–1806), tall, spare, brilliant, with 'the look of a man of genius', was informing his charitable sponsors that he would need less than they had subscribed. While Byron ran through £250 a term, White wrote cheerfully home that 'my college expenses will not be more than £12 or £15 a year, at the most . . . Our dinners and suppers cost us nothing; and, if a man choose to eat milk breakfasts, and go without tea, he may live absolutely for nothing.'

The son of a Nottingham butcher, at the age of eighteen White had published a volume of poems, *Clifton Grove*, which had sufficiently impressed such admirers as Wilberforce, Southey, and Charles Simeon the Cambridge evangelical, to decide them to club together to send him to Cambridge. Already, while drudging as a solicitor's clerk, he had managed to teach himself Latin and Greek and other subjects; now, installed as a humble but extraordinarily industrious sizar at St John's, he was determined to exploit his opportunity to the full by securing the highest academic honours and becoming a bishop or a second Bentley. That he had no grounding in mathematics he regarded only as an additional challenge.

Milk breakfasts, damp attics, and fifteen hours a day of Euripides and Euclid, however, were not a prescription for health. By the end of his first term, with the college examination and that for a university scholarship looming, he was already on the verge of nervous collapse. 'I wandered up and down, from one man's room to another, and from one college to another, imploring society, a little conversation, and a little relief of the burden which pressed upon my spirits . . . I went to our tutor, with tears in my eyes, and told him I must absent myself from the examination.' But the tutor, with an eye to Wranglers and college honours, chided him on and arranged for White to be given 'strong stimulants and supporting medicines'.

By the following June White had secured prizes in mathematics, logic, and

Latin, come top in his year's college examination, and gained a college exhibition; but though desperately in need of rest and a change of scenery, he was forbidden by his tutor even to leave Cambridge for the vacation, and had extra mathematics tuition laid on at college expense. Unwilling to show ingratitude, White laboured fatally on, having practically abandoned poetry now to the cause of the tripos. Then, one morning in July, having risen early to get up 'some rather abstruse problems in mechanics for my tutor' and studied Greek history over his breakfast, he was found by his laundress gibbering and bleeding on the floor, a book of logarithms by his head.

He tried to pass the fit off as nothing; his humour, his humility, his assiduity rose to almost saintly heights. After a brief respite in London, he was back in college in October to begin his second year. But a rapid consumption swept his enfeebled and undernourished frame and he died in college on 19 October 1806. He was buried in All Saints' Church across the street.

When Southey published White's *Remains* in 1807, it was an immediate success. White's piety, dedication, and tragic end, as expressed in his letters, more than made up for his scant poetic achievement (he is chiefly remembered for the hymn 'Oft in danger, oft in woe'). Even Byron was moved to lament his humble contemporary:

> Unhappy White! while life was in its spring,
> And thy young muse just waved her joyous wing,
> The spoiler swept that soaring lyre away,
> Which else had sounded an immortal lay.

In 1819 a monument was put up in the church, with medallion by Chantrey and verses by William Smyth, Professor of Modern History:

> Warm with fond hopes, and learning's sacred flame
> To Granta's bowers the youthful poet came;
> Unconquered powers th' immortal mind displayed,
> But worn with anxious thought the frame decayed:
> Pale o'er his lamp, and in his cell retired,
> The martyr student faded and expired.

When the church was demolished, the monument was transferred to the college antechapel. White's name is preserved on the memorial to 'Literary Men, Benefactors, and other Parishioners' in the middle of All Saints' Green.[1]

The essayist Charles Lamb (1775–1834), who had been unable to afford a university education, nevertheless nursed sentimental feelings about universities and liked nothing better than to spend his holidays from his East India House office at either Oxford or Cambridge. A contemporary of Coleridge's at Christ's

---

[1] A contemporary sizar at St John's whom White must have known was an Irishman who arrived in 1802 as Patrick Brunty but who, casting off his peasant background with his name, emerged four years later at Patrick Brontë BA. He was the father of the Brontë sisters.

Hospital, he had first visited Cambridge while Coleridge was there. In January 1801 he returned to visit a new friend, an eccentric mathematical recluse named Thomas Manning, who lived over Mr Crisp's barber's shop at 3 St Mary's Passage and who shared Lamb's gustatory enthusiasms. Lamb sent him an advance schedule for the visit:

> Embark at six o'clock in the morning, with a fresh gale, on a Cambridge one-decker; very cold till eight at night; land at St Mary's light-house, muffins and coffee upon table (or any other curious production of Turkey or both Indies). Snipes exactly at nine, punch to commence at ten, with *argument*; difference of opinion is expected to take place about eleven; perfect unanimity, with some haziness and dimness, before twelve. – NB My single affection is not so singly wedded to snipes, but the curious and epicurean eye would also take pleasure in beholding a delicate and well-chosen assortment of teals, ortolans, the unctuous and palate-soothing flesh of geese wild and tame, nightingales' brains, the sensorium of a young sucking pig, or any other Xmas dish, which I leave to the judgment of you and the cook of Gonville.

The cook of Gonville and Caius College and Trinity Hall was Richard Hopkins, who regularly advertised his celebrated brawn in the *Cambridge Chronicle*. In February 1805, Manning sent Lamb a sample of the brawn. Lamb, pretending to believe it was the gift of 'the swearing scullion of Caius' himself, wrote back:

> Richard knew my blind side when he pitched upon brawn. 'Tis of all my hobbies the supreme in the eating way . . . It is not every common gullet-fancier that can properly esteem it . . . Do me the favour to leave off the business which you may be at present upon, and go immediately to the kitchens of Trinity and Caius, and make my most respectful compliments to Mr Richard Hopkins, and assure him that his brawn is most excellent . . . We have not many such men in any rank of life as Mr R. Hopkins.

Possibly from the Cambridge brawn, certainly from a Chinese folk-tale related to him by Manning, Lamb derived the inspiration for his most famous essay, 'A Dissertation Upon Roast Pig'.

Another close Cambridge friend of Lamb's was George Dyer of Emmanuel (1755–1841), who had also been at Christ's Hospital and whom Lamb immortalised in his essay 'Amicus Redivivus'. Absent-minded, short-sighted, incorrigibly bookish, Dyer fell into rivers and walked the streets with one shoe off; he wrote the life of his friend the Cambridge Baptist preacher Robert Robinson, and compiled a gossipy informal history of the university (1814), rather over-shadowed by Rudolph Ackermann's magnificent production of the following year. He is said to have blinded himself editing the 141 volumes of Valpy's edition of the classics. His portrait (with dog Daphne) is in the Fitzwilliam Museum.

In August 1815 Charles and his sister Mary Lamb 'were driven into Cambridge in great triumph by Hell Fire Dick' (i.e. Richard Vaughan, driver of the Telegraph stagecoach from London). Mary rapturously described their weekend to Wordsworth's sister-in-law, Sarah Hutchinson:

> In my life I never spent so many pleasant hours together as I did at Cambridge. We were walking the whole time – out of one college into another. If you ask me which I like best I must make the children's traditional unoffending reply to all curious enquirers – 'Both'. I liked them all best. The little gloomy ones, because they were little gloomy ones. I felt as if I could live and die in them and never wish to speak again. And the fine grand Trinity College, oh how fine it was! and King's College Chapel, what a place!

They were in Cambridge again in August 1819, lodging over Bays the hatter in Trumpington Street (now 11 King's Parade and still in the Bays family). Lamb celebrated this visit with a sonnet, 'Written at Cambridge', in which he imagines himself in doctor's cap and gown. The following year saw a visit of special importance. Probably again staying with Bays, the Lambs bumped into Henry Crabb Robinson, also on a visit (he mentions the meeting in his diary); and Lamb wrote his misleadingly entitled essay 'Oxford in the Vacation', dated 'August 5, 1820. From my rooms facing the Bodleian' but full of unmistakable Cambridge detail. In vein similar to the sonnet, he writes:

> I fetch up past opportunities. I can rise at the chapel-bell, and dream that it rings for *me*. In moods of humility I can be a sizar, or a servitor. When the peacock vein rises, I strut a gentleman commoner. In graver moments, I proceed Master of Arts. Indeed I do not think I am much unlike that respectable character. I have seen your dim-eyed vergers, and bedmakers in spectacles, drop a bow or curtsy, as I pass.

Relinquishing momentarily the pretence to be in Oxford, he tells in a footnote of a visit to Trinity College Library, where he was horrified by the sight of the manuscripts of Milton's 'Lycidas' and other famous poems, full of too-human crossings-out: 'I wish they had thrown them in the Cam . . . How it staggered me to see the fine things in their ore! interlined, corrected! as if their words were mortal, alterable, displaceable at pleasure! as if they might have been otherwise, and just as good!'[2] It was also during this visit that the Lambs met eleven-year-old Emma Isola, granddaughter of Agostino Isola who had taught Wordsworth Italian, daughter of Gunning's fellow Esquire Bedell. Her mother having died, she was living with an aunt nearby in Trumpington Street. Greatly struck by her, the Lambs invited her to London for Christmas, and when her father died in 1823, adopted her altogether. She was to be the radiant light of their darkening years.[3]

---

[2] The novelist Maria Edgeworth, visiting Cambridge in May 1813, viewed the matter more dispassionately. 'I hear, that these corrections are all printed; and, if so, I do not see much value in the MS, except just to satisfy curiosity by shewing the handwriting of Milton . . . Besides, by this time, I had become very hungry'. (*Letters from England* (Oxford, 1971), p. 35.)

[3] A Charles Lamb Society was founded at Cambridge in 1909 by A. T. Bartholomew, Charles Sayle, and George Wherry, and held annual dinners (1909–14) at the University Arms Hotel. The society was instrumental in having a plaque placed on 11 King's Parade.

Another Christ's Hospital boy unable to go to university (his stutter prevented him delivering a required public speech) was the essayist Leigh Hunt (1784–1859), who in January 1811 stayed at Cambridge with his former schoolfellow Professor Scholefield of Trinity. Hunt dined in hall with the Fellows, who he thought 'live luxuriously, walk, ride, read and have nothing to get in this world but a good appetite of a morning', and wandered through the Backs, where the Cam ran 'through shelving banks of grass, upon which, in the summer, you may literally lie down to the water's edge with your book and your pencil'. He sat in the dean's seat at chapel, 'with my head just peering above a gorgeous cushion and huge psalm-book . . . The chanting and anthems perfectly bear one away from earth.' In the library he saw a pair of Queen Elizabeth's shoes but the Milton manuscript 'was maliciously locked up'. Hunt must be one of the few people ever sent to Cambridge for their health. Though the place was bitterly cold he seems to have taken no harm.

Lamb on his way to peer at 'Lycidas' in 1820 may well have passed the stocky studious figure, pacing Great Court deep in a book, of someone who never needed to 'fetch up past opportunities'. The stupendous powers of assimilation and memory that Thomas Babington Macaulay (1800–59) displayed from the cradle had been only too assiduously promoted by his father, the anti-slavery campaigner Zachary Macaulay. At eight Macaulay had been sent from his home at Clapham to a select boarding school at Little Shelford, run by an evangelical Fellow of Trinity called Preston, a friend of such Cambridge evangelicals as Simeon and Isaac Milner, the President of Queens'. On one occasion young Macaulay was taken to meet Milner, who pronounced: 'Sir, that boy is fit to stand before kings, and he will some day.' When Macaulay, feeling homesick, wrote home unfavourably about the people of Shelford, Zachary replied urging the eight-year-old to set about reforming them: 'the cheap Repository and Religious Tract Society will furnish tracts suited to all descriptions of persons'.[4]

Zachary himself brought Macaulay into residence at Trinity College in October 1818, carefully inspecting the young man's Jesus Lane lodgings and exacting from the tutor a promise that his laundress would be of exemplary virtue. He need not have worried. Though within easy walk of the stews of Castle End and Barnwell, and in a college where dissipation on the Byronic scale continued, Macaulay did not often take his nose from his books. He started reading at four in the morning, and complained of chapel attendance, lectures, and social obligations as irksome interruptions of his routine. For recreation he merely changed his reading matter. His father, vigilant as ever, pounced on his reported novel-reading as a grievous lapse. It was the only trait he could find to condemn.

---

[4] In 1813, while waiting in a Cambridge coffee-house for a postchaise to school, Macaulay glanced at a couple of trashy poems in a local paper. Forty years later, never having given them a thought in the meantime, he was able to repeat them by heart – an example of the power of his memory.

Macaulay's undergraduate career – up to his degree – was the triumphal course one would expect. In 1819 he won the Chancellor's Gold Medal for an English Poem – an award, first given in 1813, which had quickly become established as one of the most popular the university had to offer. The set subject that year was 'Pompeii' – a gift to Macaulay's talent for dramatic recreation of classical scenes. (He won the medal again in 1821 with a feebler affair on 'Evening'.) In 1820 he gained distinction in the Craven examination and the following year carried off one of three newly founded additional Craven awards. He was made a scholar of Trinity in April 1820, and in October took the college's Latin Declamation Prize with a speech on Dryden.

Only the whiff of politics could lure Macaulay from his books. Venturing from his lodgings to see the action during some election disturbances when the windows of the nearby Hoop Hotel were broken, he was mistaken for the Tory candidate and received a dead cat in his face. He also saw something of the famous town-and-gown Battle of Peas Hill in November 1820, the subject of many a contemporary ballad. He moved into college rooms in Bishop's Hostel in February 1821.

But for all his breadth of aptitude, mathematics, the fetish of the Cambridge system, was one subject at which Macaulay balked. 'I can scarcely bear to write on mathematics or mathematicians. Oh for words to express my abomination of that science. It is starvation, confinement, torture, annihilation of the mind.' When at last in January 1822 the moment of truth arrived, and he sat for his degree in the Senate House, his perfectionist's pride wilted under the onslaught. He quickly realised he would not be Senior Wrangler; he would not be any sort of Wrangler; there seemed any number of avid arithmetical types who were going to come out above him. After two days he withdrew; rather than be awarded a poor honours degree, he decided to accept the humble pass degree of the 'non-reading' man.

His family were aghast, taking it as a personal disgrace, a visitation of God. This was what came of novel-reading, his father fumed. But his college was not unaware of his attributes, and the days of the single mathematical tripos were already numbered. (A classical tripos, the first of the many alternative modern triposes, was introduced in 1824.) Macaulay was allowed to stay on and given a prestigious set of rooms on E staircase of Great Court (Newton's old staircase), between the main gate and the chapel, outside which, as his nephew Sir George Otto Trevelyan relates in Macaulay's *Life and Letters*, he used to stroll up and down the path each morning, book in hand,

> reading with the same eagerness and the same rapidity, whether the volume was the most abstruse of treatises, the loftiest of poems, or the flimsiest of novels. That was the spot where in his failing years he specially loved to renew the feelings of the past; and some there are who can never revisit it without the fancy that there, if anywhere, his dear shade must linger.

While awaiting a fellowship, Macaulay supported himself by teaching, and began to channel some of his energies into the Union Society. Founded in 1815, suppressed by the authorities in 1817, restored in 1821 with the proviso (skilfully evaded) that no contemporary politics were to be debated, the Union at this date met in a 'cavernous, tavernous' back room of the Red Lion in Petty Cury. In no time Macaulay, along with his Trinity contemporary Winthrop Mackworth Praed (1802–39), was dominating the proceedings.

Bulwer-Lytton, who thought Macaulay spoke as powerfully in the Union as in the House of Commons later, recalled

> that club-room, famous then,
> Where striplings settled questions spoilt by men,
> When grand Macaulay sat triumphant down,
> Heard Praed's reply, and longed to halve the crown.

He remembered an occasion when he, Praed, and others of the Union set walked with Macaulay 'along the College Gardens, listening with wonder to that full and opulent converse, startled by knowledge so various, memory so prodigious. That walk left me in a fever of emulation. I shut myself up for many days in intense study, striving to grasp at an equal knowledge.'

John Moultrie, another Union member from Trinity, remembered in *The Dream of Life*

> those nights and suppers of the gods –
> Feasts of the hungry soul, when, at the close
> Of some well argued, eloquent debate
> Held in the 'Union', which with lengthened roar
> Of cheers had shaken Petty Cury's roofs,
> Startling the jaded shopman from his sleep, –
> The leaders of the war on either side,
> (Their strife suspended) to my neighbouring rooms
> Adjourned to sup on oysters.

Moultrie sketches the two principal 'gods': first Praed,

> With that rich vein of fine and subtle wit –
> That tone of reckless levity – that keen
> And polished sarcasm – armed with which he waged
> A war of dexterous sword-play.

A dazzling Etonian who once nearly fought a duel with the President of the Union over the date of the Battle of Bunker Hill, Praed was a deft master of sparkling light verse. His academic triumphs (four Browne's Medals, college prizes for declamation in Latin and English, Chancellor's English Medals in 1823 and 1824, Seatonian Prize in 1830) matched Macaulay's, but in after-life he never quite lived up to his early brilliance and died young. Moultrie then goes on to describe Macaulay himself:

of ampler brow and ruder frame, –
A presence with gigantic power instinct,
Though outwardly, in truth, but little graced
With aught of manly beauty – short, obese,
Rough-featured, coarse complexioned, with lank hair,
And small grey eyes, – in face (so many said)
Not much unlike myself, – his voice abrupt,
Unmusical; – yet, when he spake, the ear
Was charmed into attention, and the eye
Forgot the visible and outward frame
Of the rich mind within; with such swift flow
Of full, spontaneous utterance, the tongue
Interpreted the deep impassioned thought,
And poured upon our sense exhaustless store
Of multifarious learning . . .
                            . . . he breathed
An atmosphere of argument, nor shrank
From making, where he could not find, excuse
For controversial fight.

Despite their rivalry, the two orators were good friends. Praed himself called Macaulay 'my prince of patrons, my pink of prize poets, my Cantab Cicero', and in a parody of a Union debate, written for declamation at supper parties, he fondly sketched Macaulay's style and ascendancy:

But the favourite comes with his trumpets and drums,
    And his arms and his metaphors crossed;
And the audience – O dear! – vociferate 'Hear!'
    Till they're half of them deaf as a post.

It was in company with Praed, Moultrie, Bulwer-Lytton, Henry Nelson Coleridge, and Derwent Coleridge (respectively Coleridge's son-in-law and second son) that Macaulay began writing for *Knight's Quarterly Magazine*, the first of whose six substantial numbers (they ran to over 200 pages each) appeared in June 1823. Praed, who edited it, had earlier edited *The Etonian* with the same publisher, Charles Knight of Windsor. The contributions were pseudonymous and high-spirited, and Zachary Macaulay, perusing the first issue, was shocked 'at the associations which Tom has formed. It is a loose, low, coarse, and almost blackguard work in *some* of its parts.' Macaulay nevertheless continued to contribute: it was the beginning of his literary career. Two years later, his essays in the *Edinburgh Review*, especially that on Milton, made his name overnight.

In September 1824 Macaulay was elected a Fellow of Trinity and at once left Cambridge. The larger world claimed him – parliament, high office in India, Cabinet minister – before he finally settled down to write, producing his popular *Lays of Ancient Rome* in 1842, and his monumental but unfinished *History of*

England. At the end of his life, hard on the heels of his peerage, he was proud to be appointed High Steward of his old university town.

Edward Bulwer, as he was then known, more grandly Edward George Earle Lytton Bulwer-Lytton, later Baron Lytton (1803–73), was another noted Union speaker. Modelling himself on Byron, he had already published his first poems, acquired a reputation as a pugilist, and enjoyed a tragic love affair before coming up to Trinity in 1822. In 1824, about the time of Byron's death, he even managed to initiate an affair with Byron's former lover, Lady Caroline Lamb, who apparently accepted him as a suitable Byron-substitute. Bulwer published more poems at Cambridge, won the Chancellor's English Medal for 1825 ('I had more pleasure, perhaps, in that first literary success than in any I have known since'), and was described by Praed with Nashean hyperbole in a *Knight's Quarterly* editorial as one 'who writes more verses than any man under the sun. I will engage that he shall spill more ink in an hour than a County Member shall swallow claret, and dispose of a quire in less time than an Alderman shall raze a haunch'. His Byronic life-style, however, brought him into conflict with his tutor, and he transferred to the less censorious Trinity Hall, where he imitated the 'gay life' of his elder brother Henry, who had himself transferred to the even 'faster' new college of Downing and 'had the handsomest stud, perhaps, Cambridge ever saw'. The dandy hero of his second novel, *Pelham* (1828), apparently lived more sedately, eschewing the 'varmint' life:

> I do not exactly remember how I spent my time at Cambridge. I had a pianoforte in my room, and a private billiard-room at a village two miles off; and, between these resources, I managed to improve my mind more than could reasonably have been expected. To say truth, the whole place reeked with vulgarity. The men drank beer by the gallon, and ate cheese by the hundredweight – wore jockey-cut coats, and talked slang – rode for wagers, and swore when they lost – smoked in your face, and expectorated on the floor. Their proudest glory was to drive the mail – their mightiest exploit to box with the coachman – their most delicate amour to leer at the barmaid.

Chesterton, Bulwer's 'village two miles off', was outside the limit of university authority and a favoured resort of undergraduates, as witness the first work of another Trinity student of the 1820s, Edward Fitzgerald (1809–83), best known as the translator of the *Rubáiyát of Omar Khayyám*. With as little taste for mathematics as most literary men, Fitzgerald opted for a quiet 'non-reading' life when he came up in October 1826, and took no interest in the Union or other activities. Shy, lazy, quixotic, he liked his lodgings at 19 King's Parade (marked with a plaque in 1937) so much that he even returned to them in later years. Indeed, though Cambridge seemed to have little effect on him at the time, its condition became something of a preoccupation, his visits making him increasingly critical of a system that produced 'hard-reading, pale, dwindled students . . . only fit to have their necks wrung'.

Fitzgerald's first published work, *Euphranor* (1851), brought out when he was already over forty, is a prose idyll set in Cambridge, depicting a summer day's jaunt to Chesterton by a group of young collegians, whose sparkling, almost Wildean, talk ranges over questions of youth, chivalry, and true education. The underlying argument, that education should involve physical (even agricultural) work, as well as mental, anticipates Ruskin (though Fitzgerald would have been horrified at the fetishistic extreme of compulsory games to which public-school headmasters later took such ideas). With its idealistic setting, *Euphranor* introduces a wholly new literary vision of Cambridge – a kind of Athenian home of truth and beauty.

The debate is conducted genially enough, over billiards and beer in the lilac arbours of the Three Tuns, without any scoring off any of the characters. There is perhaps overmuch parrying of erudite writers for the modern reader, who tends to feel for the indolent, cigar-smoking Lycion who, 'lying down on the grass, with his hat over his eyes, composed himself to inattention'; but the final effect is of affectionate sanity. The conclusion of the work, where the characters mingle with the crowds to watch the races on the river before returning home, was particularly admired by Tennyson:

> and suddenly the head of the first boat turned the corner; and then another close upon it; and then a third; the crews pulling with all their might compacted into perfect rhythm; and the crowd on shore turning round to follow along with them, waving hats and caps, and cheering, 'Bravo, St John's!' 'Go it, Trinity!' . . . Then, waiting a little to hear how the winner had won, and the loser lost . . . I took Euphranor and Lexilogus under either arm, (Lycion having got into better company elsewhere), and walked home with them across the meadow leading to the town, whither the dusky troops of Gownsmen with all their confused voices seemed as it were evaporating in the twilight, while a nightingale began to be heard among the flowering chestnuts of Jesus.

In Fitzgerald's final term at college, he engaged a private tutor, Williams of Corpus Christi, to coach him for his forthcoming exams; and it was in Williams's rooms that he first met a tall, broken-nosed student, eyeglass fixed quizzically in eye, with whom he at once became firm friends.

William Makepeace Thackeray (1811–63), born in Calcutta and schooled at Charterhouse, had arrived at Trinity in a 'by-term', owing to illness, in February 1829. His tutor, William Whewell ('Billy Whistle' to the students), was sufficiently impressed by the young man's means to put him straight into ground-floor rooms opposite those recently occupied by Macaulay. 'Men will say someday', Thackeray jested to his mother, 'that Newton and Thackeray kept near one another!' Having had the rooms redecorated and hung with dyed curtains on fashionable brass rods, he thought them very stylish, and did not mind about people climbing in through his window after hours.

Whewell (of whom Sydney Smith once said that 'science was his forte and omniscience his foible', and some of whose aloofness went into the character of Dr Crump in Thackeray's *Book of Snobs*) probably had little more to do with him. Intending at this stage to go for an honours degree, Thackeray engaged a private tutor and worked conscientiously from breakfast till hall (dinner was taken at 2.30); but from hall onwards there was a daily tide of temptations – such as wine parties:

> thirty lads round a table covered with bad sweetmeats, drinking bad wines, telling bad stories, singing bad songs over and over again. Milk punch – smoking – ghastly headache – frightful spectacle of dessert table next morning, and smell of tobacco – your guardian, the clergyman, dropping in in the midst of this – expecting to find you deep in algebra, and discovering the gyp administering soda-water.

Thackeray was elected a member of the Union within three days of his arrival, but his enthusiasm was dampened almost at once:

> I have made a fool of myself! – I have rendered myself a public character, I have exposed myself – how? I spouted at the Union. I do not know what evil star reigns today or what malignant daemon could prompt me to such an act of folly – but, however, I got up, and blustered and blundered, and retracted, and stuttered upon the character of Napoleon ... In endeavouring to extract myself from my dilemma, I went deeper and deeper still, till at last with one desperate sentence ... I rushed out of that quagmire into which I had so foolishly plunged myself and sat down like Lucifer never to rise again with open mouth in that august assembly.

He had many relations in the town. Several generations of Thackerays had been at Cambridge, many of them medical men. His great-uncle Thomas, surgeon at Addenbrooke's, had treated Gray, and his son Frederic had followed him in the practice. Two other cousins, George and Martin Thackeray, were respectively Provost and Vice-Provost of King's; two more Thackerays were Fellows. He duly called on them all and listened to their advice, but found their elderly respectability rather tedious.

Thackeray's letters to his mother – in contrast to Macaulay's colourless letters home – are breezy and uninhibited. He was neither quite a 'reading' nor a 'non-reading' man, neither 'varmint' nor 'Apostle', but his exuberant gregariousness took him into many circles, from the Provost's Lodge at King's to the shady purlieus of Newmarket sharpsters. He was an energetic walker – 'I walked today about twelve miles to Impington and Girton and some other places whose names I forget'; he galloped on hired hacks to Wimpole and Newmarket; he kissed a friend's 'pretty washerwoman'; he fenced every day. He extolled the college ale and found 'the plum pudding on Sundays most amiable!' On 10 March, walking by moonlight, 'I fell over head and ears in a ditch opposite Addingbrooke's Hospital. I might have drowned with the greatest facility.' On 31 March, returning from the Union, he replied to a nightcapped head that had popped out of a window to see why the fire engine was in action, that there was a fire at the back of the man's own house. The man turned out to be Henry Gunning, but the Esquire Bedell did not hold the prank against him, for on 3 May they took tea together at Dr Thackeray's. On 13 April he attended a dinner party for ten, consisting of 'soup, smelts, sole, boiled turkey, saddle-mutton, wild ducks, cream jellies etc'. Meanwhile, he laboured away at his algebra: he bought an alarm clock to help him get up to see his tutor at six, but the noise it made kept him awake and he ended by oversleeping.

On Thursday 30 April 1829, Thackeray burst into print. A new undergraduate magazine had appeared, a jocular little affair printed on six pages of coloured paper at 2½d a copy and entitled *The Snob: A Literary and Scientific Journal. NOT Conducted by Members of the University*.[5] Thackeray, signing himself merely 'T', sent in to the editor a burlesque prize poem on the subject chosen for that year's Chancellor's English Medal, 'Timbuctoo'. Appearing in the magazine's fourth issue, his squib actually stuck closer to the subject than the poem by Tennyson which won the medal:

> In Africa (a quarter of the world)
> Men's skins are black, their hair is crisp and curled;
> And somewhere there, unknown to public view,
> A mighty city lies, called Timbuctoo.
> There stalks the tiger, – there the lion roars, –
> Who sometimes eats the luckless blackamoors;
> All that he leaves of them the monster throws
> To jackals, vultures, dogs, cats, kites, and crows:
> His hunger thus the forest monster gluts,
> And then lies down 'neath trees called cocoanuts . . .

Thackeray added elucidatory footnotes in the manner of the best prize poets.

'Timbuctoo received much laud,' he told his mother. 'The men knew not the author, but praised the poem – how eagerly did I suck it in!' The editor, William Williams of Corpus, requested, 'we shall be glad to hear from "T" again'; and soon he and Thackeray were writing the magazine together. 'Myself and the Editor of the Snob . . . sat down to write the Snob for the next Thursday. We began at nine, and concluded at two but I was so afflicted with laughter during our attempts, that I came away quite ill.' (Dr Thackeray had to be called to apply leeches.) The magazine ran for eleven issues; next winter it was revived as *The Gownsman: A Literary and Scientific Journal. Now Conducted by Members of the University* for a further seventeen. Thackeray's contributions after 'Timbuctoo' are unremarkable.

---

[5] 'Snob' was Cambridge slang for a townsman. It was Thackeray himself, years later in his *Book of Snobs*, who extended the meaning to include anyone of any social rank who displayed vanity or vulgarity – 'he who meanly admires mean things is a Snob' – thus eventually reversing the word's application.

When the Long Vacation arrived, Thackeray, having done badly in his college exams, engaged his co-editor (with how much serious motivation is unclear) as his private coach, and set off with him for Paris. Though his education went forward in Paris, it did not include much mathematics, and Williams, one imagines, did not press his duties.

Significantly, by the time of his return to Trinity, Thackeray's candid reports home had ceased, and his second year remains obscure. About this time he joined a college debating society, one of whose more eminent members, W. H. Thompson, later Master of Trinity, recalled him as

> a tall thin large-eyed, full and ruddy-faced man with an eye glass fixed *en permanence* . . . We did not see in him even the germ of those literary powers which . . . he afterwards developed . . . He led a somewhat lazy but pleasant and 'gentlemanlike' life in a set mixed of old schoolfellows and such men . . . Though careless of University distinction, he had a vivid appreciation of English poetry, and chanted the praises of the old English novelists – especially his model, Fielding. He had always a flow of humour and pleasantry, and was made much of by his friends.

But the most far-reaching event was the meeting in October with Fitzgerald. They exactly shared a sense of humour, and roamed inseparably for the rest of term, discussing literature and life. A regular coiner of nicknames, Thackeray called Fitzgerald 'Fitz', 'Neddikens', or 'Teddibus'; he himself became 'Old Thack'. The friendship was temporarily curtailed by Fitzgerald's departure at the end of term, but they joined up again in Paris at Easter and were to remain long-standingly devoted, even after 'Fitz' became a dilettante recluse in Suffolk.

This second visit to Paris – clandestine and without permission – redoubled Thackeray's addiction to gambling. He was no sooner back in Cambridge than his enthusiasm was spotted by a team of professional card-sharpers, who took lodgings opposite the college and invited him over to play. At first they allowed him modest winnings, then stung him for more than he could hope to pay. He was obliged to sign promises to pay £1500 when he came of age. One of the sharpers was to be used as model for his character Deuceace.

Heavily in debt, and with predictably poor results in his 'Little Go' examination, he took fresh stock of the situation. He would never now get an honours degree; was staying on worth the expense? At the end of the summer term, having kept five terms in all, he quitted Cambridge for good. One thing he had at least learnt was when to cut his losses.

In his novel *Pendennis* (1850) Thackeray goes to pains reminiscent of Lamb's to shroud his college localities in ambiguity. When Arthur Pendennis enters the University of Oxbridge (Thackeray coined the amalgam name), his college is not the great St George's, but the little St Boniface next door; yet the description seems unmistakable:

the pretty fountain playing in the centre of the fair green plots; the tall chapel windows and buttresses rising to the right; the hall, with its tapering lantern and oriel windows; the lodge, from the doors of which the Master issued awfully in rustling silks; the lines of the surrounding rooms pleasantly broken by carved chimneys, grey turrets, and quaint gables.

Young Pen is awarded 'the best set of rooms to be had in college' and, like his creator, begins 'with tolerable assiduity'. But he is soon cutting the mathematical lectures, 'being perhaps rather annoyed that one or two very vulgar young men, who did not even use straps to their trousers so as to cover the abominably thick and coarse shoes and stockings which they wore, beat him completely'. He over-spends his allowance on jewellery, cigars, French novels, and clothes, 'appearing in the morning in wonderful shooting-jackets, with remarkable buttons; and in the evening in gorgeous velvet waistcoats, with richly embroidered cravats and curious linen'. His friend Foker gets into a scrape by painting their tutor's door vermilion, on which occasion 'young Black Strap, the celebrated negro-fighter, who was one of Mr Foker's distinguished guests, and who was holding the can of paint . . . knocked down two of the proctor's attendants and performed prodigies of valour'.

Worse is to come: in his last year Pendennis falls in with the rogue Bloundell and squanders his remaining time and money on dice. Meanwhile, the erstwhile crowds of waiters and 'skips' carrying dishes and iced champagne vanish from outside his rooms, to be replaced by pertinacious tradesmen, 'with faces sulky or piteous', presenting their bills. When Pen finally sits for his degree, he is not surprisingly 'plucked'.

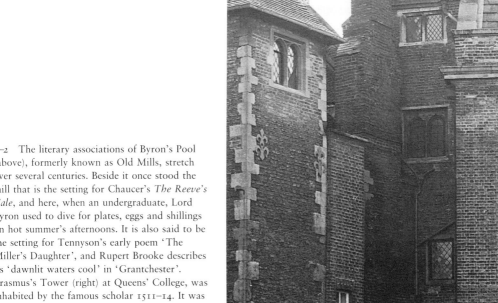

1–2 The literary associations of Byron's Pool (above), formerly known as Old Mills, stretch over several centuries. Beside it once stood the mill that is the setting for Chaucer's *The Reeve's Tale*, and here, when an undergraduate, Lord Byron used to dive for plates, eggs and shillings on hot summer's afternoons. It is also said to be the setting for Tennyson's early poem 'The Miller's Daughter', and Rupert Brooke describes its 'dawnlit waters cool' in 'Grantchester'. Erasmus's Tower (right) at Queens' College, was inhabited by the famous scholar 1511–14. It was built in 1449.

ANNO DNI · ÆTATIS SVÆ 21

7585

QVOD ME NVTRIT
ME DESTRVIT

3–4 Christopher Marlowe shared a ground-floor room in the fourteenth-century Old Court of Corpus Christi College (above) 1580–4. Today it is marked by a plaque (between the windows bottom right) commemorating him and his fellow playwright John Fletcher, who was at Corpus in the mid-1590s. The portrait (left) is thought by many to be of Marlowe. Discovered behind panelling in the Master's Lodge in 1953, it was used by a workman for mixing mortar before it was identified as an Elizabethan painting. The portrait has undergone extensive restoration.

5–6 The 'Lady of Christ's', John Milton, is shown in this portrait of 1629, painted when he was twenty-one. In the same year he took his B.A. and wrote his first masterpiece, 'On the Morning of Christ's Nativity'. 'Lycidas', a poem in memory of Edward King, a Fellow of Christ's, was written in 1637. The autograph manuscript below is part of a collection of Milton's early poems largely in his own hand preserved in the Wren Library, Trinity College.

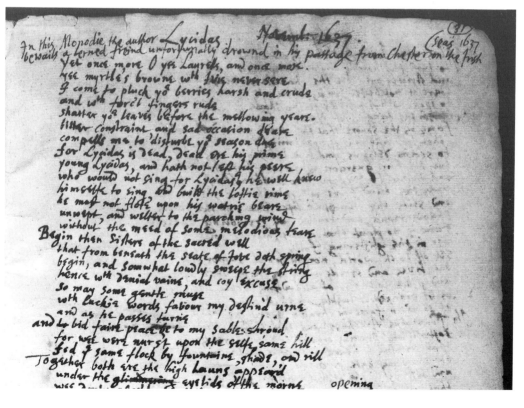

7–8 One of Milton's best-known short poems, 'On the University Carrier', commemorates a famous Cambridge character, Thomas Hobson, who died in 1631 at the age of eighty-six. This portrait was painted in 1629. The large seventeenth-century mulberry tree in the Fellows' Garden of Christ's College is traditionally, but for no good reason, known as 'Milton's'. It is shown here in a photograph of 1856. Other trees in the garden with more secure literary associations are some cypresses grown from seeds taken from Shelley's cenotaph in Rome.

9   This portrait of Samuel Pepys was painted by Lely or his studio in 1673, when Pepys was appointed
to the Admiralty. It now hangs in the hall of his old college, Magdalene.

10–11 The manuscript of Pepys's famous diary is kept with his library of books (left) which he bequeathed to the college, Magdalene. The bookcases were made specially for him. The diary records several visits to Cambridge, the first in 1660, when he stayed in the Falcon Inn (below) in Petty Cury, shown here in a mid-nineteenth-century photograph. The sixteenth-century gallery on the right survived into the 1970s.

12–14 Thomas Gray (above) and Christopher Smart (above right), utterly unlike in personality, were the most famous poets of mid-eighteenth-century Cambridge. Gray's rooms at Peterhouse were at the top of the Fellows' Building overlooking Trumpington Street. The iron bar that still survives outside his window (right) was designed to allow escape by rope ladder in case of fire.

THE

FALL

OF

ROBESPIERRE.

AN

HISTORIC DRAMA.

BY S. T. COLERIDGE,
OF JESUS COLLEGE, CAMBRIDGE.

Cambridge:
PRINTED BY BENJAMIN FLOWER,
FOR W. H. LUNN, AND J. AND J. MERRILL ; AND SOLD
BY J. MARCH, NORWICH.
1794.
[PRICE ONE SHILLING.]

15–18 'A nook obscure' is how Wordsworth (above opposite) described the rooms at St John's College (below opposite), where he lived from 1787 to 1790. They were on F staircase, above the kitchens, which he remembered as making a 'humming sound, less tuneable than bees'. Coleridge (above) published his three-act blank-verse tragedy *The Fall of Robespierre* during his last year at Cambridge.

19 Thorwaldsen's statue of Byron, 1831, was intended for Westminster Abbey, to which it was refused admission by the dean. It spent nine years in a vault of the Custom House before being placed in Trinity College Library. Byron is shown sitting amid Greek ruins, pen in one hand, the text of *Childe Harold* in the other; a Death's head peers out from behind the fallen column.

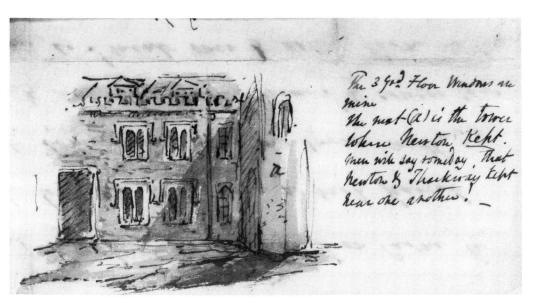

20–1 The sketch above appears in the margin of a letter written by Thackeray to his mother soon after his arrival at Trinity in 1829. This section of the letter reads 'The 3 Grd. Floor windows are mine. The next (a) is the tower where Newton kept. Men will say someday that Newton & Thackeray kept near one another!' Less than seventy years later guidebooks were observing precisely that (and pointing out that Macaulay's rooms were opposite). Edward Fitzgerald reading by lamplight (right) was drawn by his fellow undergraduate James Spedding, the future editor of Bacon and remembered by Fitzgerald as his 'earliest and dearest friend'.

22–5 'Up that long walk of limes I past/To see the rooms in which he dwelt' wrote Tennyson in *In Memoriam*, recording a visit to Cambridge in 1838 to see again the scenes he associated with Hallam who had died five years earlier. The lime walk on Trinity Backs (right) leads to New Court, where Hallam had lived. The drawings of Tennyson (above left) and Hallam are by their fellow Apostle James Spedding. Tennyson, in characteristic pose, short-sightedly holds his book close; the 'bar of Michael Angelo' – Hallam's bulging brow, as described by Tennyson – is only lightly indicated. Tennyson's Chancellor's Medal for English Poetry, won for 'Timbuctoo' in 1829, is shown above.

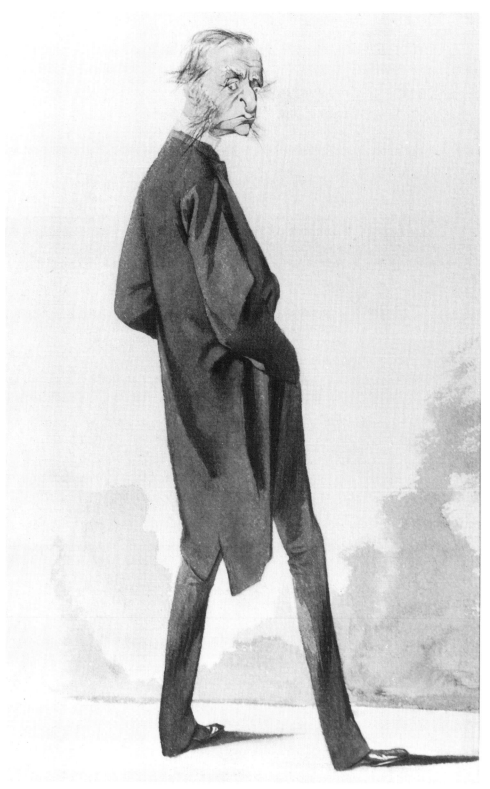

26 Charles Kingsley's career embodies the transformation of mid-Victorian Cambridge: he began as a
'blood' in the unreformed university in the late 1830s and returned twenty years later as a zealous and
inspiring teacher. *Vanity Fair*'s caricature is by 'Cecioni'.

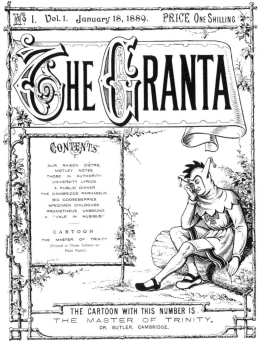

27–9 Undergraduate journalism was a new feature of nineteenth-century Cambridge; the most famous magazine was *The Granta* (its first issue is above). *The Cambridge A.B.C.* had a cover drawn by Beardsley 'for the modest sum of ten guineas' remembered one of its editors, Maurice Baring, 'and many people thought it was a clever parody of his draughtsmanship'. The vogue for novels with a university setting is exemplified by F. W. Farrar's *Julian Home* (1859): in this scene, the villain has screwed up Julian's door before an examination.

30 A detail from Robert Farren's painting *Senate House Hill: Degree Morning* (1863). The bearded man in the centre is Leslie Stephen. Henry Fawcett, the blind professor of political economy, whose biography Stephen wrote on the far left; beside him, Dr Geldart, Master of Trinity Hall, congratulates Stephen's pupil Robert Romer on being classed as senior wrangler. In the right foreground the wooden spoon is awarded to the man with the lowest marks in the mathematical tripos.

14

'Up that long walk of limes'

On the evening of 9 November 1827, a tall, swarthy, lion-headed young man stepped down from the Stamford coach at the Blue Boar in Trinity Street and made his way with his few belongings along the gaslit thoroughfare. His figure, loping in a peculiarly intense manner, attracted the notice of a proctor, who demanded why he was not in cap and gown. Peering at the official with myopic hauteur, the young man snapped, 'I should like to know what business it can be of yours, sir,' and strode on.

Alfred Tennyson (1809–92) had hardly ever before set foot outside his Lincolnshire homeland, nor mixed beyond his family, but that family, with its rankling feuds and black melancholy, had finally proved too much for him. To escape from his drunken father, the rector of Somersby, he had migrated to his grandfather's, intending to take a year's coaching in mathematics before entering the university; but when his father turned up there too, he took the next coach to Cambridge to join his elder brothers at their lodgings at 12 Rose Crescent, on the corner of Market Hill, above Pleasance's tobacco shop. Frederick (1807–98), two years older, brilliant but ungovernable, had gone originally from Eton to St John's (their father's old college), but had now transferred to Trinity. Charles (1808–79), one year older, had entered at Trinity just two weeks before. The college apparently made no difficulty over admitting a third Tennyson in the middle of term: despite his patchy and unorthodox schooling, Alfred was found 'fully competent to enter the university'.

Frederick had acquired considerable repute about the university (he won a Browne Medal for a Greek ode in 1828); the arrival of two more equally striking members of the clan heightened the effect to the point of incredulity. It did not need the information that Alfred and Charles had recently published an anonymous volume of *Poems by Two Brothers* for it to be obvious what they were. 'That man must be a poet!' exclaimed fellow freshman W. H. Thompson when he caught sight of Tennyson's figure standing 'long-haired and defiant' in the entrance to hall. From the very start, Tennyson's poetical vocation was taken as self-evident by everybody at Cambridge.

In fact, Tennyson's initial aloofness was due more to shyness than defiance. The prospect of dining in the great hall among so many strangers is said to have so panicked him that first time that he turned away, unable to face the ordeal; and initially he associated with few apart from his brothers. Despite his recent unhappiness at Somersby, some lines written soon after his arrival at Cambridge express homesickness for his childhood haunts, where even the stars seemed brighter:

> Playfellow winds and stars, my friends of old,
>   (For sure your voice was friendly, your eyes bright
>   With sympathy, what time my spirit was cold
>   And frozen at the fountain, my cheek white
> As my own hope's quenched ashes) as your memories
>   More than yourselves you look, so overcast
>   With steam of this dull town your burning eyes:
> Nay, surely even your memories wear more light
> Than do your present selves. Ye sympathize
> As ever with me, stars, from first to last.

In April 1828, having transferred with Charles to new lodgings at 57 Corpus Buildings, Trumpington Street, where he was to remain for the rest of his Cambridge career, he wrote to Mrs Russell, the aunt who was sponsoring his education:

> I am sitting owl-like and solitary in my rooms (nothing between me and the stars but a stratum of tiles). The hoof of the steed, the roll of the wheel, the shouts of drunken Gown and drunken Town come up from below with a sealike murmur . . . I know not how it is, but I feel isolated here in the midst of society. The country is so disgustingly level, the revelry of the place so monotonous, the studies of the University so uninteresting, so much matter of fact.

He described his fellow students as 'dryheaded, calculating, angular little gentlemen'.

Like Wordsworth before him, Tennyson took refuge in the associations of his surroundings. He sought out 'Milton's Mulberry' at Christ's and wrote an enthusiastic little poem about it:

> Look what love the puddle-pated squarecaps have for me!
> I am Milton's mulberry, Milton's Milton's mulberry –
> But they whipt and rusticated him that planted me,
> Milton's Milton's mulberry, Milton's Milton's mulberry.
> Old and hollow, somewhat crooked in the shoulders as you see,
> Full of summer foliage yet but propt and padded curiously,
> I would sooner have been planted by the hand that planted me,
> Than have grown in Paradise and dropped my fruit on Adam's knee –
> Look what love the tiny-witted trenchers have for me.

At Trumpington there was the pool where his childhood hero, Byron, had bathed; nearby, Grantchester Mill (which, like Wordsworth, he perhaps mistook for

Chaucer's Trumpington Mill) would give him the setting for 'The Miller's Daughter'. Similarly, the lower Cam, still very much a working waterway, may have been his model for the river in 'The Lady of Shalott', flowing down to 'many-towered Camelot':

> By the margin, willow-veiled,
> Slide the heavy barges trailed
> By slow horses; and unhailed
> The shallop flitteth silken-sailed
>   Skimming down to Camelot.

The place he could find virtues in; the preoccupations of the place he could not. His tutor, Whewell, established a tolerant relationship with him – trying to engage his attention, when he spotted him reading poetry under the desk during a mathematics lecture, by asking: 'Mr Tennyson, what is the compound interest of a penny put out at the beginning of the Christian era up to the present time?' and passing over 'certain informalities and forgetfulness of combinations as to gowns and places and times which in another he would never have overlooked'. But such forbearance did not stem Tennyson's overall contempt – comparable to Wordsworth's – for the system and the run of dons. A sonnet, 'Lines on Cambridge of 1830', later suppressed, vented an anger which did not diminish when he began to enjoy Cambridge for other reasons; indeed, when he found his feet, it was to participate in the dream of a golden dawn of reform.

> Therefore your Halls, your ancient Colleges,
> Your portals statued with old kings and queens,
> Your gardens, myriad-volumed libraries,
> Wax-lighted chapels, and rich carven screens,
> Your doctors, and your proctors, and your deans,
> Shall not avail you, when the Day-beam sports
> New-risen o'er awakened Albion. No!
> Nor yet your solemn organ pipes that blow
> Melodious thunders through your vacant courts
> At noon and eve, because your manner sorts
> Not with this age wherefrom ye stand apart,
> Because the lips of little children preach
> Against you, you that do profess to teach
> And teach us nothing, feeding not the heart.

Despite his shyness, Tennyson's majestic figure soon became familiar about the Cambridge scene. Fitzgerald, for instance, who only got to know him later, remembered Tennyson at Cambridge as 'something like the Hyperion shorn of his beams in Keats' poem: with a pipe in his mouth'. The pipe if nothing else would have drawn attention, for smoking at that date was socially taboo (and prohibited while in cap and gown). Tennyson had been addicted to tobacco since the age of fourteen, and J. W. Blakesley, a subsequent Trinity friend, complained that at college he smoked 'the strongest and most stinking tobacco out of a small blackened old pipe on an average nine hours a day'. Tennyson passed his first year quietly – smoking, reading, covering great distances with his shuffling stride over the flat countryside or watching for hours the 'wonderful sinuosities' of a pet snake slithering about the carpet of his rooms.

The following Michaelmas term brought Frederick into open conflict with the college. Having taken exception to Christopher Wordsworth's strong line on chapel attendance, he was hauled before the Master and Fellows 'smilingly and satirically impertinent', and sent down for three terms. Back at Somersby, he and his father (who had himself as an undergraduate fired a pistol through a window of Trinity Chapel) came to violent blows and he was sent packing from there too. Their grandfather, who had already disinherited the Somersby Tennysons, judged: 'Those three boys so far from having improved in manner or manners are worse since they went to Cambridge.'

Alfred tried to atone. His father had insisted that if he was a poet he must compete for the Chancellor's Medal. Tennyson had in fact drafted a hundred lines in couplets on the last year's subject, 'The Invasion of Russia by Napoleon Buonaparte' (for which his brother Charles competed; Christopher Wordsworth junior was the medallist),[1] but his heart was not in it; and when 'Timbuctoo' was announced in December as the subject for the 1829 medal (the first European explorer to return alive from the fabled city, René Caillié, had reached France in October – hence presumably the choice), he abandoned any such orthodox approach. Adapting instead an old poem of his on a totally different subject, the Battle of Armageddon, he added a new beginning and end and sent that in. Submissions were supposed to be in heroic couplets; his was in blank verse (not so very revolutionary: Seatonian Prize poems had traditionally been in blank). Worse, he seemed to cock a deliberate snook at the competition by heading his poem with an invented quotation from 'Chapman' –

> Deep in that lion-haunted inland lies
> A mystick city, goal of high emprise.

An ideal prize poem of the sort that generally won the medal might have included rhetorical evocations of Timbuctoo's remoteness and crumbled grandeur, its caravans and slavery; shown familiarity (in footnotes) with the accounts of Adams, Denham, and Mungo Park – or at least with the article in Rees's *Cyclopaedia*; speculated on the true course of the Niger; passed patriotic

---

[1] This was the second time that Wordsworth won. In 1827 when there was a tie between him and T. E. Hankinson of Corpus the Vice-Chancellor (apparently against the rules) gave a casting vote for Wordsworth. The Vice-Chancellor happened to be Christopher Wordsworth senior. After the row that ensued, Hankinson was uniquely awarded a second prize. The Trinity set thought Wordsworth's 1828 poem 'a disgrace to so clever a man' and unworthy of the medal. Having bagged most of the university prizes for two years running, he was persuaded in 1829 to stand down to give others a chance.

judgement on a French adventurer winning the laurels instead of a stalwart British major who had got there first but been cut down by infidels on the way back; and trumpeted the altruistic motivation of Christian explorers in seeking out such heathen places (a line successfully pursued by George Waddington in his 1813 poem on 'Columbus' and by Praed in his of 1823 on 'Australasia').

Poems of this sort were no doubt among the anonymous crop that arrived to be judged by William Smyth, the history professor, and his fellow examiners,[2] and it is to their credit that they picked out for the award instead one that began

> I stood upon the Mountain which o'erlooks
> The narrow seas, whose rapid interval
> Parts Afric from green Europe, when the Sun
> Had fall'n below th' Atlantic, and above
> The silent heavens were blench'd with faery light,
> Uncertain whether faery light or cloud,
> Flowing Southward, and the chasms of deep, deep blue
> Slumber'd unfathomable, and the stars
> Were flooded over with clear glory and pale.

and continued in trance-like Miltonic periods to muse over the lost legends of Atlantis and Eldorado, to speak of a Seraph descending, and to describe a mystic vision, before, working vaguely round to the given subject, it ended by lamenting, not praising, the impulse of discovery, that turns the imagined and proverbial into dismal materialistic reality.[3]

'I was never so surprised as when I got the prize,' Tennyson later remarked. Yet, though the poem was an unconventional, even dissident production, and many were mystified as to what it was all about (he himself later called it 'that wild and unmethodized performance'), it was widely acknowledged to display the mark of genius. 'Tennyson's poem has made quite a sensation,' a rival competitor, Richard Monckton Milnes, wrote home; 'it is certainly equal to most parts of Milton.' Charles Wordsworth wrote to his brother Christopher from Oxford (where the Newdigate Prize was a tamer affair):

> What do you think of Tennyson's Prize Poem? If such an exercise had been sent up at Oxford, the author would have had a better chance of being rusticated – with the view of his passing a few months at a Lunatic Asylum – than of

---

[2] There are printed copies of two unsuccessful poems in the University Library and in Trinity College Library. There were probably about thirty entrants. The following year's Newdigate Prize poem at Oxford, 'The African Desert' by G. K. Rickards, also contains much about Timbuctoo and the explorers.

[3] An apocryphal legend survives, however, that the reactionary Smyth, to whom the other examiners usually deferred, derisively pencilled on Tennyson's poem 'Look at this!' He was then taken ill or called away from Cambridge, and in his absence the others, taking the comment for the highest approval, awarded the medal to Tennyson by mistake. Another version says that he pencilled 'v.q.' ('very queer') which was mistaken for 'v.g.' ('very good').

obtaining the prize. It is certainly a wonderful production; and if it had come out with Lord Byron's name, it would have been thought as fine as anything he ever wrote.

(A very Oxford comment; though Byron was still revered at Oxford, he was by now a fallen idol among the elect at Cambridge, where 'Timbuctoo' was more likely to have been compared to Shelley.)

Though Thackeray had not submitted his squib, competition for the medal had been keen. And though winning the prize was an important first rung on the ladder of Tennyson's poetic career, the friendship which he struck up with a fellow competitor was to prove far more important. It was while hammering out their rival versions of 'Timbuctoo' that he and Arthur Henry Hallam (1811–33) became aware of each other's existence. It was to be one of the most celebrated friendships in the history of English literature.

Around Hallam's memory the eulogies of those who knew him have woven an aura of almost hallowed specialness. Tennyson called him 'as near perfection as mortal man could be'. John Kemble claimed: 'Never was a more powerful intellect joined to a purer and holier heart; and the whole illuminated with the richest imagination, with the most sparkling yet the kindest wit.' William Gladstone wrote sixty years after Hallam's death that 'it is simple truth that Arthur Henry Hallam was a spirit so exceptional that everything with which he was brought into relation during his shortened passage through this world, came to be, through this contact, glorified by a touch of the ideal'.

Hallam was remarkably precocious – he was writing tragedies and was fluent in French and Italian by the age of nine. His abilities had been zealously husbanded (like Macaulay's) by an authoritarian father, the historian Henry Hallam. While Macaulay's particular genius, however, centred on breadth of reading and infallibility of memory, Hallam's was rather different. He read widely but not deeply, had a bad memory – particularly for dates – and was bored by factual information divorced from ideas. He preferred idealistic generalities to pedantic detail, and he thrived on friendship. At Eton he enjoyed a number of extremely close friendships – particularly with Gladstone. But it was typical of his father that when Gladstone and other friends went to Oxford, Hallam was sent to Cambridge instead. Two years younger than Tennyson, but emotionally rather more experienced, Hallam came up to Trinity in October 1828, to rooms G3 in the recently completed New Court, and languished at first in solitary disaffection: 'the whole mode of existence here,' he wrote to Gladstone, '– its society, as well as its midnight lamp – its pleasures as well as its compulsions, are alike in my mind odious'. He was already suffering from headaches and fits of depression, which his contemporaries dismissed as the results of overwork, but which hindsight recognises as symptoms of the congenital vascular disease which lay in wait to kill him.

Apart from their mutual loneliness and dislike of 'the whole mode of existence here', Hallam and Tennyson did not have striking affinities: Hallam vivacious, rapid, brilliant, his emotions apparent and on the surface, loving metaphysical debate ('he could read or discuss metaphysics as he lay on the sofa after dinner, surrounded by a noisy party, with as much care and acuteness as if he had been alone', a contemporary remembered); Tennyson shy, melancholic, broody, with no talent for argument or exact dissection of things. Hallam, moreover, came from a tightly knit upper-class London family, Tennyson from a large unstable provincial one. Perhaps it was an attraction of opposites ('And he supplied my want the more / As his unlikeness fitted mine', Tennyson wrote in *In Memoriam*). The morbidly sceptical Tennyson was as much drawn to Hallam's optimism and faith as the drilled son of Henry Hallam was to Tennyson's lofty disregard of academic conventions and ambitions. In any case, their enthusiasm for poetry was shared. It must have been Tennyson who converted Hallam to Shelley. On his arrival at Cambridge Hallam had informed Gladstone that Shelley was all the vogue there, but 'For my part . . . I cannot bring myself to think *Percy Bysshe* a fine poet'; yet only months later his own 'Timbuctoo' (as unorthodox as Tennyson's) had footnotes in which he preached the new faith by means of lengthy quotations from *Alastor*.

By the end of May 1829, within a month of their meeting, Hallam had written a sonnet 'To A.T.', Shakespearean in tone, in which Tennyson is seen supplanting Gladstone in his affections. When at the beginning of June Tennyson was announced as winner of the medal, Hallam unselfishly called it a 'memorable victory . . . over prosaicism and jingle jangle'. To Gladstone he wrote: 'I consider Tennyson as promising to be the greatest poet of our generation, perhaps of our century.' When Tennyson was called upon to recite his poem at the Commencement ceremony in the Senate House and his nerves failed him (he persuaded a friend, Charles Merivale of St John's, to stand in for him) it was significant that he excused this failure to his grandfather by claiming for himself a condition that Hallam genuinely was suffering from – 'a determination of blood to the head', causing, he said, 'motes in the eyes'.

Hallam's eyes were blue and radiantly intelligent. Below them, his cheeks might be chronically flushed by blood pressure, his thin mouth a reminder of an acerbity passed over in his friends' encomiums; but above them rose a noble and impressive forehead. Once, after reading of the prominent ridge of bone above the brows of Michelangelo, he exclaimed with ingenuous delight: 'Alfred, look over my eyes; surely I have the bar of Michael Angelo!'

Hallam soon rose from his initial obscurity to the most prestigious circles. On 9 May 1829 he was elected to what was already an elite debating society, officially entitled the Cambridge Conversazione Society but better known as the 'Apostles'. Founded in 1820 at St John's, the Apostles had begun to assume importance from 1824 under the leadership of F. D. Maurice of Trinity. Meetings were held on Saturday evenings behind locked doors; after a paper had been read – 'Is there any rule of moral action except general expediency?' 'Is the existence of an intelligent

First Cause deducible from the phenomena of the universe?' 'Have the poems of Shelley an immoral tendency? ' – free discussion followed in which sincerity, lack of prejudice, and an attempt to understand the views of others were qualities preferred above the oratorical skills that counted for so much at the Union. (Macaulay and Praed were never members; on the other hand, Hallam and other Apostles also made their mark at the Union.) Members met at other times too – indeed, 'we lived in constant intercourse with one another, day by day, meeting over our wine or our tobacco', as Merivale remembered – and the 'Apostolic' atmosphere of intellectual quest, freedom, and generosity was arguably the most potent influence on maturing minds that Cambridge had to offer (even if it was also true, as Merivale admitted, that 'we soon grew, as such youthful coteries generally do, into immense self-conceit' and 'began to think that we had a mission to enlighten the world upon things intellectual and spiritual').

Hallam quickly established himself as a leading spirit in the society (and one of the most archetypally Apostolic members in its history), and it was doubtless under his sponsorship that his new friend was next suggested for election. Tennyson was admitted after the Long Vacation, on 31 October, as member number seventy. But Tennyson proved by contrast a most unApostolic member: fined for missing the next two meetings, he attended only five in all, sitting with his feet on the hob, wreathed in pipe smoke, listening with silent interest to all that was said but contributing little till the end of the evening, when he might be prevailed upon to declaim one of his latest compositions. (He carried them in his head, too lazy to write them down; on one occasion Hallam is said to have rushed unseen to a table and dashed down 'The Lotus Eaters' for posterity as it came from the poet's mouth.) When Tennyson's turn came in February 1830 to read a paper of his own, the evening ended in fiasco. He managed to prepare something on the subject of Ghosts, but when the moment approached to deliver it, consumed by nerves, he tore it up and threw it in the fire, resigning his membership. But though he did not attend any more meetings, he remained in close daily contact, and his brief membership meant much to him in bringing him into a charmed and influential circle of admirers.[4]

The society's membership at this date was particularly brilliant. John Kemble (1807–57) came from a celebrated family of actors (Tennyson and Hallam were both enamoured of his sister Fanny), and could out-row, out-debate, out-drink practically everybody; 'the world is one great thought, and I am thinking it,' he once boasted. Tennyson prophesied a great ecclesiastical career for him –

---

[4] That Hallam had begun to exert Apostolic influence for him before Tennyson was elected is indicated by the fulsome review of 'Timbuctoo' that appeared in the 22 July 1829 issue of the *Athenaeum*, then a new periodical edited by two leading Apostles, F. D. Maurice and John Sterling.

> Thou from a throne
> Mounted in heaven wilt shoot into the dark
> Arrows of lightnings. I will stand and mark.

– but in the event 'Black Jack' became a professor of Anglo-Saxon and edited *Beowulf*. Richard Chevenix Trench (1807–86), whose friendship with Kemble was almost as close as Tennyson's with Hallam, was for a time thought to be another poetical genius like Tennyson, but he became an archbishop and a philologist and looked back rather dismissively on the Apostles as 'a band of Platonico–Wordsworthian–Coleridgean–anti-utilitarians'. (An opinion of Trench's – 'Alfred, we cannot live on art' – is said to have inspired Tennyson's poem *The Palace of Art*.) James Spedding (1808–81) was a genial Lakelander with a self-mocking, whimsical humour and a great bald dome of a head that was a source of endless inspiration for Fitzgerald's and Thackeray's fantastic joking. Tennyson liked Spedding best after Hallam, valuing his critical judgement and considering him one of the wisest of men; but Spedding devoted his life's work to the narrow task of editing the works of Sir Francis Bacon. Richard Monckton Milnes, later Lord Houghton (1809–85), was elected on the same day as Tennyson, who took to him at first sight, as did most contemporaries; yet Milnes proved to have too much nervous vanity and gregariousness, too much love of paradox, to be a true Apostle. He went on to be a leading luminary of London society, and a champion of Keats, whose biography he wrote.

Tennyson did not take so readily to Thomas Sunderland (1808–67), a formidable debater whose supremacy at the Union was equal to Macaulay's before him, but who likewise lacked the finer Apostolic nature. Trench called him 'Judas', and Tennyson satirised him in 'A Character', ending:

> With lips depressed as he were meek,
> Himself unto himself he sold:
> Upon himself himself did feed:
> Quiet, dispassionate, and cold,
> And other than his form of creed,
> With chiselled features clear and sleek.

Sunderland sneered in return: 'I hear that one of the Tennysons has been writing a poem about me. Which was it? The one in the dirty shirt?' After leaving Cambridge, Sunderland became insane and his promise of a brilliant career came to nothing.

Other Apostles included W. H. Thompson (1810–86), who began at Cambridge as a sizar and ended as Master of Trinity; Henry Alford (1810–71), President of the Union and later Dean of Canterbury; J. W. Blakesley (1808–85), who became Dean of Lincoln; Charles Merivale (1808–93), who became Dean of Ely and wrote a history of Rome; the inseparable Francis Garden (1810–84) and Robert Monteith (1812–84); Edmund Lushington (1811–93), who married Tennyson's sister Cecilia; and his brother Henry Lushington (1812–55), who formed another of the close attachments of the time with George Stovin Venables (1810–88) of Jesus, who had been responsible at Charterhouse for Thackeray's broken nose and who won the Chancellor's Medal for 1831.[5]

On the fringes of the Apostles were other members of the 'set', including Tennyson's brothers; A. W. Kinglake (1809–91), who later wrote *Eōthen*, a classic account of travel in the Near East (his cousin W. C. Kinglake, at Trinity at the same time, won the Chancellor's Medal for 1830 and 1832); and W. H. Brookfield (1809–74), the college wit, universally popular for his mimicry and practical jokes. Thompson remembered a whole party of friends 'lying on the floor for purposes of unrestrained laughter' while 'Bird' Brookfield delivered a series of imaginary dialogues. He, Tennyson, and Hallam spent many convivial evenings together, to judge from Brookfield's lines –

> Blow up the fire, Gyp Haggis,
>   Bring brandywine for three;
> Bard Alfred, Bird William, and Clerk Arthur
>   This night shall merry be.

– or from the sonnet Tennyson wrote on Brookfield's death:

> Old Brooks, who loved so well to mouth my rhymes,
> How oft we two have heard St Mary's chimes!
> How oft the Cantab supper, host and guest,
> Would echo helpless laughter to your jest!
> How oft with him we paced that walk of limes,
> Him, the lost light of those dawn-golden times,
> Who loved you well! Now both are gone to rest.

There was, in fact, as much laughter among that brilliant Trinity intake as idealism. Tennyson himself was no mean mimic, enthralling supper parties with impersonations of George IV, of Satan squatting toad-like at Eve's ear, of a man on a close stool, or, pipe-stop in mouth, of a giant squawking and flapping bird. In *The Princess* (1847) he writes how

> They boated and they cricketed; they talked
> At wine, in clubs, of art, of politics;
> They lost their weeks; they vext the souls of deans;
> They rode; they betted; made a hundred friends,
> And caught the blossom of the flying terms.

The Dean was indeed vexed one night when there was excessive noise from Hallam's rooms. According to Tennyson's version, when Hallam apologised, 'I'm very sorry, sir, we had no idea we were making a noise,' the Dean frothed, 'Well,

---

5 Lushington and Venables, Garden and Monteith, Kemble and Trench, Milnes and Stafford O'Brien – passionate 'arm-in-arms' were *de rigueur*, and that between Tennyson and Hallam in no way exceptional for the time.

gentlemen, if you'll all come down into the court, you'll *hear* what a noise you're making.'

There were amateur dramatics, too, in particular a performance of *Much Ado About Nothing* at the Hoop Hotel on 19 March 1830, with Hallam as Verges, Kemble as Dogberry, and Milnes as Beatrice, in which a sofa collapsed beneath the weight of Beatrice, who disappeared with an unfeminine expletive amid tumbled petticoats and general hilarity.

Never had there been so much debate about poetry. Many of the Apostles wrote poetry; all of them discussed it. Although it remained fashionable for more dandyish students to affect the Byronic manner, the more advanced souls (like the Apostles) sought a more inspirational pabulum (one of the earliest 'dislodgements' of Byron had been effected by Derwent Coleridge and Praed in the *Knight's Quarterly* for October 1823). This they found in the works of Wordsworth and Coleridge (whom Hallam made a pilgrimage to Highgate to meet), Keats and Shelley. Few as yet shared such tastes. When in November 1828 the Union debated – or tried to debate – the motion 'Is Wordsworth or Lord Byron the greater poet?' the proceedings terminated in uproar. Shelley was thought even more *avant-garde* than Wordsworth. Hallam had brought back a copy of the first (Pisa, 1821) edition of *Adonais* from Italy, and in 1829 he and Milnes had five hundred copies – the first English edition – printed in Cambridge by Metcalfe. These they distributed, with the fervour of evangelicals distributing tracts, wherever they went. In November 1829 a historic Oxford–Cambridge debate took place when, at the invitation of Gladstone and the Oxford Union, the three most prominent Cambridge debaters – Hallam, Milnes, and Sunderland – travelled to Oxford to defend Shelley (an Oxonian the Oxford side professed never to have heard of) against Byron (a Trinity poet vigorously belittled by the Trinity team). To Cambridge's dawn-golden convictions oxford (as the Apostles styled it) replied with profound sangfroid, confusing Shelley with Shenstone and certainly never noticing that among the Shelley poems quoted by the Cantabs were some by Tennyson slipped in by 'Old Brooks' as one of his practical jokes before the expedition set out.[6]

The following April, Hallam accompanied Tennyson to Somersby, and their destinies looked set for yet closer intertwining as they discussed a projected joint volume of poems and as Hallam fell in love with Tennyson's sister Emily. Neither hope was to be realised. Hallam's father – alarmed at the appearance of such a product of their union – forbade his participation in the book, even though it was

---

[6] Permission for the expedition was extracted from Christopher Wordsworth under the impression that it was his brother they were going to defend, rather than the atheist Shelley. Shelley's name was in fact not wholly unknown at Oxford: the poet Beddoes had produced an edition of his *Posthumous Poems* in 1824, while still an undergraduate at Pembroke College.

already set up in type, so that when *Poems, Chiefly Lyrical* came out in June 1830, Tennyson was its sole author. Even greater was Henry Hallam's alarm when his son announced his engagement the following Christmas, with its prospect of marriage into the 'black-blooded' Tennysons. He forbade Arthur to see Emily again until he came of age and made intractable difficulties over any question of a settlement. Hallam sublimated his frustration by the enthusiastic promotion of his friend's poems.

The Apostles' political idealism reached a climax in the summer of 1830 – as, just over a century later, did that of another generation – by practical involvement in Spanish affairs. Byron at Missolonghi had made the cause of oppressed foreign peoples topical and romantic; now the exiled Spanish dissident General Torrijos drew on the sympathies of English liberals to involve themselves in his attempt to overthrow the tyrannical Ferdinand VII. Their heads ruled by their hearts, the Apostles plunged into the adventure. Trench summed up their mood: 'anything seems to me preferable to rotting in England, one's energies turning inward and corrupting: it is action, action, action that we want'. Kemble and Trench sailed with Torrijos for Gibraltar. Hallam and Tennyson travelled overland with money and messages for insurgents in the Pyrenees. Though the episode ended tragically, with Torrijos shot and the would-be revolutionaries reassembling in Cambridge disillusioned and wiser, Tennyson never forgot his days in the valley of Cauteretz, where Hallam nursed him through an illness and where he entered on an important period of poetry-writing. The black sombreros and voluminous cloaks that he was to affect for the rest of his life were mementoes of those sunlit Pyrenean days.

The following October term coincided with agricultural riots and widespread lawlessness in England. Hallam wrote to Trench in December: 'while I write, Madingley, or some adjoining village, is in a state of conflagration, and the sky above is coloured flame red'. 'Captain Swing' and his rick-burners were active in the vicinity, and the undergraduates formed volunteer groups to put out fires and defend the town. Over fifty years later, Tennyson remembered how he had helped put out a blazing farmhouse at Coton:

> I well remember that red night
> When thirty ricks
>
> All flaming, made an English homestead Hell –
> These hands of mine
> Have helped to pass a bucket from the well
> Along the line.

While he sympathised with the people, he could not support lawlessness. In 'Swing, at Cambridge', a poem written jointly by Lushington and Venables, Tennyson's reactionary attitude towards trouble-makers (so different from his encouragement of revolution in another country a few months earlier) is under-lined when the students prepare to defend Cambridge from attack:

Unto the poet wise we spoke,
'Is any law of battle broke,
By pouring from afar
Water or oil, or melted lead?'
The poet raised his massive head –
'Confound the laws of war.'

In December, William Wordsworth stayed at the Master's Lodge on one of his visits and reported 'a respectable show of blossom in poetry. Two brothers of the name of Tennyson, in particular, are not a little promising.' (Charles's *Sonnets and Fugitive Pieces*, published in Cambridge that year, had been praised by Coleridge.) Wordsworth attended the Commemoration Day service in the chapel, where Spedding and Hallam gave declamations – 'it was verily splendid to see the poet Wordsworth's face, for he was there,' Monteith wrote to Milnes, 'kindle as Hallam proceeded with it'. Spedding invited the poet to coffee in his rooms; all the college's leading lights attended – except, curiously, Tennyson and Hallam. They had already taken the coach for Somersby, where Hallam was to propose to Emily.

Tennyson stayed just one more term at Cambridge before the death of his father in March 1831 terminated his university career. His last night as an undergraduate was spent with Spedding and Thompson in Corpus Buildings, dancing nostalgic quadrilles (he was a keen dancer) in the bare rooms. At 2.30 in the morning he and Charles boarded the coach across the way at the Bull, and Tennyson's last memory was of Thompson's affectionate face illuminated by a gas lamp. He never took his degree, though both Charles and the reprobate Frederick returned in the following October and took theirs with Hallam in January 1832. All three Tennysons left considerable bills, which their grandfather eventually had to pay off.

Tennyson, in Hallam's words, 'resisted all attempts to force him into a profession, preferring poetry, and an honourable poverty'. Hallam himself moved back to London and went through the motions of studying for the bar, but emotionally he was killing time before he could see Emily again. In the summer of 1832 he and Tennyson journeyed to the Rhine, but the jaunt lacked the excitement of their Spanish vacation. Then Tennyson retired to Somersby to brood over the savage reviews that had greeted his 1832 volume. Only occasionally did he dash up to London to see Hallam and his other friends. In the autumn of 1833, perhaps impelled by some premonition, he came to see Hallam off on a Continental tour with his father. It was to be the last time he ever set eyes on his best friend and most unselfish champion.

Hallam died suddenly in Vienna of a cerebral haemorrhage on 15 September 1833. For years he had put a brave face on his ill health, and probably could have died at any time; but his death came like a bolt of fate to the circle of Cambridge friends. Henry Alford described it as 'a loud and terrible stroke from the reality of things upon the faery building of our youth'. For Tennyson the tragedy was to constitute the central trauma of his life: redoubling his fatalistic morbidity, it provided the inspiration for some of his greatest poetry. Under the double shock of Hallam's death and the hostile reviews, he refrained from publication for a decade, leading a wandering, introspective life, slowly accumulating the body of lyrics that eventually made up his elegiac masterpiece, *In Memoriam A.H.H.* (1850). During the course of those years he often revisited places sanctified by their association with Hallam, and in 1838 (as he tells in section LXXXVII of the poem) he came back to Cambridge to muse – no more now than an anonymous figure shrouded in his Spanish cape – over the scenes where he and his companions had walked and talked and where, in those first-floor rooms in New Court, there had been no doubt whose was the noblest and most penetrating mind.

> I past beside the reverend walls
>   In which of old I wore the gown;
>   I roved at random thro' the town,
> And saw the tumult of the halls;
>
> And heard once more in college fanes
>   The storm their high-built organs make,
>   And thunder-music, rolling, shake
> The prophet blazoned on the panes;
>
> And caught once more the distant shout,
>   The measured pulse of racing oars
>   Among the willows; paced the shores
> And many a bridge, and all about
>
> The same grey flats again, and felt
>   The same, but not the same; and last
>   Up that long walk of limes I past
> To see the rooms in which he dwelt.
>
> Another name was on the door:
>   I lingered; all within was noise
>   Of songs, and clapping hands, and boys
> That crashed the glass and beat the floor;
>
> Where once we held debate, a band
>   Of youthful friends, on mind and art,
>   And labour, and the changing mart,
> And all the framework of the land;
>
> When one would aim an arrow fair,
>   But send it slackly from the string;
>   And one would pierce an outer ring,
> And one an inner, here and there;
>
> And last the master-bowman, he,
>   Would cleave the mark. A willing ear
>   We lent him. Who, but hung to hear
> The rapt oration flowing free

'Up that long walk of limes'

From point to point, with power and grace
    And music in the bounds of law,
    To those conclusions when we saw
The God within him light his face,

And seem to lift the form, and glow
    In azure orbits heavenly-wise;
    And over those ethereal eyes
The bar of Michael Angelo.

15

'The light sarcastic eye'

Another name was on the door: Tennyson's disillusionment was just. The liberal impetus of his Trinity generation had passed to Oxford, which grew clamorous with movements and ideas, while at Cambridge the eighteenth century continued to flow on into Victorian times. Even Darwin, Tennyson's Cambridge contemporary, was stimulated at Cambridge to an interest in hunting, smoking, and beetle-chasing rather than in scientific discovery. Sir Walter Besant, who came up to Christ's in 1855, wrote later of 'the dullness, the incapacity, the stupidity' of the dons of his day, the utter idleness of the undergraduates. In literature, the fifty years after Tennyson's departure bubble with parody and burlesque, belles-lettres and sentiment, producing no one much more eminent than a string of editors of *Punch*. Greatness is mimicked, as in the parodies of C. S. Calverley, or recalled, as in Augustine Birrell's enquiry into why all great poets were Cambridge men (he was Tennyson's son-in-law); occasionally it visits (Tennyson's own last visit to Cambridge was in 1886); but for more than half a century it is not produced by Cambridge.

In such circumstances, Charles Kingsley (1819–75) acquires unwonted stature. If his 'Muscular Christianity', the evangelical influence of Charles Simeon, and the ecclesiological activities of the Cambridge Camden Society constituted the three nearest approaches to a Cambridge 'movement', Kingsley perhaps had the widest appeal. Yet his choice of college exemplifies at once the ambiguity of his position, for Magdalene, which he entered in 1838 (he lived on c staircase in the front court) was notoriously sporty and his student career hardly suggested a moral force in the making. Though shy and stammering at first, he was soon outstripping his contemporaries at their own pursuits: sinking pewters of ale, smoking as heavily as Tennyson, rowing in the college's second boat, and hunting, shooting, and fishing in all weathers (he thought nothing of climbing out of college at three in the morning to walk nine miles to Duxford in pouring rain in the hope of hooking trout). He attended Professor Sedgwick's famous horseback geology lectures, taken at a gallop over the Cambridgeshire countryside; mathematical lessons with the Senior Tutor were palliated with oysters and cigars. Kingsley's wife, whom he met during his first vacation, later compared him to the hero, Lancelot Smith, of his first novel, *Yeast* (1848), whom another character describes as

> one of a set who tried to look like blackguards, and really succeeded tolerably. They used to eschew gloves, and drink nothing but beer, and smoke disgusting short pipes, and when we established the Coverley Club in Trinity, they set up an opposition and called themselves the Navvies. And they used to make piratical expeditions to Lynn in eight oars, to attack bargemen and fen girls, and shoot ducks, and sleep under turf-stacks, and come home when they had drunk all the public-house taps dry.

In his last year, however, Kingsley suddenly reformed. He plunged into desperate cramming, resulting in headaches and the application of leeches but also a first in classics and a second in mathematics. Ordained in 1842, he took a position at Eversley near Reading, his home for the rest of his life.

Having turned a new leaf, Kingsley looked back on Cambridge with polemical censure in his second novel, *Alton Locke* (1850), in some chapters of which his young Chartist tailor visits Cambridge and is disgusted by the behaviour of the upper-class undergraduates. The noble buildings and institutions have been prostituted to the use of the idle rich, he feels, in violation of the spirit of their foundation. As Locke wanders King's Parade in the moonlight, he reflects bitterly on the circumstances that exclude him from his rightful inheritance.

But Kingsley, though a lifelong champion of working men's education, later toned down some of these passages when he had opportunity to see for himself that reform was under way. For in 1860, to his surprise, he was appointed Regius Professor of History, and, returning to Cambridge, detected 'increased sympathy between the old and young, increased intercourse between the teacher and the taught'.

He himself contributed significantly to the improved atmosphere. Though not a professional historian, Kingsley was an inspiring lecturer who achieved a rapport with his students far removed from his predecessor Gray's total aloofness. At his inaugural lecture he 'was received with deafening cheers upon the mention of his name before he came in, again when he came in, and a third time when he ended his lecture'. Cheering became traditional at his appearances. 'His eye used to glisten, his voice in its remarkable sea-like modulations to swell like an organ as he recounted something great, till his audience listened, quite spell-bound, fixed, till the climax came, and then rushed into a cheer before they were well aware of it.' He would stammer, 'Gentlemen, you must not do it. I cannot lecture to you if you do', but the cheering went on. He drew similarly packed audiences when he preached in Great St Mary's. The student Prince of Wales (later Edward VII), who attended tutorials at Kingsley's Cambridge address, 13 Fitzwilliam Street, came away as instilled with an interest in history as he had previously been disaffected by it at Oxford.

Consciousness perhaps of the academic shortcomings which 'proper' historians picked on in his lectures led Kingsley to pepper his popular last novel, *Hereward the Wake* (1866), with footnotes and scholarly references. The resistance of Hereward, 'Last of the English', against the Norman conquerors is set largely in and around the Isle of Ely, and abounds with evocations of the ancient fenland scene:

> He held on over the Fleam-dyke: but he feared to turn downwards into the Cambridge flats, and kept his vantage-ground upon the downs; till, on top of the Gogmagog, he struck the old Roman road, which men call 'Wort's Causeway' at this day. Down that he turned, short to the right, toward the green meadows, and the long line of mighty elms, and the little village which clustered, unconscious of its coming glories, beneath the new French keep, beside the Roman bridge . . .
>
> The Wake was, of course, too wise to go through Cambridge street, under the eyes of the French garrison. But he saw that the Roman road led straight to a hamlet some mile above the town; and at the road end, he guessed, there must be either a bridge or a ford. There he could cross the Cam . . .
>
> Into the ford – by Chaucer's after-famous mill – he dashed, making more splash than ever did geese in Shelford Fen; and out again, and on to the clay wold, and away for Coton and Madingley rise, and the black wall of oak, and ash, and elm.
>
> And as he entered the forest at Madingley, he rose in his stirrups, with a shout of 'A Wake! A Wake!' which was heard, for aught he cared, in Cambridge Castle.

Kingsley, brought up in Lincolnshire, was one of the first writers to find the fens romantic. In a lecture delivered in 1867 to the Mechanics Institute in Cambridge, he rhapsodised over those vanished wastes where once 'high overhead hung, motionless, hawk beyond hawk, buzzard beyond buzzard, kite beyond kite, as far as eye could see', where the coot clanked and the bittern boomed, 'while clear above all sounded the wild whistle of the curlew, and the trumpet note of the great white swan'.

Kingsley's publishers, Macmillan, began in Cambridge in 1843 when two enterprising young Scotsmen, Daniel and Alexander Macmillan, took over a bookshop at 17 Trinity Street; two years later they moved to No. 1 on the corner by Great St Mary's – a bookshop since 1581 – and began to issue their own publications. Their premises were always much more than a shop. Wordsworth had visited them at No. 17, and No. 1 became one of the cultural meeting places of Cambridge, an informal club where don and undergraduate, writer and booklover, from Cambridge and beyond, chatted, smoked, and exchanged points of view. Here Kingsley came up from Eversley 'in a sort of sailor's dress' to submit the manuscript of *Alton Locke*; here F. D. Maurice and others propagated their Christian Socialism; here Thomas Hughes, author of *Tom Brown's Schooldays*, appeared; here Thackeray lunched in November 1851 before lecturing on the English humorists; here Tennyson gave one of his incantatory renderings of

Maud. With several bestsellers under their belt, the Macmillans eventually transferred their publishing interest to London, and a nephew, Robert Bowes, joined the bookshop, which became Macmillan & Bowes. (His son became a partner in 1899; in 1907 the shop became Bowes & Bowes. It is now the Cambridge University Press shop.)

Like Kingsley, William Cory (1823–92), originally William Johnson, was an influential educator, though his influence remained largely limited to Eton and King's (he was passed over for the professorship in Kingsley's favour, and again in 1869 on Kingsley's retirement). Now remembered mainly as the author of the 'Eton Boating Song' and of 'They told me, Heraclitus, they told me you were dead', Cory was a first-rate classicist who came up to King's in 1842 and won the Chancellor's English Medal for 1843 with his poem 'Plato'. He was elected to the Apostles and to a fellowship at King's, but returned to Eton where he taught until 1872, when he left under a cloud (because of a homosexual scandal) and was obliged to change his name. He published two slender volumes of verse, *Ionica* and *Ionica II* (the latter a curiosity printed by the University Press without title, author's name, or punctuation); and his *Letters and Journals*, published in 1897, exude a High Victorian platonic educational spirit. His spiritual progeny (and pupil at Eton) was Oscar Browning, who resigned his own teaching post there in similar circumstances three years after Cory (see p. 178, below).

Although likewise a classical scholar, minor poet, and influential teacher, Charles Stuart Calverley (1831–84) was otherwise totally different. From Harrow Calverley went first to Balliol College, Oxford, where he was sent down for what the Master termed 'desultory and idle habits, and wicked acts of gross immorality' – mainly smoking, keeping dogs, and scaling walls after hours.[1] He transferred in 1852 to Christ's College, Cambridge, where the authorities were apparently more indulgent.

Calverley, who won several classical awards and graduated in 1856 as Second Classicist, could write as fluently in Latin and Greek as in English, and the bulk of his work consists of classical poetry translated into English or – very odd to modern tastes – English classics turned into Latin or Greek. But he was principally known as a mimic and parodist, whose imitations of Browning, Tennyson, and other poets are not only witty in themselves but studied replicas, metrically and stylistically, of their originals.

Stocky, curly-haired, bearded, 'the hero of a hundred tales', Calverley combined mental brilliance with extraordinary physical powers. His feats of leaping were legendary. Wearing cap and gown and with his hands in his pockets, he once jumped over a horse drawing a cart in Green Street. On another occasion, finding himself locked out of his first-floor rooms in the front court of Christ's, he

---

[1] 'That is the Chapel, that is the Master's Lodge', Calverley is reputed to have told some visitors he was showing round Balliol, 'and that, if I'm not mistaken' – picking up a pebble and lobbing it at a window – 'is the Master himself'.

bounded onto the pediment over the staircase entrance and dived through the window. His most celebrated exploit took place one Sunday at Trumpington when he unhooked the inn sign outside the Green Man and made off with it in the direction of Cambridge. The innkeeper and numerous customers gave chase, but Calverley, burdened as he was, managed to race them back to Christ's, where he called on the porter to bar the gate and carried his trophy in triumph to his rooms. When the Dean, roused by the uproar outside the college, demanded the meaning of the disturbance, Calverley, ever ready with the apt quotation, replied: 'Sir, an evil and adulterous generation seek after a sign, but no sign shall be given' (Matthew 12:39).

Calverley was another great Victorian tobacco addict and became a cherished customer of Bacon's, the Cambridge tobacconists, to whom there are references scattered about his works and outside whose former premises on the corner of Rose Crescent and Market Hill still hang some verses from his 'Ode to Tobacco' cast in bronze.[2] Bacon's appear again with other local tradesmen in his humorous self-portrait, 'Hic *Vir*, Hic Est':

> Past the Senate-house I saunter,
>   Whistling with an easy grace;
> Past the cabbage-stalks that carpet
>   Still the beefy market-place;
> Poising evermore the eye-glass
>   In the light sarcastic eye,
> Lest, by chance, some breezy nursemaid
>   Pass, without a tribute, by.
>
> Once, an assuming Freshman,
>   Thro' these wilds I wandered on,
> Seeing in each house a College,
>   Under every cap a Don:
> Each perambulating infant
>   Had a magic in its squall,
> For my eager eye detected
>   Senior Wranglers in them all.
>
> By degrees my education
>   Grew, and I became as others;
> Learned to blunt my moral feelings

---

[2] Bacon's, founded in 1805, and trading in Cambridge from 1810 until their demise in 1983, are probably the only tobacconists to be the subject of a *Times* leader (22 October 1935). Calverley was not the only writer to owe them a debt, metaphorical or otherwise. The Tennysons were regular customers (Alfred still owed them 2s 10d in 1833), and others included Fitzgerald, Samuel Butler, Walter Besant, Leslie Stephen, and F. C. Burnand. Professor Kingsley was in the shop every other day, stocking up with pounds of Bird's Eye Mixture and barrels of fresh clay pipes. A typical entry under his name in the ledger for 1861 reads: '2 lb mixture, 20 dozen pipes, box Vesuvius, £1 2s 0d.' (Vesuviuses were extra-powerful matches that enabled outdoor smokers like Kingsley to light up in gales and downpours.)

> By the aid of Bacon Brothers;
> Bought me tiny boots of Mortlock,
> And colossal prints of Roe;
> And ignored the proposition
> That both time and money go.

Calverley was elected to a fellowship at Christ's in 1857 and taught there until his marriage in 1863; three years later a skating accident put paid to a promising legal career but he continued to produce translations and parodies until his early death. W. W. Skeat (1835–1912), the editor of Chaucer, who became professor of Anglo-Saxon in 1878, was a close friend of Calverley's at Christ's, as was Sir Walter Besant (1836–1901), who studied under Calverley and recalled how he 'kept a kind of open house for his intimates, with abundance of port and claret'. At a time when the academic study of English literature was unknown, Calverley caused a sensation by holding an examination for his friends in the *Pickwick Papers*, with questions ranging from 'What kind of cigars did Mr Ben Allen chiefly smoke?' to 'Who, besides Mr Pickwick, is recorded to have worn gaiters?' Besant took first prize, Skeat second, and as a result of the publicity *Pickwick* sold better for a while than any other book in Cambridge. Besant also recalls being invited to Calverley's rooms to meet a charming young Frenchman, 'who told quantities of stories in a quiet, irresponsible way, as if he was an outsider looking on at the world' and sang Italian arias with Calverley. This was George du Maurier, the author of *Trilby*.

Indolently brilliant (his friends often had to drag him from bed to attend – or give – lectures), scholarly without ever appearing to work, unconventionally athletic, a master of pastiche and parody, 'C.S.C.' became a kind of English archetype; his books were required reading for generations of undergraduates and the inspiration for a whole school of succeeding Cambridge versifiers, including A. C. Hilton, J. K. Stephen, A. A. Milne, J. C. Squire, and most of the early contributors to *The Granta*. Yet he never ventured successfully beyond translations and humorous verse, and his expulsion from Oxford (where he would never have been heard amid the great Victorian flowering of literary talent) and subsequent predominance at Cambridge only emphasise the contrast between the two universities at the time.

The first of the Calverley school, Arthur Clement Hilton (1851–77), who had begun writing charades and skits at Marlborough, brought out while at St John's a celebrated magazine, *The Light Green*, almost entirely written by himself, the two issues of which (May and November 1872) contained parodies of Swinburne, Tennyson, Edward Lear, and others, including such classics as 'The Vulture and the Husbandman' (a parody of Lewis Carroll's 'The Walrus and the Carpenter') and 'The Heathen Pass-ee' (a parody of a parody: Bret Harte's 'Heathen Chin-ee' was modelled on Swinburne). Slightly younger, James Kenneth Stephen (1859–92), who came up to King's in 1878, was President of the Union in 1880 and a Fellow of King's from 1885. Still remembered by Etonians for his nostalgic poems 'My Old School' and 'The Old School List', he also wrote many clever parodies and, like Calverley, was credited with legendary powers of extempore wit and composition. He returned to Cambridge in 1891 to take pupils and was an early contributor to *The Granta*, but his health had been impaired[3] and he died insane the following year.

Stephen came from a distinguished literary family with several Cambridge connections, none more aptly personifying the mid-Victorian don than his uncle Sir Leslie Stephen (1832–1904). Son of Sir James Stephen (Kingsley's predecessor as professor), father of Virginia Woolf, Leslie Stephen entered Trinity Hall in 1850 and remained pleasurably immersed in Cambridge for the next fourteen years. For him, Cambridge was tobacco parliaments at midnight in college rooms, sipping wine beneath the cascading chestnuts of the Fellows' Garden while nightingales sang along the Backs, tender friendships (he wrote the biography of his fellow collegian Henry Fawcett, the blind professor of political economy and Postmaster-General), vigorous bumping races (he rowed every year for his college), mammoth walks (he thought nothing of walking to London), and mountaineering in the vacations (he had smoked his pipe on top of the Eiger). Edward Fitzgerald would have applauded Stephen's integration of physical and mental fitness, but his response to questions of intellectual moment was less vigorous. He accepted ordination as a requirement for a fellowship, and it was years before his unbelief finally troubled him enough to resign. But at last he did uproot himself to London, where he became eminent as a critic and as compiler of the *Dictionary of National Biography*.

Leslie Stephen's attitude towards Cambridge remained one of waggish affection. In his essay on Coleridge in *Hours in a Library*, he writes:

> Cambridge, the mother of poets, received him with the kindness she has so often shown to her children. We – I speak as a Cambridge man – we flogged (or nearly flogged) Milton into republicanism; we disgusted Dryden into an anomalous and monstrous preference for Oxford; we bored Gray, till half stifled with academic dulness, he sought more cheerful surroundings in a country churchyard; we left Byron to the congenial society of his bear; we did nothing for Wordsworth, except, indeed, that we took him to Milton's rooms, and there for once (it must really have done him some good) induced him to take a glass too much; and we, as nearly as possible, converted Coleridge into a heavy dragoon.

The same sentimentally humorous tone pervades his *Sketches from Cambridge* (1865),[4] in which Stephen depicts the types and mores of his day – the wine parties and riots (not, he laments, what they were), the dull shuffling

---

[3] Curiously, like Calverley's, by a knock on the head. Calverley's was sustained while skating, Stephen's by collision with a windmill. Hilton too was once concussed, by a jam jar.
[4] Itself a kind of up-market version of John Delaware Lewis's more satirical *Sketches of Cantabs* of 1849.

mathematical men, the reeking Cam ('that big sewer at the back of the college'),[5] and the laissez-faire dons ('Hallo! easy all! Hard word here. Smith, what does it mean?' asks a rowing-minded lecturer. 'I don't know', says Smith. 'No more don't I. Paddle on all!'). Oxford is gently mocked as a hotbed of disputatiousness – but even Stephen at last apparently had enough of mid-Victorian 'paddle-on-all' Cambridge.

A somewhat later Trinity Hall don was Edward Carpenter (1844–1929), who also threw up a safe career as Fellow and curate of St Edward's Church, under the influence of Walt Whitman's poetry and the realisation of his own homosexuality, to don sandals and live on the land near Sheffield with working-class lovers. Carpenter's ideas were to inspire many later writers, including E. M. Forster in his homosexual novel, *Maurice*.

If dons were complacent, the undergraduate 'Bucks' remained often as uninhibited as in the days of Gray. Sir Francis Cowley Burnand (1836–1917) chronicles a mid-Victorian Etonian's life at Trinity in his *Records and Reminiscences*, with supper parties, theatrical jinks, and general high-spirited fun filling most pages; his equally diverting *Personal Reminiscences of the A.D.C.* described how in 1855 he founded the Amateur Dramatic Club (the first such undergraduate society at Cambridge). The club gave its first performance without permission in hired rooms at the back of the Hoop Hotel, with a speaking-tube run from the bar to the green room to give warning in case the proctors arrived, and a ladder and gowns laid ready for a quick getaway into the back yard. But the authorities turned a blind eye and the ADC went on to become an important ingredient in the Bohemian student life of the time. Its staple fare was burlesque and farce ('We aimed low, and hit the mark exactly'), of which Burnand was a prolific composer. He was later editor of *Punch* in succession to the equally fertile Tom Taylor (1817–80), another Trinity humorist, and antecedent to Sir Owen Seaman of Clare: from 1874 to 1932 *Punch* was solidly in Cambridge hands.

The gallimaufry life of the public-school set is likewise portrayed in *The Cambridge Freshman*, a novel by 'Martin Legrand', pseudonym of James Rice of Queens' (1843–82), for many years Walter Besant's literary collaborator; and in *The Foster Brothers* by James Payn of Trinity (1830–98), another friend of Besant and Calverley, who borrows Thackeray's 'St Boniface' for its setting. But the best of its fictional evocations is the two-volume *Charlie Villars at Cambridge* (1868) by George L. Tottenham of Trinity (1844–1910), a novel so graphic in its detail that it might have been compiled expressly for the social historian. Without

---

[5] Letter to the *Cambridge Chronicle*, 24 September 1859, describing a visit by the Poet Laureate, Tennyson, with F. T. Palgrave: 'The two were seen in Trinity walks with their handkerchiefs up to their olfactories, to prevent their inhaling the odours of the two filthy mud banks on each side of the watercourse called the Cam.' Gwen Raverat in *Period Piece* recalls Queen Victoria eyeing all the pieces of paper floating in the river and asking the Master of Trinity what they were. 'Notices forbidding bathing, Ma'am,' he replied with great presence of mind.

artistic aspirations to plot or characterisation, *Charlie Villars* follows its Harrovian hero episodically from the moment he first arrives at Cambridge station to his graduation. There are descriptions of dinner in hall, where the students hack mangled joints and the gyps scoop leftovers into their pockets; of billiards at Brown's in Ram Yard and chops at Litchfield's in All Saints' Passage; of races at Newmarket and the Drag at Histon; of acting at the ADC and spouting at the Union; of Fifth of November fisticuffs and arm-in-arms through the Backs at midnight with one's chum. There are impromptu pony-trap races:

> Over the ruts – across the grass – they went, Egerton leading – through the turnpike – down the road to the railway bridge, where Castleton came up and tried to pass; but Egerton, standing up, gave his pony a few cuts with the whip, which sent him along at an unapproachable pace. Through Barnwell, frightening all the curs of the place, – past Midsummer Common they rattled, both standing up now like charioteers of old, – up Jesus Lane – every one making way for them, and past Death's, where Castleton made a final effort, and got his head in front; but trying to pass between Egerton and a waggon, caught his wheel . . .

There is cat-hunting to hounds through the streets of Cambridge; cribbing at exams; wild dinners with the Beef-Steak Club; 'larking' with hacks; and, on rainy days, a visit to Callaby's nefarious menagerie on Midsummer Common, where one can buy a dog (trained to return to its proprietor), take pot shots at a pigeon tied to a string, or drop a terrier among imprisoned rats.

More homiletic is *Julian Home: A Tale of College Life* (1859) by F. W. Farrar (1831–1903), who came up to Trinity in 1852, won the Chancellor's English Medal, and was an Apostle. Moral didacticism is as evident here as in Farrar's earlier school story, *Eric, or Little by Little*, and his college characters are of the stock variety: the industrious Julian, who spurns an inheritance in order to come up from 'Harton School' (Harrow; Farrar wrote the book while a teacher there) to 'St Werner's College, Camford' (Trinity, Cambridge) as a sizar; the exalted fellow-commoner Vyvyan Bruce, sneering in the butteries at the sizars dining off leftovers; the idle Kennedy, giving in to temptation when he finds himself (as he thinks) alone in his tutor's study with the draft Greek examination on the desk; or the villain Brogten, who morally blackmails Kennedy and who screws Julian into his room on the morning of a vital scholarship exam, only to be rescued from the river at 'Gower's Mill' (Chaucer's Mill) by – of course – Kennedy and Julian themselves. The book ends with the double wedding of Julian and Kennedy and their virtuous sisters.

Samuel Butler (1835–1902), satirical author of *Erewhon* and *The Way of All Flesh*, grandson of the Butler who defeated Coleridge for the Craven award, came up to St John's from Shrewsbury School in 1854. At Cambridge he pursued his interests in art and music, coxed the college boat (a mishap with the steering rope nearly cost Lady Margaret the Headship of the River), and joined the 'Upware

Republic' – an undergraduate allegiance of the 1850s which met at the lonely fenland inn known as the 'Five Miles from Anywhere: No Hurry' for shooting, fishing, and drinking. (On 10 February 1855, according to a surviving record, Butler and two friends skated on the Cam from Waterbeach to Upware in seventeen minutes – 'splendid ice!').

In his autobiographical novel *The Way of All Flesh* (1903) Butler casts light on student life at the opposite end of the social scale from Charlie Villars. Until they were swept away in the 1860s to make way for Scott's new chapel, there existed at St John's a congeries of tumbledown rooms, reached by a winding passage from the first court, and known as the Wilderness or Labyrinth, where sizars and scholarship men were housed in industrious obscurity.

> In the labyrinth there dwelt men of all ages, from mere lads to grey-haired old men who had entered late in life. They were rarely seen except in hall or chapel or at lecture, where their manners of feeding, praying and studying, were considered alike objectionable; no one knew whence they came, whither they went, nor what they did, for they never showed at cricket or the boats; they were a gloomy, seedy-looking confrerie, who had as little to glory in in clothes and manners as in the flesh itself . . . I have seen some of these men attain high position in the world of politics or science, and yet still retain a look of labyrinth and Johnian sizarship.

Simeonism is rife among the Labyrinth, and the 'Sims' go about at night dropping tracts into the letter-boxes of students they consider in need of saving. Butler's hero, Ernest Pontifex, tired of receiving such exhortations, has a parody printed and delivered to the letter-boxes of the Simeonites – an incident based on fact, for Butler himself performed such a prank. Despite this resistance, when Ernest is eventually lured to hear an evangelical preacher, the effect is devastating. Repenting of his indolent ways, he determines to turn over a new leaf, beginning by locking away his smoking apparatus under the bed. For a week or two he is a changed man. Then the old lazy doubts creep back. Exactly where in the Bible, after all, is tobacco forbidden?

Butler's first appearance in print was an article contributed in 1858 to the very first number of the college magazine, *The Eagle* (the first college magazine at either Oxford or Cambridge). To the fifth number he contributed an account of an economical Continental tour he had made, signed 'Cellarius', and concluding with his pleasure to be back at 'dear old St John's', where, looking out on the Backs from his college window (his rooms were on D staircase of New Court), he commented: 'for a continuance, I would rather have this than any scene I have visited during the whole of our most enjoyed tour'. After taking his degree in 1859, however, Butler resisted the twin temptations of ordination (which his family expected) and a 'continuance' at St John's (his tripos results promised a fellowship) and disappeared to New Zealand for five years to take up sheep-farming. From there he sent two more articles to *The Eagle* as 'Our Emigrant'.

Among the Labyrinth's 'grey-haired old men' was the Dorset poet William Barnes (1801–86), who came up to St John's in his forties as a 'ten-year man'. These mature students, under an archaic Elizabethan statute, were allowed to take a Bachelor of Divinity's degree by keeping their names on the books for ten years, the only residence requirement being three terms during the final two years. Barnes entered his name in 1838 and came to Cambridge for the first time in the summer of 1847, leaving his wife in charge of his school in Dorchester. He wrote to her: 'I am in that part of the college which the men call the Wilderness, one side of the first or oldest court. I ascend to my room by a dismal dusty decayed staircase of dark oak, trodden by gownsmen of many generations.' But he missed Dorset and his family, and 'at last, in 1850, at a more trying cost of time in residence in Cambridge than even of money, I took my degree'. (The 'ten-year men' regulation was abolished in 1858.)

Two widely travelled Victorian writers were both educated at Caius. George Alfred Henty (1832–1902), the prolific and popular writer of boys' fiction, was born at Trumpington. His family moved to Kent when he was five. After a boyhood of fragile health and butterfly-collecting, Henty came up to Caius in 1852 and took up rowing, boxing and wrestling in preparation for the globe-trotting years that were to provide the diverse scenes of action for his books; but his studies caused a collapse at the end of his first year, and no sooner had he returned after taking a year off than the Crimean War broke out and he threw up the university to become a war correspondent.

Charles Montagu Doughty (1843–1926), author of *Travels in Arabia Deserta* and the epic poem *The Dawn in Britain*, entered Caius in 1861. A shy and rather humourless man, resentful of lectures and compulsory chapel, his chief interests at that time were geology and natural science. He haunted the Barnwell gravel pits, the Cherry Hinton chalk pits, and the local coprolite diggings for fossils; but as Caius did not favour the new natural science tripos he transferred for a while to Downing. He graduated in 1865 after a spell studying glaciers in Norway. Doughty's literary taste ran to nothing later than the Elizabethans, and his account of his harrowing vicissitudes in Arabia, first published by the University Press in 1888, was couched in a style, compounded of Chaucer, Spenser, and Arabic, that discouraged a popular audience (but greatly influenced T. E. Lawrence). Doughty was made an honorary Fellow of Caius in 1907 and awarded an honorary doctorate in 1920. His Arabian notebooks were acquired for the Fitzwilliam Museum in 1922.

The firm of Morris & Company, founded by equally confirmed Chaucerians and medievalists, was active at Cambridge in the 1860s and 1870s, redecorating Peterhouse and Queens' College halls and Jesus College Chapel, and decorating the new All Saints' Church in Jesus Lane. The Oxonian William Morris (1834–96) once wrote: 'As to Cambridge, it is rather a hole of a place, and can't compare for a moment with Oxford'; and the *Oxford and Cambridge Magazine* which he and his friends had produced in 1856 had been largely an Oxford affair. (The main

Cambridge contributor was Vernon Lushington, an ex-midshipman who rose to be President of the Union.)

John Ruskin (1819–1900) was another Oxonian who paid visits to Cambridge, where his friends included William Whewell, now Master of Trinity, F. W. H. Myers, Fellow of Trinity and one of the founders of the Society for Psychical Research, and Oscar Browning (1837–1923) of King's. Ruskin lectured to the Cambridge School of Art in 1858 and delivered the Rede Lecture in 1867. He too thought Oxford the superior place, and his *Seven Lamps of Architecture* (1849) criticised the exterior of King's College Chapel in terms as pedagogic as Gilpin's strictures on its interior eighty years before:

> What a host of ugly church towers have we in England, with pinnacles at the corners, and none in the middle! How many buildings like King's College Chapel at Cambridge, looking like tables upside down, with their four legs in the air! . . . Knock down a couple of pinnacles at either end in King's College Chapel, and you will have a kind of proportion instantly.

Elsewhere in the same book he called the chapel 'a piece of architectural juggling', and on a visit to Cambridge in 1851 wrote that he found it 'uglier even than my remembrance of it'. Matthew Arnold (1822–88), also from Oxford, admired the Chapel when he visited Cambridge in 1853 as a schools inspector but felt that 'the Middle Ages and all their poetry and impressiveness are in Oxford and not here . . . It seems so strange to be in a place of colleges that is not Oxford.'

A fourth Oxonian, Oscar Wilde (1854–1900), paid two visits to Cambridge. In November 1879, as yet comparatively unknown, he was the guest at King's of Oscar Browning (see chapter 16, below). They attended a performance at the ADC together, and afterwards the cast were treated in Browning's rooms to the egotistical wit of the Cambridge Oscar, the paradoxical wit of the Oxonian. ('I wish he was *not* called Oscar,' Wilde lamented. They were both named after a Norwegian king.) On the second visit, in November 1885, Wilde was the guest of a literary group known as the Cicadas of which his young friend H. C. Marillier of Peterhouse was a member. Wilde saw that year's Greek play, the *Eumenides*, and is said to have first invented his story 'The Happy Prince' afterwards for the benefit of his hosts. He wrote to Marillier: 'I remember bright young faces, and grey misty quadrangles, Greek forms passing through Gothic cloisters, life playing among ruins, and, what I love best in the world, Poetry and Paradox dancing together!'[6]

Seven of the age's leading novelists – Dickens, George Eliot, Turgenev, Stevenson, Hardy, Trollope, and Henry James – paid visits to Cambridge.

---

6 Wilde kept up a stream of epigrams to the delighted undergraduates who accompanied him to the station, timing the most brilliant for the very moment the train pulled out. The effect was rather spoilt when the train came shunting back and redeposited him opposite the place where they were still standing.

Charles Dickens (1812–70) came three times on his public reading tours, reciting extracts from his works at the Guildhall. On the first visit, 17 and 18 October 1859, when he stayed at the Eagle Hotel, his appearances on stage were greeted by prolonged cheering, and hundreds had to be turned away. Dickens called the second night's audience 'the finest I have ever read to. They took every word of the *Dombey* in quite an amazing manner, and after the child's death, paused a little, and then set up a shout that it did one good to hear. Mrs Gamp then set in with a roar, which lasted until I had done.' Of his second visit, on 28 March 1867, when he read the first and last chapters of *Doctor Marigold* and the trial scene from *Pickwick*, the *Cambridge Chronicle* reported that 'the rapid change of his voice from the pathetic to the ludicrous were a study; he is a perfect author as far as physiognomical performance is concerned'; and Dickens himself wrote: 'The reception at Cambridge last night was something to be proud of in such a place. The colleges mustered in full force from the biggest guns to the smallest, and went far beyond even Manchester in the roars of welcome and the rounds of cheers . . . The place was crammed, and the success the most brilliant I have ever seen.' Dickens's last appearance, on 18 March 1869, was billed as 'One Farewell Reading' (he died the following year). No doubt Henry Fielding Dickens, his sixth son, who caused him such enormous pride by winning a scholarship at Trinity Hall, was in the audience.[7]

George Eliot (1819–80) first visited Cambridge with George Henry Lewes in February 1868 as guests of W. G. Clark, Vice-Master of Trinity and Public Orator, and of Oscar Browning (then still a master at Eton). Browning, who travelled down with them and saw them established at the Bull, wrote later: 'We dined in the evening, a small party, in Mr Clark's rooms. I sat next to her, and she talked to me solemnly about the duties of life . . . The next day she breakfasted with me in my rooms at college.' Browning ever after kept her picture above his desk.

She and Lewes next came in May 1873 as guests of F. W. H. Myers, and as the author of the recently published *Middlemarch* she was much feted. But when taken to see the boat races she fell in the estimation of the students, after a particularly exciting finish, by pronouncing that 'all human joys are transient'. Myers, however, to judge by the epic prose with which he immortalised the visit, was even more carried away than Browning:

> I remember how, at Cambridge, I walked with her once in the Fellows' Garden of Trinity, on an evening of rainy May; and she, stirred somewhat beyond her wont, and taking as her text the three words which have been used so often as the inspiring trumpet-calls of men – the words *God, Immortality, Duty* –

---

[7] In his first term (October 1868) Dickens sent 'Harry' 'three dozen sherry, two dozen port, and three dozen light claret' – more generous lubrication than even Byron had enjoyed – but warned him: 'Now, observe attentively. We must have no shadow of debt. Square up everything whatsoever that it has been necessary to buy. Let not a farthing be outstanding on any account.'

pronounced, with terrible earnestness, how inconceivable was the *first*, how unbelievable the *second*, and yet how peremptory and absolute the *third*. Never, perhaps, have sterner accents affirmed the sovereignty of impersonal and unrecompensing Law. I listened, and night fell; her grave, majestic countenance turned towards me like a Sibyl's in the gloom; it was as though she withdrew from my grasp, one by one, the two scrolls of promise, and left me the third scroll only, awful with inevitable fates. And when we stood at length and parted, amid that columnar circuit of the forest trees, beneath the last twilight of starless skies, I seemed to be gazing, like Titus at Jerusalem, on vacant seats and empty halls – on a sanctuary with no Presence to hallow it, and heaven left lonely of a God.

In May 1877 it was Myers's fellow spiritualist, the moral philosopher Henry Sidgwick, who was the host. George Eliot visited the two new ladies' colleges and was especially interested in Girton, to which she had subscribed. She used her experiences at Cambridge as basis for a poetic dialogue, *A College Breakfast Party* (1878). She was also a frequent guest at W. H. Hall's estate at nearby Six Mile Bottom (The Cottage, now The Hall, near The Lodge of Byron fame), and in October 1878 she and Ivan Turgenev (1818–83), great admirers of each other's works, reciprocated toasts there – 'to the greatest living novelist'.

Turgenev, who lived mostly outside Russia, had come to Six Mile Bottom ostensibly for the partridge shooting (said to be the finest in England; he was the author of *A Sportsman's Sketches*). He and George Eliot also visited Newmarket to watch the Cambridgeshire Stakes, but mostly there was serious talk, some of it recorded by the ubiquitous Oscar Browning. On 24 October, after his fellow novelist's departure, Turgenev was driven over by Henry Sidgwick to see something of Cambridge. He had visited Cambridge once before, in May 1871, when he had stayed at Trinity, probably as the guest of W. G. Clark. On this second occasion he lunched with Henry Fawcett at 18 Brookside and was afterwards taken by Mrs Fawcett and Mrs Sidgwick to see Newnham College, where he was introduced to young Jane Harrison, already famed as the cleverest woman in England and an ardent admirer of Russian literature. 'What would I not give to see colleges for women like this in my own country!' Turgenev told Mrs Fawcett as he left. Two days later he was in Oxford. 'I visited both the Universities – Cambridge and Oxford,' he wrote to Tolstoy. 'What incredible and subtle things they are, these English educational establishments!' He returned to shoot at Six Mile Bottom in 1880 and 1881.[8]

Also in Cambridge in October 1878 was Robert Louis Stevenson (1850–94), visiting his friend Sidney Colvin, Slade Professor of Art, with whom he

---

[8] Constance Garnett (1861–1946), the translator largely responsible for bringing Turgenev and the other great Russian writers to the English reading public, studied classics at Newnham in 1879–82. 'The beauty of Cambridge was overwhelming', she recalled. 'I was constantly wanting to cry. I had never imagined such a lovely place. I had never seen a beautiful building before.' (She came from Brighton.)

occasionally stayed between 1878 and 1885 at his rooms in Trinity, on A staircase, Great Court. Stevenson, at work on three projects simultaneously – *Providence and the Guitar*, *The New Arabian Nights*, and *Travels with a Donkey* – found his college surroundings unconducive to writing, as he told W. E. Henley:

> Here I am living like a fighting-cock, and have not spoken to a real person for about sixty hours. Those who wait on me are not real. The man [Colvin's gyp] I knew to be a myth, because I have seen him acting so often in the Palais Royal. He plays the Duke in *Tricoche et Cacolet*; I knew his nose at once. The part he plays here is very dull for him, but conscientious. As for the bedmaker, she's a dream, a kind of cheerful, innocent nightmare; I never saw so poor an imitation of humanity. I cannot work – *cannot*. Even the *Guitar* is still undone; I can only write ditch-water. 'Tis ghastly; but I am quite cheerful . . .

An unpublished novel featuring Cambridge people was never completed.

Thomas Hardy (1840–1928), who as a young man had hoped to study at Cambridge but had been unable to meet the entrance requirements, stayed at Queens' on 20 June 1873 with his close friend and mentor Horace Moule. An enigmatic poem, 'Standing by the Mantelpiece', subtitled 'H.M.M. 1873', apparently refers to their conversation that evening, during which Moule unconsciously touched the candle-wax as it was 'shaping to a shroud' – a sign, according to folk belief, that death soon awaited him. Early next morning, Hardy's diary records, Moule took him to King's College Chapel and 'opened the great West doors to show the interior vista: we got upon the roof, where we could see Ely Cathedral gleaming in the distant sunlight. A never-to-be-forgotten morning.'

The visit was to be invested with retrospective poignancy, for Moule, who was privately racked by frequent depressions, committed suicide in his college rooms that September – a tragedy that deserves the name 'Hardyesque' and helped to darken the novelist's perception of life. When Hardy returned to Cambridge in October 1880 with his first wife, Emma, for a week's visit as guests of Moule's brother, he pencilled '(Cambridge) H.M.M.' against the section of *In Memoriam* in which Tennyson revisits a Cambridge haunted by memories of Hallam, and marked the line 'Another name was on the door'. At evensong at King's his eye dwelt significantly on the candles:

> The reds and the blues of the windows became of one indistinguishable black, the candles guttered in the most fantastic shapes I ever saw, – and while the wicks burnt down these weird shapes changed form; so that you were fascinated into watching them, and wondering what shape those wisps of wax would take next, till they dropped off with a click during a silence. They were stalactites, plumes, laces; or rather they were surplices, – frayed shreds from those of bygone 'white-robed scholars', or from their shrouds – dropping bit by bit in a ghostly decay. Wordsworth's ghost, too, seemed to haunt the place, lingering and wandering on somewhere alone in the fan-traceried vaulting.

Hardy paid several later visits to Cambridge, most notably to attend the Milton tercentenary celebrations in 1909 and to receive an honorary doctorate in June 1913 (wearing the wrong gown). In September of the same year he was installed as honorary fellow of Magdalene (wearing his doctor's gown over a surplice).

Anthony Trollope's novel *John Caldigate* (1879), though nominally set in and around Cambridge, lacks local colour. His protagonist is heir to an unprepossessing estate in the Cambridgeshire fens, but after a frivolous career at the university running up debts he absconds to Australia to prospect for gold. He returns rich to claim the hand of Hester Bolton of Puritan Grange, Chesterton, but former mining associates turn up with incriminating evidence and he is thrown into Cambridge gaol for bigamy. He is finally exonerated by the sharp eye of a postal clerk named Bagwax, who reveals that a postmark is a forgery. (Though Trollope's grandfather, father, brother, and uncle studied at Cambridge, he himself never went to university. He probably got his background for the novel from visiting his favourite nephew, A. A. Tilley, who entered King's in 1871 and was later a Fellow of the college.)

In his essay 'English Vignettes' (1879), Henry James (1843–1916) mentions spending 'a beautiful Sunday morning walking about Cambridge . . . and attempting to *débrouiller* its charms'. These comprised

> the loveliest confusion of Gothic windows and ancient trees, of grassy banks and mossy balustrades, of sun-chequered avenues and groves, of lawns and gardens and terraces, of single-arched bridges spanning the little stream, which is small and shallow, and looks as if it had been turned on for ornamental purposes. The thin-flowing Cam appears to exist simply as an occasion for these brave little bridges – the beautiful covered gallery of John's or the slightly-collapsing arch of Clare.

James found particularly 'heart-shaking' the horse-chestnuts of Trinity Hall, whose 'giant limbs strike down into the earth, take root again and emulate, as they rise, the majesty of the parent stem'. James revisited Cambridge in July 1884, lunching with F. W. H. Myers at Leckhampton House and taking tea with the undergraduate A. C. Benson at King's after attending a service in the chapel. But his most memorable visit was to be twenty-five years later still.

16

'With the wind in their gowns'

The university's revised statutes of 1882, by freeing Fellows of colleges at last from the twin requirements of ordination and celibacy and so encouraging them to stay on at Cambridge instead of disappearing to country livings, resulted in a conspicuous intellectual revival, noticeable first in science and philosophy, but by the end of the century in literature also. Not only did the houses of the new Cambridge families – Darwins, Maitlands, Verralls, Cornfords, Keyneses, and so on – provide extracollegiate meeting grounds for dons and undergraduates, but from them emerged a number of writers born and bred in the town.

Life in one such household has been captivatingly recalled by Gwen Raverat, née Darwin (1885–1957), in her *Period Piece: A Cambridge Childhood* (1952). Granddaughter of the evolutionist, she was born at Newnham Grange, Silver Street (now part of Darwin College). Her father, George Darwin, was professor of astronomy, and Uncles Frank (lecturer in botany) and Horace (Mayor of Cambridge), as well as Grandmamma, built themselves houses on the Huntingdon Road. All five uncles (for 'a father is only a specialized kind of uncle') are portrayed as lovably eccentric, sharing the family hypochondria, relaxed erudition, and engaging remoteness from reality. *Period Piece* is full of horse-trams and chaperones, beggars and dancing-bears, penny-farthings and lamplighters, games of hide-and-seek with the Butler boys in Trinity Master's Lodge and of pirates on the river. Though the scene is predominantly an upper-class academic one, with all its straitlaced Victorian absurdities, perhaps no more evocative or entertaining book has ever been written about Cambridge.

Uncle Frank's daughter Frances (1886–1960), who appears in *Period Piece* (it was she who informed Gwen one day, as they snuggled under the wooden bridge that connected the Darwins' garden with Sheep's Green, that Christianity was untrue), was to show literary inclination much sooner than Gwen (whose success with *Period Piece* in her late sixties, after a distinguished career as a wood-engraver, took her family by surprise). At the age of sixteen, Frances Darwin (Frances Cornford as she later became) wrote a neat little poem, 'Autumn Morning at Cambridge', which already has her recognisable attributes:

I ran out in the morning, when the air was clean and new
And all the grass was glittering and grey with autumn dew,
I ran out to an apple-tree and pulled an apple down,
And all the bells were ringing in the old grey town.

Down in the town off the bridges and the grass,
They are sweeping up the old leaves to let the people pass,
Sweeping up the old leaves, golden-reds and browns,
Whilst the men go to lecture with the wind in their gowns.

Most of her poems were to be equally brief, their scene typically morning or sunset, the season autumnal. The leading Cambridge representative of the 'Georgian' style, Frances Cornford became a close friend of Rupert Brooke, who respected her judgement even though he rather scoffed at her poems as 'the old, old heart-cry business'.

Not everyone found the new academic suburbia as innocuous as Gwen Raverat. Although Cambridge never put on quite such a 'base and brickish skirt' as Gerard Manley Hopkins deprecated at Oxford, the change seemed ominous enough to some. A. C. Benson, in the *Cambridge Fortnightly* of 1888, complained that since 1882 Cambridge wore 'a worse, an altered face':

> thou art made
> A land of villas – load by load
> The waggons grumble past, and trade
> Is busy on the Barton Road.

The hero of H. G. Wells's novel *The New Machiavelli* (1911), who studies at Trinity in the 1890s, likewise castigates

> those roads and roads of stuffy little villas. Those little villas have destroyed all the good of the old monastic system and none of its evil . . .
>
> Some of the most charming people in the world live in them, but their collective effect is below the quality of any individual among them. Cambridge is a world of subdued tones, of excessively subtle humours, of prim conduct and free thinking; it fears the Parent, but it has no fear of God; it offers amidst surroundings that vary between dinginess and antiquarian charm the inflammation of literature's purple draught; one hears there a peculiar thin scandal like no other scandal in the world – a covetous scandal – so that I am always reminded of Ibsen in Cambridge. In Cambridge and the plays of Ibsen alone does it seem appropriate for the heroine before the great crises of life to 'enter, take off her overshoes, and put her wet umbrella upon the writing-desk'.

University reform needed to go further than letting wives in, Wells suggested. The entire academic system needed turning upside down, not simply domesticating. 'I should have had military manoeuvres, training ships, aeroplane work, mountaineering and so forth, in the place of the solemn trivialities of games, and I should have fed and housed my men clean and very hard – where there wasn't any audit ale, no credit tradesmen, and plenty of high-pressure douches.'

Before the reforms threw it open and it became a focal point of Cambridge's regeneration, King's had been the university's most stagnant backwater, a privileged preserve of Etonians who could there acquire degrees and life fellowships without the indignity of university examinations. Vestiges of former days – 'strange mastodons and plesiosauri, learned lizards in human form, with caps and gowns' – were still to be seen when E. F. Benson (1867–1940) followed his brother A. C. Benson (see below, p. 204) up to the college in 1887, as he recounts in *As We Were: A Victorian Peepshow* (1930). Eccentric dons still abounded: J. E. Nixon, one-armed tennis-player, glee-singer, quixotic solver of practical problems such as how to turn envelopes inside out for reuse; Mr Mozeley, who only emerged from his rooms at three minutes to five, and could be sent back into them with a whistle in his direction; Walter Headlam, the renowned Greek scholar, who lived oblivious to time or season amid a chaos of books and papers; and, most legendary of all, Oscar Browning (universally known as 'the O.B.'), obese, hyperbolic, paradoxical, courting royalty, and attended in his turn by undergraduate acolytes. He rode a tricycle, listened to essays with a red bandanna over his face and strummed in his spare moments on harmonium-like instruments nicknamed OBeophones. After leaving Eton to avoid a homosexual scandal similar to that which had ruined William Cory's career, but apparently without Cory's sense of shame, Browning transferred his multifarious activities back to King's for the next four decades, making the college a leading centre for history, if also a vortex of scandal and controversy. E. F. Benson sums him up as 'a genius flawed by abysmal fatuity'; A. C. Benson, writing in 1905, called him 'a genius and a bore, a man of light and darkness; Hyperion and a satyr, Jekyll and Hyde'. Browning's figure – caricatured, vilified or eulogised – inevitably recurs through much of the literature of the period.

Equally antediluvian, to E. F. Benson's taste, were the fictions of 'Alan St Aubyn', pseudonym of Mrs Frances Marshall, wife of a Tiverton bookseller, who resided at 20 Brookside between the late 1880s and 1897 while her three sons were at university. In her hands the university novel, always a perilously homiletic genre, declined into saccharine melodrama. The best of her five Cambridge novels, *A Fellow of Trinity*, published while Benson was an undergraduate, shows similarities to Farrar's *Julian Home*. Again there are the self-righteous sizar and the cocksure fellow-commoner; but now too there are gambling hells at Chesterton where vague but terrible crimes are perpetrated, a fashionable element of supernatural menace – bedmakers' ghosts and knockings in the cloister on the eve of a boating catastrophe – and a new sentimental love element (that generally in her novels leads to a 'dear little house' in the suburbs of the sort Wells excoriated). Some of her melodramatic touches were founded on fact (an oarsman apparently *was* transfixed by the bow of a following boat during the May races one year, while the ducking of an undergraduate in King's fountain is based on Robert Ross's unfortunate experience (see p. 181 below)); nevertheless, her picture of academic life was so far removed from the reality on which it was supposed to be based that a reaction was inevitable, and E. F. Benson, worldly, flippant, witty, was the man to introduce it.[1]

'Did you ever go to a gambling-hell on the Chesterton Road, Tom?' laughs the hero of Benson's early novel, *Limitations* (1896); Tom replies: 'No. Do you ever have ennobling thoughts when you look at the stately chapel? Of course you don't. You think it's deuced pretty, and so do I, and we both play whist with threepenny points.' Benson's two further Cambridge novels, *The Babe B.A.* (1897) and *David of King's* (1924), develop the protest. They sparkle like cocktails, shun plot and didacticism, and come no closer to melodrama than a vigorous game of croquet. They are also – an innovation in Cambridge novels – brilliantly funny, their fizzy superficialities a welcome relief after the stagelit portentousness of Mrs Marshall. *David of King's* parades the same *fin-de-siècle* circus of eccentrics, this time under fictitious names, who appear in *As We Were*. 'A.G.', whose egoistic garrulity is wonderfully caught, is clearly 'O.B.', while 'Mr Crowfoot' with his glee-singing and practical dodges is Nixon. Some of the scenes – the game of tennis in which 'A.G.' is hit in the stomach and Crowfoot's bowler hat falls off, or the Great Rag – are comic gems.

If Benson's dons are plesiosauri, his undergraduates are modern pragmatists who saunter their way through the university untortured by the moral dilemmas of Victorian heroes. When a friend, getting out of his depth at cards, has taken to cheating, the Babe accepts his denial so absolutely that the man at once owns up.

> The Babe got up, went to the door and sported it. Then he sat down again on the arm of the chair.
> 'Poor chap', he said. 'It's beastly hard lines, and I fully expect it's as much our fault as yours.'

– an outcome that contrasts with those beloved of Dean Farrar or Mrs Marshall, in whose pages the unfortunate would probably have had to expiate his lapse by a lifetime of missionary work in the tropics. Again, when one of David Blaize's friends is drinking too much, David spends each evening with him, quietly pacing him glass for glass; the friend soon stops drinking. Somehow, Benson's heroes get firsts without 'sapping' and rugger blues without competing. They enjoy cigars and champagne without qualms of conscience and without hiding their surprise when the champagne makes them tipsy. Somewhere a long way outside the college gates lurk marriage and careers; but just now their world is a pleasant limbo of ripping friendships, picnics up the river, and a total avoidance of earnestness, priggishness, or any other tommy-rot.

---

[1] Novels can exert unpredictable influences, however. The mathematician G. H. Hardy recounts in *A Mathematician's Apology* how reading *A Fellow of Trinity* while a Winchester schoolboy decided him to go to Trinity instead of New College, Oxford. The final scene in particular, in which the hero 'drinks port and eats walnuts for the first time in Senior Combination Room ... fascinated me completely, and from that time, until I obtained one, mathematics meant to me primarily a Fellowship of Trinity'.

The Babe B.A. was originally serialised in *The Granta*. Since the *Snob* of Thackeray fame, there had been an increasing spate of university magazines of one sort and another, mostly of short duration, including Morris's *Oxford and Cambridge Magazine*, George Otto Trevelyan's *The Bear* (itself a parody of one called *The Lion*), and Hilton's *Light Green*. But two were to achieve longevity and to become staple weekly features of Cambridge life – *The Cambridge Review* and *The Granta*. The former, in which dons and undergraduates collaborated, was founded in 1879 by a group including J. G. Frazer of Trinity (later famous as the author of *The Golden Bough*), and its declared aim was to be 'a fair representative of the life and thought of the University'. It carried university and college news, book reviews and obituaries, essays and poems, and during its twentieth-century heyday was to provide a forum for the exposition and debate of new ideas in Cambridge.

The Granta began less auspiciously. Indeed, it first appeared in November 1888 under the title of *The Gadfly*, its main feature being a satirical portrait of 'Oscar Browning at Home', apparently written by Robert Ross (1869–1918), a long-haired aesthetic freshman of King's and already a friend of Oscar Wilde (whose foul-weather champion and literary executor he later became):

> In the corner of the room on a soft lounge hung with delicate silk material, sat – or, rather lolled – the object of the visit. Two Arab boys severally support on each side an ash tray and a gold cigarette box. The occupant of the sofa from time to time languidly whiffs a weed of delicate flavour vulgarly known as tobacco, but of a brand grown only in Paflagonia, imported for O.B.'s express purpose.

The gold-brocaded curtain under which one enters, the Persian wallpaper, the faint smell of incense, the clutter of Renaissance masterpieces – all evoke an interestingly Wildean atmosphere. After noting Browning's resemblance to a Caesar and, by his sofa, the direct telephone to Marlborough House, the interviewer takes leave by asking: 'Do you believe in the personal existence of a Deity?' 'Do I believe in myself?' is the laconic answer.

Wilde had written to Ross only the previous month: 'Do you know Oscar Browning? You will find him everything that is kind and pleasant', and Ross, who was reading history under Browning, later struck up a decidedly intimate friendship with him (they holidayed together the following year on the Isle of Wight). But his freshman interview showed lack of judgement, and Browning, missing the affection beneath the satire, was apparently incensed. At all events, *The Gadfly* (in the words of *The Granta*) 'was written on Tuesday, printed on Wednesday, published on Thursday, sold on Friday, suppressed on Saturday, and wept for on Sunday'. However, its secret editor, Walter Murray Guthrie (1869–1911) of Trinity Hall, was not daunted. He seems to have led a double life, for he too was actually on friendly terms with Browning (who did not suspect him of being the editor) and even went so far as to unite in a pledge with some of the O.B.'s supporters that 'they would neither wash nor shave until they had brought condign and personal vengeance on the head of the editor of *The Gadfly*'. Soon afterwards he found a means of retribution. Learning that the O.B. was intending to bring out a serious educational journal of his own entitled *The Granta* (Roger Fry had designed 'a beautiful cover, the chief feature of which was a panoramic view of the Cambridge spires and towers'), Guthrie at once registered the identical title for himself. In Browning's words, 'Early the following term I saw the countryside placarded with posters announcing that a new *undergraduate* paper, *The Granta*, was to be published. I was horrified.' His own journal never appeared, and he never forgave what he called this 'act of literary piracy'.

In its first term *The Granta*, subtitled 'A College Joke To Cure the Dumps', managed to steer a safe course between acceptable badinage (the first issue contained a cartoon of the Master of Trinity 'printed in three colours on plate paper' as the first in a long-running series of 'Those in Authority') and further publicity-engendering controversy (Ross was ducked in King's fountain for an article satirising an election of college Dean).[2] But generally for its first fifty years it was to retail between its light-blue, jester-adorned covers a vigorous but conservative brand of varsity humour – the sort that features freshmen, bedmakers, and proctors – together with sports news and Union gossip. Described as '*Punch* with a little Cam water', it liked to think itself the Cambridge *Punch* (and to think *Punch* the London *Granta* – not without justification, since many contributors graduated from one to the other). Under the founding editorship of Guthrie, Lionel Holland, and R. C. Lehmann (an ex-Cantab already on *Punch* who took *The Granta* under his wing for its first six years), it published contributions from, among others, J. K. Stephen, Owen Seaman, T. R. Glover (later Public Orator), E. E. Kellett (an Oxford-educated master at the Leys School and minor literary figure), and Barry Pain (who penned the most brilliant bits of his *In a Canadian Canoe* series with the printer's devil waiting at the foot of his staircase).

'When I was at school', A. A. Milne once reminisced, 'a copy of *The Granta* came down to us; and after a friend and I had looked through it together, he said to me, "You ought to go to Cambridge and edit that paper," and I said, "Henry" (or whatever his name was), "I will". And I did. It's a horrible story, isn't it?' Alan Alexander Milne (1882–1956) came up to Trinity from Westminster in 1900 (his rooms on P staircase in Whewell's Court would be inherited by his son, Christopher Robin Milne, in 1939) and began contributing what he called 'Milnicks' to *The Granta* under the initials 'A.K.M.' (a confusing vestige of collaboration with his brother Ken). Milne's first moment of glory came when,

---

[2] E. F. Benson was one of those who ducked him. The involvement of a tutor, Arthur Tilley, exacerbated the offence. Ross himself was 'seized with a violent brain attack, the result of the outrage preying on his mind' (another version says he caught pneumonia) and had to be taken home; he contemplated suicide; he contemplated bringing criminal charges. Tilley eventually made a public apology to him in hall but Ross left Cambridge soon afterwards never to return.

stopping at Bletchley on the return journey from a football fixture at Oxford, he heard 'no less a person than the Captain of the Side say to no less a person than one of the "blues" in the side: "Did you see those awfully good verses in *The Granta* this week – a new sort of limerick by somebody called A.K.M.?" I plunged a glowing face into the ginger-beer. This was authorship.' Milne's contributions remained modest, however, until at the beginning of his second year he received a totally unexpected invitation to take over the editorship, thus fulfilling his schoolboy ambition though dismaying his tutor, who foresaw that he would neglect his studies and lose the chance 'to become something respectable like an accountant'. After two happy terms filling the paper with his own productions, Milne took a third in his mathematical tripos and moved on, not to accountancy, but to *Punch*.

Milne wrote of the predominant undergraduate style of the time that 'Calverley was our hero'. A particularly celebrated parody, J. K. Stephen's take-off of Robert Browning, published in the *Cambridge Meteor* in June 1882, included the lines

> There's a Me Society down at Cambridge,
> Where my works, *cum notis variorum*,
> Are talked about . . .

This referred to the Cambridge University Browning Society (formed on the model of the national society), which met in the early 1880s under the presidency of Professor Westcott and with A. C. Benson as secretary. According to E. F. Benson's *As We Were*, Robert Browning (1812–89) once paid a visit to the society and was afterwards invited to tea at Newnham College. There, his undergraduate hostess,

> in a frenzy of diffidence and devotion, told him that she had woven a crown of roses for him . . . and might she have the extreme honour of placing it on his head. The poet most good-naturedly consented, and with trembling hands she deposited the decoration on that august brow. So there he sat, bland and ruddy, and slightly buttery from the muffins, with the crown of pink roses laid upon his white locks, and looking like a lamb decked for sacrifice. By his side was an occasional table on which were placed the volumes of his complete works, and opposite him on the wall there happened to hang a mirror . . .

Conceivably Benson derived the story from his brother (who himself apparently found Browning so disappointing when he met him at breakfast with Sidney Colvin that he allowed the society to fold); but more likely it is mere embroidering on Max Beerbohm's famous cartoon 'Robert Browning taking tea with the Browning Society'. Girton College also boasted a Browning Society for a while, but it was dissolved in 1886 and its remaining funds spent on chocolate.

A more reliable reminiscence of Robert Browning in Cambridge is that of Edmund Gosse (1849–1928), the ubiquitous literary socialite who was at home in most of the Cambridge households and who held the newly founded Clark Lectureship at Trinity College from 1884 to 1888. According to Gosse, Browning, much feted on a visit to Cambridge in June 1888 (in his last year of life),

> proposed a temporary retreat from too full society, and we retired alone to the most central and sequestered part of the beautiful Fellows' Garden of Trinity. A little tired and silent at first, he was no sooner well ensconced under the shadow of a tree, in a garden-chair, than his tongue became unloosed. The blue sky was cloudless above, summer foliage hemmed us round in a green mist, a pink mountain of a double-may in blossom rose in front. We were close to a hot shrub of sweetbriar that exhaled its balm in the sunshine. Commonly given to much gesticulation, the poet sat quite still on this occasion; and, the perfect quiet being only broken by his voice, the birds lost fear and came closer and closer, curiously peeping. So we sat for more than two hours . . .

Apparently oblivious to his surroundings, Browning talked about his youth and career and at one point, recounting an Italian anecdote, demonstrated how he would have made it into a poem. 'The speed with which the creative architect laid the foundations, built the main fabric, and even put on the domes and pinnacles of his poem was, no doubt, of uncommon interest. He left it, in five minutes, needing nothing but the mere outward crust of the versification.'

Gosse's tenure of the Clark Lectureship (which he initially liked to refer to as a professorship) was controversial. Leslie Stephen, the first lecturer, had resigned after two terms, weary of addressing 'a number of young ladies from Girton and a few idle undergraduates and the youthful prince', and Gosse, a boyish-looking thirty-five with recommendations from Browning and Tennyson, took over. At a time when English studies were unknown in the university (in 1871 a parent had complained to *The Times* that his son had returned after three years at Cambridge 'utterly ignorant of his native language'), and thirty years before the English faculty was founded, the lectureship was a pioneering innovation. But Gosse, while enthusiastic and, to his packed audiences, an inseminator of enthusiasms, was a wayward scholar. His life of Gray was packed with inaccuracies (an interleaved copy exists at Pembroke annotated by the Gray scholar Leonard Whibley, who held that every sentence was 'incorrect or inadequate or misleading'), his edition of Gray's works unreliable. When his Clark lectures were published in 1885 as *From Shakespeare to Pope* they were savaged by the critic Churton Collins, who, having failed to get the first professorship of English at Oxford, resented the appointment at Cambridge of a 'dilettante' like Gosse. Collins exposed every error in Gosse's book and expressed outrage that such a work should be 'dated from Trinity College, Cambridge, and published by the University Press'. It was the scandal of the year, and to 'make a Gosse of oneself' became slang at Oxford for committing a 'howler'. Nevertheless, one Trinity undergraduate wrote that Gosse's lectures had 'lit candles that no Quarterly Reviewer could blow out', while Gosse himself found Cambridge 'entirely enthusiastic and scornful of my assailants', feeling 'more attached to this dear place than ever'. The mere sight of Trinity's battlements 'against a deep purple sky and the hall with its coloured festal lights' gave him 'an indescribable feeling of joy' while of the spectacle of young men at play in the Backs he thrilled: 'how beautiful and really how Greek it is!' At the conclusion of his lectureship seventeen students showed their loyalty and appreciation by presenting him with a piece of plate, while Tennyson is supposed memorably to have told Gosse that Churton Collins was 'a Louse upon the Locks of Literature' (but apparently the tale is another Gosse exaggeration).

Gosse's friend and fellow man of letters Maurice Baring (1874–1945) spent one year (1893–4) at Trinity and in his summer term helped H. Warre Cornish and R. Austen Leigh, both of King's, to edit *The Cambridge A.B.C.* They persuaded Aubrey Beardsley to design the cover 'for the modest sum of ten guineas . . . and many people thought it was a clever parody of his draughtsmanship'. Baring admitted that 'in spite of having learnt nothing in an academic sense at Cambridge, I am glad I went there', though while there 'I hid my literary aspirations'. While at Trinity he played a practical joke on Gosse by sending him a telegram announcing his own death.

In June 1886 the American writer Oliver Wendell Holmes (1809–94) visited Cambridge, first as the guest of Gosse in Nevile's Court, then a few days later to receive an honorary doctorate. Gosse described Holmes as like 'a delightful elderly bird, that sings whenever you ask it to. He is rather fragile, but has the most delightful readiness in going to bed – has been there twice already today – before dinner.' On the second occasion he was the guest of Alexander Macalister, the professor of anatomy (Holmes was professor of anatomy at Harvard). As he received his degree, the undergraduates in the Senate House sang 'Holmes, Sweet Holmes'.[3] In the evening he witnessed the annual procession of boats on the Cam, a river he judged 'about as wide as the Housatonic . . . as that slender stream winds through "Canoe Meadow", my old Pittsfield residence'. On the following day, the author of *The Autocrat of the Breakfast Table* was accorded a ceremonial breakfast party in the Combination Room of St John's, at which W. E. Heitland, the classical scholar, read a poem specially written in commemoration of the occasion.[4]

Sherlock Holmes paid a visit to Cambridge some time in the 1890s, according to Sir Arthur Conan Doyle's story 'The Missing Three-Quarter'. The lynchpin of the Cambridge side has disappeared on the eve of the Varsity match, and the clues lead to Dr Armstrong, opposite whose house in the town's 'busiest thoroughfare'

---

[3] When Henry Wadsworth Longfellow received an honorary doctorate in 1868 they shouted 'Three cheers for the red man of the West'.

[4] His compatriot Francis Bret Harte (1836–1902) lectured at the Guildhall in 1880 on life in California, the *Cambridge Chronicle* speaking of his 'well-deserved popularity and undoubted genius'.

Holmes and Dr Watson lodge at a small hotel. Holmes first follows Armstrong's carriage on a bicycle hired next door, but is given the slip near Chesterton. Ever resourceful, he next borrows Pompey, 'the pride of the local draghounds', from Dixon of Trinity, and doctors the carriage wheel with aniseed. Doyle's topography is vague, but Holmes and Watson must cover at least six miles on foot, dashing about the Cambridgeshire roads with their hound, before they approach the solution to the mystery. 'This should be the village of Trumpington to the right of us', Holmes cries at last. 'And, by Jove! here is the brougham coming round the corner! Quick, Watson, quick, or we are done!'[5]

The novelist John Cowper Powys (1872–1963) genuinely did cover great distances along the Cambridgeshire roads in the 1890s. In his *Autobiography* he describes how he came up in 1891 to Corpus Christi (his family's traditional college: William Cowper's brother John was an ancestor) with a loaded revolver in his pocket as defence against rowdies, having heard dark rumours about the antics of the 'fast' set towards freshmen. When rowdies did indeed burst into his rooms, the mere production of the weapon had a suitably evaporative effect on their intentions.

Powys's rooms, overlooking Old Court and the tower of St Bene't's, were 'part and parcel of one of the most romantic relics of medieval scholasticism that I have ever seen'. (His younger brother Llewelyn, also a novelist, occupied the same rooms twelve years later.) But orthodox undergraduate pursuits held little interest for him and

> the university *as* a university had not the least influence upon my taste, my intelligence, my philosophy or my character! . . . I obeyed their rules, I 'kept' my chapels, I passed my examinations, I took my degree. I was studious. I was quiet. No Proctor ever had to pursue me. No Dean ever had to interview me. I slipped into the place, and I slipped out of the place, totally uninfluenced.

Though studying history, he was untouched by the history of his surroundings and left Cambridge 'without having so much as even stepped into some of the most beautiful and famous of the courts, halls, chapels, libraries, gardens that are its glory'. The teachers he found uninspiring, the students unimaginative. In his last year he competed for the Chancellor's Medal; the subject was 'The English Lakes', but though he spent his vacation walking near Ullswater to gain first-hand

---

[5] In 'The Creeping Man', Holmes and Watson visit Camford; a third story, 'The Three Students', is set in 'one of our great university towns'. They again visit Cambridge in Randall Collins's novel *The Case of the Philosophers' Ring* (1980), in which Bertrand Russell summons them to investigate the theft of Wittgenstein's mind. Whether Holmes was himself a Cambridge man has been hotly debated. Dorothy L. Sayers claimed he was at Sidney Sussex and Christopher Morley, Peterhouse. W. S. Baring-Gould, in his biography of Holmes, compromised by sending him first to Christ Church, Oxford, then to Gonville and Caius. Trevor H. Hall has argued that Holmes was at Trinity c. 1870 (he points to the existence of a Sherlock Road and a Sherlock Close in Cambridge); but the Sherlock Holmes Society of London's 1989 Cambridge expedition plumped for Trinity Hall.

impressions, the prize went instead to A. A. Jack of Peterhouse.[6] Powys preserved nothing that he wrote at Cambridge.

But if Powys gained little from Cambridge, 'wherever I go I shall carry with me to the end what I learnt from Cambridgeshire while I was at Cambridge'. Its flat roads were ideal for his addiction to long country walks. If accompanied, he would act Coleridge, spouting wild heterogeneous monologues as he went along, but if alone would imitate Wordsworth, striding in a mystic reverie of identification with the fields and sky, with his oak stick 'Sacred' that he clutched in his hand, with the mud on his boots and with the scraps of grass sticking in the mud. The turnip fields, the milestones, the weedy estuaries and swamp-pools, an ancient fragment of lichened wall 'somewhere in the umbrageous purlieus to the rear of the Fitzwilliam Museum' from which, passing on his way to take tea with a local novelist (almost certainly 'Alan St Aubyn') he derived 'a sort of Vision on the Road to Damascus', the 'greatest event in my life at Cambridge' – all these fed the manic fervour for incidentals that contributed to the unique quality of his writing.

> Oh how can I express my deep, my indurated, my passionate, my unforgettable, my *eternal* debt, to that dull, flat, monotonous, tedious, unpicturesque Cambridgeshire landscape? How those roads out of Cambridge . . . come back to my mind now! Those absurd little eminences known as the Gog and Magog hills; that long interminable road that leads to some pastoral churchyard that once claimed precedence of Stoke Poges as the site of the Elegy: that more beguiling, but not *very* beguiling road that led in the Ely direction, past the place where my father's father, when a fellow of Corpus, used to go courting: those meadows towards Grantchester where there is that particular massive and wistful effect about the poplars and willows . . . these are my masters, my fellows, my libraries, my lecture-halls; these are my Gothic shrines!

---

[6] And not to J. H. B. Masterman, to whom Powys erroneously gives it in his *Autobiography*. Masterman was the previous year's winner.

17

Prelude to Bloomsbury

Edward Morgan Forster (1879–1970) arrived at King's in October 1897 (in his own words) 'immature, uninteresting, and unphilosophic'. Brought up by women, dismissed as deficient by Tonbridge School, a latent homosexual, with few obvious recommendations for conventional success, he might at any other college have passed through his academic career untouched and unwoken.

King's, however, had by now a special atmosphere that made it precisely the place for self-discovery. Although the college had ended its Etonian exclusivity, it retained an Etonian tradition of free association between teachers and students that made it uniquely friendly and liberal. The influence of Oscar Browning especially (who was something more than the satirical figure beloved of novelists) was great in introducing a more humane educational atmosphere not only to King's but to Cambridge as a whole. For Browning, a university was not just a machine for the production of an intellectual elite, as Cambridge had so often tended to be in the past: he believed it should serve more genuinely to open up the minds of all who came to it, and that those who came to it should be drawn from a wider field. Calling from his window to anyone who was passing to come and share his lobsters or play duets, and keeping open house at his Sunday *soirées* for dons and undergraduates alike, Browning was a prime example of a King's don who did not shroud himself in remoteness.

Another was Goldsworthy Lowes Dickinson (1862–1932), who had come up to King's from Charterhouse in 1881 expecting (not unlike Forster) nothing much from the place and who, under Browning's influence, had experienced self-revelations comparable to those Forster would undergo. At Cambridge Dickinson had come to appreciate, for instance (what no amount of schoolboy cramming could effect), the proper significance of Greek culture, and had come under the spell of Goethe and Shelley, the twin lodestars of his subsequent life. It was in the first flush of his enthusiasm for Shelley that he won the Chancellor's Medal for 1884 with a poem on Savonarola composed in imitation of 'Adonais'.

Later, after unsatisfactory attempts to find a career outside Cambridge, Dickinson had been drawn back inevitably into the 'exquisite enclosure' of King's, where he held a fellowship from 1887 until his death, teaching history, propagating liberal opinions, and writing books – *The Greek Way of Life*, *A Modern Symposium*, *The International Anarchy*, and so on – that enjoyed considerable influence at the time but have proved too elegantly static in style for later tastes.

'Goldie' had his absurdities. A homosexual, he cultivated intense platonic crushes for undergraduates, especially if they wore shiny leather boots; the self-declared reincarnation of a Chinaman, he sported a mandarin's cap as he pottered about his rooms over the 'Jumbo Arch', doing battle with 'so-called inanimate objects' such as typewriters and hot water bottles. But he represented in many ways the best spirit of King's, and his memory is kept green by Forster's biography of him. In its pages, Forster not only pays affectionate tribute to one of the seminal influences in his life, but evokes with discerning hindsight the particular qualities with which turn-of-the-century King's was invested by Browning, Dickinson, and others. For them, Cambridge was a place where youth and age might learn from one another, where knowledge brought insight rather than mere academic trophies, where young men with their minds just waking up could learn to discover themselves:

> Cambridge shared with ancient Athens the maieutic power which brings such minds into the light. The Cephissus flows with the Cam through this city, by the great lawn of King's under the bridge of Clare, towards plane trees which have turned into the chestnuts of Jesus. Ancient and modern unite through the magic of youth.

At King's, Forster was to claim in his second novel, *The Longest Journey*,

> They taught the perky boy that he was not everything, and the limp boy that he might be something. They even welcomed those boys who were neither limp nor perky, but odd – those boys who had never been at public school at all, and such do not find a welcome everywhere. And they did everything with ease – one might almost say with nonchalance – so that the boys noticed nothing and received education, often for the first time in their lives.

All this maieutic power did not, however, immediately manifest itself to Forster. As a freshman he lived in lodgings (probably 10 Peas Hill), frittered his time away on golf and bagatelle, and clung to his connections with the school he had so much disliked. At first he seemed to have been tipped more into E. F. Benson's King's than Dickinson's, for, reading classics, he came under the one-armed glee-singing Nixon and went for occasional walks with Walter Headlam that were relieved by the great scholar's giddy fits and habit of walking straight through fields of standing corn.

Things improved when Forster moved into college in his second year, inhabiting w7 at the top of the recently built neo-Gothic Bodley's building beside the river. He began to make friends and to feel a greater sense of belonging. Now too he got to know Dickinson, joining his Discussion Society. (His initial meeting with Dickinson in his freshman year had not been auspicious: they had lunched in silence on 'Winchester cutlets' – a kind of rissole that Dickinson enjoyed – and Forster had left 'unprepossessing and unprepossessed'; it was only when Forster borrowed a fashionable book and, returning it, confessed he hadn't liked it, that Dickinson's face lit up with interest.) But possibly even more important than his friendship with Dickinson was the fact that instead of Nixon he now came under Nathaniel Wedd, a young radical atheistical don, who perhaps contributed more than anyone towards Forster's awakening. Wedd's challenging attitude towards all received values taught Forster to think for himself, while his impatience with 'sets' or aesthetic elites (such as the so-called 'Best Set' of A. C. Benson's day) encouraged Forster to be similarly catholic and all-embracing in his friendships. It was Wedd who encouraged him to write.

In his first year, Forster later recalled, he wasn't sure of his clothes, in his second he was too sure of himself, in his third he was 'just right. Without arrogance and with exultation, with occasional song and dance, I owned the place.' What he was to write of Dickinson's settling down at King's in the 1880s could apply equally to himself:

> As Cambridge filled up with friends it acquired a magic quality. Body and spirit, reason and emotion, work and play, architecture and scenery, laughter and seriousness, life and art – these pairs which are elsewhere contrasted were there fused into one. People and books reinforced one another, intelligence joined hands with affection, speculation became a passion, and discussion was made profound by love.

Forster floated, busy–idle, on a stream of friendships and ideas. Among his close friends was H. O. Meredith, a fellow classicist, whose relationship with him was to be the basis for Clive Durham's with Maurice Hall in Forster's posthumously published novel *Maurice* (Maurice and Clive meet at Cambridge, though their college is not named). Like Durham in the novel, Meredith attacked and destroyed his friend's vestigial Christian beliefs, and introduced him to the revelation of homosexual love (Forster and he became lovers after Cambridge in London). Another friend, A. R. Ainsworth, a disciple of G. E. Moore (whose sister he later married), was to be the model for Ansell in *The Longest Journey*. E. J. Dent (later professor of music) was to be the model for Philip Herriton in *Where Angels Fear To Tread*. Another King's contemporary was Percy Lubbock (1879–1965), who later became Pepys Librarian at Magdalene and was the author of several travel and critical books. With these and other friends Forster breakfasted, walked, and took tea, analysing beauty and discussing books and art. In the evenings they met again at the discussion groups run by Dickinson and M. R. James (then Dean of the college – see p. 206 below). Forster in his third year won a college prize with an essay on the eighteenth-century novelists, and contributed short pieces (his first appearances in print) to *The Cambridge Review* and a new college magazine, *Basileon*. At the end of the year, though he only took a second, his college renewed his Exhibition and he stayed on for a fourth year to read history.

His hope was to study under Dickinson, but Browning stepped in – 'You're not coming to me at all, you *must* come to me' – and so it was to the spread bandanna that Forster's history essays were read. He began work on an unpublished, untitled apprenticeship novel (already attacking his bourgeois background) and – most important event – was elected to the Apostles in February 1901 as member number 237.

The Apostles – whose general aims and procedures had not changed since Tennyson's day, though each generation expressed different preoccupations within the same candid atmosphere – had recently entered on one of their most brilliant periods of activity. All the giants of Cambridge philosophy – J. E. McTaggart, A. N. Whitehead, Bertrand Russell, and, most importantly, G. E. Moore (see p. 194 below) – were senior Apostles ('angels'), as were Dickinson, Browning, Wedd, Roger Fry, and G. M. Trevelyan. The active younger members included both Meredith (who sponsored Forster's election) and Ainsworth. With the influence of Moore predominant, the elevated philosophical level of discussion must have been awesome at first; and although from now on the society *was* Cambridge for Forster, its atmosphere of truth-seeking and friendship probably counted for more with him than the outcome of some of the topics of debate. Forster's mind worked intuitively rather than logically, and his inability to follow argument is reflected in the opening scene of *The Longest Journey*, where a philosophical discussion based loosely on an Apostles meeting is under way in Rickie Elliot's rooms at King's (based on Forster's own). The argument (whether the cow in the meadow is still there when no one is looking at it) seems closer to Berkeley than anything the Apostle disciples of Moore were likely to have been discussing; even so, Rickie's attention wanders. Like Tennyson,

> He preferred to listen, and to watch the tobacco-smoke stealing out past the window-seat into the tranquil October air. He could see the court too, and the college cat teasing the college tortoise, and the kitchen-men with the supper-trays upon their heads. Hot food for one – that must be for the geographical don, who never came in for Hall; cold food for three, apparently at half a crown a head, for some one he did not know; hot food, *à la carte* – obviously for the ladies haunting the next staircase; cold food for two, at two shillings – going to Ansell's rooms for himself and Ansell, and as it passed under the lamp he saw that it was meringues again. Then the bedmakers began to arrive, chatting to each other pleasantly, and he could hear Ansell's bedmaker say, 'Oh dang!' when she found she had to lay Ansell's tablecloth; for there was not a breath stirring. The great elms were motionless, and seemed still in the glory of midsummer, for the darkness hid the yellow blotches of their leaves, and their outlines were still rounded against the tender sky.

Though the scene is not an accurate portrait of an Apostles meeting or of current Apostolic argument, Rickie and his friend Ansell do in the course of the novel act out one debate that was current, between proponents of attitudes designated 'King's' and 'Trinity'. 'Trinity men', of whom Ansell is representative (Lytton Strachey was a real-life example), were intellectual elitists: Ansell will not even admit the existence of the conventionally minded Agnes, who bursts in on their meeting and to marry whom Rickie abdicates his intellectual standards, ending up teaching in a pretentious minor public school ('Sawston' = Tonbridge). 'King's men' on the other hand (like Browning, Dickinson, or Forster himself) want to know and like everybody. The distinction is exemplified by a visit Rickie and his friends pay to a dell he has discovered on the Madingley Road. An aesthetic Trinity type exclaims, 'Procul este, profani!' as they enter, but Rickie felt 'if the dell was to bear any inscription', he would have liked it to be "This way to heaven", painted on a sign-post by the high-road'. Rickie's fate exemplifies the dangers of the King's attitude but also shows how salvation can come not only from one's intellectual peers but also from unsophisticated 'naturals', like his illegitimate out-of-doors half-brother in the story.[1]

Like Rickie, Forster had

> crept cold and friendless and ignorant out of a great public school, preparing for a silent and solitary journey, and praying as a highest favour that he might be left alone. Cambridge had not answered his prayer. She had taken and soothed him, and warmed him, and laughed at him a little, saying that he must not be so tragic yet awhile, for his boyhood had been but a dusty corridor that led to the spacious halls of youth.

Forster left Cambridge for Italy at the end of 1901; but his connection with the Apostles remained close and he often returned for meetings and to see friends. He did not hold any official position at Cambridge, however, until 1927, when in the wake of the success of his Clark Lectures, *Aspects of the Novel*, he was made a Supernumerary Fellow of King's for three years. In 1945 he was made an Honorary Fellow, and from then until his death he resided at Cambridge.[2] In the meantime, it was through his Apostolic connections that he became a semi-accredited member of the group known as Bloomsbury.

The origins of Bloomsbury, indeed, were firmly rooted in turn-of-the-century Cambridge, even though not one of the disparate embryo Bloomsburyites who arrived at Trinity in October 1899 remotely resembled at that date a prophet of cultural revolution. If Forster had seemed dowdy and unprepossessing, Giles

---

[1] The novel's title is taken from a passage in Shelley's 'Epipsychidion' which J. T. Sheppard of King's had quoted during the Apostles debate on 'Trinity versus King's' in 1903. Another example of the unsophisticated type who provides enlightenment and emotional reassurance where intellectuals have failed is the garden boy in the posthumous story 'Ansell', with whom a Cambridge graduate spends his vacation after his crate of dissertation notes has fallen in a ravine. (Forster's own preference, like that of Edward Carpenter, was for working-class lovers.)

[2] See below, chapter 24.

Lytton Strachey (1880–1932) was so sapless and arrogant that even the mildest of 'bloods' would feel an urge to duck him in the fountain – 'You'd never think he was a general's son', commented the head porter, watching his stooped stick of a figure traverse the court. Clive Bell (1881–1964), by contrast, offspring of sporting gentry, strode about Great Court in full hunting regalia, clutching horn and whip. Thoby Stephen (1880–1906), elder son of Sir Leslie Stephen and brother of Vanessa and Virginia Stephen, resembled an E. F. Benson hero in his languid pragmatism and tall, handsome physique. Saxon Sydney-Turner (1880–1962), retiring, nocturnal, painstakingly erudite, withdrew with the years into a spectral persona. Leonard Woolf (1880–1969), son of a successful QC, was a poker-faced Jew who came to Trinity from St Paul's crammed with dead languages and as ignorant of the existence of living art, he later confessed, as any public-school product of the time.

'It began casually in what was called the screens,' Woolf recalls in his first volume of autobiography, *Sowing*; '. . . I was looking at the notices on the board after dining in Hall and said something to a man standing next to me. We walked away together and he came back to my rooms.' This was Sydney-Turner, with whom Woolf was to share rooms in Great Court for the last three of his five years at Trinity. Woolf recalls how he 'seemed to glide, rather than walk, and noise-lessly, so that one moment you were alone in a room and the next moment you found him sitting in a chair near you though you had not heard the door open or him come in'.

Clive Bell was Sydney-Turner's neighbour in New Court. Pink-faced and bubbling with talk, he gradually, under the influence of his new friends, turned from his sporty preoccupations to more intellectual ones and eventually, after Cambridge, to an abiding interest in art. He got on best with Stephen, whose elder sister Vanessa he subsequently married. Stephen's own chief qualities were his great personal charm and his towering heroic presence. His death at the age of twenty-six came as a great blow to all his friends. (Virginia Woolf was to use her memory of him as the basis for the character Percival in *The Waves*, and to some extent for Jacob in *Jacob's Room*.)

Strachey, who came from the same kind of 'intellectual aristocracy' as the Stephens, arrived at Trinity after two years at Liverpool University and rejection by Balliol. For his first year or so he too lodged in New Court, 'with a beautiful view of weeping willows'; then in 1901 he moved to the top of K staircase in Great Court (the 'Mutton-Hole Corner' where Byron was falsely reputed to have kept his bear) – 'nice and rather quaint with sloping roofs, etc.' Here he remained for the next five years, gradually developing the notorious theatrical eccentricities – floppy hats, a moustache, sneering silences, squeaky laughs, acid repartee – that camouflaged what he felt were his underlying ugliness and unlovableness. He soon became a byword for decadence: *The Granta*, in a spoof interview, depicted 'The Strache' reclining in silk pyjamas on a sofa, a volume of French poetry in his jaundiced hands and bottles of absinthe nearby. His cheeks are white and hollow, the room reeks of Gallic tobacco, his shrill paradoxical talk parrots Oscar Wilde's at Oxford twenty years before.

Strachey contributed 'Ninetyish' poems to *The Cambridge Review*, and delivered outrageous essays, flouting Christianity and other received beliefs, to the college's sober-minded Sunday Essay Society. Other more conventional essays, on Warren Hastings and on English letter-writers, failed (to his chagrin) to win college prizes. But he did win the Chancellor's Medal for 1902 with 'Ely: An Ode', an evocation of the neighbouring cathedral town's history, put together in something of a hurry and concluding with a totally irrelevant but suitably ingratiating catalogue of poets, from Spenser to Tennyson, who had mused by the Cam.

Strachey, Bell, Woolf, Stephen, Sydney-Turner, and a sixth, A. J. Robertson, formed themselves into a reading club which met at midnight on Saturdays in Bell's rooms to declaim favourite poetry at length – the whole of Shelley's *Prometheus Unbound* or *The Cenci*, for instance, or Milton's *Comus*. 'As often as not it was dawn by the time we had done', Bell recounts; 'and sometimes we would issue forth to perambulate the courts and cloisters, halting on Hall steps to spout passages of familiar verse, each following his fancy as memory served'. The Midnight Society, as it was called, lasted until 1902, and was the original germ, so Bell claims, of Bloomsbury itself. (But Bell may have overemphasised its importance; Woolf scarcely mentions it.)

They belonged to other, similar societies too: they read Shakespeare aloud once a week at the old-established college Shakespeare Society, and formed the X Society in order to read non-Shakespearean plays, including not only other Elizabethans but also more contemporary dramatists such as Ibsen and Shaw. (A. A. Milne, who had known Sydney-Turner at school, was admitted as a 'reading visitor'.) Breaking up from one or other group late on summer nights, they would wander through the cloisters, according to Woolf's version, to look out through the ironwork at the Backs and listen to the nightingales, before drifting away to bed chanting Swinburne.

Swinburne's influence is apparent in a collection of their own verse published anonymously in 1905 by Elijah Johnson, the Trinity Street bookseller, under the title *Euphrosyne*. Sydney-Turner contributed nearly half the poems, Bell about a third, and others were by Strachey (including 'The Cat'), Woolf, the slightly younger Walter Lamb (brother of the Bloomsbury painter Henry Lamb), and 'Brighton' Bell (apparently no relation, but his identity is now forgotten). Clive Bell's 'The Trinity Ball: Midnight' is a splenetic atheistical outburst 'Against God and his crapulous spawn', apparently composed in a mood of intoxicated reaction against the May Week festivities. Other poems (especially Strachey's 'When We Are Dead a Thousand Years') resemble the early poems of Rupert Brooke.

The literary enthusiasm of their coterie in a university where English literature was as yet neither taught nor widely read by students was unusual, and soon attracted the attention of the Apostles. Strachey, Sydney-Turner, and Woolf were elected to the Apostles in 1902 (Stephen was not – his nickname, 'the Goth', underlined a certain unsuitability – nor was Bell, to his lasting disappointment). Strachey's admission brought a breath of iconoclasm and wit to a society in danger of being over-ponderously philosophical – though Desmond MacCarthy (1877–1952), a brilliant raconteur who became a leading journalist and theatre critic, continued to inject urbane worldliness into their meetings on his weekend visits from London. Strachey's election also, as Russell noted, introduced (or reintroduced: Strachey liked to think of Tennyson and Hallam as a precedent) homosexual relations among members. The following year, John Maynard Keynes (1883–1946) of King's was elected, and he and Strachey became close friends.

The influence of G. E. Moore (1873–1958) over the Apostles remained paramount. Guileless, almost childlike in his directness, without the argumentative skilfulness of Russell, Moore was constantly demanding 'What *exactly* do you *mean*?' in an attempt to penetrate to the very root of things. His *Principia Ethica*, published in 1903, with its proposal that 'By far the most valuable things, which we know or can imagine, are certain states of consciousness which may be roughly described as the pleasures of human intercourse and the enjoyment of beautiful objects', was to be largely accepted by the Apostles and afterwards by Bloomsbury as the expression of an ideal code of values. Under Moore, 'states of consciousness' became the Apostles' chief preoccupation – good ones being induced by communion with love, truth, and beauty; and although there was some minor dissension between 'King's' and 'Trinity' as to whether 'good' states might also be pleasurable, or pleasurable ones good, all shared a conviction – similar to that experienced by the Apostles of seventy years before – that they were participating in some kind of spiritual renaissance. As Strachey boasted to Woolf in 1904, 'We are . . . like the Athenians of the Periclean age. We are the mysterious priests of a new and amazing civilization . . . We have mastered all. We have abolished religion, we have founded ethics, we have established philosophy, we have sown our strange illumination in every province of thought, we have conquered art, we have liberated love.'

It was one May Week afternoon in Stephen's rooms in New Court that Woolf first set eyes on Thoby's sister Virginia. She had come down with Vanessa for the Trinity Ball (at which Vanessa also first met Clive Bell), and 'in white dresses and large hats, with parasols in their hands, their beauty literally took one's breath away, for suddenly seeing them one stopped astonished and everything including one's breathing for one second also stopped'.

His future wife's impression of him on this occasion has not been recorded. A clever young man differentiated from all the other clever young men she was being introduced to at Cambridge mainly by the praises Thoby sang of him and by his uncontrollable fits of trembling, it is doubtful whether he took her breath away. It would be another ten years before their feelings for one another reached the point of marriage, ten years during which she received declarations of love from several other Cambridge men, including Strachey (whose proposal of marriage she initially accepted). But the meeting in Thoby's rooms was nevertheless a significant moment for them, for the group, and for literature. It was Virginia Woolf who gave their group its chief literary claim to importance. It was the addition of Vanessa and Virginia, with their beauty, their artistic imaginations, and their role as witty hostesses over their Bloomsbury salons, that kept the Midnight/Apostle association together after Cambridge and gave it a new epicentre from which its influence spread. Retrospectively it was Virginia Woolf also who cast a literary glow over their Cambridge – which, with London and Cornwall, became one of those points of 'literary geography' that send out vibrations through her writings. Though her attitude to it was far from uncritical, Cambridge remained a significant symbol to her, as witnessed by her descriptions of it in *Jacob's Room*, *A Room of One's Own*, and elsewhere.[3]

The daughters of Sir Leslie Stephen naturally felt in their element at Cambridge, though Virginia in particular felt bitter at being excluded from its male preserve. (In 1903 she complained to Thoby: 'I have to delve from books painfully and all alone, what you get every evening sitting over your fire and smoking your pipe with Strachey etc.') Their cousin J. K. Stephen was dead, but his sister Katherine was Vice-Principal (later Principal) of Newnham,[4] and, more immediately, a maiden aunt, Caroline Emelia Stephen, had settled since 1895 at The Porch, 33 Grantchester Street. It was with 'the Quaker', as they called her, that the Stephen sisters stayed on their May Week visits while Thoby and their younger brother Adrian were at Trinity, and that Virginia stayed, in 1905, while recuperating from the first of her many breakdowns. She continued to visit The Porch until her aunt's death in 1909, after which she stayed with the Darwins or Cornfords, attending Gwen Darwin's wedding to the painter Jacques Raverat in 1911. But Cambridge, attractive though it was, seemed narrowly provincial in many ways: 'No place in the world can be lovelier,' she wrote during her 1904 visit; but 'Lord! how dull it would be to live here! There seem to be about ten nice and interesting people, who circulate in each other's houses – Darwins, Maitlands, Newnham etc.'

One by one the Bloomsburyites departed from Cambridge. Bell went to Paris and developed his interest in art. Woolf stayed on to cram for the Civil Service exam, then disappeared for seven years to Ceylon. Keynes went to the India Office, Sydney-Turner to the Treasury. Strachey, after taking a second in history, twice competed for a Trinity fellowship without success. His dissertations on Warren Hastings were too indigestibly factual for those who judged them – a

---

[3] See below, chapter 21.

[4] Principals of Newnham had a habit of being related to famous writers: the first, A. J. Clough (1871–92), was the sister of the poet A. H. Clough; E. M. Sidgwick (1892–1910) was the wife of the philosopher Henry Sidgwick; Katherine Stephen (1911–20) was Virginia's Woolf's cousin; B. A. Clough (1921–3) was A. H. Clough's daughter; Pernel Strachey (1923–41) was Lytton Strachey's sister.

criticism he presumably learned from, since his later biographical works –
Eminent Victorians, Queen Victoria, Elizabeth and Essex – were more often to be
censured for the opposite fault of bending fact to effect. Possibly his abnormal
appearance and life-style contributed to his rejection. Disappointed, he wrote:
'Cambridge is the only place I never want to leave, though I suffer more there than
anywhere else.' His six years at Trinity had meant much to him, and he had found
its milieu ideally congenial:

> The real enchantment of Cambridge is of the intimate kind; an enchantment
> lingering in the nooks and corners, coming upon one gradually down the
> narrow streets, and ripening year by year. The little river and its lawns and
> willows, the old trees in the old gardens, the obscure bowling-greens, the crooked
> lanes with their glimpses of cornices and turrets, the low dark opening out on
> to sunny grass – in these, and in things like these, dwells the fascination of
> Cambridge.

But Cambridge, which had rewarded him for his dashed-off prize poem, turned
unimpressed from his labours on Warren Hastings, and in October 1905 he
quitted Mutton-Hole Corner for the last time – though his love for the place
brought him repeatedly back in the following years, often staying for months at
a time in lodgings. His younger brother James came up the term he left and
commandeered his rooms.

18

Edwardian excursions

The Granta's caricature of Strachey in *fin-de-siècle* pose might have stood for the self-image of other undergraduates of the day, who distinguished themselves from the average Edwardian student in his Norfolk jacket and flannel trousers by their floppy hats and monocles, silk cravats and waistcoats, buttonholes and silver-tipped canes, who hung Beardsley illustrations on their walls and carried the works of Dowson and Baudelaire. The showy aestheticism of such 'decadents' was accompanied by other influences that were even more widespread. Homosexuality was one, permeating Edwardian Cambridge in all degrees of intensity from fashionable affectation to passionate involvements of the *Maurice* kind. Interest in the supernatural was another, ranging from a vogue for ghost stories to the 'magick' of Aleister Crowley. In religion, there was a distinct polarisation between the atheism of Clive Bell's 'The Trinity Ball' and Roman Catholicism.

The original founders of the *fin-de-siècle* movement – Swinburne, Wilde, Dowson, Lord Alfred Douglas – had been Oxford men. Robert Ross, despite his year at King's, later confessed that 'it has always been my ambition to be mistaken for an Oxford man'. Strachey's first preference had been for Oxford. It was natural, therefore, that Oscar Wilde's younger son Vyvyan, though brought up in exile under the assumed name of Holland and in strict quarantine from any contact with his father's 'undesirable' milieu, should long also to go to Oxford. Instead Vyvyan Holland (1886–1967) was circumspectly sent to Cambridge, where he arrived at Trinity Hall in 1905 to read law. The Master and dons knew his real identity, but, as he relates in *Son of Oscar Wilde*, 'I was not supposed to know that they knew, which put me into a cruelly awkward position.' His father's works, after a period of virtual suppression, were just being rediscovered, and it was at Cambridge that Holland read them for the first time.

Trinity Hall at this date was scarcely the place for an aesthete: rowing was 'almost compulsory', and the college was packed with 'Philistines' and 'hearties'. It was curious, therefore, that the following year saw the arrival of someone even more incongruous than Holland. Ronald Firbank (1886–1926) already knew Lord Alfred Douglas (Wilde's lover and the chief cause of his tragic downfall) and by the time of his arrival at Cambridge had fashioned himself into the model of a decadent dandy. He quickly made his rooms (F2 in the main court) the most elegant in college, with oriental rugs and red silk curtains, a grand piano, a velvet sofa, innumerable vases of flowers on innumerable little tables, and liberal scatterings of cushions and books of verse. According to Holland, his arrival caused a sensation in literary circles – he had already published a book, *Odette d'Antrevennes* – and Holland called on him at once, finding him full of stories of Bohemian life in Paris.

For the next two years, Firbank's rooms became the setting for sumptuous dinners and witty talk among a select circle of friends that included, in addition to Holland, Rupert Brooke, E. J. Dent, and Shane Leslie from King's, Forrest Reid from Christ's, and Charles Sayle of the University Library. Brooke had arrived at Cambridge deep in decadence – a phase he only slowly emerged from. Dent was a Fellow of King's and a friend of Brooke's, who, writing to Clive Carey in 1915, looked back with amusement: 'Do you remember an absurd thing at the Hall called Firbank who tried to look rather like Lord Alfred Douglas of the sonnets? a great adorer of Rupert? He has written a novel . . . It is very 1890 – incredibly artificial and absurd . . . '

Forrest Reid (1875–1947), venturing outside his native Belfast for the first and last time in his life to read modern languages at Cambridge at the age of thirty, was a peripheral member of the group; he disliked Firbank, whom he remembered lounging in evening dress on the hearthrug of his orchid-crammed rooms, smoking 'drugged cigarettes'. Reid had published two novels, already displaying the pederastic inclinations that were to motivate his books; and his distrust of Firbank was intensified when the latter begged an autographed copy of one of them, then promptly sold it to a bookseller. Reid made one lasting friend at Cambridge, with Sayle's colleague at the library, A. T. Bartholomew; but he looked back on his Cambridge years as a 'blank interlude', particularly condemning the ossified attitudes towards the teaching of English literature (which as yet could only be studied as part of the modern languages tripos). 'English is taught exactly as if it were a dead language', he complained. The Irish Society, to whom he read a paper, had never even heard of Yeats.

Charles Sayle (1864–1924), son of Robert Sayle the Cambridge draper, had been educated at Rugby and Oxford, where he fell in with the poets Ernest Dowson and Lionel Johnson and was rusticated because of a homosexual scandal. Back in boorish and unenlightened Cambridge ('in Cambridge they say "you mustn't", in Oxford we used to say "oh do"'), he worked as a bibliographer at the University Library and was a member of the literary group that invited Wilde in 1885. It was to visit Sayle that Dowson came to Cambridge in 1889 (Dowson agreed in finding the Cantabs 'sadly wanting' in any comprehension of the *Yellow Book* gospel). Sayle's 'decadent' connections, his homosexuality and Catholic leanings, his bibliographical enthusiasm and the handful of slim volumes he had published were all recommendations to the Firbank set, mitigating the disparity in age (he was by now over forty).

Sir Shane Leslie (1885–1971), later to become the gossipy aristocratic author of over seventy books, shared Firbank's Catholic fervour and portrayed the High Church enthusiasms of his set and period in his novel *The Cantab* (1926), set in the King's of 1905. Published only two years after E. F. Benson's *David of King's*, it reworks many of the same anecdotes, and parades (under fresh pseudonyms) the same eccentric dons, together with later members such as Brooke ('Adolphus Briggs'). But in contrast to Benson's limpidity, Leslie's style is heavily baroque. Where Benson's heroes call the chapel 'deuced pretty' and think no more about it, Leslie's hero is carried into mystic transports by its catholic fabric:

> In wonderful raiment the beams of the morning sun crept upon Edward's swooning eyes. Yellow and scarlet patches broke through the argentine glaze without a half-tint or a semi-tone to modify their clash. The sun's rays collected in the fine Venetian gold, in the fantastic flesh pinks and languishing rose, melting and emblazoning the glass to cyclamen and peach-blossom and heliotropic sanguine, but cooling into clotted clarets and the murrey hue of bull's blood. Slowly the sun stole along the Chapel like the face of a mighty dial, dwelling an hour upon each window and stirring blobs, blurs and blotches of glaucous greens, cinereal amethysts and gorgeous oranges, while the heraldry aloft blazed in asteriated sapphire and aureate sateen. All the trimmings of the original Deuteronomic rainbow preserved in Amber!

The novel caused something of a scandal at the time, certain episodes of 'sexual reality' being considered so offensive by Leslie's Catholic bishop and by the magistrature that he was obliged to suppress the first edition; but the passages in question (they include a description of men changing in a boat-house after rowing and a panegyric to a woman's navel) seem remarkably innocuous by modern standards.[1]

Catholic enthusiasms were particularly fanned by the presence in Cambridge of Monsignor Robert Hugh Benson (1871–1914), younger brother of A. C. and E. F. Benson, who appears in *The Cantab* as 'Father Robert Rolle'. Despite being the son of an Archbishop of Canterbury, Hugh Benson was converted to Catholicism and ordained at Rome in 1904. He returned to Cambridge (he had originally studied at Trinity), first to study theology at Llandaff House, then to officiate at the Roman Catholic church. An electrifying preacher, he was keenly interested in spiritualism and the supernatural, and assiduous in the conversion of undergraduates. ('I can see him sitting in the firelight of my room at King's', Leslie

---

[1] Leslie's first appearance in print was with a poem in *The Cambridge Review* in 1906 lamenting a cormorant ('scaly legate from the termless ocean') which roosted on the top of King's College Chapel until shot by a 'low-minded sportsman'. When the porters at King's intended removing the swallows' nests from beneath the college gateway, Leslie wrote an entreaty in his best Greek from the swallows to Provost M. R. James and they were reprieved.

recalls, 'unravelling a weird story about demoniacal substitution, his eyeballs staring into the flame, and his nervous fingers twitching to baptise the next undergraduate he could thrill or mystify into the fold of Rome.') With the same literary facility as his brothers, Benson poured out historical romances of a Catholic propagandist nature in his spare time. In 1905, having read *Hadrian the Seventh* by the then unknown Frederick Rolfe ('Baron Corvo'), Benson wrote to its author, and Rolfe came to Cambridge in August to meet him at the start of a walking tour together, during which they decided to collaborate on a novel about St Thomas of Canterbury and even talked of living together. Rolfe shared Benson's interest in the supernatural, and on one occasion persuaded him to participate in a remote-control magical experiment, the alleged outcome of which was the manifestation in the middle of Benson's room at the Catholic rectory of a figure on a horse. But the literary collaboration came to nothing and, like most of Rolfe's friendships, his relationship with Benson ended acrimoniously. Benson put Rolfe into his novel *The Sentimentalists*, while Rolfe caricatured Benson as the Reverend Bobugo Bonsen in *The Desire and Pursuit of the Whole*. Rolfe appears in *The Cantab* as 'Baron Falco'.

Firbank, Holland, and Leslie all came under Monsignor Benson's spell at Cambridge, and Firbank was received into the Catholic Church by him in December 1907. (Legend has it that Benson made Firbank, who detested games,[2] take up rowing as a penance, and he actually rowed for a while in his college's second boat, before both his physical strength and his spiritual obedience collapsed.)

Firbank never took any exam at Cambridge and left without a degree, having resided for only five out of his nine terms. Later he went to live at Oxford, where he would have felt more at home in the first place, and where he wrote many of his novels. Shane Leslie was rusticated for his part in a bonfire rag (he had the misfortune to hand a plank from a fence to the Proctor). Holland abandoned Cambridge for a year to travel in America, then briefly came back into residence in 1908. In their last term he and Firbank invited Robert Ross down to dinner at Trinity Hall. Brooke was among the guests, and there was the usual abundance of flowers and champagne.

Lord Alfred Douglas too had once dined in the same room, but more recently had become embroiled in a recriminatory and absurd dispute with both *The Granta* and *The Cambridge Review*. Firbank had been instrumental in persuading Douglas to contribute an article to the May Week 1908 issue of *The Granta*; but in December the editor, Ragland Somerset of Queens', published an attack on Douglas under the heading 'Celebrities I Have Not Met, Yet Still Am Happy', satirising Douglas's arrogance and taking particular exception to his

---

[2] Encountering Firbank returning to college in sporting costume one day, Holland enquired what he had been doing. 'Oh, football.' 'Rugger or soccer?' 'Oh – I don't remember.' 'Well, was the ball round or egg-shaped?' 'Oh, I was never near enough to it to see that!'

claim that when he was at Oxford 'Socialists were put under the pump'. A Fabian Society had recently been formed at Cambridge and Somerset announced that a Socialist friend of his, 'who strips at 14 stone 6', would 'dearly love to try a round or two at the pump' with Douglas. When *The Cambridge Review* weighed in in February 1909 on a different subject, Douglas vilified Cambridge journalism, in the pages of his own *Academy*, as 'unworthy of even the lowest gutter rags of London'. In the end, he sued *The Cambridge Review* and two of its editors were sent down. There was general hostility against Douglas, and Firbank, known to be his friend and stigmatised by association with the scandal, possibly left the university prematurely as a result.

Aleister Crowley (1875–1947), the 'Beast 666' of black-magic notoriety, enjoyed a chequered association with Cambridge. At the age of ten he was sent to a school kept at 51 Bateman Street by a Plymouth Brethren zealot, an experience he later called 'a boyhood in hell'. The regime involved a bread and water diet, vicious lashings for petty misdemeanours, cricket in which it was forbidden to score runs, and preaching on Parker's Piece. 'Morally and physically, it was an engine of destruction and corruption' and he called down a curse on the place (the headmaster duly went insane and the school was closed). His years at Trinity, 1895–8, were happier. Having inherited a fortune, he was able to dress the dandy, buy books 'literally by the ton', and spend his vacations mountaineering or learning Russian in St Petersburg. Crowley refused to attend chapel ('it involved early rising') or to dine in hall, and claimed to have done only one day's work for the tripos (he did not take a degree). Instead, he represented the university at chess, enjoyed a 'very intense' sexual life, and published several works at his own expense. *Aceldama: A Place to Bury Strangers In*, a Swinburnian poem with mystical overtones, appeared in 1898 in an issue of eighty-five copies ('in a sense I have never written anything better', he recalled); the same year he produced *The Tale of Archais* and *Jephthah, A Tragedy*, as well as a novel, *White Stains*, which has been called 'the most disgusting piece of erotica in the English language'. In 1904 the Cambridge publisher Elijah Johnson brought out *In Residence: The Don's Guide to Cambridge*, a collection of Crowley's undergraduate verse reprinted from *The Granta* and other papers. 'People who wanted to read them', Crowley's preface explains, 'had to buy these papers, which were messy and lumpy, while the reader's attention was unpleasantly distracted by the dung heap on which these pearls were cast'. The book concludes with a fourteen-page puff for 'The Works of Mr Aleister Crowley', which apparently already number forty-eight, and offers a £100 prize for the best essay about them. There are also jokey advertisements, presumably from Crowley's pen, for local tradesmen such as the tobacconist Colin Lunn. Crowley's continuing influence at Cambridge as a poet is measured by the disproportionate space given to him in Aelfrida Tillyard's anthology *Cambridge Poetry 1900–1913*. In his *Confessions* Crowley describes Great Court as practically the only spot in England worth preserving, and expresses a wish for the 'haunted room' over the main gate to be converted into 'a vault like that of Christian Rosencreutz to receive my sarcophagus'. This was unlikely, the college having latterly forbidden him to set foot within its courts.

Four other later well-known poets (apart from Brooke) were at Cambridge in the early years of the century: T. E. Hulme, J. C. Squire, Siegfried Sassoon, and James Elroy Flecker.

Hulme (1883–1917) was more of a poetic theoriser than a poet (his 'Complete Poetical Works' comprises just five short pieces), but his modernist views contributed significantly to the development of the imagist movement. He came up to St John's in 1902 with a mathematics Exhibition, and was soon exercising his propensity for vigorous argument. He 'would start an argument with the coach of the boat during an outing, with the lecturer in the middle of his lecture, or with the waiter in Hall', a friend recalled. J. C. Squire, also at St John's, called him 'a huge, ham-faced, idle man, but one of great wit and lightning intellect'. His pugnacity and flouting of morals and rules were not appreciated by the authorities, however. There were constant rows in his rooms in Third Court, he was ejected from the New Theatre, arrested on Boat Race night, and finally sent down. According to Squire, his departure from Cambridge in March 1904, riding astride a coffin on a hearse, was the 'longest mock funeral ever seen in the town'.

For the next two years, though lodging in London, Hulme commuted regularly to Cambridge in order to attend philosophy lectures. In 1912, with the help of Squire, he even managed to get himself reinstated at St John's, and took lodgings in the town, inviting down his London friends, including Ezra Pound, to deliver talks. But again scandal and controversy began to surround his name. One member of St John's wrote to *The Cambridge Magazine* in disgust that the college should be associated with a translator of Bergson – still considered a charlatan in some Cambridge philosophical circles. Others besieged the Master with renewed complaints about Hulme's moral conduct, particularly his alleged influence over choirboys, the morals of one of whom he was accused of perverting 'by day and night'. Once again Hulme was obliged to remove his name from the books – perhaps a unique instance of a student being sent down twice from the same college.

The career of Sir John Collings Squire (1884–1958), who entered St John's in 1903, could not have been more different. He contributed weekly reports on Union debates to *The Granta* in the form of verse parodies, and joined an amateur touring company to perform melodramas around East Anglia (he married the sister of a fellow undergraduate actor). But perhaps his most important commitment was as one of the original members of the Cambridge University Fabian Society, founded in 1906, of which Ben Keeling of Trinity was the leading light. Fabianism quickly became fashionable among the leading student intellectuals, with Pigou's *Wealth and Welfare* (and his 'I often think that we here with our greater opportunities are trustees for the poor') supplanting Moore's *Principia Ethica* as a major influence. As secretary of the society, Squire invited Keir Hardie, H. G. Wells, George Bernard Shaw, and others to come and talk.

Wells used his visit as the basis for a scene in *The New Machiavelli* in which a leading socialist comes to speak at King's. Wells makes the pertinent comment that for all the students' socialist fervour, it required 'a sort of inspiration' for them to connect the idealised Working Man displayed on the posters in their rooms with real-life bedders and gyps. 'On the whole it is a population of poor quality round about Cambridge, rather stunted and spiritless and very difficult to idealise. That theoretical Working Man of ours! – if we felt the clash at all we explained it, I suppose, by assuming that he came from another part of the country.'[3]

(Bernard Shaw returned to Cambridge in May 1911 to address the freethinking Heretics Society, founded in 1909, at the Victoria Assembly Rooms. Invited to talk about religion, he treated his audience to 'a typically Shavian outburst' in which he preached his theory of the Life Force and claimed: 'We are all experiments in the direction of making God'. The press condemned this 'detestable outrage', this 'dissemination of poisonous theories amongst young persons', and wanted Shaw 'thrown into the Cam'. The following term G. K. Chesterton replied to Shaw's views 'before one of the largest Guildhall audiences Cambridge has known'. Other notable Heretics speakers included Arthur Machen (1910), T. E. Hulme (1912), Frank Harris (1912), Rupert Brooke (1913), T. S. Eliot (1915: see below, p. 237), Rebecca West (1919), Walter de la Mare (1920), Edith Sitwell (1921), Arthur Waley (1921), E. M. Forster (1923), and Virginia Woolf (1924: see below, p. 247).)

Siegfried Sassoon (1886–1967), who entered Clare in 1905, tried reading first law, then history, but failed to bring his mind to bear on either. What he really wanted to be was a poet, and he spent his afternoons drifting along the river reading William Morris, 'pretending that I had been at Cambridge with Tennyson, and having long talks with him and Edward Fitzgerald. At any moment they might come along the river-bank and get into my punt.' He dreamt of redeeming his idleness, like Tennyson, by winning the Chancellor's Medal, and in his second year attempted a poem on that year's unpromising subject of 'Edward the First'. He studied 'Professor Tout's monograph' on the king and dutifully began turning it into verse, but 'instead of seeming to be Edward the First, it was obviously only Professor Tout talking in very prosy blank verse'. Nevertheless he felt certain of winning, and when he didn't, his disillusionment with Cambridge was complete, and he decided not to return.

James Elroy Flecker (1884–1915) had already scraped through Oxford, but the Levant Consular Service sent him back to Cambridge for two years (1908–10) to learn oriental languages before posting him abroad. Attached to Caius, he lodged in Jesus Lane. If Cambridge was a surrogate Oxford for Firbank and Holland, it

---

[3] Wells scandalised Fabians in 1909 by getting the treasurer of the Cambridge Fabians pregnant and eloping with her; sexual intercourse had allegedly occurred 'within the very walls' of Newnham College.

was the merest parody of Oxford for Flecker, who wore a pretentious blazer of his own design and tried to teach the locals proper Oxford punting. Flecker took an interest in a few younger literati such as Francis Birrell (son of Augustine Birrell, grandson of Tennyson, friend of the Bloomsbury group) and met Brooke through the Fabians. Flecker's interest in oriental poetry, which was to result in his poem *The Golden Journey to Samarkand* and his play *Hassan*, began at Cambridge, where he contributed oriental tales to *The Cambridge Review*. Also from Cambridge dated the beginnings of the tuberculosis that was to kill him.

The novelist Hugh Walpole (1884–1941) was at Emmanuel (1903–6) where he belonged to the Mildmay Essay Club and competed against Brooke for the 1906 Winchester Reading Prize (neither won it). J. C. Squire remembered Walpole as giving the impression 'of a thin, spectacled, governess-like youth, with very little to say, extremely unlike the portly novelist of later years', and Walpole himself recalled 'my shabby furtive career at Emmanuel with no honour and much timidity'. He took a third in history. An early novel of his, *The Prelude to Adventure*, is a psychological thriller about a Cambridge undergraduate who murders a fellow student, and whose sense of guilt intensifies in proportion as he achieves college success. Finally he is released of his burden in a mystic moment on the rugby field, going on to score a brilliant winning try for the university. The book has interest as a late example of the university novel genre. Although there are touches of Alan St Aubyn in the supernatural devices (druidical stones in the murder wood), the psychological element is new and the aloof college swell, traditionally the villain, is here transformed into a tragic hero.

While a student, Walpole 'fell idealistically in love' with A. C. Benson, then a Fellow of Magdalene: 'most purely, let it be said, but I suppose Benson saw more in it than met my innocent eye'. Walpole was only one in a series of young men whom Benson took under his avuncular, affectionate wing (Percy Lubbock, the mountaineer George Mallory, and George Rylands were others), with motives that were complex and unsatisfied and analysed in perplexity in his diary. Benson administered to Walpole's religious crises, encouraged his writing, invited him to his country house at Haddenham; and the image of the shy young man and the repressed elderly man cycling together about the empty Cambridgeshire lanes is a telling vignette of Edwardian Cambridge.

The eldest of the Benson brothers and the most literarily prodigious of them, Arthur Christopher Benson (1862–1925), after taking his degree at King's, had taught for twenty years at Eton before returning to Cambridge in 1904. Between his election as Master of Magdalene in 1915 and his death ten years later, he expended a fortune on improvements to what had been a run-down and impoverished college, money raised by the extraordinary popularity enjoyed by the stream of mellifluous, spinsterish books that flowed from his pen. Neither he nor his friends could ever equate this torrent of mediocrity with his genuinely shrewd and forceful personality. 'My desire is to write a great and beautiful book', he once lamented, 'and instead I have become the beloved author of a feminine tea-party kind of audience'. His ruminating essays, *From a College Window* (1906), are typical of what he could turn out by the bookful:

> And thus I went slowly back to College in that gathering gloom that seldom fails to bring a certain peace to the mind. The porter sate, with his feet on the fender, in his comfortable den, reading a paper.[4] The lights were beginning to appear in the court, and the firelight flickered briskly upon walls hung with all the pleasant signs of youthful life, the groups, the family photographs, the suspended oar, the cap of glory. So when I entered my book-lined rooms, and heard the kettle sing its comfortable song on the hearth, and reflected that I had a few letters to write, an interesting book to turn over, a pleasant Hall dinner to look forward to . . . I was more than ever inclined . . . to purr like an elderly cat.

Apart from his reputation as the author of the words for Elgar's *Land of Hope and Glory*, Benson's chief claim to fame (appropriately for a Master of Pepys's old college) is the diary which he kept for nearly forty years. Running to four million words, it was written up each day as a sort of literary blood-letting to assuage his repressed emotions and the lurking dark anxieties that periodically erupted into paralysing depressions. It comprises one of the best portraits of Edwardian Cambridge, its pages peopled by white-haired patriarchal dons (the Master of Trinity is described as looking exactly like Blake's picture of God in the Job designs) and fresh-faced undergraduates. Benson records his daily bicycle rides, 'spinning before the wind' over the flat countryside, and the triumphs and absurdities of college and university affairs, and draws often caustic portraits of his contemporaries – including even his best friends. An account of the Pepys Dinner of 1911, for instance, at which Hilaire Belloc and G. K. Chesterton were guests, cruelly portrays the two writers in their cups – Belloc 'dirty, unkempt, frowsy', quarrelling and falling 'into instantaneous slumbers', lighting his cigar at both ends, dropping down steps 'at an involuntary run', Chesterton sweating so much that when he held his cigar downwards, 'the sweat ran down and hissed at the point'. A selection from the diary was published by Percy Lubbock after Benson's death, and the 180 manuscript volumes were then judiciously sealed up for the next fifty years. Recently, further selections have been made available by David Newsome in *Edwardian Excursions* (covering the period 1898–1904) and in his biography of Benson, *On the Edge of Paradise*.

It devolved on E. F. Benson (who had little in common with A. C. apart from an equally vast output – they each wrote over a hundred books) to clear out the Master of Magdalene's rooms after his death. He found the study 'piled high with boxes containing manuscripts, a towering cliff of them from door to window', including several shelves of unpublished stories, essays, poems, and novels thrust aside by the relentless spate of composition. Vast amounts of this material E. F.

---

[4] The porters apparently did not enjoy much peace after the book's publication, with a constant succession of tourists demanding to be shown The Window. This was ironic, since in real life Benson disliked a room with a view and lived gloomily behind heavily shrouded windows.

Benson decided to burn. 'Morning and afternoon, with the clothes-basket going heavy to the furnace and returning hungry, I voyaged on not yet seeing land, till I felt that I was losing all power of discrimination as to what ought to be kept and what destroyed.' Many of Benson's collection of books went to found the English Faculty Library.[5]

Benson used to tell ghost stories to the boys at Eton and left a bale of unpublished ones at his death; his friend and King's contemporary Montague Rhodes James (1862–1936) used to tell them to the choristers at King's. As a distinguished medievalist (he had been Director of the Fitzwilliam Museum, and catalogued all the Cambridge college libraries), M. R. James had the background to become, incidentally to his other achievements, one of the genre's most adept exponents, many of his ideas for stories being picked up on his antiquarian travels. His *Ghost Stories of an Antiquary* (1905) and *More Ghost Stories* (1911) were published while he was Provost of King's, but there is surprisingly little use of Cambridge as a setting. ('The Tractate Middoth' is supposedly set in the old University Library; a posthumous story describes what two King's students of the sixteenth century, dabblers in magic, meet on the road back from visiting a witch at Fenstanton.[6]) The success of James's stories is largely due to their evocation, against precise foregrounds full of antiquarian exactness, of unnameable antagonistic forces – things furry, skeletal, distortedly grotesque, insuperably malevolent. James recounts in *Eton and King's* how he would invent ghost stories 'at fever heat' for the delectation of the Fellows in the Combination Room after dinner on Christmas Eve.

Another head of college who turned his hand to the genre was Arthur Gray (1852–1940), Master of Jesus. His *Tedious Brief Tales of Granta and Gramarye*, all set in Jesus College in bygone centuries, are spooky stories of boarded-up rooms and hidden treasure, of necromancers and alchemists and disembodied voices on ancient staircases. Again the author's knowledge of local history and topography (he wrote histories of his college and of Cambridge town and university) makes them all the more convincing (he even uses authentic names of former students). One is almost persuaded to set off at once with lantern and spade and Loggan's plan of the college to search for John Badcoke's treasure; and one would certainly not want to be near the staircase known as Cow Lane on the night of 2 November.

---

[5] As part of his scheme to improve the image of Magdalene, Benson founded an Honorary Artistic Fellowship, the first three holders of which were Thomas Hardy, Rudyard Kipling, and T. S. Eliot, who all donated important manuscripts of their poetry to the college and whose portraits hang in the hall. The present holder is Will Carter, of the nearby Rampant Lions Press.

[6] Probably based on fact: two King's Fellows in the 1550s, John Walker and William Cobbe, 'studied and were conversant in the black art' and were intimate with John Heron, necromancer of Chislehurst, Kent.

19

'Ten to three'

'Rupert Brooke, isn't it a romantic name?' wrote Lytton Strachey to Virginia Stephen in 1908, after meeting Brooke on an Apostles reading party in Wiltshire; ' – with pink cheeks and bright yellow hair – it sounds horrible, but it wasn't.'

Pink cheeks, bright yellow hair, grey-blue eyes, Peter Pan humour, a Hellenic balance of intellect and body that seemed the very apotheosis of the Athenian dreams of the dons by the Cephissus/Cam: no one seemed better than Rupert Chawner Brooke (1887–1915) to exemplify the golden youth of Edwardian Cambridge or, in retrospect, the entire English generation lost in the First World War. At Rugby, where his father was housemaster and house was also home, he had already been outstanding: captain of the house, member of the school teams, with a space in the school chapel between Matthew Arnold and Arthur Hugh Clough (so he joked) already reserved for his plaque. Much of the posthumous interest in him derived from the way his life seemed to progress with the inevitability of a Greek tragedy to the filling of that space – though it was an inevitability he rebelled against as each act unfolded.

From Rugby he won a classics scholarship to King's – a college with something of a family tradition. His father had been its first non-Etonian Fellow, while his uncle, Alan England Brooke, was currently Dean (later Provost). But Brooke did not look forward to Cambridge; he was reluctant to abandon the known world of Rugby, and, given the choice, would have preferred the university of his favourite decadent writers (including his literary mentor at Rugby, St John Lucas). At the beginning of October 1906 he wrote to fellow Rugbeian Geoffrey Keynes (1887–1982): 'I expect to turn up early on Thursday morning, if I have not, ere that, killed myself in the train that bears me from Rugby. I shall live in Cambridge very silently, in a dark corner of a great room, clad perhaps in cowl and scapular.'

Keynes, studying science at Pembroke, younger brother of John Maynard Keynes, was a native of Cambridge (his father was lecturer in political economy and later Registrary of the University; his mother was later Mayor) and at first he and a few other Rugbeians were Brooke's only contacts in the town. In the 'gaunt *Yellow Book* wilderness' of his rooms (A14), Brooke looked dolefully down at the terribly old or terribly young people in King's Parade 'from the lofty window where I sit and moan'. Nor did he take to his staircase neighbour, the aging Oscar Browning, who at the earliest opportunity invited the rosy-cheeked freshman in for lunch.

If he was slow to be impressed by Cambridge, Cambridge was not slow to notice him. His enthusiasm for theatre took him along to watch a rehearsal of that year's Greek play, the *Eumenides* of Aeschylus, and he was offered the part of the Herald on the spot. He had no lines and little to do – 'I wear a red wig and cardboard armour and luckily am only visible for one minute. I put a long horn to my lips and pretend to blow and a villain in the orchestra simultaneously wantons on the cornet' – but his debut on 30 November clad in a girlish short tunic elicited reactions out of all proportion to his dramatic significance. The audience, packed with Edwardian hellenists and paedophiles, opened its eyes. A. C. Benson noted in his diary how 'A herald made a pretty figure, spoilt by a glassy stare', while Edward Marsh still remembered eleven years later how Brooke's 'radiant, youthful figure in gold and vivid red and blue, like a Page in the Riccardi Chapel, stood strangely out against the stuffy decorations and dresses'. Marsh, son of the Master of Downing and an Apostle at Trinity in the previous decade, was later to be Brooke's patron, literary executor, and first biographer.

The part of the Priestess was taken by Justin Brooke (no relation; his father was the founder of Brooke Bond Tea), a third-year student at Emmanuel with whom Brooke struck up a warm friendship. Justin had been at Bedales, the progressive coeducational school, and in time the Bedalian passion for drama and fresh-air group activities supplanted Brooke's current pose of Dowsonesque urban disillusion. Justin introduced him to another Bedales-and-Emmanuel product, the Frenchman Jacques Raverat (see above, p. 195). The three of them were soon inseparable.

Equally important was his friendship with a fellow King's freshman, Hugh Dalton (later Lord Dalton, the Labour politician), who fanned his interest in socialism. They founded a college society called the Carbonari to debate politics and recite poetry; and in their second term it was Dalton who introduced Brooke to the Cambridge Fabian Society (of which Brooke was later President). In addition to providing a focus for Brooke's socialist beliefs, the Fabians had the attraction of being the only undergraduate society that admitted women. The Treasurer was a first-year Newnham girl, plain, plump, and maternal, called Katharine ('Ka') Cox, who was destined to play a leading part in Brooke's personal Greek tragedy.

Brooke's first appearance in Cambridge print came in February 1907 when his poem 'The Call', inspired by the recent death of his elder brother, came out in *The Cambridge Review*, for which he also undertook poetry reviews. In the May Week issue of the college magazine *Basileon* he published three poems, including 'Dawn', the first of his so-called 'ugly' poems ('Opposite me two Germans snore and sweat'). Brooke was to contribute frequently to these two magazines, as also later to *The Gownsman*. In May Geoffrey Keynes invited Brooke to hear Hilaire Belloc speak to a Pembroke undergraduate society, the Martlets, and Brooke afterwards had the honour of escorting the great man home: 'He was wonderfully drunk and talked all the way'.

'Go back to Cambridge for my second year and laugh and talk with those old dull people on that airless plain! The thought fills me with hideous *ennui*', Brooke wrote to Lucas at the end of the Long Vacation. To Keynes he confessed: 'Though Cambridge is loathsome, yet . . . what I chiefly loathe and try to escape is not Cambridge nor Rugby nor London, but – Rupert Brooke.'

For his second year he moved into E1, on the ground floor of Gibbs's Building (at the end furthest from the chapel). 'I have new and more nauseous rooms', he informed Lucas. A new recruit to the Carbonari this term was Arthur Schloss, who changed his name in 1914 to Arthur Waley (1889–1966). He had followed Brooke from Rugby to King's where, under the influence of Dickinson in his mandarin's cap, his interest was first aroused in Chinese literature, of which he was to become a pre-eminent translator. He, Brooke, and Dalton would ride out of town on summer evenings to recite Swinburne by the light of their cycle lamps at some favourite spot.

Another old acquaintance was Rose Macaulay (1881–1958), who had been born at Rugby, where her father, like Brooke's, had been a master. He was now a lecturer in English at Cambridge, and Rose, who had recently graduated from Oxford, used to cycle over from their house at Great Shelford to take tea with Brooke or to see her uncle, W. H. Macaulay, Senior Tutor at King's. Brooke in return often went to Shelford for Sunday lunch and tennis. He and she and Frances Darwin were rival competitors for the *Westminster Gazette*'s weekly poetry prize; but he was possibly less impressed by this shy, rather gangling older girl than she was by him (two of her early novels, *The Secret River* (1909) and *Views and Vagabonds* (1912), contain many echoes of her feelings for him). Her first volume of poems, *The Two Blind Countries* (1914), contains several about Cambridge – notably 'Trinity Sunday' and 'The Devourers', full of mysterious intuitions of the primeval world beneath the feet of the scarlet doctors going to St Mary's – of 'wild wet things that swam in King's Parade'.

The Bedalian contingent thought it was time Cambridge put on some serious drama, in addition to the ADC's farces and the annual Greek play. A number of leading dons agreed, and it was decided to attempt a production of Marlowe's *Doctor Faustus*. This time, Brooke was cast as Mephistophilis, Justin Brooke as Faustus. Also in the (mainly Rugbeian and Bedalian) cast were Geoffrey Keynes, A. S. F. Gow (see p. 264 below), Denis Browne (the musician who was to serve with Brooke in the war and describe his death and burial), and H. St John Philby (the Arabian explorer and father of the spy 'Kim' Philby). Though the two performances at the ADC Theatre in November 1907 met with scathing censure from some elderly quarters (there were no sets, no music, frequent black-outs, and no list of actors, and Mephistophilis could barely be heard), it was decided to go ahead and found the Marlowe Dramatic Society, with Brooke as President, Keynes as Secretary, and Francis Cornford, a young classics don from Trinity, as Treasurer.

Brooke's second appearance on the Cambridge stage, despite his inadequacies as an actor, again attracted keen interest from his elders. Charles Sayle was introduced to him by Geoffrey Keynes (a member of the bibliographical Baskerville Club Sayle had founded), and was soon besieging him with gifts and *tête-à-tête* dinners at his curious narrow house at 8 Trumpington Street. Sayle's diary is full of entries that thrill to the touch of Rupert's hand or the colour of Rupert's eyes, but though Brooke accepted the gifts and dinners and was in Sayle's house every other day, presumably his breezy frankness helped him avoid the pitfalls of association with Edwardian Cambridge's bachelor dons.

Brooke was elected to the Apostles in January 1908 as member number 247. James Strachey, who had attended the same preparatory school and for long had hero-worshipped Brooke, had brought his idol's qualifications to his elder brother's attention well in advance; and though Lytton was not overly impressed, he and Brooke shared certain literary interests (such as the poetry of Donne) and the society's numbers did urgently need replenishment (there had been no election since James Strachey's own two years before). Once elected, Brooke found himself amid further homosexual entanglements – to which he generally responded with hearty heterosexual sarcasm.

Although he had carried off the poetry prize at Rugby and repeatedly won the *Westminster Gazette*'s prizes, Brooke competed without success for the Chancellor's Medal. In his first year – the year Sassoon tusselled with 'Edward the First' – Brooke too 'tried feebly to drivel about him, but failed', and presumably did not submit anything. (That year's examiners included Rose Macaulay's father and 'Goldie' Dickinson.) In 1908 he tried again, and Sayle, who saw the finished poem, on 'The Fenland', on the day it was submitted, thought it 'very fine stuff indeed', better than any prize poem he had read for years. J. T. Sheppard, Brooke's classics tutor, also admired it, later considering it discreditable to the examiners (M. R. James and A. W. W. Dale of Trinity Hall) that it had not won. The poem was apparently afterwards destroyed, presumably in disgust at the outcome.

The tercentenary of Milton's birth fell in 1908, and Christ's invited the new Marlowe Society to put on a production of *Comus* as part of the celebrations. As Justin Brooke was taking his finals, it fell to Rupert Brooke to stage-manage virtually the whole thing. It was through *Comus* that he first met Frances Darwin, who undertook the designs, and Gwen Darwin, who helped with the costumes (see p. 176, above). E. J. Dent arranged the music, Albert Rothenstein did the scenery, and there were Newnham girls in the cast – the first women to appear in an undergraduate production.

It was a hectic summer term, with new relationships developing on all sides. For Brooke, the highlight in his emotional life came during a Fabian dinner party in

Ben Keeling's rooms at Trinity, where the guests included H. G. Wells and one of the founding London Fabians, Sir Sydney Olivier, who brought three of his daughters. When the youngest, fifteen-year-old Noel Olivier, dropped her coffee cup, Brooke helped her pick up the pieces. 'My long dead life thrills strangely and opens its eyes,' he reported to Raverat afterwards. He wrote to her – was answered – and for the next few years kept 'accidentally' popping up at her school (Bedales) or wherever she might be, till at last she agreed to a secret engagement.

He had pledged the cast of *Comus* not to get engaged to one another, but such an unprecedented gathering of the bright young things of Cambridge inevitably had its romances, and Frances Darwin and Francis Cornford (who played Comus) were married the following year. (Cornford, twelve years older than his wife and already the author of a skit on university politics, *Microcosmographia Academica*, later became professor of ancient philosophy.) It was during the preparations for *Comus* that Frances turned her first impressions of Brooke into what she later called 'a rather bad epigram about him', published under the title 'Youth' in her first collection:

> A young Apollo, golden-haired,
> > Stands dreaming on the verge of strife,
> Magnificently unprepared
> > For the long littleness of life.

The first performance of *Comus* followed a banquet on 10 July 1908, with Thomas Hardy, Edmund Gosse, Robert Bridges, Laurence Binyon, Henry Newbolt, and Alfred Austin mixing with the Cambridge *monde* in the audience at the New Theatre in Regent Street. Brooke, as well as managing, played the Attendant Spirit, dressed once again in a skimpy tunic that showed off his (rather bandy) legs and in which he was afterwards unable to sit down at the dance given by the Darwins. The production was again not without its critics – notably Lytton Strachey in the *Spectator*. ('So at last you have heard *Comus*', someone remarked to Gosse. 'Overheard it', was his reply. Bridges left before the end.) But it was generally agreed to be an improvement on *Faustus*.

For his twenty-first birthday on 3 August, Brooke received from Geoffrey Keynes an edition of Blake. (Keynes, who had 'discovered' Blake in Elijah Johnson's bookshop, was, among his diverse later distinctions, to become a leading Blake authority and to do much to bring about Blake's modern reputation.) The gift coincided with a new 'mystical' phase of Brooke's poetry, though his own mysticism consisted mainly of celebrating everyday objects such as fluff and clean plates.

'If I had rooms on the second floor, instead of the ground!' Brooke lamented at the beginning of his third year, as work for his tripos again took second place to other activities. He continued to attend the Apostles and Carbonari, and to dine out with dons (the fastidious A. C. Benson on closer inspection was left rather unimpressed), and in February took part in the Marlowe's next production, Ben

Jonson's *The Silent Woman*. In the summer there was a memorable May picnic when Justin Brooke reappeared with an open car and swept a crowded party – Ka Cox and Dorothy Lamb, Jacques Raverat and his future wife Gwen Darwin, Geoffrey Keynes and his future wife Gwen's sister Margaret – off to the banks of the Ouse near St Ives. When Brooke finally sat his exams, he found time to write letters and poems in the examination room.

He did not get a first – by some accounts he was lucky to scrape a second. If he was to stay on for a fourth year and try for a fellowship, there must be changes. He decided to switch from classics to English for his dissertation, and to move not merely from the ground floor but right out of college. Strolling in Grantchester that June, Brooke enquired at the Orchard tea-rooms whether the landlady, Mrs Stevenson, had rooms to let. She had – a sitting-room and a bedroom with meals for thirty shillings a week. The move marked the beginning of a new phase, in a setting which he described three years later:

> But Grantchester! ah, Grantchester!
> There's peace and holy quiet there,
> Great clouds along pacific skies,
> And men and women with straight eyes,
> Lithe children lovelier than a dream,
> A bosky wood, a slumbrous stream,
> And little kindly winds that creep
> Round twilight corners, half asleep.[1]

It was from the Orchard on 12 June 1909 that Brooke attended a notable lunch party in Geoffrey Keynes's rooms at Pembroke. Keynes, Sayle, and A. T. Bartholomew, all fans of Henry James, had invited the great novelist to spend the weekend at Sayle's house. After the lunch (which was attended by James, Keynes, Brooke, Sydney Cockerell, Director of the Fitzwilliam Museum, and R. C. Punnett, professor of genetics) James is said to have enquired whether Brooke was thought a good poet, and on being reassured that he wasn't, replied: 'Thank goodness. If he looked like that and was a good poet too, I do not know what I should do.' James had a busy weekend at Cambridge seeing all the sights – 'how intensely venerable!' he exclaimed with lifted hands and proper American appreciation of Erasmus's Tower – but was rather overwhelmed by the scintillating breakfast conversation in Maynard Keynes's rooms at King's. Sunday dinner with J. W. Clark, the antiquarian and Registrary of the University, when French literature was discussed and 1847 port consumed, was perhaps more in his

[1] There are no 'little kindly winds' anywhere in Cambridgeshire. The passage in 'The Old Vicarage, Grantchester' leading up to these lines, with its derogatory remarks on various other Cambridgeshire villages ('Barton men make cockney rhymes' etc.), possibly derives from local folk rhymes ('Barton bulldogs, Barrington bears, Haslingfield worry-cats, Harlton catch-hares' etc.). See Enid Porter, *Cambridgeshire Customs and Folklore* (Routledge, 1969), pp. 376, 387. In 1913 Brooke contributed a spoof Cambridgeshire folk song to *The Cambridge Review*.

line. On the Monday, a trip on the river was suggested. 'The process of pushing off from the landing stage', Geoffrey Keynes recalls, 'was marred when Sayle dropped the pole with a crack on the large, shiny, yellowish dome of James's bald head'. Nevertheless, his hour and a half on the Cam, with Brooke in white shirt and flannels propelling the punt for some time, remained indelibly impressed on James's memory. 'He reappears to me', he wrote after Brooke's death, 'as with his felicities all most promptly divinable, in that splendid setting of the river at the "backs", as to which indeed I remember vaguely wondering what it was left to such a place to do with the added, the verily wasted, grace of such a person.' Sayle, however, added insult to injury by his tactless habit of constantly finding words for James – inevitably wrong words – as he stammered and stuttered through his convoluted and inimitable sentences; and finally James left rather suddenly, a day early, leaving his pyjamas behind in his haste.

In July Brooke described his new surroundings at Grantchester for his cousin, Erica Cotterill:

> It is a lovely village on the river above Cambridge. I'm in a small house, a sort of cottage, with a dear plump weather-beaten kindly old lady in control. I have a perfectly glorious time, seeing nobody I know day after day. The room I have opens straight out onto a stone verandah covered with creepers, and a little old garden full of old-fashioned flowers and *crammed* with roses. I work at Shakespeare, read, write all day, and now and then wander in the woods or by the river. I bathe every morning and sometimes by moonlight, have all my meals (chiefly fruit) brought to me out of doors, and am as happy as the day's long. I am chiefly sorry for all you people in the world. Every now and then dull bald spectacled people from Cambridge come out and take tea here. I mock them and pour the cream down their necks or roll them in the rose-beds or push them in the river, and they hate me and go away.

Rooms over a tea-room at Grantchester, however, soon proved as attractive to visitors as the ground floor of Gibbs's Building. Flecker came over; Raverat stayed down the lane at the Old Vicarage; Eddie Marsh came down. Then Augustus John, commissioned to paint a portrait of the Newnham classicist Jane Harrison, turned up with his caravans. Maynard Keynes reported that 'John is encamped with two wives and ten naked children' and that 'Rupert seems to look after him and conveys him and Dorelia and Pyramus and David and the rest of them about the river'. John frequented the Cambridge hostelries, 'and has had a drunken brawl in the streets, smashing in the face of his opponent'. Lady Ottoline Morrell, currently in love with John, posted down in her finery (she was the second 'wife' that Keynes mentioned), but was so repelled by the gipsy life and the food that she left again almost at once. Grantchester was momentarily the focus of scandalised gossip for all Cambridge.

Brooke's first letters from Grantchester are headed 'Arcady', and the change of scenery seemed to exert a potent effect on him, transforming him overnight from a blear-eyed decadent into a prophet of eternal youth. 'We'll be children seventy years, instead of seven', he told Raverat, promising him a heaven here and now 'of Laughter and Bodies and Flowers and Love and People and Sun and Wind'. Full of new-found pastoralism, he boasted to the Carbonari next term that 'we of the country abide, perdurable, slow of brain, with hearts that change from glory to glory, like a pool at evening', while his luckless audience were dismissed as 'noisy, quick-witted, little, dark, shifty-eyed, bitter-tongued, little men of the city'. To the Apostles he hoped that he and they would commit suicide when middle age approached – age being incompatible with the pursuit of truth. For them, already divided between 'Trinity' and 'King's', Brooke postulated a new division, between 'Cambridge' and 'Grantchester', of the former later writing

> For Cambridge people rarely smile,
> Being urban, squat, and packed with guile.

– of the latter

> They love the Good; they worship Truth;
> They laugh uproariously in youth;
> (And when they get to feeling old,
> They up and shoot themselves, I'm told).

Brooke offered 'Grantchester' as the new brand of salvation to a society whose members had customarily regarded themselves as the 'saved', even if the term had had different connotations at different times. To the Apostles of Tennyson's day, intellectual salvation had lain through a proper enthusiasm for Wordsworth and Shelley; to those of the 1890s, through rigorous metaphysical integrity; to the disciples of Moore, through the cultivation of 'good states of mind'. Now Brooke offered his own recipe – night bathing, socialism, mystical delight in homely objects, and the pursuit of eternal youth. The Apostles were not wholly taken with the mixture – Maynard Keynes called Brooke and his followers 'Neo-Pagans' – but plenty of less intellectually demanding friends were enthusiastic. Oliviers, Raverats, Cornfords, Darwins – the gay spirits of Orchard breakfast parties, the burnt-skinned plungers into Byron's Pool – collectively believed in tents and chastity, wind in the hair and poems among the tea-cups, hikes and bikes and Donne beneath the Grantchester apple blossoms. To the Neo-Pagans, if not to the Apostles, the archetypal 'unsaved' person might be personi-fied by the 'Fat Lady Seen from the Train' of Frances Cornford's first volume, *Poems* (1910):

> O why do you walk through the fields in gloves,
>   Missing so much and so much?
> O fat white woman whom nobody loves,
> Why do you walk through the fields in gloves
> When the grass is soft as the breast of doves
>   And shivering-sweet to the touch?
> O why do you walk through the fields in gloves,
>   Missing so much and so much?

Fat, loveless, untanned, wearing gloves,[2] and presumably middle-aged – such a person represented the antithesis of Neo-Pagan youth.[3]

The Brooke who had once desponded at the prospect of a second year in Cambridge at King's was all eagerness for a fourth at Grantchester. When in January 1910 his father died and he had to step in for a term as caretaker housemaster, he wrote: 'Oh, and I'm so sad and fierce and miserable not to be in my garden and little house at Grantchester this term. I love there so much – more than any place I've ever lived in.' He was back at the Orchard in time to throw his traditional May party. He had now settled on the Elizabethan dramatist John Webster as the subject for his fellowship dissertation; but 'the apple blossom and the river and the sunsets have combined to make me relapse into a more than Wordsworthian communion with nature, which prevents me from reading more than 100 lines a day, or thinking at all'.

July 1910 was spent with Dudley Ward on a caravan tour of the New Forest, delivering Fabian speeches on village greens, while August saw a repeat performance of *Faustus*, put on for the benefit of some visiting Germans, with Cornford this time in the title role and Brooke as the Chorus. Neo-Pagans flocked back to Cambridge for the occasion, Noel Olivier being put up at the Old Vicarage with three other girls, one of whom, Sybil Pye, recalled Brooke reciting Milton in ultra-Bedalian style from the branches of a tree, declaiming his *Faustus* lines to the Stevensons' bull-terrier, and canoeing them back from Cambridge in the dark, knowing every twist of the river. After the performance there was a torchlit procession in costume to the Cornfords' new house at Conduit Head, followed by suitably pagan dancing round a bonfire.

October 1910 brought E. M. Forster to the Orchard, and also the poet Edward Thomas, who thought Brooke had 'the look of a great girl'. In December Brooke delivered his lecture *Democracy and the Arts* to the Cambridge Fabians, before resigning office as President. A knowledge of German being in those days thought essential to English studies, he spent the first four months of 1911 in Munich and Vienna.

Germany evoked from Brooke almost his only note of intemperate hatred. 'It has changed all my political views,' he told Marsh. 'I am wildly in favour of nineteen new Dreadnoughts. German culture must never, never prevail.' It also evoked nostalgia for home. There was always 'an attitude of Jacques or a slow laugh of Ka's or a moon at Grantchester' getting between him and the

---

[2] Brooke to Gwen Darwin, December 1909, about a fancy-dress party they were going to, Brooke as the West Wind: 'May *non*-dancers dispense with gloves? However proper at a dance, I feel they'd be wrong for a wind. (Moreover I hate them.)'

[3] D. B. Wyndham Lewis, humorous columnist in the *News Chronicle*, produced a riposte:

> Why do you rush through the fields in trains,
> O thin pale girl with the Bloomsbury brains?
> Why do you rush through the fields in trains
> Missing so much and so much?

Munich carnival or the beer-swillers at the next table, and he was glad to get back.

Before leaving for Germany, he had moved from the Orchard into rooms at the Old Vicarage. The rent was the same, but in place of a perfumed tea-garden, bright and sociable, he now looked out on a dank, rank, overgrown, mysterious terrain of ancient trees and tangled undergrowth, permeated by the 'thrilling-sweet and rotten' river smell, and bounded at the far end by the 'yet unacademic stream' itself as it flowed through a 'tunnel of green gloom',

> Green as a dream and deep as death.

The house was a tumbledown affair dating from about 1683, end-on to a bend in the lane. A gothic folly in the manner of a medieval oratory, put up at the bottom of the garden by the eccentric previous owner, Samuel Page Widnall, added a touch of fantasy to the rural circumstances of the present tenants, Mr and Mrs Neeve, with their hens and hives. Brooke liked to spin legends about Widnall (whom he apparently confused with another local family called Shuckburgh); though Widnall dressed somewhat clerically, he was never rector and is not known to have committed the Satanic deeds Brooke attributed to him (his interests lay more with printing and photography than with necromancy). The previous year, when Lytton Strachey had contemplated taking rooms at the Old Vicarage, Brooke had reported:

> The garden is the great glory. There is a soft lawn with a sundial and tangled, antique flowers abundantly; and a sham ruin, quite in a corner; built fifty years ago by Mr Shuckburgh, historian and rector of Grantchester; and *most* attractive. He used to feast there nightly, with . . . I don't know whom. But they still do, spectrally, in the evenings; with faint lights and odd noises. We of the village hate passing. Oh, I greatly recommend all the outside of the Old Vicarage. In the autumn it will be very Ussher-like.

In his famous poem in celebration of the house, written two and a half years later, Brooke worked up these supernatural ideas (including the reference to Edgar Allan Poe's story 'The Fall of the House of Usher'), adding some more eminent ghosts whose memory was evoked by his daily bathes in the pool where Byron had once dived for shillings:

> Still in the dawnlit waters cool
> His ghostly Lordship swims his pool,
> And tries the strokes, essays the tricks,
> Long learnt on Hellespont, or Styx.
> Dan Chaucer hears his river still
> Chatter beneath a phantom mill.
> Tennyson notes, with studious eye,
> How Cambridge waters hurry by . . .
> And in that garden, black and white,
> Creep whispers through the grass all night;

And spectral dance, before the dawn,
A hundred Vicars down the lawn;
Curates, long dust, will come and go
On lissom, clerical, printless toe;
And oft between the boughs is seen
The sly shade of a Rural Dean . . .
Till, at a shiver in the skies,
Vanishing with Satanic cries,
The prim ecclesiastic rout
Leaves but a startled sleeper-out,
Grey heavens, the first bird's drowsy calls,
The falling house that never falls.[4]

The summer of 1911 was a halcyon, somnolent one of peace and promise. 'There is no wind and no sun,' Brooke wrote to Ka Cox that July, 'only a sort of warm haze, and through it the mingled country sounds of a bee, a mowing machine, a mill, and a sparrow. Peace! And the content of working all day at Webster. Reading and reading and reading. It's not noble, but it's so happy. Oh *come* here!' The constant thought of Ka, indeed, had been strangely getting between him and his books. He had to keep breaking off from Webster to write to her, imploring her to come. At last she did come, if only for two days, staying properly in the Neeves's part of the house. Everything boded well. His burgeoning relationship with her might remedy his sense of emptiness as one after another of his friends got married. There was the prospect of a fellowship. There was a contract from Sidgwick & Jackson to publish his first book of poems. Like the church clock, the clock of experience stayed temporarily on the gentlest of hours.[5]

Bloomsbury experienced as yet no dissociation of attitude. Virginia Stephen came for a week, sleeping in the bed lately occupied by Ka, and the chief Bloomsburyite and chief Neo-Pagan worked happily side by side under the chestnuts, she on her long-gestating first novel, *The Voyage Out*, he on the proofs of his poems. On one occasion she supplied him with an image. What was the brightest thing in nature? he enquired, and she, looking around, suggested a sunlit leaf. Straightway a blank in one of his puzzle-like manuscripts was filled. One night Brooke said, 'Let's go swimming quite naked', so the two of them did. (Back in Bloomsbury she was disappointed no one thought this so very daring.)

---

4 According to Peter Underwood's *Gazetteer of British Ghosts* (Souvenir Press, 1971), poltergeist manifestations have indeed been reported in the folly, and mysterious footsteps heard walking about the top floor of the house. Other footsteps, going from the garden into the house, have been attributed to the ghost of Brooke himself. But none of the house's recent owners has observed these phenomena.

5 In prosaic reality, the church clock had stuck at neither ten to three (as Brooke claimed in his poem) nor half-past three (as he first wrote) but at a quarter to eight. After Brooke's death, the hands were set at ten to three as a gesture of sentimental piety, and stayed that way until the clock was finally repaired in the 1920s.

She was impressed more by Brooke's force of personality and powers of leadership than by his poems. 'I didn't think then much of his poetry, which he read aloud on the lawn, but I thought he would be Prime Minister.'

Few retained her sense of critical objectivity about his poems. His coevals – doting females and idolising males – were content to accept the appearance of a poet for the actuality of poetic achievement, while his elders – Sayle, Benson, Dickinson, Dent – were generally too infatuated to provide the firm critical response he needed. The image of Brooke sitting absorbed on the lawn over his proofs is one of a *Wunderkind* as yet largely innocent of self-critical awareness, banked round by a glamorous precocity. The poems he is finalising are, in Virginia Woolf's words, 'all adjectives and contortions'; they have the immediate appeal of self-dramatising poses, but he had yet to learn from Donne and Marvell some sense of disciplined argument, and to acquire through the catharsis of deepening experience – the botched love affair with Ka, the travels to the South Seas, the taste of war – a less egoistic voice.

The repose was not to last. *Poems* appeared in November 1911, but Noel Olivier had refused its dedication. By the end of the year Brooke was nervously exhausted from work on his dissertation – only to learn that it had failed to secure him a fellowship. Then, at Lulworth in January 1912, he stumbled on the fact that Ka was having an affair with Henry Lamb, a married painter and peripheral Bloomsburyite, whose sister Dorothy had acted in *Comus*. Suddenly his world seemed to collapse. A new Brooke began to appear, in Virginia Woolf's words 'jealous, moody, ill-balanced' – or perhaps the old Brooke turned inside out. The benevolent guru became the fallen despot, ignominiously discovering that his charmed reign had been based on unsound premises. Although Ka had acted in obedience to his own principles of freedom by choosing someone else, he clamoured for her back. When, after an emotional pursuit of her across Europe, she capitulated, the falsity of his triumph turned him against her again. His emotional wellsprings were poisoned.

He threw over all connection with Bloomsbury on a wild charge of culpability, publicly snubbing the Stracheys. He dropped the Fabians and decried feminism. He picked out and entered a new world, hard, purposeful, pragmatic – America, Marsh, Churchill, the Asquiths. He transferred his affections to an actress. He reverted to that *alter ego*, the 'Rupert Brooke' at whom he had once laughed. His final incarnation, the crusading sub-lieutenant, more military in appearance than his fellow soldiers, is a throwback to school and head of house and the blank space in Rugby Chapel. In his poems, the world-weariness of his 'decadent' days is revived, tricked out in the colours of the momentary Cause. The obsession with death, transformed for a while at Grantchester into lust for life, returns with grim urgency. He seizes the outbreak of war with avid opportunism. 'Come and die. It'll be great fun', he writes to John Drinkwater.

Sitting in May 1912 in the Café des Westens, Berlin, 'sweating, sick, and hot', watching the despised culture of Charlottenburg go by, trying not to hear the

'*Temperamentvoll* German Jews' arguing at the neighbouring tables, pencilling therapeutic octosyllabics into the manuscript book Maynard Keynes had given him, Brooke sat perched between two worlds. The Neeves would welcome him back, there could still in theory be innocence and bathes, but Grantchester and all it stood for, he knew, were already out of reach. 'I've a fancy you may be, just now, in Grantchester', he had written to Ka. 'I envy you, frightfully. That river and the chestnuts – come back to me a lot. Tea on the lawn. Just wire to me and we'll spend the summer there; with Goldie to tea every Sunday and a fancy dress ball on Midsummer night.' But he must have known she would not wire – that bee-loud enclave was lost. There was just time to recapture the mood before the actuality vanished for ever, to retreat one last time from 'the lies, and truths, and pain' he was experiencing into those deep meadows of forgetfulness. 'The Old Vicarage, Grantchester' was a poem he could have written any time during these two years: all that had been lacking was the distance, geographical and emotional, that focussed it. Now the words came so easily he scarcely noticed he had written them. The editors of that year's *Basileon* were begging a contribution; he wired them to hold the press – 'A masterpiece on its way'. To Frances Cornford he mentioned having 'scrawled in a Café a very long poem about Grantchester, that seemed to me to have pleasant silly passages'; to Sibyl Pye he called it 'a long lanky lax-limbed set of verses'. He little knew that post-war generations would cut their literary teeth on the Grantchester clock, the English unofficial rose, the honey for tea.

Brooke won his fellowship in 1913 at the second try – 'I dined solemnly with very old white-haired men at one end of a vast dimly-lit hall, and afterwards drank port somnolently in the common room, with the College silver and seventeenth-century portraits and a sixteenth-century fireplace and fifteenth-century ideas. The perfect don, I' – but immediately went off for a year to America and the South Seas. He made noises occasionally about the life he was going to lead in Cambridge –

> Oh, but I'm going to have the loveliest rooms in King's . . . I'm going to get up such performances, that'll turn old Cambridge upside-down . . . I'm going to have my great play in the Grantchester Garden, with Clothilde dancing in it. I'm going – oh, Hell, I don't know what I'm going to do. But every morning I shall drift up and down the Backs in a punt, discussing everything in the world, with anybody who desires.

– but increasingly it was pie in the sky. He had thrown in his lot with London society and *Georgian Poetry* – in the first volume of which, edited by Marsh and published by Harold Monro (the Caian who ran the Poetry Bookshop), the Grantchester poem reappeared.

All who met him attested to Brooke's magnetism and talent, yet talent for what precisely none could tell. Could he ever have focussed himself into the defined role of politician, don, poet, impresario, or critic? His humour resisted such narrow formulations – except when, unbalanced by his emotional crisis, he donned khaki. Only a fortnight before war broke out, he accepted an invitation from Professor Quiller-Couch to teach at Cambridge next term. Among a host of speculations is that of the influence he might have had – salutary, surely – if he had been present during the seminal first decade of Cambridge English. But in the event one can only ponder with Virginia Woolf: 'What would he have been, what would he have done?'

20

Cambridge in khaki

'Cambridge has seen many strange sights. It has seen Wordsworth drunk; it has seen Porson sober. Now I am a greater scholar than Wordsworth, and a greater poet than Porson . . . ' Thus Alfred Edward Housman (1859–1936), classical scholar and author of *A Shropshire Lad*, greeting his appointment as Kennedy Professor of Latin at Cambridge in 1911. Rupert Brooke greeted the news from Munich with a parody of some of Housman's best-known lines:

> Emmanuel, and Magdalene,
>   And St Catharine's, and St John's,
> Are the dreariest of places,
>   And full of dons.
>
> Latin? so slow, so dull an end, lad?
>   Oh, that was noble, that was strong!

Instead of shooting himself, as a 'Grantchester' poet would do when middle age dulled his muse, Housman had cravenly opted for a professorship in an extinct tongue:

> Those who don't care for song now hear you
>   In curious, some in languid rows.
> Undishonoured, clean and clear, you
>   Teach and lecture, safe in prose.

In fact Housman, who attributed his *Shropshire Lad* creative upwelling of 1895 to a 'relaxed sore throat' he had had at the time, looked forward to the 'exhalations of the Granta' repeating the effect; and he was no sooner installed than he was complaining encouragingly about the damp climate. But in the end Brooke's jokey prognostication proved to have some justice. Housman published only a further slim volume of *Last Poems* during twenty-five years at Cambridge.

After failing his Greats at Oxford, Housman had passed many years in the obscurity of the Patents Office before the distinction of his classical papers brought him a professorship at University College, London. With the Cambridge appointment the Oxford disgrace was finally retrieved. He was elected to a fellowship at Trinity and moved into the stony gloom of Whewell's Court, where he was to live for the rest of his life in spartan rooms overlooking Sidney Street. At intervals he brought out volumes in his monumental edition of Manilius – usually with prefaces acidly dissecting the faults of previous editors – and during term time he gave lectures which were models of both exact textual scholarship and stoical delivery. A gourmet, Housman brought his informed taste to bear on the college Wine Committee, enlivened the Kitchen Suggestion Book with crisp (sometimes metrical) comments ('for the first time in my experience the Christmas sideboard has been disgraced by tinned tongue, of which the waiters themselves are ashamed', or 'the salmon today was tasteless, and the lamb both tasteless and tough'), provided turtles for the soup at Audit Feasts, and belonged to an elite bachelor dining club, founded in the eighteenth century, known as The Family.[1] But he remained an aloof, cryptic figure, repulsing the advances of acquaintance-ship, never discussing his poems, and taking long solitary walks in an odd button-topped cap, greeting no one he passed. Two (male) photographs above his chimney-piece alone testified to buried passions.

Housman harboured ambivalent feelings about Cambridge similar to those of Gray (whom he resembled in many ways). He could be sharply critical of it, as well as comfortably vegetative in it. Cambridge, he once pronounced, was 'an asylum – in more senses than one'. Generally as publicity-shy as Gray, he could be prevailed upon on college occasions, such as the Master's eightieth birthday, to produce scrupulously polished prose addresses; but he turned down the Oratorship and similar opportunities for public creativity.

He relented only once, on 9 May 1933, when he delivered the Leslie Stephen lecture on literature and for the first time addressed a Cambridge audience not as the editor of Manilius but as the author of *A Shropshire Lad*. Taking as his theme *The Name and Nature of Poetry*, he defined poetry, to a packed Senate House, as the transmission of emotion rather than intellect. Even verse with little meaning could have great poetic impact, he declared, appealing 'to something in man which is obscure and latent, something older than the present organisation of his nature, like the patches of fen which still linger here and there in the drained lands of Cambridgeshire'. But really poetry could only be defined by the symptoms it produced. 'Experience has taught me, when I am shaving of a morning, to keep watch over my thoughts, because, if a line of poetry strays into my memory, my skin bristles so that the razor ceases to act.' Another symptom consisted of 'a constriction of the throat and a precipitation of water to the eyes'.

---

[1] Other members included A. C. Benson, M. R. James, D. A. Winstanley (historian of Cambridge), and S. C. Roberts (later Master of Pembroke). Roberts was much given to the production of donnish little spoofs and pastiches, such as his Boswellian *Doctor Johnson in Cambridge*, his *Distinguished Visitors* ('Bertie Wooster in Cambridge' and 'Mr Mulliner in the Combination Room'), and *Zuleika in Cambridge* (in which Max Beerbohm's heroine, having caused havoc at Oxford, fails to have any effect at Cambridge).

Such a romantic admission of faith, in defiance of the analytical critical spirit that had evolved at Cambridge by that date, was received with surprising enthusiasm, the published lecture selling in thousands, to the disgust of F. R. Leavis. 'The leader of our doctrinaire teachers of youth', Housman chuckled, 'is reported to say that it will take more than twelve years to undo the harm I have done in an hour'. But by his later years (he died at the Evelyn Nursing Home on 30 April 1936) Housman had become an anachronistic relic at Cambridge.[2] To the end he maintained his stoicism (willing himself to continue lecturing even when he could barely cross the court to the lecture room) and his silence about the feelings of the heart. He was as chary of association with E. M. Forster when the latter called on him in 1927 as he had been in 1918 when André Gide arrived with letters of introduction.[3] Yet behind an infinitely greater devotion to textual analysis than a Leavis could muster, Housman concealed passions for the positive usefulness of all poetry that contrasted with the partisan spirit of Leavis's 1930s.

Housman's quarter century at Cambridge was to witness a dramatic turnabout in the study of English, the year of his appointment as professor seeing also the belated first step in the establishment of a proper English school – the founding of the King Edward VII Professorship of English Literature by the newspaper magnate Lord Rothermere. Cambridge's tardiness in accepting English studies (there were already English schools at Oxford and London, but Cambridge continued to believe that 'Englishmen did not need to be taught English') turned out ultimately for the best: the professorship carried the stipulation that the incumbent 'shall treat the subject on literary and critical rather than on philological and linguistic lines', thus introducing a liberal note into Cambridge English from the start (by contrast with Oxford English, which had been stiffened with compulsory Anglo-Saxon and language studies to give it a semblance of proper academic rigour). The first appointee to the new post, A. W. Verrall (1851–1912), though a classicist, was a classicist who, unusually for the time, had

---

[2] His antipathy to the philosopher Ludwig Wittgenstein, who lived above him in the 1930s, is illustrated by an occasion when Wittgenstein, suffering from an attack of diarrhoea, begged to use Housman's private lavatory to save a long journey across Whewell's Court. Housman, taking his stand as a 'philosophical hedonist', refused permission.

[3] Gide, who stayed first at Byron's Lodge, Grantchester, to be near his beloved protégé Marc Allégret, who was studying with a tutor in the village, caused a minor scandal by attempting to seduce the tutor's nephew. He later moved to Cambridge, staying at Merton House, Queen's Road, the home of Harry Norton, a Fellow of Trinity. It was in Cambridge, at 27 Grange Road, that Gide first met Dorothy Bussy (sister of Lytton Strachey), who became his official translator. 'I felt more at home in the remotest of African oases than I do here in Cambridge', Gide wrote (in French) to Arnold Bennett on 16 July 1918; 'and I realize it is no accident that the Grantchester church clock has for so many years been stopped. Several hours left over from my youth awaited me on the Cam that I am now living at last as if in some desperate dream, canoeing, reading Herrick, bathing . . . ' As well as Housman and the Strachey clan, he met the Raverats, Lowes Dickinson, Maynard Keynes, Roger Fry and others of the Bloomsbury circle, and read Rupert Brooke's letters in manuscript. His Cambridge adventure with Marc caused a crisis in his marriage.

endeavoured to treat Greek and Latin works as living literature, not merely as grammatical texts. Already a sick man, Verrall had to be carried to his lectures where, arranged on the table like an eastern guru, he held forth with great learning and insight on the new subject. He died the following year, however, and the choice of his successor was to be even bolder.

Sir Arthur Quiller-Couch (1863–1944), like Housman, arrived at his professorship by an unacademic route. Having failed to win a fellowship at Oxford (where he had read classics), he had turned his hand to the manufacture of popular novels, stories, essays, and anthologies -- most notably the *Oxford Book of English Verse* (1900). There was some suggestion that his appointment had been a political one; and, feeling unqualified for the job, he confessed to arriving in Cambridge 'in a hideous funk'. He need not have worried: his lectures throughout the thirty-two years of his tenure were to be among the most popular in the university.

'Q' – the pseudonym he employed and was universally known by – accepted a fellowship at Jesus and divided his life between term-time bachelor quarters on C staircase, First Court, and vacations with his family in his beloved Cornwall, where he presided over the little port of Fowey. (As time went on, his terms tended to grow shorter, his lectures fewer, and his actual appearances at the lectures he had scheduled rarer.) A man of panache and generosity, dedicated to old-fashioned standards, he spoke out against the debunking fashions of Bloomsbury and what he considered the ugliness and muddled thinking of poetry like T. S. Eliot's. His lectures, stylishly prepared and sonorously delivered, were generally attended by capacity audiences (unlike Housman's specialist communications), and were even reported, often verbatim, in the local press. They also reached a wide audience beyond the university in such collections as *On the Art of Writing* (1916), *On the Art of Reading* (1920), and *Cambridge Lectures* (1943). Often there was a preponderance of women present (especially during the war); but legends of his continuing to address his audience as 'Gentlemen' even when no male was present are attributable less to misogyny (he liked women) than to a stickling for proper academic formulae.[4]

Q was one of the forces behind the founding of an English tripos in 1917 (though Professor Chadwick was equally influential: subsequent students owed much to the Anglo-Saxon professor's refusal to have compulsory Anglo-Saxon in the syllabus). Something of Q's approach to his subject may be judged from a sentence in his second lecture: 'Yes, I seriously propose to you that here in Cambridge we *practise writing*: that we practise it not only for our own improvement, but to make, or at least try to make, appropriate, perspicuous, accurate, persuasive writing a recognizable hall-mark of anything turned out by our

---

[4] An apocryphal story relates that Q once arrived to find a hundred women and one man in the audience. 'Sir!' he began. Next time there were only the hundred women. He glared about, waited, collected up his papers, announced, 'No attendance this morning, I see!' and left.

English School.' 'Germanic' scholarship – the narrow study of texts, sources, influences – though useful, was not the main aim of the school as he saw it, so much as the comprehension of the total meaning and value of great works of literature. This would necessitate the concomitant study of life, art, and history – 'literature cannot be divorced from life'. The new tripos (or semi-tripos, since at first students could take English only in one part of the course; it was not until 1926 that they could take it in both parts) was not to be a soft option.

Q continued to turn out Oxford anthologies, and collaborated with John Dover Wilson (1881–1969) in the *New Cambridge Shakespeare* enterprise (the first volume, *The Tempest*, appeared in 1921). Correct, suave, flamboyantly dressed ('his bedder plays draughts on his cast-away suits', joked a college rhymester; a passionate boating man, Q would appear at the May Races in yachting trousers and reefer jacket), he became one of the best-loved and best-abused figures about Cambridge.[5]

A figure occasionally seen accompanying Q along the river bank was that of his friend J. M. Barrie (1860–1937). Rather shy, Barrie usually stipulated that his visits should be times when 'we could be together without my having to meet people', but in December 1922 he accepted an invitation to dinner at Trinity expressly so he could meet Housman. It turned out to be 'one of those dire dinners of dons and wines . . . The awful feeling that you will never be able to speak or think again!' and next day he wrote to Housman:

> Dear Professor Houseman,
> I am sorry about last night, when I sat next to you and did not say a word. You must have thought I was a very rude man: I am really a very shy man.
> > Sincerely yours, J. M. Barrie.

Housman replied:

> Dear Sir James Barrie,
> I am sorry about last night, when I sat next to you and did not say a word. You must have thought I was a very rude man: I am really a very shy man.
> > Sincerely yours, A. E. Housman.
> P.S. And now you've made it worse for you have spelt my name wrong.

In August 1914 the nine-year old Graham Greene (1904–91) was spending his summer holiday at Harston House, five miles from Cambridge, the home of his uncle Sir Graham Greene (who had earlier lived at Grantchester; the family are connected with Greene King, the East Anglian brewers). In *A Sort of Life*, he recalls the constant passing of troops in the first days of war, and once going out with a basket of apples from the orchard for soldiers resting on the village green.

---

[5] The teetotalism of fellow Cornishman A. L. Rowse was tested when he stayed with Q at Jesus in 1937. At dinner he was offered wine from Q's own cellar, then port, then whisky; there was beer for breakfast and oysters with stout for lunch. 'Longing for the simple life of All Souls, I staggered back and went straight to bed.'

When his eldest brother cycled in from Cambridge with the evening paper announcing the fall of Namur, the boys were delighted, hoping the war would continue long enough for them to be involved. The garden of Harston House, with orchard, stream and islanded lake, provided the setting for Greene's 1963 story 'Under the Garden'.[6]

The First World War completely dislocated Cambridge, emptying it of undergraduates, filling it with soldiers and refugees, disfiguring it with hospital sheds and encampments. The university's reaction to the war was passionate, and polarised. At one extreme were belligerent patriots like Brooke. Housman, who donated all his private savings, certainly sympathised with the war effort. Sir Owen Seaman, interpreting his wartime duty as editor of *Punch* as the maintenance of national morale, revisited Cambridge in late 1914 and composed a poem, 'Cambridge in Khaki', in which he held up his alma mater as an example of a community doing its bit. An army is 'bedded out on King's Parade', he reports, the scholars' walks 'ring to the hustling clank of spurs and sabres', the 'buttery becomes a mere canteen', the 'grass of many an ancient court' is churned by cavalry, troopers doze 'on Parker's sacred Piece', an airship is 'lashed for the night' in Jesus Close:

> O Cambridge, home of Culture's pure delights,
>   My fostering Mother, what a desecration!
> Yet England chose you (out of several sites)
>   To be a bulwark and to save the nation;
> Compared with this proud triumph you have won,
>   Pray, what has Oxford done?

Q too described garrison Cambridge, in a letter to a friend serving in France that was published in *The Cambridge Review* in February 1915 under the title 'To the Front from the Backs'. Though he delighted in the spectacle of 'crowds of Tommies navigating the Backs in Canadian canoes and other bounding shallops', he wandered pensively at night in the Fellows' Garden, 'carefully hiding the ardent tip of my cigarette (lest it should attract a Zeppelin)', musing on the mess his generation had made of things.

Out at Shelford, Rose Macaulay was certainly 'doing her bit', first as a VAD nurse, scrubbing floors at a military convalescent home on the Gog Magogs, then as a land-girl on Station Farm. Her poem sequence 'On the Land: 1916' describes the camaraderie and exhilaration as well as the hardships of farm work. In 'Spreading Manure', she battles with the Cambridgeshire mud, thinking enviously and with something of a Brookeian death wish of the mud of Flanders:

> I think no soldier is so cold as we,
>   Sitting in the Flanders mud.

---

[6] Greene renewed his connection with the area in the 1950s, during his love affair with Catherine Walston, wife of the socialist millionaire Lord Walston, who had estates at nearby Thriplow.

> I wish I was out there, for it might be
> A shell would burst, to heat my blood.

Another poem, 'All Souls' Day, 1916', describes Cambridge 'carried and stormed' by the influx of military, while meanwhile

> The keen breeze searches the chill bones
> Of Cambridge men, not these,
> Of Cambridge men keeping their terms
> In trenches overseas;
> And of colder Cambridge men who lie
> In No Man's Land, at ease.

The character Basil Doye in her novel *Non-Combatants and Others* (1916) in many ways resembles Brooke. Basil goes off to fight in France and later Greece, leaving the heroine with her unrequited love and her memories.

When the fated news came, in April 1915, of Brooke's death in the Aegean, Frances Cornford, his closest Cambridge friend, gave expression in an elegy, 'Contemporaries', to her sense of the futility of things:

> Can it be possible when we grow old
> And Time destroys us, that your image too,
> The timeless beauty that your youth bestowed
> (As though you'd lain a moment since by the river
> Thinking and dreaming under the grey sky
> When May was in the hedges) will dissolve?
>
> . . . .
>
> Most loved, on you
> Can such oblivion fall? Then, if it can,
> How futile, how absurd the life of man.

She would name the child she was bearing in the dead poet's memory, but not even the name would take – her son, a poet of a different stamp, would grow up to reject its connotations (see p. 257 below). Later that year, another Cambridge poet, Charles Hamilton Sorley (1895–1915), son of the professor of philosophy, educated at King's College Choir School and Marlborough, was killed at the battle of Loos, aged twenty. Another, Ferenc Békássy (1893–1915), a Bedalian of Hungarian birth whom Brooke had known in the Apostles and who had graduated from King's only the previous year, was killed in June on the enemy side, aged twenty-two. In Békássy's own words,

> He went without fears, went gaily, since go he must,
> And drilled and sweated and sang, and rode in the heat and dust.

But the readiness to fight of Brooke and Békássy was anomalous among Apostle/Bloomsbury circles, where the general conviction was pacifist and where Brooke's fate was received with mixed emotions. Dean Inge's recitation of

Brooke's sonnet 'The Soldier' ('If I should die . . . ') in an Easter sermon at St Paul's, the poet's death on Skyros on St George's Day, Churchill's reverberant obituary of him, and ultimately Edward Marsh's idealising *Memoir* – all transformed Brooke into a hero of the hour (albeit a hero who had done nothing heroic, who had died not in battle but of a mosquito bite, and whose patriotic utterances reveal themselves, under closer analysis, as expressions of his emotional unbalance). This idolatry of Brooke greatly dismayed his former Cambridge friends – biassed in their turn by their pacifism and by his rejection of them for the more pragmatic world of Marsh and Churchill. While *The Times* and the *Morning Post* rang with Churchill's and Abercrombie's eulogies, *The Cambridge Magazine* (an increasingly pacifist journal run by C. K. Ogden of Magdalene) printed a long obituary by E. J. Dent that emphasised Brooke's dislike of the romantic and sentimental, his 'austere concentration on what was real and intellectual', and ended: 'It was grotesquely tragic – what a characteristic satire he would have written on it himself! – that he should have died . . . just after a sudden and rather factitious celebrity had been obtained by a few poems which, beautiful as they are in technique and expression, represented him in a phase that could only have been temporary.' Harold Monro, in a perceptive appraisal of Brooke's poetry in the same magazine a fortnight later, wrote: 'One fears his memory being brought to the poster-grade. "He did his duty. Will you do yours?"' E. M. Forster complained to a friend in August that Brooke 'goes down to posterity as a sort of St Sebastian, haloed by the Dean of St Paul's, and hymned by the *Morning Post* as the evangelist of anti-Germanism. As far as I dare speak for Rupert, how he would hate it, or rather laugh at it.'

Whether the Brooke legend was inspiring, grotesque, or merely laughable, the fact remained that he and many of the youth of England lay dead. Goldsworthy Dickinson's feelings about the carnage caused him, as he later wrote, 'to retire altogether from such life as there was in the place. I lived and ate alone, when I was in Cambridge, and saw almost nobody.' He was particularly disillusioned by the realisation that academics, beneath a veneer of scholarly detachment, were 'just like other men, blindly patriotic, savagely violent, cowardly or false'. Everything that his Cambridge had stood for – youthful vitality, truth-seeking, the patient development of individual minds – had been destroyed, replaced by militarism, jingoism, and herd reactions. Forster, visiting Dickinson in 1915, saw a symbolic vignette of militaristic 'obscenity' in a group of Welsh soldiers laughing aloud at a lone undergraduate in his cap and gown. 'They had never seen anything so absurd, so outlandish. What could the creature be? To me the creature was the tradition I had been educated in, and that it should be laughed at in its own home appalled me.'

The author and literary critic Hugh I'Anson Fausset (1895–1965), then an undergraduate at Corpus (he won the Chancellor's Medal in 1918), was also appalled at the combination of 'great learning and little minds' in the patriotic dons. A Fabian fellow student had opened his mind to the 'train of sordid financial greed, of shifty diplomacy, and international panic' which had caused the war. This friend was killed in France. Another, returning horribly wounded 'talked to me late into the night, the firelight playing over his prematurely seamed features', showing how 'the very quick of his being was shattered'; he too was later killed. Fausset sought escape from the 'ugly reality' through singing in the choir at King's, reading and writing poetry (he took a copy of Shelley into services), through eccentricities of dress (black hat and big bow tie), and through art: walking through the Grantchester meadows or sitting on Madingley Hill 'painting the sea of ripening corn that stretched from my feet to the island of green poplars and the peeping pinnacles of King's which was Cambridge', he felt he had 'slipped back into an Eden before the Fall'.

Siegfried Sassoon, having won the MC and the sobriquet 'Mad Jack' for his courage in the trenches, had been invalided home and in June 1917 returned to Cambridge to be interviewed for a post as instructor of cadets. After the front line (or even after the horrors of Liverpool Street Station, where his train had been bombed), Cambridge seemed to him intolerably peaceful and smug. 'The streets were empty, for the Cadets were out on their afternoon parades – probably learning how to take compass-bearings, or pretending to shoot at an enemy who was supposedly advancing from a wood nine hundred yards away. I knew all about that type of training.' He was interviewed in the converted library of his college by a don in uniform, who greeted him as if he had just won a scholarship. Sassoon was in fact at that moment gathering his resolve to refuse to serve any further. He had already contributed several anti-war poems to *The Cambridge Magazine*, in which eventually more than thirty first appeared – including 'To Any Dead Officer', 'Does it Matter?' and 'Fight to a Finish'. He sat in King's Chapel after the interview, trying 'to recover my conviction of the nobility of my enterprise'. Cambridge presented itself to him as the image of all he opposed. He reminded himself how Cambridge had dismissed Bertrand Russell from his lectureship for his pacifist activities. '"Intolerant old blighters!" I inwardly exclaimed. "One can't possibly side with people like that. All they care about is keeping up with the other colleges in the casualty lists."'[7]

One cadet undergoing 'that type of training' in August 1917 was Beverley Nichols (1898–1983). Arriving at Magdalene, where he was billeted, he was standing in the porter's lodge wondering where to report when he was 'picked up' by A. C. Benson who, having spotted Nichols's curly head, hauled him off for tea. Benson, who hated the 'wastage of this hideous war' and saw Nichols's cadetship as part of the waste, pulled strings for him, socially and literarily (selling his first works to an American magazine for $500). A year later, now a subaltern stationed

---

[7] After the war Sassoon often visited the psychiatrist who had treated him for 'shell shock', W. R. R. Rivers, at St John's, where he was a Fellow. His poem 'To a Very Wise Man' is about Rivers; another, 'Early Chronology', was written after a convivial evening in his New Court rooms in August 1919.

at Jesus, Nichols found himself the butt of a vindictive colonel and a 'snarling, smouldering, bitter gang' of shell-shocked officers. Unpleasantnesses included being commanded to instruct a squad in bayonet practice when he had not yet been taught it himself. But while visiting Milton's mulberry tree at Christ's, fate again intervened. This time it was the Vice-Chancellor, Sir Arthur Shipley, who hauled him off to tea and ultimately got him out of Cambridge on a mission to America. Nichols's pacifism later found expression in *Cry Havoc* (1933).

Though attacked in some quarters for what was considered its unpatriotic stance, *The Cambridge Magazine* enjoyed a wide readership, both within and beyond the university, particularly on account of the digest of foreign press opinion about the war that it carried. Certainly, at a penny, it was value for money. A letter of support published in March 1917 contained the signatures of, among others, Thomas Hardy, Arnold Bennett, J. C. Squire, Sir Arthur Quiller-Couch, and Jerome K. Jerome; the latter (serving in France) called the magazine in a separate endorsement 'the only paper from which one obtains the undoctored and undistorted fact'. Fausset recalled:

> It was because the atmosphere was so rank with grandiloquent falsehood that one turned eagerly each week to *The Cambridge Magazine* for Sassoon's latest poem. His cynicism may at times have been cruel, but it was like drinking a draught of cold water in those stifling days to read words which cut like a knife alike through the sanctimoniousness of politicians or prelates and the credulity of the conventional-minded who took such patriotic pride in being deceived.

A less likely contributor than Sassoon was Ogden's friend T. E. Hulme (see above, p. 202), who, as aware of war's horrors as Sassoon but as convinced of the war's necessity as Sassoon was of its unnecessity, sent belligerent articles from France under the pseudonym 'North Staffs', with titles like 'Why We Are in Favour of This War'. He crossed swords with Russell, whom he attacked as a typical misguided pacifist, and who, along with Dickinson and Sassoon, was one of the paper's chief anti-war contributors. (Though he was killed in action in 1917, Hulme's name was not included in his college's roll of honour.)

But the most vehement rejection of wartime Cambridge came from an outsider – D. H. Lawrence (1885–1930). Overwhelmed by the madness of the war, Lawrence had conceived of a community of thinkers ('Rananim') living together on an island somewhere far from the sick world, working to bring a spiritual rebirth from the ruins of civilisation. He was having difficulty finding recruits, but Lady Ottoline Morrell, whom he had recently met, had introduced him to her latest lover, Russell, who was sufficiently infected by Lawrence's enthusiasm to invite him to Cambridge to make further contacts. ('It was only gradually', Russell later wrote, 'that we discovered that we differed from each other more than either differed from the Kaiser'.) Lawrence was particularly keen to meet Dickinson, who had formulated the idea of a League of Nations, and Maynard Keynes, who he hoped would be able to design a new economic system for the world. 'I feel frightfully important coming to Cambridge – quite momentous the occasion is to me,' Lawrence wrote to Russell, and arrived to stay the weekend at Trinity on 6 March 1915, a few days after completing his novel *The Rainbow*.

The visit proved a bitter disappointment. He sat in hall next to G. E. Moore, who had never heard of him, surrounded by carapaced elderly dons whose eyes seemed wilfully closed to the implications of the war. G. H. Hardy, the mathematician, to whom he held forth after dinner on socialism, was the only one he found sympathetic; as for the rest of the dons, according to Russell, 'He hated them all with a passionate hatred and said they were "dead, dead, dead".'[8]

But Lawrence's moment of greatest horror apparently came the following day, Sunday, at King's, when he encountered Keynes. As he afterwards told David Garnett,

> We went into his rooms at midday, and it was very sunny. He was not there, so Russell was writing a note. Then suddenly a door opened and K was there, blinking from sleep, standing in his pyjamas. As he stood there gradually a knowledge passed into me, which has been like a little madness to me ever since. And it was carried along with the most dreadful sense of repulsiveness – something like carrion – a vulture gives me the same feeling.

What Lawrence experienced in that instant was a sense of what seemed the repellent evil of homosexuality. 'Truly I didn't know it was wrong, till I saw K that morning in Cambridge. It was one of the crises of my life. It sent me mad with misery and hostility and rage.'

Keynes, Lawrence, and Russell dined together that night in Russell's rooms in Nevile's Court (the cloisters of which had been turned into a military hospital). Russell described it to Lady Ottoline as 'an interesting but rather dreadful evening. Keynes was hard, intellectual, insincere'. Pressed by the others about his purpose in life, Keynes displayed a Bloomsburyan desire for nothing more than 'a succession of agreeable moments' – exasperating to Lawrence at what he considered a moment of profound crisis in the destiny of the world. Keynes's own account of the occasion (he remembered a breakfast party rather than a dinner party) supplies circumstantial detail but shows no memory of the purpose of the meeting. 'We sat round the fireplace with the sofa drawn across. Lawrence sat on the right-hand side in rather a crouching position with his head down. Bertie stood up by the fireplace, as I think I did, too, from time to time.' In Keynes's version, Lawrence, 'morose from the outset', could hardly be got to talk, though Keynes and Russell tried to provoke him into speech – 'You know the sort of situation where two familiar friends talk *at* a visitor.' This conflicts with Russell's account of Lawrence and Russell getting at Keynes, and much of Keynes's account

---

[8] His poem 'From a College Window' (1918), its title taken from Benson, satirises the academic who sees the suffering and humanity of the street outside yet remains content to stay 'Beyond a world I never want to join'.

seems deliberately misleading (he dates the meeting as 1914, and confuses the issue further by using his account as a peg on which to hang an analysis of the proto-Bloomsburyites' beliefs of a decade earlier). But there was no doubt about Lawrence's reaction: his repugnance possibly sharpened by awareness of homosexual tendencies in himself, he afterwards compared Keynes and his fellow Bloomsbury homosexuals with rats, scorpions, and black beetles. He seems not to have met Dickinson at Cambridge; his disillusion, if he had, might only have been reinforced.

In wartime Cambridge, Lawrence had encountered everything that he feared and despised: a military encampment, narrow-minded self-interest, the dry academic mentality, Bloomsburyan aesthetic escapism, homosexuality. 'I went to Cambridge and hated it beyond expression', he told his friend Barbara Low. To Russell himself he confessed: 'It is true Cambridge made me very black and down. I cannot bear its smell of rottenness, marsh-stagnancy. I get a melancholic malaria. How can so sick people rise up? They must die first.' In his haste to get away he left his umbrella behind.

21

The door to Mortmere

When Cambridge did 'rise up' again, it was to enter on a particularly diverse and lively interwar period, reaching its apogee in the late 1920s. While Housman still dined in rigid propriety on Trinity high table and Q still proceeded in morning dress to deliver his lectures, elsewhere Bowes & Bowes was stacked with the latest works by T. S. Eliot; a Cambridge psychologist, Ernest Jones, was attempting to psychoanalyse Hamlet; the Festival Theatre in Newmarket Road under Terence Gray was calling itself the most progressive in England; I. A. Richards was dissecting the psyches of poets and readers of poets in his critical laboratory; and William Empson, *enfant terrible* of the new movement, was peeling apart familiar texts with his scalpel intellect to reveal onion-like layers of unsuspected meaning.

When the Cambridge courts began to fill with students again, it was with an unwontedly mature intake. The arrival in 1919 of four hundred naval officers whose education had been interrupted by the war was celebrated by Rudyard Kipling in his poem 'The Scholars':

> Hallowed River, most gracious Trees, Chapel beyond compare,
> Here be gentlemen tired of the seas – take them into your care.
> Far have they come, much have they braved. Give them their hour of play,
> While the hidden things their hands have saved work for them day by day.

Rose Macaulay in her poem 'Cambridge' (1919) predicted an unbridgeable divide between 'warriors' and 'schoolboys':

> They shall speak kindly one to another,
>   Across gulfs of space.
> But they shall speak with alien tongues,
>   Each an alien race.
>   They shall find no meeting place,
> No common speech at all;
> And the years between, like mocking owls,
>   Shall hoot and call.

Malcolm Muggeridge (1903–90), who arrived at Selwyn from secondary school in 1920 aged seventeen, describes the ex-servicemen he met as tragic figures, obsessed with their wartime experiences, 'minor Robert Graveses, Richard Aldingtons, Ernest Hemingways, Siegfried Sassoons born to blush unseen'. Among those arriving were Vladimir Nabokov, who had fled with his family from the Russian Revolution; and J. R. Ackerley, Gerald Bullett, F. R. Leavis, J. B. Priestley, and Basil Willey, who had all served in the war and who almost all opted for the new English tripos.

To Vladimir Nabokov (1899–1977), arriving at Trinity in 1919, Cambridge presented itself less as an intellectual challenge than as a 'mild masquerade' in which he idly participated while discovering the depth of his feelings for his abandoned homeland. He shared rooms, first on R staircase of Great Court, then at 2 (now 38) Trinity Lane, with another Russian *émigré* called Kalashnikoff; they and a third, Prince Nikita Romanov, were given to unspecified nocturnal pranks, one of which nearly had Nabokov sent down. While a student, Nabokov carried on simultaneous love affairs with a Danish war widow, an *émigrée* from St Petersburg, a Polish Jewess whose brother was at Peterhouse, and a waitress. His lodgings in Trinity Lane seemed 'intolerably squalid' after the aristocratic spaciousness he had been accustomed to; in an article entitled 'Cambridge' published in an *émigré* paper in 1921, he describes the dirty red divan, the gloomy fireplace, the absurd ornaments. Disconcerted by the Leninist 'drivel' with which pipe-sucking undergraduate socialists assailed him, he spoke in November 1919 at the Magpie & Stump debating society, describing Bolshevism as a loathsome disease. He tried in particular to explain the Russian situation to his contemporary R. A. Butler, on whom the character Nesbit in his autobiographical *Speak, Memory* is based. Nabokov stayed the course and took a degree in French and Russian (he had first planned to study ichthyology); but while keeping goal for his college he was mentally formulating Russian verses, and at night he sat up late practising recondite Russian phrases out of a tome bought on David's bookstall.[1] Cambridge supplied an irrelevant but conducive frame for his growing ambition to be a Russian writer: though his memories of it in *Speak, Memory* are vividly nostalgic, elements of his novel *Glory* (largely set in Cambridge) tend towards caricature.

After serving on the Somme and being taken prisoner, J. R. Ackerley (1896–1967) arrived at Magdalene in 1919 to study law (he soon changed to English). He did not enjoy Cambridge much, living in digs at 49 Bridge Street and mixing little; but poems of his appeared in *Cambridge Poets 1914–20* and in *Poems by Four Authors*, a collaboration with A. Y. Campbell, Edward Davison

---

[1] Gustave David (1860–1936), originally from Paris, first set up his bookstall in Cambridge market in 1896. From it could often be bought at unbelievably cheap prices some of the finest and rarest of books, and many great Cambridge bibliophiles – Maynard and Geoffrey Keynes, for example – here laid the foundations of their collections.

(editor of *The Cambridge Review*) and Frank Kendon published by Bowes & Bowes in 1923. A. C. Benson, the Master of his college, to whom he showed the manuscript of his play *The Prisoners of War*, thought it too unrelievedly tragic to be performed (it was staged in 1925). Ackerley played Achilles in the Marlowe Society's 1922 production of *Troilus and Cressida*, his good looks causing a stir. A homosexual, he met E. M. Forster soon after leaving Cambridge, and through him obtained a posting in India. Forster encouraged his literary career (as novelist, poet, playwright, autobiographer, and for twenty-five years literary editor of *The Listener*); Ackerley in return became Forster's confidante.

The novelist Gerald Bullett (1893–1958) had already published his first book by the time he arrived at Jesus in 1919 to read English (he took a first). His novella *Men at High Table* (1948) is a combination-room dialogue among the Fellows of Pentecost College, Cambridge, during a Second World War air raid.

J. B. Priestley (1894–1984) at Cambridge wrote less out of ambition, like Nabokov, than from the need to earn money. An ex-officer's grant took him to Trinity Hall in 1919, but it was freelance journalism and coaching – 'anything to earn a guinea or two' – that kept him there. He later liked to maintain that he had found Cambridge less educative than the wool office in Bradford where he had worked before the war; but he appreciated the freedom, when he could raise the means, to shut himself up 'with a tin of tobacco, a case of beer, and the whole of the Elizabethan drama'. Priestley recalled:

> The Cambridge I knew was crowded and turbulent. Men who had lately commanded brigades and battalions were wearing the short tattered gown and broken mortar-boards of the undergraduate. Freshmen who had just left school, nice pink lads, rubbed elbows with men who had just left Ypres and Scapa Flow. All the colleges were crammed full. (I spent a year in a disused porter's lodge.) The older dons hurried from one crowded lecture room to another with a bewildered air. The pubs did a roaring trade. Nearly all meetings were riotous. College rooms were loud with argument until dawn. Some men had money and chucked it about. Others better known to me, had to live with the grim frugality of the medieval scholars. Fathers of families went down to the river on winter afternoons and were cursed for their clumsiness. Porters reprimanded their late commanding officers. It was a queer time, perhaps the queerest Cambridge had ever known.

His first two volumes were published in 1922 by Bowes & Bowes: *Brief Diversions* was a slim collection of 'Tales, Travesties and Epigrams', mainly reprinted from *The Cambridge Review* (he was a friend of Davison); *Papers from Lilliput* was a more substantial collection of early essays, already showing command of a form he was so brilliantly to make his own. But one senses that the bluff, practical Priestley found Cambridge something of a waste of time. In *English Journey* (1934) he calls Cambridge 'a lovely old place, far lovelier now than Oxford' but wished 'it were not so primly pleased with itself, as if it were a hard-working charitable spinster and the Absolute its delighted vicar'. His friend Kingsley Martin, later editor of the *New Statesman*, who first met him at Trinity

Hall, once told him: 'In spite of Cambridge, you have kept up a Redbrick personality ever since'. Always impatient with academicism, Priestley later reacted to the teaching of his contemporary Leavis with the heartiest contempt.

Leavis's day, however, was not yet. Basil Willey (1897–1978), who had a long and distinguished association with the English Faculty (author of *The Seventeenth Century Background* and other literary studies, he taught English at Pembroke and in 1946 succeeded Q in the professorship), looked back on the pre-Leavis twenties as the 'golden or heroic age of Cambridge English'. Only later did he begin to feel out of place among what he called an increasingly 'specialised, doctrinaire and sectarian Faculty'.

Willey's sentiments were shared by his friend E. M. W. Tillyard (1889–1962). Born in Cambridge (his father was Mayor and editor of the *Cambridge Independent Press*) and educated at the Perse School and Jesus College (of which he was later Master), Tillyard was a classicist who had been seconded after the war to lecture for the new tripos, at a time when the teaching was still in the hands of a select band of 'amateurs' such as Q himself and the eccentric but inspiring Mansfield Forbes of Clare. In his book *The Muse Unchained* (1958),[2] Tillyard tells the history of English teaching at Cambridge, and celebrates the catholicity, liberality, and absence of partisan controversy of the Faculty's early years. The high point, for Tillyard, was 1929 (the first year when students could graduate in English in both parts of the tripos), with Muriel Bradbrook, Alistair Cooke, and William Empson taking firsts in Part I, and Ronald Bottrall, Humphrey Jennings, and T. H. White in Part II. By the middle thirties, most of the original teachers had departed and the liberal mood was being soured by the moralistic influence of Leavis, over which Tillyard, an implacable opponent of Leavis, draws a hasty curtain.

Cambridge English in the 1920s had many inspiring teachers – Forbes at Clare, Willey and Aubrey Attwater at Pembroke, Tillyard and Q at Jesus, L. J. Potts at Queens', T. R. Henn at St Catharine's, F. L. Lucas and George Rylands at King's, H. S. Bennett at Emmanuel.[3] But the seminal spirit of the 'golden age' was undoubtedly Ivor Armstrong Richards (1893–1979) of Magdalene, who, after training in philosophy under Moore, began to lecture in literary criticism in 1922, pioneering a far more analytical approach than had hitherto been general. He and A. C. Benson in the early 1920s began giving undergraduates unattributed passages of verse to comment on, a method Richards subsequently developed into 'practical criticism' classes at which the students' resulting 'protocols' (as he called them) were analysed. (His *Practical Criticism* of 1929 was a collection of students'

---

[2] Tillyard's title is presumably a riposte to Stephen Potter's satirical study of 'Eng. Lit.' at Oxford, *The Muse in Chains* (1937).

[3] Not to forget the medieval historian G. G. Coulton at St John's, who for long bore sole responsibility for the period 1000–1500. A fierce anti-Roman Catholic, Coulton subsequently achieved immortal obloquy as Hilaire Belloc's 'Remote and ineffectual don / That dared attack my Chesterton.'

protocols with commentary.) Kathleen Raine remembered Richards illustrating a lecture on Shelley's 'Ode to the West Wind' by drawing electrical circuits on the blackboard; Tillyard recalled diagrams illustrating how part of the impact of a poem came through the throat muscles of the reader.[4] Richards's forensic, agnostic method encouraged his students to approach all poetry – whether familiar classics or the latest productions of Eliot and Pound – on its own merits and with avoidance of 'stock responses'.

Eliot's influence was particularly high at Cambridge, even while the general public found him baffling. (Even Oxford was less keen: the Fellows of All Souls, for instance, having perused *The Waste Land*, turned him down for a fellowship.) Willey recalls Tillyard mentioning, as they walked to Grantchester, that there was 'a new chap called T. S. Eliot for whom one should be on the look-out', and how Eliot's influence soon pervaded critical attitudes – down with Milton and Shelley, up with Dryden and Donne. Tillyard thought Eliot 'the man really responsible for introducing into Cambridge a set of ideas that both shocked and satisfied'. Richards thought him 'the one hope for the then brand-new English tripos . . . I was soon full of dreams of somehow winkling Eliot out of his bank and annexing him to Cambridge.' Muriel Bradbrook claims Eliot's critical essays were 'canonized in the Cambridge of the time' and that 'our working implements were the books of Eliot and Richards'. James Reeves, who entered Jesus in 1928, considered Eliot's influence 'paramount, though not unchallenged' (Q scorned 'the T. S. Eliot game', Lucas, librarian at King's, went so far as to ban his works from the college library). Malcolm Lowry once claimed he learnt nothing at Cambridge except 'a great deal of Eliot'. Leonard Woolf assured Eliot in 1930 that his poetry was a constant subject of discussion among 'the Cambridge younger generation'. The culmination was F. R. Leavis's championing of Eliot in *New Bearings in English Poetry* (1932).

In fact Eliot (1888–1965) had visited Cambridge in 1915, arriving from Oxford only days after D. H. Lawrence's departure, to speak in Russell's rooms to the Moral Science Club; he also addressed the Heretics. Though he found Russell 'unbalanced', they got on well and stayed up talking until one. On that occasion Eliot compared Cambridge men with Harvard types, 'serious, industrious, narrow and plebeian'. Soon afterwards he met Vivien Haigh-Wood, then living as a governess at 26 Malcolm Street, Cambridge; they were married in June 1915. Though Eliot was not tempted by Richards's invitation to become a Cambridge don, 'he got into the way of coming fairly often to stay with us in Cambridge, at first on King's Parade directly opposite the gate of King's'. In 1924 he lectured on George Chapman to the Cambridge Literary Society, then accepted the 1926 Clark lectureship. Delivered on Tuesday afternoons in the hall of Trinity, his eight lectures on Metaphysical poetry were initially packed out ('the whole of Newnham and Girton' attended the first) though they proved dull, recondite and

---

[4] It is not clear whether this is related to the symptom Housman complained of in his 1933 lecture.

semi-audible. A few chosen undergraduates were allowed to meet Eliot for coffee on the Wednesday mornings; these included Empson and John Hayward, then an undergraduate at King's, later Eliot's friend and literary adviser.[5] Eliot made many subsequent visits to Cambridge. In May 1936, while visiting Maynard Keynes (Willey, invited to lunch, recalls Eliot as 'immaculate, impenetrable, inscrutable; uttering little, but looking very handsome, melancholy and wise'), he motored with the dean of Trinity's wife to Little Gidding (his poem *Little Gidding* was written in 1941). In November 1936 he gave a talk to the English Club on 'The Idiom of Modern Verse'; in 1938 he received an honorary degree; in 1939 he was elected an Honorary Fellow of Magdalene and gave the Boutwood Foundation lectures at Corpus, published as *The Idea of a Christian Society*; and during the war years he visited John Hayward at Merton Hall.

In Eliot's absence, however, Richards with his practical criticism classes remained the principal direct influence. Empson claims that when his audience overflowed the hall, Richards 'would then lecture in the street', something unknown since the Middle Ages. Bradbrook recalls the atmosphere at a Richards lecture as 'a cross between a Welsh revivalist meeting . . . and the British Association's lectures in elementary science'. Christopher Isherwood (1904–86), who came up to Corpus Christi from Repton in 1923 to read history, describes in his fictionalised autobiography *Lions and Shadows* (1938) the inspiration he and his fellow Reptonian Edward Upward (b. 1903), also reading history at Corpus, drew from Richards's lectures:

> Here, at last, was the prophet we had been waiting for – this pale, mild, muscular, curly-headed young man . . . But, to us, he was infinitely more than a brilliant new literary critic: he was our guide, our evangelist, who revealed to us, in a succession of astounding lightning flashes, the entire expanse of the Modern World . . . Poetry wasn't a holy flame, a fire-bird from the moon; it was a group of interrelated stimuli acting upon the ocular nerves, the semi-circular canals, the brain, the solar plexus, the digestive and sexual organs. It did you medically demonstrable good, like a dose of strychnine or salts.

Isherwood and Upward apparently found little else at Cambridge to enthuse over: *Lions and Shadows* otherwise presents two highly imaginative adolescent minds at total war with academic reality. Through the eyes of the narrator and his friend 'Allen Chalmers' (Upward), Cambridge is depicted as a surrealist, threatening ambience, through which they move like spies, in a conspiracy of two, sharing a secret terminology and relating the hostile phenomena around them to a private mythology. 'Cambridge exceeded our most macabre expectations. Both Chalmers and myself were overpowered, by the leisure, by the politeness, by the extravagance, by the abundance of alcohol and rich food . . . The whole

---

[5] Another American-born lecturer of 1926 was Gertrude Stein, who addressed the Literary Society on 'Composition and Explanation'. She was accompanied by the three Sitwell siblings.

establishment seemed to offer an enormous tacit bribe. We fortified ourselves against it as best we could . . . swearing never to betray each other, never to forget the existence of the "two sides" and their eternal, necessary state of war.' The facts that Isherwood's sitting-room was filled with menacing and useless brown chairs or that Upward's rooms in Old Court were supposed to be haunted were received with a delighted sense of inevitability. The dons were sinisterly benign – a mythical history don called Laily was invented to represent all the donnish attributes they loathed – while the students arranged themselves into repellent but alluring sets. In his own novel *No Home but the Struggle* (the third part of his trilogy *The Spiral Ascent*), Upward portrayed how in his first year, before Isherwood came to join him, he had been drawn in among the hearties, playing poker, taking town girls up so-called Fornication Creek, and climbing into college drunk. Isherwood, when he arrived, was sucked as insidiously into a circle of upper-class snobs that they dubbed the Poshocracy. To keep them alert in future against such self-betrayals, they created a mythical 'Watcher in Spanish', visible only to themselves, whose propensity was to appear silently at their elbow at moments when they were being insincere and in danger of being incorporated into the 'Combine'.

All around them, Isherwood and Upward diagnosed sham values, mysterious hints. The pair of cleaned shoes deposited by a college servant on the chapel steps, the waiter murmuring in one's ear in hall, a reptilian shopman praising one's choice of tie – all seemed symptoms of the conspiracy. Yet hidden among the duplicity, like openings in a metaphysical labyrinth, lay escape routes into dissident reality. 'One evening, as we were strolling along Silver Street, we happened to turn off into an unfamiliar alley, where there was a strange-looking rusty-hinged little old door in a high blank wall. Chalmers said: "It's the doorway into the Other Town."' Another time, wandering over a foggy bridge, they spotted the name beneath the gas-lamp – Garret Hostel Bridge. '"The Rat's Hostel" Chalmers suddenly exclaimed . . . Now we both became abnormally excited: it seemed to us that an ill-important statement had been made. At last, by pure accident, we had stumbled upon the key-words which expressed the inmost nature of the Other Town.'

Gradually, the Other Town became dissociated in their minds from Cambridge altogether. Cambridge was irredeemable, but somewhere there existed a locality, a village, inhabited by all their fantastic creations. They named it Mortmere, and began to channel their alienation from university life into outrageous surrealist stories about its inhabitants. Peopled by necrophiles, poshocrats, coprophagists, pornographers, and anarchists, subject to horrendous disasters that they detailed with tea-table blandness, Mortmere could be neither rationalised nor categorised. 'Every brick of Mortmere village is strange', as Isherwood said.

With hopes of a generous allowance from his wealthy gentry family, Isherwood was not unduly worried if his academic results suffered from the effects of all this imaginative excitement. But Upward (who became a schoolmaster) needed a degree. Having taken a third in the first part of his tripos, Upward tried to appease the authorities by competing for the Chancellor's Medal for 1924 – 'If Chalmers won the Medal – well, it was a disgrace he shared with Tennyson: if he failed to win it, there was always the precedent of Rupert Brooke, who had been defeated by an embryo don' (in fact by Sir Geoffrey Butler, their history tutor). With the Watcher in Spanish doubtless in minatory attendance, Upward turned out a piece in polished couplets on the subject 'Buddha' and shared Tennyson's disgrace. He also, disliking Cambridge history for its 'fact-grubbing passionlessness, its dull indifference to human affairs', switched to English and ultimately took a respectable second.

Isherwood, however, had decided he had had enough of academicism. After dropping Bishop Stubbs's unloved *Charters* into the Cam, he sat through the first part of his tripos writing limericks and blank verse in answer to every question. Summoned by his tutor, he was recommended to avoid a scandal by voluntarily removing his name from the college books.

Isherwood celebrated his premature departure from Cambridge in an unpublished Mortmere poem, 'The Recessional from Cambridge', addressed to their tutor by the disgraced students Hynd and Starn as they board the midnight express for Mortmere:

> Therefore, we leave you, snug in Cambridge town
> With your cigar, your glass of old dry sherry,
> Your smirking and plump-busted secretary,
> Curtly dictating with closed eyes and frown:
> 'Dear Starn, the Master has removed your name
> From the college books. Personally, I will not blame . . . '

> Outcast, subject to disapproving glances,
> We pack our suitcases and pay our bills,
> Casually scatter tips and arsenic pills
> And leave, two idiots, who have missed their chances.
> Yes, tutor, two young men must go alone
> Into the night, because Beauty ailed them at the bone.

In fact, far from going alone, all the mad surrealist characters they have created detach themselves from their Cambridge haunts to pile aboard with them:

> You will not, any more, I think, discern
> Miss Belmane sketching in the college courts,
> And Sergeant Claptree, with his limp and warts
> Is hardly to be expected to return.
> I do not think that you will ever see
> Gunball again near Coton, fishing from a tree.

> And scarcely any longer shall you find
> The Reverend Welken poring over tomes
> In Corpus library, for now he roams

>   Past other shelves. When the sexton has climbed
>   High up St Mary's tower to set the clocks on
>   He'll spy no more the sauntering shape of Reynard Moxon.[6]

The Cambridge they abandon is reviled as the graveyard of love, poetry, and the imagination, the Mortmere towards which they speed eulogised as the cradle of all that is creatively vital. It took Isherwood several years to emerge from the influence of Upward and Mortmere – not finally until his departure for Berlin in 1929.[7] Upward himself was to resolve the passionate hatreds aroused in him by Cambridge by a commitment to Marxism, as expressed in his trilogy of novels.

If Richards was the presiding magus of Cambridge criticism, William Empson (1906–84), Richards's pupil at Magdalene, was its most impressive neophyte, producing at Cambridge not only some of his best poetry but his most influential contribution to criticism. Empson had already graduated in mathematics when he switched to English in his fourth year. Arriving at his third supervision under Richards fresh from reading *A Survey of Modernist Poetry* by Robert Graves and Laura Riding, which contained a multi-interpretative analysis of a Shakespeare sonnet, Empson commented that one could probably apply the technique to almost any poetry. Richards suggested that he go off and try. Two weeks later Empson returned 'with a thick wad of very illegible typescript under his arm – the central 30,000 words or so' of what was to become *Seven Types of Ambiguity*, a work which took analytical criticism to its limit by examining poetry microscopically and isolating every conceivable meaning – often meanings in seeming contradiction to the obvious ones. Submitted in 1929 as part of his tripos, the work gained Empson a starred first and was published the following year to considerable acclaim. This was an extraordinary achievement for a student in his early twenties who had only just taken up literary criticism.

In addition to this pioneering critical work, Empson found time to turn out a torrent of book, theatre, and film reviews for *The Granta*, and to produce a substantial corpus of poetry of his own, dense with difficult, scientific imagery, that was to make him one of the most influential poets of his generation. Many of his poems first appeared in Cambridge magazines: 'Sleeping Out in a College Cloister', for instance, in the *Magdalene College Magazine*, 'Camping Out' (with

---

6   The same characters again board a train for Mortmere at the start of the only Mortmere story ever published – Upward's 'The Railway Accident', written in 1928 as a kind of farewell to the imaginary domain.

7   In Isherwood's second novel *The Memorial* (1932) the character Maurice loathes Cambridge with a more basic relish, wanting to blow up the whole place with dynamite; he lets off an aerial torpedo on Guy Fawkes night, is involved in a fatal smash-up on the Newmarket Road, drives a motor-boat up the Backs, swamping the punts, nearly kills a cyclist during an evening spin, and carts an uprooted signpost back to college. Isherwood himself had in fact acquired a powerful AJS motor-cycle in the spring of 1924 but, nervous of riding it, used to wheel it through the streets, pretending it had broken down.

its arresting first line 'And now she cleans her teeth into the lake') in *Experiment*, one of two rival literary publications that burst into life in October 1928 – both with editorial roots in Magdalene. *Experiment*, which ran for seven termly issues and was the more *avant-garde* of the two, was edited by a team including Empson himself, his fellow mathematician Jacob Bronowski of Jesus, and Hugh Sykes Davies of St John's. Among its other contributors were Malcolm Lowry, T. H. White, the American poet Richard Eberhart (studying at St John's), Kathleen Raine, Humphrey Jennings (the film producer), James Reeves, and Elsie Phare (the first woman to win the Chancellor's Medal). As well as poems and stories, the magazine carried articles on modern art and aesthetics and extracts from *Seven Types of Ambiguity*, and was distributed in Paris and Toronto as well as Cambridge. It expired just when it seemed to be achieving real significance – the final issue contained an extract from James Joyce's 'Work in Progress'. Its rival, *The Venture*, which ran for six issues and was edited by Michael Redgrave and Robin Fedden of Magdalene and Anthony Blunt of Trinity, was more conservative and 'arty', containing essays on art by Blunt, and poems, stories, and decorations by John Lehmann, John Davenport, George Rylands, Julian Bell, and others. Although *The Venture* announced itself as 'a protest against the more licentious forms of Free Verse, Surréalisme, and Art Without Tears', in its last number it offered a reconciliation with *Experiment* by including a poem by Empson and a story ('Goya the Obscure') by Lowry. Most of the contributors to *Experiment* and *The Venture* were also represented in two volumes of *Cambridge Poetry*, published in 1929 and 1930 by the Woolfs' Hogarth Press. (F. R. Leavis, no friend to university anthologies, reviewed the first very favourably, singling out the work of Empson and Eberhart for special praise.) Heffer's produced a series of individual poems, 'ideal as Christmas cards', under the title *Songs for Sixpence*.

The contributors to *Experadventure* (as *The Granta* burlesqued the two magazines) and *Cambridge Poetry*, however, constituted less a coherent move-ment than a largely fugitive alignment. Kathleen Raine (b. 1908), for example, who came up to Girton in 1926 to read botany, tried to ally herself with the group that centred on Empson, contributing her early poems to *Experiment*; but for her, while Cambridge provided a point of departure in one sense (as an escape from the cultural desert of her home town, Ilford), it also proved a blind alley. It was to be some years before she realised that her particular talent was for something very different from the productions of Empson or Bronowski. She regretted later not having met Vernon Watkins (1906–67), who had come up to Magdalene in 1924 to read modern languages but had quickly realised that the Cambridge teaching and ethos were deadly to his gift, and returned to Wales. (A friend of Isherwood's, he had shown some of the Mortmere stories to a don, who pronounced them childish.) Both Watkins and Raine were poets of the Imagination – a 'meaningless' word, according to Raine, in the positivist scientific context of Cambridge. Lacking the strength of character at that date to follow

Watkins's example, however, and unsure what to do with her life, she followed the literary crowd, contracting two successive failed marriages to Cambridge poets – Hugh Sykes Davies and Charles Madge – before ultimately finding, partly through her growing interest in Blake, her real path. After a life's work devoted to the study of the Imagination, she looks back on the Cambridge of that date, in which 'clever manipulation of natural fact passed for poetry', as 'intellectually insignificant'.

Equally individualistic were the group's two novelists, T. H. White (1906–64) and Malcolm Lowry (1909–57). White, who studied English at Queens' (1925–9), was scholarly, loquacious, insatiable for knowledge, and already busily writing – he contributed a column as 'Our Cambridge Correspondent' to the *Saturday Review*, was included in *Cambridge Poetry 1929*, and published his first volume of poems, *Loved Helen*, while at Cambridge. From Cambridge White derived two lasting benefits. It was there that he first became interested in Malory – an interest that later germinated his cycle of Arthurian novels, *The Once and Future King*. (But the essay on Malory that he submitted for the first part of his tripos was apparently too 'original' for the examiners, one of whom turned out to be a Malory expert, and he did badly. In Part II he redeemed this failure by taking a starred first.) The other benefit White took from Cambridge was his friendship with his tutor, L. J. Potts ('the greatest literary influence in my life'), a lifelong friend, confidant, and trusted literary adviser who read all White's books as he wrote them. White jested that Potts was his model for the murdered don in his early detective thriller, *Darkness at Pemberley*, set partly in a Cambridge college unashamedly based on Queens'. The ingenious and villainous murderer, a chemistry lecturer named Mauleverer, he claimed was based on his Director of Studies at Queens', R. D. G. Laffan. Mauleverer and Inspector Buller of the Cambridge police play out their final deadly battle of wits in the labyrinthine chimneys of an ancient mansion in Derbyshire.

Lowry, from a prosperous Liverpool family, had already had a taste of Cambridge before he came up to the university, for he attended the Leys School in 1923–7. It was at the Leys that he first began to play the ukulele, drink, and write. Encouraged by his housemaster, W. H. Balgarnie,[8] he contributed a stream of stories, poems, and even hockey reviews to the *Leys Fortnightly*. He also dodged games to attend the Festival and New Theatres, wrote love letters during geometry, swam at Byron's Pool (which he claimed 'smelt of people's feet'), and shared a study with the future film star, Michael Rennie. After six months as a deckhand on a voyage to the Far East (the inspiration for his first novel, *Ultramarine*, largely written at Cambridge), a spell in America with his hero

---

[8] Balgarnie was the model for the schoolmaster in *Goodbye Mr Chips* (1934) by another Leys pupil, James Hilton (1900–54). Hilton, who took a first in English from Christ's, later worked in Hollywood (where he and Lowry once met up); his novel *Lost Horizon* (1933) added Shangri-la to the dictionaries.

Conrad Aiken, and three months as a student at Bonn, his return to Cambridge in October 1929 to read English at St Catharine's seemed 'a horrible regression'. But if he struck his contemporaries, with his traveller's tales and epic boozing, as frighteningly mature, he probably seemed the reverse to the dons, and remained fundamentally insecure and shy. The university in fact showed unusual indulgence towards him: strings had to be pulled to admit him to the college in the first place; he cut lectures and tended to meet his supervisor, if at all, in the pub; and finally he was allowed to submit extracts from *Ultramarine* as part of his tripos (he scraped a third on the strength of it).

Lowry lost no time in seeking out the editors of *Experiment* and *Cambridge Poetry*. Hugh Sykes Davies (1909–84), at *Experiment*, was immediately impressed by Lowry's prose style and used an excerpt from an early draft of *Ultramarine* (the death of the carrier pigeon) in the next issue. 'Mostly our contributors wrote stream-of-consciousness stuff of unutterable boredom . . . Malcolm came along doing the same kind of thing, but his stuff was different.' Of the editors of *Cambridge Poetry*, John Davenport (1908–66) of Corpus (who later collaborated with Dylan Thomas on *The Death of the King's Canary*) became a friend for life. Witty, bibulous, name-dropping, monocle-wearing, larger than life (by 1940 he weighed nineteen stone), a character in other writers' lives who never wrote a book of his own, he was a fair match for Lowry. Davenport, who had rooms at the Eagle, has described Lowry's freshman rooms at 2 Bateman Street as a confusion of books and bottles, barbells and ukuleles, with international restaurant bills pinned to the walls. The books showed Lowry's breadth of reading: 'Like other undergraduates of that time he had the Elizabethans, Joyce and Eliot, but few undergraduates then knew Knut Hamsun and Hermann Bang, B. Traven and Nordahl Grieg' or the whole of Ibsen and Strindberg. Davenport included a poem of Lowry's in the next anthology.

It was Davenport who introduced Lowry to the salon kept by Charlotte Haldane (wife of Professor J. B. S. Haldane the biochemist) at Roebuck House beside the river at Chesterton, also frequented by Empson, Redgrave, and Hugh Sykes Davies. Charlotte, herself a novelist and former journalist, fell for Lowry, whom she called 'the most romantic undergraduate of that period in Cambridge'. Lowry in turn was infatuated by her, though too terrified of her amatory enthusiasms to respond fully. (As Dana Hilliot, the deckhand hero of *Ultramarine*, laments, 'I pursue women from street to street, from lamp to lamp, from Petty Cury to old Chesterton, always remaining a virgin. When they speak to me I run away.') Mrs Haldane's third novel, *I Bring Not Peace* (1932), is dedicated to Lowry, and its central male character, James Dowd, an ex-undergraduate turned cabaret singer, is clearly based on him (some of the songs Dowd sings are acknowledged to be by Lowry himself). When the heroine first encounters Dowd, he is drunkenly nursing his smashed ukulele after walking into a door; but as in real life, the protagonists' romance comes to nothing. The novel ends with a suicide based on an actual event in Lowry's first term, when a fellow St Catharine's freshman, Paul Fitte (whom Lowry had met in Germany), gassed himself in his Trumpington Street lodgings, apparently as a result of blackmail. Lowry, the last person to see Fitte alive (according to one version, he even helped Fitte seal the windows and door) gave evidence at the inquest, and, in addition to the use of it in Mrs Haldane's novel, the incident resurfaces in Lowry's own writings – as in the suicide of Peter Cordwainer in *October Ferry to Gabriola*. Despite Charlotte Haldane's adulation of him, Lowry, perhaps conscious of having failed a test, later used to sneer about 'Chaddy Haldane's addled salon'.

For his second year Lowry moved into college, barricading himself in his rooms (D2) with bottles of beer, jazz records, and Norwegian literature. He showed little interest in his English course, and had fallen out with Tom Henn ('I was bitterly hurt when my supervisor in his last interview with me before I left college said, "You are not nearly so unusual a type as you think you are!"' – *Ultramarine*). Sykes Davies, having himself only just graduated, was asked to take him over, which involved meeting him in pubs, his favourites being the Bath, the Eagle, and the Red Cow. According to Davies, Lowry drank a 'kind of fake champagne' called Moussec, and was only completely sober for 'an hour or two a month'. (In fact Lowry would drink anything alcoholic, including a ninety-five per cent alcohol solution of limonene which a science friend was using in experiments: 'true fire water'.) In the pub, Lowry would read aloud chapters of his novel to anyone willing to listen, or indulge in friendly fisticuffs. During vacations he made trips to Scandinavia or stayed with Aiken at Rye. In their last term, he and Davenport took part in the annual Footlights revue, Lowry contributing lyrics and music.

Lowry's memories of Cambridge were to become a significant part of his strangely obsessive subconsciousness, with images of the university recurring throughout his works. A novel, *In Ballast to the White Sea*, lost when Lowry's Canadian beach-house was burnt down, seems to have been largely set in Cambridge, while in one of his stories, 'Through the Panama', the gateway to hell is revealed to its hero in the form of the entrance to St Catharine's College. In *Ultramarine*, Hilliot looks back constantly to Cambridge, from which he has been sent down; he parries the invitation of a *danseuse* in a Chinese bar to 'come upstairs' by saying, 'My supervisor would strongly object to it. Not to mention the proctors!' and later reacts to the squalor and enmities of the forecastle in a nostalgic soliloquy:

> If I could only shut my ears to this, and my eyes, and . . . be walking down Bateman Street, Cambridge, Eng., that day in late February with spring approaching and the grey birds sweeping and dipping in curves and spirals about the singing telegraph wires – or weren't there any? – and later the two undergraduates fighting outside 'The Red Cow'. And the green buses. Station – Post Office – Chesterton, which always swirled so surprisingly from behind corners as though they had some important message to deliver!

In chapter 3 of *Under the Volcano*, the Consul, lying drunk in a Mexican street, is rescued by a passing motorist with a 'King's Parade voice' and a Trinity tie, 'mnemonic of a fountain in a great court'. In chapter 6, the Consul and his half-brother Hugh Firmin reminisce boozily about their supervisor Carruthers, who used to pass out with drink at supervisions, and the day the Consul brought a horse into the college buttery ('Apparently it took about thirty-seven gyps and the college porter to get it out'). Hugh muses on 'the harbour bells of Cambridge! Whose fountains in moonlight and closed courts and cloisters, whose enduring beauty in its virtuous remote self-assurance, seemed part, less of the loud mosaic of one's stupid life there', than of the dream of some ancient monk who had once inhabited the spot.

Nicholas Monsarrat (1910–79), also from Liverpool, studied Law at Trinity in 1928–31, and was aware of Lowry's existence and reputation though his own Cambridge scarcely overlapped. For Monsarrat Cambridge was a 'golden age of privilege allied to laziness, a dreamlike progress' marred only by the occasional exam to be 'scraped through' before enjoying 'the next act of this first-rate comedy of manners'. Dress was important: displaying the correct arrangement of buttons on one's waistcoat, 'always wearing complete suits, not grey flannels and sports coat'. Poker was played, champagne drunk, Joe Venuti span on the gramophone, one went daily to the 'flicks', drank 'emerald-green beer, the very last word in decadent indulgence' at the Festival Theatre, and dined twice a term, in green silk dinner jacket, with the Lucullans. Instead of studying for one's finals, one shot up to 'metrops' in Lord Gentil-Jones's open Bentley, dined with debs at Quaglino's, then sprinted to catch the 10.12 ('The Flying Fornicator') from Liverpool Street. Although the future author of *The Cruel Sea* sent weekly contributions to *Granta* they were neither printed nor returned: 'all my stuff, exquisitely witty and polished, simply disappeared without trace'. He scraped a third; then had to face his father's interrogation: 'How much do you actually owe?'

Although the more 'advanced' elements now tended to put down the Bloomsbury aesthetic, there remained a strong element of 'Bloomsbury-by-the-Cam', especially at King's, where Maynard Keynes (whose rooms in Webb's Court were decorated by Vanessa Bell and Duncan Grant) gathered about him a number of younger Apostolic Fellows, including Gerald Shove, Frank Ramsey, Richard Braithwaite, and W. J. H. ('Sebastian') Sprott. The salon at The Pavilion, West Road, of another of the group, F. L. ('Peter') Lucas, who taught English at King's, and his novelist wife E. B. C. ('Topsy') Jones, provided a Bloomsburyan counter-attraction to the Haldanes' salon at Chesterton, just as *The Venture* countered *Experiment*. Lucas's first pupil at King's, George ('Dadie') Rylands, managed the Woolfs' Hogarth Press while working on his fellowship dissertation, and after gaining his fellowship in 1927, provided yet another Bloomsburyan link (Lytton Strachey often stayed in his rooms, which were decorated by Strachey's intimate friend Dora

Carrington).[9] Older Bloomsbury affiliates at King's included J. T. Sheppard (later Provost) and 'Goldie' Dickinson (whose rooms in Gibbs's Building were decorated by Roger Fry).

It was through Dickinson that the Chinese poet Hsü Chih-mo (1896–1931) came to study at King's in 1921–2 and was introduced into Bloomsbury circles, acquiring in the process a taste for Shelley and the belief that the free pursuit of adventure by the soul was the highest ideal. Putting the principle at once into action, he divorced his wife (who had been sharing his cottage at Sawston), wrote his first poems, and devoted himself to the enjoyment of life, later recalling that the spring of 1922 'alone in all my life was natural, was truly joyful!' Hsü went on to become one of the first 'modern' Chinese poets. Two famous poems and a prose essay about Cambridge, in which he describes the Cam with its bridges and willows as 'the most beautiful river in the world', have secured for the town a special place in the Chinese affection. It was Hsü who gave Dickinson his mandarin's cap.

The Woolfs themselves still often came down for the weekend. In 1924 Virginia Woolf expounded to the Heretics Society her belief that rigid narrative structures in fiction were dispensable – a theory triumphantly implemented in her own novels. In October 1928 she delivered two lectures on 'Women and Fiction' to the Arts Society at Newnham and the ODTAA[10] Society at Girton, lectures subsequently expanded to form her feminist masterpiece *A Room of One's Own*. In the first chapter she contrasts a sumptuous lunch party at King's (where she had been the guest of Rylands) with dinner at 'Fernham College' (Newnham) – prunes and custard. She felt vehemently about the male-dominated system at Cambridge, of which she gives telling examples – such as her being refused entry to Trinity Library. In the audience at Girton, where she arrived accompanied by Vita Sackville-West, were Kathleen Raine, who remembered them as 'the two most beautiful women I had ever seen', and Muriel Bradbrook, who later recalled how 'we enjoyed Mrs Woolf but felt her Cambridge was not ours'. Mrs Woolf for her part commented in her diary on the chocolate-coloured corridors of Girton – 'like vaults in some horrid high church cathedral – on and on they go, cold and shiny' – and on their inhabitants – 'intelligent, eager, poor; and destined to become schoolmistresses in shoals'. Much as she was attached to Cambridge, she retained a non-native's idealised notion of it – as when, in a famous passage of *Jacob's Room*, she speaks of the Cambridge sky as 'lighter, thinner, more sparkling than the sky elsewhere' – and her Cambridge characters tend towards caricature. The Trinity dons in *Jacob's Room*, hunched vegetatively over their texts, are as whimsical as the girl undergraduates in her piece about life at Newnham, 'A

---

9 Beverley Nichols, attending a party in Rylands's rooms, passed out in the bedroom to awake with a beard in his face and someone 'murmuring phrases of adoration. I have never been attracted by beards . . . and Mr Lytton Strachey swiftly found himself flat on the floor.'
10 Acronym for 'One Damned Thing After Another'.

Woman's College from Outside' (reprinted in *Books and Portraits*) with their mirrors, kisses, and dreams.

Second-generation Bloomsburyites were also now arriving. John Lehmann (1907–87), who came up to Trinity in 1927, frequented the Lucases' salon, contributed to *The Venture*, and appeared in both volumes of *Cambridge Poetry*. He later made the transition to Bloomsbury itself, being taken on by the Woolfs, on the recommendation of Rylands, to manage the Hogarth Press. His elder sister Rosamond Lehmann (1901–90) – they were the children of R. C. Lehmann, the founder of *The Granta* – had been one of the first graduates in the English tripos. Her first novel, *Dusty Answer* (1927), set partly in Girton, brings alive the echoing corridors and dowdy rooms that Mrs Woolf had hurried past. Rich in scenic evocation in the Woolf manner, the book is permeated with contemporary pessimism: all the heroine's attempts at relationships, both with men and with her glamorous fellow student Jennifer, end unsuccessfully, and the lesson she draws is to be totally independent, to have not just a room but a life of one's own.

Another Bloomsbury arrival of 1927 was Julian Bell (1908–37), son of Clive and Vanessa Bell, who read history and English at King's. Large, genial, extrovert, Bell represented the antithesis of the Empson/*Experiment* group. He did not subscribe to the adulation of T. S. Eliot, Pope being his favourite poet and the heroic couplet his preferred form; he attacked the fashion of obscurity, and Empsonian criticism as an encouragement to obscurity; and he tilted (in a poem in *The Venture*) at Wittgenstein, whose linguistic philosophy trespassed unwelcomely, in Bell's view, into the closed preserve of the artist:

> In every company he shouts us down,
> And stops our sentence stuttering his own;
> Unceasing argues, harsh, irate and loud,
> Sure that he's right, and of his rightness proud.
> Such faults are common, shared by all in part,
> But Wittgenstein pontificates on Art.

Bell's interest in politics and communism was fanned by membership of the Apostles. In the anti-war demonstration of 1933 he drove a car through the streets of Cambridge with fellow Apostle Guy Burgess as navigator. Bell stayed at Cambridge until 1932 but failed to secure a fellowship at King's. He taught for a while in China before volunteering as an ambulance driver in the Spanish Civil War, in which he was killed.

A writer outside such groupings was Charles Percy Snow (1905–80), who came up to Christ's in 1928 from Leicester with a postgraduate scholarship in science. After taking his PhD and becoming a Fellow of his college, Snow spent some years researching into vitamins before a humiliating failure convinced him he was in the wrong profession. 'By training I was a scientist: by vocation I was a writer', he later declared, and in about 1935, still at Cambridge, he began planning the sequence of eleven novels, *Strangers and Brothers*, that was to make his name.

(Three of them are set in Cambridge – a Cambridge of Machiavellian college elections and endless combination-room intrigue.) Snow later acquired further fame from his pronouncements (in Cambridge) on what he considered the rift between the two 'cultures' (science and the arts) of which he claimed membership. This invited refutation, especially since it came from a product of the Cambridge of Richards, Empson, Bronowski (who in his own career, and in his *Science and Human Values* (1961) denied such a rift), Russel (mathematician, philosopher, and 1950 Nobel laureate for literature), and Wittgenstein, where links between scientific and literary disciplines were close. The challenge was to be taken up by the most determinedly Cambridge product of all.

22

'The Ogre of Downing Castle'

Frank Raymond Leavis (1895–1978) was the son of a Cambridge tradesman who sold musical instruments ('Leavis spells pianos') on the corner of Parker's Piece opposite Downing College. The first townsman since William Whitehead to achieve literary fame, Leavis remained unshakeably a Cambridge man all his life, hardly ever quitting the place and exhibiting to a marked degree certain arguably East Anglian characteristics: dogged resilience and independence of mind, humourless puritanism, a level, acute but unsoaring percipience, and the besieged combativeness of a Hereward defending ancient springs against rapacious incursions.

Of Huguenot origin (and supposedly connected with the ducs de Lévis), the Leavises settled early in the nineteenth century on the Cambridgeshire/Norfolk borders. Leavis's great-great-grandfather was a gardener at Elm, near Wisbech, his great-grandfather a basketmaker there. His grandfather, Elihu, was a piano-tuner in Cambridge, later retiring to a cottage at Denver; 'when I was about five years old he bicycled with me in front of him, the thirty miles from Cambridge, through Ely, along the fen dyke that banks the Great Ouse'. Leavis's father (Harry) and uncle (Frederick) were born at Cambridge; by 1896 Frederick was publican of the Six Bells pub off Mill Road – a fact subsequently not referred to on Harry's (more puritanical) side of the family. Leavis was born over his father's early premises at 68 Mill Road. Harry, a cultured and radical man greatly admired by his son, was killed in a motorcycle accident near Trumpington in 1921.

At the Perse School (where he was some years junior to Tillyard), Leavis acted Macbeth, shone at rugger, and was remembered as a quiet, industrious boy with deep, already scrutinising eyes. From school he went straight to the war as a stretcher-bearer. In 1918, still in a state of shock from the butchery he had witnessed on the Somme and from the effects of gas, he took up a scholarship at Emmanuel to read history; but after taking a poor second in the first part of the tripos he switched to English, came under the influence of Richards, and secured a first (despite his father's death on the day of his first exam).

Leavis's primary ambition was to teach – and the new faculty was desperate for teachers. But for many years he progressed inexplicably slowly, picking up teaching jobs where he could – bicycling to Girton on Wednesday afternoons, for example, to give supervisions in a converted army hut. It was at Girton that he met Queenie Dorothy Roth (1906–81), an equally aggressive and puritanical spirit, then working as a Research Fellow on her *Fiction and the Reading Public*, a work that, like Leavis's own first publication, *Mass Civilization and Minority Culture* (1930), decried the lowering of cultural standards in modern society. They were married in 1929 and were to enjoy a lifelong collaboration, with Mrs Leavis being by some accounts the more trenchant force behind her husband.

Though he was appointed to a probationary lectureship in 1927, Leavis's views, personality, and perhaps even trivial details like his dislike of wearing ties gained him official disfavour. When, in 1926, wanting to quote from James Joyce's *Ulysses* (then a banned book) in his lectures, he wrote to the Home Office for permission to import a copy, he was summoned to see the Vice-Chancellor, who handed him a communication from the Public Prosecutor disclosing that the Cambridge police had been monitoring his lectures and ending with the recommendation that he 'should be suitably and firmly dealt with'. A turning point came in 1932, when he was appointed Director of English Studies at Downing and published his first major critical work, *New Bearings in English Poetry*, when his wife published *Fiction and the Reading Public*, and when together they launched the quarterly journal *Scrutiny*.

Scrutiny, which was to run on a shoestring budget until 1953, became the principal sounding-board for Leavis and a clique of collaborators on a wide range of cultural issues, and much of Leavis's published criticism (all the chapters of *Revaluation* and much of *The Great Tradition*, for example) began as contributions to its pages. The first issue contained a manifesto claiming, 'the general dissolution of standards is commonplace. Many profess to believe (though fewer seem to care) that the end of Western civilization is in sight'; a demolition of Virginia Woolf by Muriel Bradbrook ('to demand thinking from Mrs Woolf is clearly illegitimate: but . . . such a smoke screen of feminine charm is surely to be deprecated'); a favourable review of Aldous Huxley's *Brave New World* (as a portrayal of what science was likely to do to the world); and warnings about the inevitability of the next war from Goldsworthy Lowes Dickinson (who died three months later). Although the editorship was at first credited to L. C. Knights and Donald Culver, it was the Leavises who from the start dictated the tone of the journal and did much of the writing and most of the administrative work; and the loaded, bristling, partisan style for which *Scrutiny* became known derived directly from their prejudices and preoccupations. Response to the journal, as to everything the Leavises did, was polarised. Received in many quarters with hostility (two major Cambridge bookshops refused to stock it), it was elsewhere greeted as the very trumpet call of Cambridge English and of everything Cambridge English ought to be: 'We were, and knew we were, Cambridge – the essential Cambridge in spite of Cambridge', Leavis was later to boast. Meanwhile, the Leavises' Friday tea parties at their home at 6 Chesterton Hall Crescent became the rallying-ground for contributors, colleagues, and supporters. These included co-editors L. C. Knights, Donald Culver, and Denys Thompson; D. W. Harding, Muriel Bradbrook, and H. A. Mason; and D. J. Enright, who began contributing while an undergraduate at Downing and later became Leavis's editor at Chatto & Windus.

Leavis's rise in the English faculty never accelerated – frustrated, he maintained, by enemies on the Board, to whom his whole attitude towards literature and criticism came as an unwelcome challenge. For Leavis, English was the central discipline which should inform all others, a discipline, moreover, that must be immediate, moralistic, and uncomplacent if it was to be valid at all; whereas many of his seniors in the faculty – Quiller-Couch, Tillyard, Lucas, Willey – still saw English as a kind of modern extension of the classical discipline. (Willey, in his 1946 inaugural lecture as professor, significantly entitled *The 'Q' Tradition*, declared: 'Long may Classics keep its honourable place in the front of the battle! We will follow, proud to be second . . . In so far as English is true to its aim, it must keep in touch with classical antiquity . . . I would never, for my part, wish anyone to embark upon the study of English at Cambridge without a thorough previous grounding in Classics.') Recognition of Leavis's highly original work and of his powers as a teacher was consequently grudging. Downing appointed him college lecturer in 1935 and elected him to a fellowship the following year, when the university also promoted him to assistant lecturer; but it was 1954 before he was made a member of the Faculty Board, 1959 before he became a university reader. He was all the time aware of others – 'charlatans' and 'dull mediocrities', he called them – being promoted over his head. 'I was, in my academic career (if that is the word), made to feel irretrievably an outlaw, and I remained to the end conscious of being looked on by those in power as a deplorable influence', he wrote in 1972. Nevertheless, despite interludes as visiting lecturer at Oxford, York, and Bristol and in the United States, Leavis stubbornly refused to be budged from his home town.

After *New Bearings*, a steady stream of books – about twenty in all – established and reinforced his reputation as one of the greatest of living literary critics. Yet though highly influential for the fresh perceptions they offered of major novelists and poets, his critical writings were also notorious for their dogmatic and proselytising tone, their stodgily uncompromising style, and their manner of ranking writers as if in some league system of importance, with the implication that only those in the top division (pre-eminently Lawrence and Eliot) need to be bothered with. This led him to relegate Browning and to celebrate Milton's 'dislodgement', or, in his belligerent introduction to *The Great Tradition*, to bring down a string of major English novelists (Fielding, Scott, Dickens, Thackeray, Trollope, Hardy) as if tackling a deficient team on the college rugger field. Such methods did not lack their attraction for hard-pressed students. As Donald Davie has said of *Scrutiny*, 'Every issue of the magazine made me a present of perhaps a dozen authors or books or whole periods and genres of literature which I not only *need* not, but *should not* read. To be spared so much of literature, and at the same time earn moral credit by the exemption – no wonder that I loved *Scrutiny*, and Leavis's *Revaluation*, and his *New Bearings in English Poetry*!'

The reputation that took the most resounding fall beneath Leavis's flying tackle, however, was that of C. P. Snow. Snow represented everything that Leavis detested: fiction with no moral guts, the superficial 'culture' of Sunday newspapers and Brains Trust pundits, the enemy Cambridge of high-table complacency. When Snow, in his much-publicised 1959 Rede Lecture,[1] *The Two Cultures and the Scientific Revolution*, declared in the Senate House that scientists not only had as much right to the title of intellectuals as their literary colleagues, but were infinitely more important for the future of the world (which Snow seemed to measure solely in terms of material improvement), he was setting himself up in the Leavises' eyes as the personification of the degenerate standards of 'technologico-Benthamite' society they had been against from the start. In fact Leavis bided his time (a Cambridge biochemist, Michael Yudkin, did some preliminary loosening up of the victim in *The Cambridge Review*); but he decided to act when he saw Snow's lecture going through edition after edition and Snow's reputation as an oracle soaring (between the Rede Lecture and his death Snow received thirty-one honorary degrees, mainly from American universities, and had a college in the University of Buffalo named after him). Leavis chose as the occasion of his attack a Cambridge lecture of his own, the Richmond Lecture,[2] delivered in the hall of Downing College on 28 February 1962 under the title *Two Cultures? The Significance of C. P. Snow*.

Opening with magnificent sarcasm – 'If confidence in oneself as a master-mind, qualified by capacity, insight and knowledge to pronounce authoritatively on the frightening problems of our civilisation, is genius, then there can be no doubt about Sir Charles Snow's. He has no hesitations' – Leavis began at once ruthlessly to sabre his enemy. Snow was 'intellectually as undistinguished as it is possible to be'. As a novelist, Snow 'doesn't exist; he doesn't begin to exist. He can't be said to know what a novel is. The nonentity is apparent on every page of his fictions.' Snow was 'utterly without a glimmer of what creative literature is, or why it matters'. Leavis took an example.

> Among the most current novels of Snow's are those which offer to depict from the inside the senior academic world of Cambridge, and they suggest as characteristic of that world lives and dominant interests of such unrelieved and cultureless banality that, if one could credit Snow's art with any power of imaginative impact, one would say that he had done his university much harm – for this is a time when the image of the ancient university that is entertained at large

[1] The most prestigious public lecture at Cambridge, founded by Sir Robert Rede in 1524.
[2] Founded during the Second World War by Sir Herbert Richmond, Master of Downing. The speaker is invited by, and the lecture delivered to, the undergraduates of Downing.

matters immensely. Even when he makes a suspect piece of research central to his plot, as in that feeble exercise, *The Affair*, he does no more than a very incompetent manufacturer of whodunnits could do: no corresponding intellectual interest comes into the novel; science is a mere word, the vocation merely postulated.

Snow's 'literary intellectuals', Leavis claimed, were merely *New Statesman* opinionators and Sunday paper reviewers, his comparisons between scientific and literary values meaningless. Worst of all, his insistence that material progress was the world's first priority was a pernicious untruth: there were higher values at stake than (Snow's word) 'jam'. Had Snow never read Lawrence? Instead of turning universities into technical colleges, or technical colleges into 'universities', universities should be properly rearranged around vital English schools. 'I mustn't say more now about what I mean by that, I will only say that the academic is the enemy and that the academic *can* be beaten, as we who ran *Scrutiny* for twenty years proved.'

Though the lecture was supposedly a private occasion, two press representatives were admitted (the pro-Leavis Ian Binney for *Varsity*, the anti-Leavis L. P. Wilkinson for *The Times*), and news of its content spread so rapidly that the text was soon afterwards printed in the *Spectator*. (Philip Snow's claim that the *Spectator* bought the text before the lecture was even delivered is untrue.) Enormous controversy was aroused. Snow, then in the middle of writing *Corridors of Power*, was greatly shaken. He decided not to reply: although he accepted the Downing undergraduates' offer to deliver the following year's Richmond Lecture, he made no reference in it to Leavis. The Leavisites maintained that Snow had failed to answer the case; the supporters of Snow, that Leavis's attack was a publicity-seeking outburst motivated by jealousy of Snow's creative talent and success. Others, while pleased to see Snow hit the floor, called 'foul' at the brutal way it had been done. No personal attack had caused such a rumpus in English literature since Churton Collins rumbled Gosse. Privately, Snow remarked to his brother that the adverse publicity had ruined his hopes for a Nobel Prize that year.

Although Leavis retired from teaching at Cambridge shortly after his Richmond Lecture, his lean and wiry figure – clad in open shirt and sandals, a knapsack of books over his shoulder, his mouth thin and disapprobatory, his tanned cranium fringed with white tufts – continued to be seen for another decade or two about the streets (where, according to one witness, he rode a tall, ancient bicycle 'with the high-shouldered erectness of a Spanish master of *haute école*', or, according to another, observed a version of the Scout's Pace – forty paces running, forty walking, the forty running generally coinciding with the approach of one of his enemies in the faculty). Although he eventually fell out even with Downing (resigning his honorary fellowship in 1964 in anger at the college's appointment of his erstwhile disciple H. A. Mason as the first Leavis Lecturer), his name continued to be almost synonymous with the college to a worldwide audience, who, while absorbing his influence via the teaching of his pupils and pupils' pupils, were often unaware of his actual position in the university.

Among those who knew him, as colleagues or pupils, opinions remained polarised. On the one hand, Elsie Phare, who was supervised by Leavis at Newnham in the late 1920s, thought 'he looked rather like one's idea of Shelley; thin, ethereal, with an open-necked shirt. His classes were momentous . . . He was not formidable, indeed rather shy and gentle.' Muriel Bradbrook, her contemporary at Girton, remembered his reading from Eliot, Richards, and Empson ('how many people have been taught poetry written by a contemporary undergraduate?') and using Q's *Oxford Book of English Verse* as a fertile source of 'horrendous examples'. To her he seemed 'the most engaging mixture of the Prophet Elijah and Peter Pan'. Sebastian Moore, a Catholic monk and another early pupil, believed that he 'associated literature with the hunger for ultimate meaning without which we would not be human'. H. A. Mason similarly felt that 'what he offered was a real *askesis* [spiritual self-discipline and training], a discipline impossibly hard to live up to'. Thom Gunn, who attended Leavis's practical criticism classes in the 1950s, considered that Leavis's 'discriminations and enthusiasm helped teach me to write, better than any creative writing class could have'.

On the other hand, Richard Eberhart, who was supervised by Leavis in 1929, saw 'the fallacies in Leavis: a biting iconoclast, unbalanced'; his fellow American poet John Berryman in 1937 similarly called Leavis 'a vacant popularizer, vacant and impudent'. William Empson thought Leavis went wrong from the moment in the 1930s when he denounced his former hero I. A. Richards and his Benthamite values; he recalls T. S. Eliot in his Faber office looking at the latest *Scrutiny* and commenting 'how *disgusting* the behaviour of Leavis was, what mob oratory his arguments were, couldn't something be done to stop him? – and then, with cold indignation, "Of course, I know it's going to be me next" '. Sylvia Plath described the Leavis of 1955 as 'a magnificent, acid, malevolently humorous little man who looks exactly like a bandy-legged leprechaun'. Simon Gray, a little later, found the self-appointed Leavis coterie 'a pretty grisly gang'. J. B. Priestley, attacking Leavis in *Thoughts in the Wilderness* (1957), complained: 'To be an author, in his view, is to invite damnation, for only a few – D. H. Lawrence, himself, and a favourite pupil or two – will be saved.' Robert Graves called Leavis 'a detestable fellow'. The poet George Barker observed of a disciple that *rigor Leavis* had set in. Leonard Woolf complained that Leavis's savaging of his wife's novels completely ignored their subject, 'the deepest and most important things in the world'. George Steiner in 1962, while remembering how as a schoolboy he had waited 'for those grey, austerely wrapped numbers of *Scrutiny* as one waits for a bottle flung into the ravening sea', condemned the latter-day Leavis as arrogant, outmoded, narrow, insular. Donald Davie, also originally a supporter, expressed similar disillusionment in 1976, calling Leavis 'the god that failed'. Tom Sharpe condemned Leavis retrospectively in 1980 as 'poisonous'; the unlikeable Dr

Sydney Louth in his novel *The Great Pursuit* (1977) is clearly a lampoon of Leavis. Derek Brewer (1985), while conceding the importance of Leavis's struggle to preserve literary culture, felt he was a critical literalist in the tradition of Bentley's Milton: 'What is missing is any sense of recreation, of sympathetic participation in other people's interests, of concern with other possible hypotheses about life.' Robert Houghton (1988), comparing Leavis's reported last words, *I am wretched, I am in despair*, to those of the religious reprobate, concludes that 'the attempt to live one's life, especially "religiously", largely in and through literature must fail'. For Clive James (1989), Leavis 'had given up his sense of reality, and all in pursuit of the very study which, he went on insisting, was the only thing that could give you a sense of reality'. What especially alienated many writers was the sense Leavis gave that the critic was more important than the creative artist. The creative content of *Scrutiny*, for example, was negligible – Davie has written of the humiliation he experienced when he submitted a poem for inclusion – and creative writing played no part in Leavis's view of the function of a university. 'Writers in residence' were a particular anathema to him.

To much of the Cambridge academic establishment, Leavis himself was anathema. If he largely created for himself the Enemy he pitched his battles against ('a fabled, heraldic monster with many heads', in Steiner's words), he himself had also become a kind of mythical villain, object of irrational hatreds, for many of his colleagues ('The Ogre of Downing Castle' in the words of an Oxford supporter, Howard Jacobson). Yet to his own select circle he could do no wrong: his disciples hung in adulation around him, his supervisions were monologue expressions of his own opinions, and students who came to him with flexible and unformed minds went away happily moulded in his own image. Equally hated and worshipped, for half a century Leavis exerted a seminal and unignorable influence not only at Cambridge but over the wider spheres of English taste, thought, education, and culture.

23

'Be comfortable while you can'

Writing to the *New Statesman* in December 1933, Julian Bell claimed (with some partisan exaggeration):

> In the Cambridge that I first knew, in 1929 and 1930, the central subject of ordinary intelligent conversation was poetry. As far as I can remember we hardly ever talked or thought about politics . . . By the end of 1933, we have arrived at a situation in which almost the only subject of discussion is contemporary politics, and in which a very large majority of the more intelligent undergraduates are Communists or almost Communists.

In fact, in 1933 only an intellectual minority among undergraduates – some Apostles and a few others – were as yet committed communists, and concern about politics was only just becoming general. But as the thirties developed, it seemed true that politics drove out poetry. The decade of the Spanish Civil War and the rise of Hitler and Mussolini saw even *The Granta* throw off its levity and turn serious. Moreover, most of the figures who had given Cambridge English in the late twenties its special vitality were dispersed in the thirties – Mansfield Forbes dying in 1936, Richards and Empson abandoning Cambridge for the Far East; while the ascendancy of the Leavises, who have themselves been compared by some with dictators, seemed to dampen literary creativity.

The most typical Cambridge poet of the decade was Rupert John Cornford (1915–36), whose name is often associated with Bell's although they were in fact neither friends nor contemporaries. The son of Francis and Frances Cornford, born and brought up in Cambridge, John Cornford (he early jettisoned the too-romantic first name) had embraced communism by his teens and from then on regarded all literature, culture, and teaching that did not promote the Marxist struggle as reactionary time-serving. He entered Trinity in 1933 and took a double first in history (even though he regarded Cambridge history as a Fascist rationale of the doomed bourgeois system); but his academic work took second place to his political campaigning, his impassioned, fierce, long-haired, grubbily dressed figure being ubiquitous at Cambridge protest meetings. Cornford had no time for socialising or cultural chat, and in his poem 'Keep Culture Out of Cambridge', after sneering at the contemporary intellectual fashions – Eliot's *Waste Land* futility, Freud's 'obscure important names / For silly griefs and silly shames', the disjointed imaginations of Dali and the Surrealists – he pushes them all impatiently aside:

> There's none of these fashions have come to stay
> And there's nobody here got time to play.
> All we've brought are our party cards
> Which are no bloody good for your bloody charades.

As one critic, John Press, had commented, 'unfortunately they were no bloody good for poetry', either, and Cornford's poetry, like so much written in the thirties, is stifled by his Marxist commitments – save in a few final personal statements like 'To Margot Heinemann', written from the Spanish Civil War to his girlfriend at Cambridge. Cornford resigned his research scholarship in 1936 to fight in Spain, with *Das Kapital* and his father's First World War revolver in his knapsack, and was killed on or about his twenty-first birthday.

If literary Cambridge in the twenties seemed contraposed between Magdalene and King's, in the thirties the chief contraposition was between Leavis's stronghold at Downing and that of his opponent Tillyard at Jesus. Alistair Cooke of Jesus (b. 1908) took a first in English, edited *The Granta* in 1931, and founded the University Mummers, the first mixed drama group. Robert Gittings (1911–92), poet and biographer of Keats and Hardy, who read history at Jesus, won the Chancellor's Medal for 1931 with his poem 'The Roman Road'. (He remembers the runner-up, T. F. A. Ragg of Jesus, reciting his own version in the college hall through loud-hailers with jazz accompaniment supplied by Cooke and other *Facade*-inspired friends.) Gittings's success earned him the notice of Bronowski and James Reeves; other Jesus contemporaries included the Australian poets John Manifold and David Campbell. Gittings stayed on at Jesus until 1940 to do research and to teach. One of his pupils was Terence Tiller (1916–88), who himself won the Chancellor's Medal in 1936 with a sonnet sequence on 'Egypt' (an appropriate subject for him, since he taught during the war at Cairo University). Many of the poems in Tiller's first three volumes were directly influenced by people and events at Cambridge. Cooke, Gittings, and Tiller all later worked for the BBC; Cooke becoming famous for his 'Letters from America', Gittings writing scripts during the war, and Tiller working in the Drama Department for thirty years after the war.

Gavin Ewart (b. 1916) came up to Christ's in 1934. After two years reading classics without enjoyment, he switched to English under Leavis, which 'went down as stimulating as new wine'. Ewart was also friendly with Rylands, Blunt, and Snow. Many of the poems in his first volume, *Poems and Songs* (1939), date from his Cambridge days, and have overtones of the growingly unsettled atmosphere of the times. In number XXXVI he advises his contemporaries to enjoy themselves while they may:

> O listen to the band excite the dancers,
>   Walk over the lawns, admire the architecture,
> Be like that flower expansive in your leisure
>   Or reading Auden in a Cambridge theatre.
>
>   . . . .
>
> Be comfortable while you can, be bored,
>   Be gay, be undergraduate, be clever,
> Smoke cigarettes and flick the ash away,
>   Either be mean or be the generous giver.

Ewart's often splenetic wit found fit object in his poem 'Cambridge', in which he castigates the uninvolved existence of dons amid a turbulent world, and finally in 'Fed Up and Going Down', written in his last term, in which he extends his contempt to the whole Cambridge scene, impatient as he now was for London.

> Goodbye to spectacles and to straight hair,
> Goodbye to all the mannered pathics,
> Goodbye to Boat Clubs drowned in seas of beer,
> And spotty scholars reading Clathics.
>
> Goodbye to all the flowers of culture,
> Goodbye to all the local whoredom,
> Goodbye to lectures early in the morning,
> Goodbye to flicks and blinds and boredom.

The American poet John Berryman (1914–72) arrived at Clare in 1936 to study English on a two-year scholarship, as he later recounted in a sequence of poems in *Love & Fame* (1971). 'The Other Cambridge' describes his first impressions:

> Spires, gateways; bells. I like this town:
> its bookshops, Heffer's above all and Bowes & Bowes
> but Galloway & Porter too, & Deighton Bell
> & sparkling Gordon Fraser's in Portugal Place
>
> for days outranked for me the supernatural glass in King's Chapel,
> the Entrance Gateway of John's, the Great Court of Trinity.
> Slowly, as rapidly my books assembled every afternoon,
> I strolled to look & see, & browsed, & began to feel.

In November he attended T. S. Eliot's talk on 'The Idiom of Modern Verse', thinking Eliot looked 'a very shy, neurotic man'. Berryman became friendly with Gordon Fraser (1911–81), whose picture-gallery-cum-bookshop was something of a literary meeting place at this date, and whose Minority Press, started while Fraser was still an undergraduate at St John's, had published a remarkable series of little books, including three by Leavis – *Mass Civilization and Minority Culture*

(1930), *D. H. Lawrence* (1930), and *How to Teach Reading* (1932) – as well as works by L. C. Knights, T. F. Powys, John Middleton Murry, and the first book by the Swedish Nobel Prize winner Pär Lagerkvist to be translated into English. (Fraser's firm later became best known for its greetings cards, which he also first produced in Cambridge.) It was at Fraser's house at 274A Mill Road, in March 1937, that Berryman participated in a week-long drunken party, the principal guest at which was Dylan Thomas, who had come to give a reading at St John's.[1]

Berryman's supervisor was Rylands, who was kind to the 'lonely & ambitious young alien' and invited him to a party at which Auden and Keynes 'sat on the floor in the hubbub trading stories'. In his second year, he moved from Memorial Court into digs at 34 Bridge Street and 32 Thompson's Lane; got engaged to a Newnham student, 'the most passionate & versatile actress in Cambridge'; and won the Oldham Shakespeare Scholarship. He failed, however, to secure a first.

On 27 February 1935 T. E. Lawrence (1888–1935), author of *Seven Pillars of Wisdom*, bicycled into Cambridge from Bridlington, having left the air force after thirteen years in the ranks. It was his second visit – in December 1925 he had motorcycled from Cranwell to see E. M. Forster at King's, 'the splendiferous college with the extra splendiferous (and rather horrible) chapel'. (He told his biographer Liddell Hart in 1934 that King's Chapel left him cold, having been built when architecture 'had become a game – competitive – instead of an art'; the only Cambridge buildings he admired being Jesus chapel and the tower of St Benet's. Corpus library he liked for its manuscripts and its proportions. The Backs were 'fine' so long as one saw them 'without preparation'. Trinity 'was all wrong'.) This time he stayed overnight with his younger brother A. W. Lawrence, then reader in classical archaeology in the university, at 31 Madingley Road; the following day he bicycled on to London. It was the last time the brothers met: three months later 'Lawrence of Arabia' was killed in a motorcycle accident in Dorset.[2]

Patrick White (1912–90), Australian winner of the 1973 Nobel Prize, studied modern languages at King's in 1932–5, after Cheltenham College and three years as a 'jackeroo' in the outback. At that date he was writing poetry rather than prose and his chief influence was Housman. He used to wander past Housman's house, hoping to meet him and be invited in, and was in the Senate House audience for Housman's celebrated *Name and Nature of Poetry* lecture (see p. 222). Still discovering his homosexuality, White learned, like Housman, to write about his feelings with discretion. His first poems appeared in the *London Mercury* in 1934; a collection, *The Ploughman and Other Poems*, was printed at his mother's

---

[1] Glyn Daniel, who attended the reading, remembers Thomas arriving 'much the worse for wear after a long liquid session in Fleet Street' and dinner at the Blue Boar. After reading for a short while, he suddenly announced loudly 'I am a Dionysiac poet, a Dionysiac poet' and slumped to the floor.

[2] His famous Brough Superior motorcycle was bought by King & Harper Ltd, 6–7 Bridge Street, who resold it in March 1936.

expense in Sydney, and a play, *Bread and Butter Women*, apparently written while at King's, was put on there. White fell in love with a fellow King's student and for a while they shared rooms on the ground floor of Gibbs's Building. Together they went for six-mile walks through a countryside he later recalled as 'a grey country . . . of many, many greys: boots clattering through grey streets; the mirror-grey of winter fens; naked elms tossing rooks into a mackerel sky'. Evenings they would spend at the Cosmopolitan cinema, watching French and German films, or listening to music on a friend's gramophone at Corpus (sometimes climbing out after hours down a rope). But overall he was disappointed by the academic routine and the uninspiring dons and he failed to make the stimulating friendships he had hoped for. A lasting sense of regret stayed with him, that his life at Cambridge had been too self-contained. 'I didn't make the most of Cambridge', he admitted in 1973, and his time there is passed over in his autobiography, *Flaws in the Glass*. He took a lower second, refused to accompany his sister to the May Balls and, disappointing his mother who planned a diplomatic career for him, set off for London to be a writer.[3]

Also at King's was the American novelist Frederic Prokosch (1908–89), who spent two years, 1935–7, researching Chaucerian manuscripts. Already author of an acclaimed first novel, *The Asiatics*, he was working on his second. While at King's he purportedly took tea with A. E. Housman in the Whim ('He had the air of an illustrious but exhausted old field marshal. He seemed, as I watched him, to be receding into an earlier era'), had lunch with E. M. Forster at the Copper Kettle (Irish stew), and took Walter de la Mare, on a poetry reading visit, to Grantchester. In the Leavises' garden fashionable writers were clinically dissected while Queenie poured the tea and Prokosch furtively disposed of his cake behind a bush. But the reminiscences fail to convince.

Robin Maugham (1916–81), nephew of W. Somerset Maugham and himself a prolific novelist and travel writer, studied at Trinity Hall in 1934–7; his father (Lord Chancellor of England) allowed him to read English for the first two years on condition he studied law (which he hated) in the third. Despite his uncle's admonition that 'undergraduates are a notoriously dangerous audience. You must be prepared not only to be booed but also to see your set broken up and all the props destroyed' (did he speak from experience? He had himself had a play put on at Cambridge in 1904), Maugham wrote a play which was successfully put on by the ADC. He also challenged a college hearty to a duel, wrote for *Granta* and, a committed socialist, worked in his spare time in the Cambridge juvenile employment office, learning the truth about child exploitation. Summer holidays were spent with uncle Willie at his Villa Mauresque.

P. D. James (b. 1920), the thriller writer, spent her teens in Cambridge, living first at Magrath Avenue, then at Roseford Road. She attended the

---

[3] At the time of his Nobel Prize, the college library possessed none of his works, since he had never donated any and the college had not thought to buy them.

Cambridgeshire High School for Girls, where she won the school's short story prize and had her work published in school magazines. 'I remember my time at the High School with great affection. The longer I live, the more I realise how well we were taught.'[4] Her first job, on the outbreak of war, was with the Ration Office, billeted in Christ's College, but she married soon afterwards and moved to London.[5]

Two novels evoke retrospectively the atmosphere at Cambridge in the thirties. Bryan Forbes's *Familiar Strangers* (1979) portrays the ambience at Trinity in which Burgess and Philby avowed their allegiance, while Jack Trevor Story's *Hitler Needs You* (1970), set wholly in working-class Cambridge, shows that the political atmosphere was just as acute in the town's radio factories and jazz clubs. (In real life Story (1917–91) had worked as a butcher's boy delivering sausages to the colleges, then for Pye, and had played guitar with the town's Quincagintas jazz band.) Indeed, with the mysterious deaths of tea girls, the threat of instant redundancy hanging over those who failed to keep their noses clean, and Nazi infiltrators up every street, Cambridge town, if Story is to be believed, was the more perilous place. (Novels actually written in the thirties are less rewarding: L. S. Howarth's *Ladies in Residence* (1936) features a token communist poet, but in none of them is there the critical evaluation of a privileged institution during a time of social and political upheaval that one might have expected.)

In fact one of the most critical views of 1930s Cambridge comes from the Irish playwright Sean O'Casey (1880–1964), invited in January 1936 to address the Shirley Society at St Catharine's. Although he spent under a day in the place, he devotes an entire chapter of autobiography to the experience. Eschewing the dons' table in hall, he dined with the students; then followed an encounter with a reactionary professor: 'You're not a bit funny, O'Casey; Cambridge is too big to be impressed by Irish wit.' A tour of the colleges made O'Casey feel that medievalism had stultified the place for too long. As for Cambridge town: 'it sidles and lurches round the colleges, looking like a shabby fellow waiting for a job from a rich relative.' The room he lectured in was spartan but 'crowded to the doors'. Having duly preached his revolutionary message, he was afterwards led up a stone staircase, like a Dublin tenement, to a bleak room lit by a single bulb, where drama, religion and socialism were discussed until the early hours. (The light being cut off at the official bedtime hour, he and the students continued by torchlight.) Finally he was shown his guest room at St John's, 'a slum room', worse than anywhere he had ever lived, unheated. Unable to sleep for the cold, he spent the night fully dressed, in overcoat and muffler, pacing up and down till

---

[4] She took the name of her poetry-reading (and writing) detective, Adam Dalgliesh, from her English mistress at school, Miss Dalgliesh. In *An Unsuitable Job for a Woman*, set in Cambridge, Dalgliesh investigates the death of a history undergraduate.

[5] An earlier 'queen of crime', Margery Allingham (1904–66), spent 1919 as a boarder at the Perse High School for Girls; the novelist Jean Rhys (1890–1979) had spent four terms at the same school in 1907–8.

'dawn came to the coldest spot in England'. Later he learnt that the room's previous occupant had died of pneumonia. Paradoxically, what shocked the socialist O'Casey was not the privilege of Cambridge but the poverty: students living in dingy rooms, skimping their meals, studying arid texts. And these were tomorrow's educators of the poor. 'I saw things in Cambridge that no man ought to speak about that "knows his catechism"', he told Lady Rhondda.

The poet Nicholas Moore (1918–86), son of G. E. Moore, was born in Cambridge and up to the age of thirty spent most of his life there. He achieved some fame in the 1940s and 1950s and a large number of his poems refer to his Cambridge memories, particularly of his undergraduate days at Trinity (1938–40). Like Ewart, Moore abandoned classics for English, which he studied under Tom Henn at St Catharine's (Trinity still regarded the subject with suspicion). He remembered Henn constantly holding up a student of a few years before, Patric Dickinson (1914–94), as his ideal – scholarly, handsome, athletic (he won a golf blue), and a poet into the bargain. Moore founded and edited the poetry magazine *Seven* while an undergraduate, and in 1940 he and his Trinity contemporary Alex Comfort (b. 1920), who was studying medicine, edited a third Hogarth Press anthology of *Cambridge Poetry*.

When the Second World War broke out and Cambridge was again invaded by the military, its youth again conscripted, its colleges once more taken for hospitals and billets, reactions were perhaps less ideologically acrimonious than the first time. Frances Cornford, still writing in her miniaturist Georgian idiom, seemed confident, in 'A Wartime Sketch', that her Cambridge would survive the upheavals of war:

> Drink the unflowing waters with green hair
> You Cambridge willows, calm and unaware;
> Soon he will vanish like a summer's midge,
> That calm-struck soldier leaning on the bridge,
> And things be always as they always were.

But Moore, a conscientious objector and left-wing sympathiser, struck an angry note in his 'Epistle from Cambridge', printed in the leading literary magazine *Horizon* in February 1941, condemning the Cambridge establishment and local war profiteers.

> Here is a town that is warm, not afraid of the winter,
> Well-fed on its learning. Here are people who find
> Delight in things of the mind, and dull shopkeepers
> Who make their living from it. This is the city.
> These walk by the riverside, find it pretty,
> Curse Hitler, and hope his bombs will never fall
>
> Over this little world that belongs to them all.
> These are the narrow and powerful. They have claws
> To snatch at a profit, who dream to feather a nest

Where no stranger or foreigner comes. They love their homes.
But even here now is the dissident voice of the few
Who have learnt their history, who have watched, and know,

Hear the acknowledged words of the politicians,
And make protest about their living conditions.
O, the Cam is idle. The water flows to no good,
Here in this hospitable and devilish town,
Where no one cares for anyone but his own.
The narrow and powerful rule, the protests go down.

In Helen Foley's novel *A Handful of Time* (1961), Fanny stands on Garret
Hostel Bridge listening to Chamberlain's announcement of war: 'Through the
open windows of Trinity Hall came the modified boom of fate and then
the wireless was switched off, there was silence, and for a minute no one on the
bridge but Fanny.' Her friend Frances attends E. M. Forster's 1941 Rede lecture
(he eyes his mostly female audience like a 'retired greengrocer eyeing wilted
vegetables'), and Lord David Cecil's Clark lectures on Hardy; returning one
evening to their lodgings in Little St Mary's Lane, she is handed a telegram by
Fanny that tells her her lover is a prisoner of war. Later, in the Eagle and the Bath,
they watch off-duty bomber crews inscribe their girlfriends' names on the ceiling
with lipstick. Hearing them chatter about Shakespeare, an American snaps: 'Some
day after the war I'm going back to see all those places I've been bombing. Yeah,
I'd kind of like to see them.'

C. P. Snow, still tutor at Christ's, was appointed college air warden at the start
of the war, and reported developments in letters to his brother Philip in Fiji. The
war gave him a heightened sense of the importance of his *Strangers and Brothers*
series. When the first came out in 1940 he wrote with relief: 'If I die now I shall
die pretty cheerful.' The drafts of two more he stored in a steel cabinet at Christ's
as a precaution against bomb damage. Snow left Cambridge in 1942 to undertake
administrative work for the Civil Service.

Over at Trinity, Snow's counterpart as air warden was a classics don, A. S. F.
Gow (1886–1978), who in earlier days had been friendly with both Brooke and
Housman. For the benefit of former pupils now scattered all over the world, Gow
began to produce monthly news letters, subsequently collected as *Letters from
Cambridge 1939–1944*, which preserve a don's-eye record of the exigencies of
the time – air raid practices, dwindling numbers of students, influxes of military
trainees, rationing, the occasional real air raid, and so on. The novelist Anthony
Powell, once Gow's pupil at Eton, arrived at Trinity in January 1941 on an eight-
week politico-military course. An incident when one of his fellow officers was
ragged by having a dummy planted in his bed was the germ for a similar incident
in his novel *The Valley of Bones*. Gow invited Powell to dinner and gave him a
copy of his book about Housman in exchange for one of Powell's early novels,
which Gow read during his 'weary hours' at his warden post.

Powell's friend John Hayward (1904–65), editor, anthologist, bibliographer, was also in Cambridge during the war, evacuated from London on account of his disability (he suffered from muscular dystrophy) as a guest of Lord Rothschild at Merton Hall. While still a King's undergraduate he had produced a pioneering edition of Rochester and first met T. S. Eliot, whose friend, literary adviser, and 'keeper of the archive' he became. (He was also the original 'Man in White Spats' in *Old Possum's Book of Practical Cats*.) Hayward brought the Eliot papers to Cambridge for safety and during the war years sorted them and had them bound by Gray & Son, the Cambridge binders. (He eventually bequeathed the collection to King's, together with early editions of Rochester and other valuable books and manuscripts.) Eliot himself, then writing *Four Quartets*, sent him drafts for his comments, and came to stay at Whitsun 1941, looking 'very haggard and washed out and dispirited' from colds, tooth trouble and overwork. During this visit Eliot called on Leavis (one of the very few occasions they met); Leavis recalled Eliot's cigarette ends piling up in the fireplace while they chatted and his seven-year-old son, evidently a budding critic himself, producing Eliot's poems and quizzing him about variant readings, the meaning of certain phrases, and the musical structure of *Ash-Wednesday*.

The Australian novelist Martin Boyd (1893–1972) also spent the war years in Cambridge, having been first introduced to the town by his friend Hugh l'Anson Fausset and thinking it 'a sort of City of God'. In 1940, having inherited money, he bought a cottage with nine acres at Little Eversden, seven miles south-west, and grew his own food. In 1942, due to the exigencies of wartime life, he moved into a top-floor flat at 1 Jesus Lane, and began an intensely creative life, feeling deeply the madness of the war and writing his major novel *Lucinda Brayford*. Like Fausset during the first war, he drew consolation from the services at King's, feeling there 'secluded from the evil pagan world'. (A homosexual, he also developed a crush on a chorister.) Thwarting the authorities' efforts to turn him into a farm labourer, he attended pacifist meetings at the Quaker Meeting House, got to know Bertrand Russell, and ate daily in the Peacock, a restaurant opposite Trinity run by Hungarian refugees, where intelligent conversation could be had. He met John Hayward at a literary society at King's (neither of them was impressed when Arthur Koestler came to speak); Hayward, a 'blend of Dr Johnson and Oscar Wilde', tended to dominate proceedings. During these Cambridge years Boyd felt 'more alive than at any time since my adolescence', with 'friendships of the heart and mind'. He completed his novel on the last day of war and then went to bed, exhausted, for three days. Hayward helped him find a publisher. Subsequently Boyd lodged with a Monsignor at St Peter's Terrace. Though he returned to Australia in 1948, he maintained his Cambridge connections: he lived at Trumpington Hall in 1955–6, and in 1961 held an exhibition of his drawings and paintings in Cambridge.

Robert Nichols (1893–1944), the First-World-War poet, also attended the King's literary meetings. Boyd remembers his outdated slang: 'Cheerio chaps! Had a champion evening', while Edmund Blunden recalls his enthusing over a copy of *Amarynthus the Nympholept* by Horace Smith, found on a stall in the market. He was then living at 12 Newnham Terrace, shared with the mystical artist Cecil Collins, bombed out from London. Nichols died in Cambridge. By 1948 Collins, whose paintings often contained images of fools, had moved into the stable at 7 Grange Road of Enid Welsford, author of *The Fool: His Social and Literary History*.

The Spanish poet Luís Cernuda (1902–63), in exile from his Francoist homeland, taught at Emmanuel for two years during the war (1943–5). Nicholas Moore remembers his mother taking Spanish lessons from him. Now considered by some the equal of Lorca, Cernuda began his sequence *Vivir sin estar viviendo* while at Cambridge; his poem 'El árbol' was inspired by the great oriental plane at Emmanuel.

Among students who had their careers disrupted by the war were D. J. Enright (b. 1920), Raymond Williams (1921–88), Donald Davie (b. 1922), and David Holbrook (b. 1923). All four were grammar-school boys who came up to read English – Enright to Downing in 1938, Williams to Trinity in 1939, Davie to St Catharine's in 1940, Holbrook to Downing in 1941 – but who were only allowed a year or two at the university (on condition of enrolling as officer cadets) before being called up. For most of them Cambridge still seemed as insufferably 'public school' as Malcolm Muggeridge had found it in 1920, though there was by now an active left-wing sub-culture (a flourishing Socialist Club, a bookshop in Rose Crescent selling Stalinist paperbacks, showings of Russian films, and so on), and both Williams and Holbrook were drawn strongly into left-wing politics at Cambridge. John Cornford continued to be regarded as a hero, and communism was as much the intellectuals' avocation during the second war as pacifism had been during the first.

Even Frances Cornford must have known that things would not after the war 'be always as they always were'. Once again, an entire generation of Cambridge youth and talent had been wiped out, and in her poem 'In the Backs', published in her collection *Travelling Home* (1948), she reflected on the memories of all those over the centuries (they included many personal friends like Rupert Brooke, and her son John Cornford) who had added their lustre to Cambridge and were now dead.

> Too many of the dead, some I knew well,
> Have smelt this unforgotten river smell,
> Liquid and old and dank;
> And on the tree-dark, lacquered, slowly passing stream
> Have seen the boats come softly as in dream
> Past the green bank . . .

Mid-Term Tea at Mr Oscar Browning's,

31–2 The flamboyant and snobbish Oscar
Browning, Fellow of King's, is caricatured above
by Max Beerbohm in 'Mid-Term Tea at Mr
Oscar Browning's': 'O.B.' introduces
undergraduates to an assembly of European
royalty. The photograph of 1885 (right) provides
a real life parallel: J. K. Stephen (seated, with
pipe) is to the right of his pupil the Duke of
Clarence, eldest son of the future Edward VII. In
front of them lies the composer C. V. Stanford.

33–5 King's College in the early twentieth century, under the Provostship of M. R. James, acquired its special reputation as a relaxed, liberal community in which friendly relations between undergraduates and dons were encouraged. The portrait of James (above left), famous medievalist and ghost-story writer, is by William Strang. E. M. Forster has left memorable pictures of the turn-of-the-century college in his novels *The Longest Journey* and *Maurice* and in his biography of his close friend Goldsworthy Lowes Dickinson, who was in many ways the quintessential King's don. Forster appears left, photographed c. 1901, at about the time he was elected to the Apostles, surrounded by memories of Italy – on the walls behind him are photographs of the *Apollo Belvedere* and Raphael's *Pope Julius II*. The portrait of the young Dickinson (above right) is by the art critic Roger Fry, another friend of Forster's, and, like him, closely associated with the Bloomsbury Group.

36–7 Trinity, in contrast, liked to see itself as worldly, patrician, rather exclusive, and disdained the idealistic visions of fellowship characteristic of King's. Yet it was at Trinity that the nucleus of the Bloomsbury Group was created, although the group's idealisation of human relationships and aesthetic pleasure owed more to current concerns in the Apostles, and in particular to the philosophy of G. E. Moore (right), than to the intellectual traditions of any one college. The photograph above of Trinity's Shakespeare Society, taken in Nevile's Court, shows two prominent members of the group, Lytton Strachey (front row, far left) and Leonard Woolf (front row, far right). Thoby Stephen, son of Leslie Stephen and brother of Virginia Woolf and Vanessa Bell, is second from left in the back row.

38 The voluminous diary of A. C. Benson (left), Master of Magdalene and best-selling belletrist and novelist, is a detailed and occasionally catty portrayal of Edwardian university and literary personalities. His brother E. F. Benson (right) wrote an equally vast amount; his books include light-hearted versions of the 'varsity novel'. The third brother, R. H. Benson (centre), was a Catholic priest, a prolific writer, a dabbler in the supernatural and – briefly – a close friend of Baron Corvo.

39–40 Cambridge in khaki. Siegfried
Sassoon (above) published many of his most
bitter anti-war poems in *The Cambridge
Magazine*, one of the few outlets for
unofficial views of the war's progress.
C. H. Sorley (right), son of the professor of
philosophy, and one of the most promising
poets of his generation, was killed in action,
aged twenty.

41 Rupert Brooke was not, by all accounts, an especially good actor, but his performances on the Cambridge stage were memorable. In his first year he played the Herald in *The Eumenides*, a non-speaking role, in 'a red wig and cardboard armour'.

42–3 'Grantchester! ah, Grantchester!/ There's peace and holy quiet there…' Brooke decided to move to Grantchester at the end of his third year so that he could work at his fellowship dissertation without distractions from Cambridge's too hectic social life. Lodging first at the Orchard tearooms, in 1910 he moved into the Old Vicarage, where he lived for two years. The youthful following that he gathered round him in this liberating pastoral setting was christened 'the Neo-Pagans' by its Bloomsbury elders. In the photograph above, Brooke is writing in the garden of the Old Vicarage. The ground-floor windows behind him opened on to his room. Brooke is seen right reciting – perhaps his own poems – to Dudley Ward and Jacques Raverat.

44–6 Brooke first met Frances Darwin (left, with her father Francis Darwin) in the Marlowe Society's production of *Comus*. She described him in a poem written at that time as 'A young Apollo, golden-haired...'. It was while acting in *Comus* that she met her future husband, the classics scholar Francis Cornford.

The two most famous literary critics at Cambridge in the 1920s represented very different traditions. Sir Arthur Quiller-Couch (below left), better known as 'Q', was Edward VII Professor of English Literature from 1912 to 1944. He was one of those responsible for setting up the English tripos in 1917 and his lectures were immensely popular, both inside and – in printed form – outside the university. He stood out against modernism in literature and criticism and thus inevitably appeared old-fashioned in comparison with I. A. Richards (below right), who was propagating a scientific approach to literature based on the discipline of practical criticism. Richards was, wrote Christopher Isherwood, 'the prophet we had been waiting for'.

47–9 Contrasting methods of boating on the Cam: Vladimir Nabokov (above left) later wrote of this 1920 photograph, 'it was not unnatural for a Russian, when gradually discovering the pleasures of the Cam, to prefer, at first, a rowboat to the more proper canoe or punt'. The punt above right is being steered by Edward Upward, c. 1925. Upward's pro-Soviet views were an extreme example of those political attitudes current in undergraduate circles that so dismayed Nabokov. During Upward's Cambridge years, however, Marxism had yet to replace Mortmere, the anarchic world he invented with Christopher Isherwood (right), who describes it as 'our private place of retreat from the rules and conventions of university life'. Isherwood gave this photograph to Upward.

50–2 1930s literary Cambridge was dominated by the ascendancy of the Leavises (left) and by the call to political commitment. John Cornford (right), son of Frances Cornford, became a communist in his teens and devoted his poetic energies to Marxism. He left his academic career to fight in Spain, where he was killed, aged twenty-one. The sense of mission shared by many writers of the decade is characteristic of the Leavises, although they remained aloof from politics. Writers unwilling to align with any party found Cambridge had little to offer: Kathleen Raine (above, photographed by the Cambridge firm Ramsey and Muspratt) remembers it as entirely antipathetic to her poetic gifts.

53–5 'Forster's gnomish figure...stooped
and ordinary-looking in a cheap cloth
cap...added an undeniable touch of
literary romance to the Cambridge scene.'
E. M. Forster's retirement at King's,
1945–70, brought a civilising influence to
the university that is fondly recalled by
many who knew him when they were
undergraduates. In the photograph right,
Forster (with stick) is sitting on the wall
outside King's, the Old Schools in the
background. Beside him is a college
porter, C. E. Fuller. The 1950s, best
remembered for students' aggressive
aspirations, threw up several permanent
literary reputations, among them those of
the poets Sylvia Plath and Ted Hughes
(seen above in a photograph taken in
Cambridge in 1957) and Thom Gunn
(left, a photograph first published in the
undergraduate newspaper *Varsity*).

56 The 1960s and 70s saw writers adopting a more fiercely critical attitude to Cambridge than ever before. David Hare's *Teeth 'n' Smiles*, set at a Jesus College May Ball, condemns the social arrogance of a university that is made to represent much of the worst in modern Britain. This photograph is of the first production, starring Helen Mirren (right), in 1975.

57–8 The literary associations of Cambridge town, as distinct from the university, have continued to increase. Among writers with no primary connection with the university are the thriller writer P. D. James, who grew up in Cambridge in the 1930s (pictured, opposite above, by Jesus Lock in 1982); and the novelist Tom Sharpe whose *Porterhouse Blue*, a comic send-up of college life, was televised in 1987 starring David Jason and John Sessions (seen, opposite below, outside the Anchor pub during filming).

59–60 Among Cambridge-educated writers to gain recent prominence has been the novelist Salman Rushdie, who read history at King's. In 1993 he marked the fourth anniversary of the Iranian *fatwa* that forced him into hiding by delivering a speech in the college chapel (above). His fellow Booker prizewinner Ben Okri (below) has been a Fellow Commoner in the Creative Arts at Trinity, one of a number of writers in residence appointed by Cambridge colleges in recent years.

24

Glittering prizes

Although the Second World War, like the First, was eventually to be followed by a particularly lively decade, the Cambridge to which Raymond Williams, Donald Davie, and David Holbrook returned in 1945 and 1946 seemed as restrictive, provincial, and dull to men who had seen overseas service as the Cambridge of 1918 and 1919 had done. They worked hard to make up for lost time, completed their degrees, and moved on. Williams migrated to Oxford in 1946, not returning until 1961 to take up a lectureship in English and a fellowship at Jesus (he became Professor of Drama in 1974); even then he continued to feel the same sense of alienation from the university establishment that he had experienced from the start. Holbrook escaped to London. The author of numerous educational and critical books as well as novels and poetry (and well known for his anti-pornography campaigning), he later came back to the area to teach at village colleges and was a Fellow of King's in the sixties. Eventually he returned to his own college, Downing, as Director of English Studies.

Donald Davie stayed at Cambridge until 1950, doing research and teaching, living with his wife in 'four draughty and mouse-infested rooms over the village store in Trumpington'. But a sense of restlessness, and a poet's ambivalent feeling towards Cambridge, which seemed to offer no compromise between his rural surroundings and the rarefied atmosphere of combination rooms and high tables, urged him to move on, as expressed in his early poem 'On Bertrand Russell's *Portraits from Memory*':

> It was the Muse that could not make her home
> In that too thin and yet too sluggish air,
> Too volatile to live among the loam,
> Her sheaves too heavy for the talkers there.

In 1950 Davie transferred to Dublin University, in 1957 to California. He returned to Cambridge in 1958 as a lecturer and a Fellow of Caius, but again moved on in 1964 to become Professor of English at Essex. In 1968 he returned to America. When Davie's first book of poetry was published in 1955, his name became associated with the new wave of poets, mainly from Oxford and Cambridge, collectively known as the 'Movement'.

Davie is very typical of a trend among post-war poets to combine their poetry with academic careers, a combination that might once have seemed anomalous but which now, in the wake of such charismatic critics as Leavis and of the boom in 'Eng. Lit.' studies, seemed to accord a kind of double glamour. Other Cambridge poets who have subsequently taught at universities include Charles Tomlinson (b. 1927), who studied under Davie at Queens' in 1945–8 and was first introduced by Davie to the American writers who have had a great influence on his work; Nathaniel Tarn (b. 1928), who studied at King's and has since held positions at American universities; D. J. Enright, who did not return to Cambridge after the war but instead carried the torch of Leavisite enlightenment into Egypt and Japan; Eric Mottram (1924–95) who, after taking a double first in English at Pembroke in 1947–50, went on to combine a professorship of American literature at King's College, London, with authorship of over twenty books of poetry; Thom Gunn; John Holloway (Professor of Modern English at Cambridge from 1972 to 1982); and Peter Redgrove (appointed Resident Author at Falmouth School of Art in 1966).[1]

E. M. Forster returned to King's in 1945. He had maintained his Cambridge connections since going down in 1901, and in 1927 had delivered the Clark Lectures at Trinity, afterwards published as *Aspects of the Novel*, blending critical perception with characteristic informality of style ('ramshackly' was his own word). They were so well received (although Leavis predictably dismissed them as 'intellectually null') that King's elected Forster as Supernumerary Fellow until 1933. In 1931 he lectured to the English faculty on 'The Creator as Critic' and in 1941 delivered the Rede Lecture (on Virginia Woolf). But he did not reside more than a few weeks each year, living mostly with his mother at Abinger Hammer in Surrey. After her death in 1945, however, he was appointed an Honorary Fellow and invited – unusually for an Honorary Fellow – to take up residence. At first, though assigned a study on A staircase, Forster actually lodged with his friend L. P. Wilkinson (classicist Fellow of King's and university Orator) and his wife at 3 Trumpington Street, but when they moved in 1953 he took up permanent residence in college. It was an arrangement, comparable to that of W. H. Auden later at Christ Church, Oxford, which provided a home for an eminent bachelor writer in his old age and at the same time reflected literary prestige onto the host college.

Forster lived in his spacious, sunlit rooms at King's until his death at the age of ninety-one in 1970. Speaking at the Founder's Feast in 1952, he confessed: 'I have to tell you that I do not belong here at all. I do nothing here whatsoever. I hold no College office; I attend no committee; I sit on no body, however solid, not even

---

[1] Iris Murdoch, who has combined an academic career with writing fiction, spent 1947–8 studying philosophy at Newnham, before returning to Oxford.

on the Annual Congregation; I co-opt not, neither am I co-opted; I teach not, neither do I think.' Yet, like his mentor Dickinson before him, he became a quintessential ingredient in the spirit of the place, mixing on equal terms with freshmen and Fellows, giving encouragement to each new generation of 'Rickies'. Undergraduates were encouraged to drop in without ceremony, and to call him Morgan. (He preferred those from humble backgrounds; 'the higher up the social scale, the bigger the starting handicap', Wilkinson noted.) One remembered Forster reading the opening chapter of his unfinished novel *Arctic Summer* to a group who at once 'started arguing about it exactly as though he weren't in the room, or as if he'd been reading someone else's stuff'. He would fuss over his coal fire, lay the luncheon table for guests, greet a stream of visitors with unfailing courtesy, host the Apostles, and make room on his bookshelves for new acquisitions by donating old ones, often valuable, to the college library. (On his eightieth birthday he gave his first edition of Blake's *Songs of Innocence*.) For all Forster's approachability, however, Simon Raven, who studied at King's from 1948 to 1952, suspected him latterly of being 'bone idle', noting that he never seemed to have anything to do or anywhere to go, 'so that very often, if he happened on friends by the way, he would turn round and go wherever they were going instead . . . He was merely killing time'. In a television interview in 1959 Forster described Cambridge as 'a place for the very young and the very old. Middle-aged people ought to go away and get other experiences.'[2]

After *A Passage to India* (1924) Forster published no more novels, though he continued to tinker with his homosexual novel, *Maurice*, and to show it in typescript to friends. Although he had begun *Maurice* as early as 1913, he did not feel able to publish it in his lifetime. By the time it was published in 1971 (it was filmed in 1987), it had inevitably become a period piece, not only on account of its pre-First World War setting (partly Cambridge) but also because of the changed social attitude towards homosexuality. Forster's *Commonplace Book*, kept between 1925 and 1968, includes vignettes of his daily life in Cambridge: college friends, sunsets over the Backs, evenings at the theatre, Indian miniatures in the Fitzwilliam, a don's funeral, a student drowned ('that dirty little prettified river'), the experience of nearly dying in an Addenbrooke's ward, near-misses with a car in Queen's Road or a motor-bike on Peas Hill. In 1948, while still lodging at Trumpington Street, midway between Thomas Gray's old rooms at Pembroke and Edward Fitzgerald's in King's Parade, he compared himself to those two previous writers as the 'academic gentle gentlemanly type', living in

---

2 Forster refused to install a telephone. On one occasion, when an American film studio rang to offer an enormous sum for *A Passage to India*, the porter asked them to hold on while he crossed the court, climbed Forster's stair, and knocked on his door. 'There's a Mr Hollywood on the line for you, sir.' Forster, implacably opposed to the book's being filmed, feigned innocence: 'Hollywood? I don't think I know any Mr Hollywood. You'd better tell him I'm out.'

a 'small enclosure reserved for old dears', though he thought himself more important as a writer than either of them, having 'taken more trouble to connect my inner life with the world's.'

Forster's eightieth birthday in 1959 was celebrated by a lunch party in the college hall attended by an illustrious literary gathering that included several aging Bloomsburyites – Leonard Woolf, Duncan Grant, Clive and Vanessa Bell, David Garnett – as well as the Greek poet George Seferis (then ambassador to Britain; he was also guest of honour at the college's Founder's Feast in 1957, and received an honorary degree from the university in 1960). Forster's ninetieth birthday was celebrated by a concert in the chapel, for which he chose the music; on the same day he was awarded the OM. In his final years Forster's gnomish figure shuffling between his rooms and the Backs, stooped and ordinary-looking in a cheap cloth cap and grubby raincoat, added an undeniable touch of literary romance to the Cambridge scene.

'I have met E. M. Forster', says Jim in J. G. Ballard's autobiographical novel *The Kindness of Women* (1991); 'he tottered into the Provost's sherry party yesterday. Whiskery old gent with sad eyes, like a disappointed child-molester.' Ballard (b. 1930), best known for his science-fiction novels and experimental stories, was educated, like Jim, at the Leys School before studying medicine for two years at King's (1949–51). Jim's room, facing the 'organ-weary chapel', is hung with surrealist reproductions and he has Camus and Boris Vian on his shelves ('Nobody's heard of them here'). His principal relationships are with the female cadaver he has to dissect and with Miriam, a Perse sixth-former who works as an assistant to a Chevrolet-driving, Tiger Moth-flying psychology lecturer. Jim takes Miriam (whom he later marries) on his motorbike to see the American bases at Lakenheath and Mildenhall, where the concrete of the nuclear weapons silos seems more meaningful than the university's 'primped and polished stone'. Jim can only experience Cambridge through the pain of his wartime trauma in Shanghai: the view from the Anatomy Library of Cambridgeshire meadows reminds him too vividly of 'the abandoned paddy fields near Lunghua', while the cadaver he dismantles represents for him 'all the victims of the war in China'. At the cinema he compulsively watches newsreels of hydrogen bomb tests. While he goes through the motions of getting drunk on the river with Addenbrooke's nurses and playing tennis with his fellow Kingsmen, the university remains 'a foreign city' to him. Ballard himself while at King's won a short story competition run by *Varsity* and was already thinking of becoming a writer; he would sometimes chat to Simon Raven in the Copper Kettle, though Raven, two years older, 'seemed to belong to another generation'. Ballard dismisses the Cambridge of 1950 as 'a shabby, seedy place deluded by its own self-importance; the teaching was abysmal and the colleges were little more than dons' dining clubs'.

In an article entitled 'The Varsity Match', Donald Davie observed that each new 'wave' of English poets over the last fifty years had been 'formed or fomented or dreamed up by lively undergraduates at Oxford, who subsequently carried the group-image to London'. Only afterwards and incidentally, according to Davie, have such 'waves' picked up recruits at Cambridge ('Isherwood in one generation, Thom Gunn in another'). This perpetuates an image of undergraduate poets conspiring to form putsches. In fact, if Cambridge has tended to take second place in such 'waves', that may be because Cambridge poets have been more concerned with poetry than with putsches. Even so, it is worth recalling that Stephen Spender, writing of the 1920s 'wave', admitted that he and its other Oxford members were aware at the time of Isherwood and Upward distantly looming as yet greater 'peaks' behind the more immediate one of Auden; while Edward Lucie-Smith has similarly confessed that in his time 'we Oxford poets had an inferiority complex about our Cambridge contemporaries. The chief cause was Thom Gunn.' Although such writers as John Wain, Kingsley Amis, Philip Larkin, Davie, and Gunn seemed to some at the time to represent a concerted attack on the literary establishment, they had little in common beyond their middle-class Oxbridge backgrounds and their broad intellectual attitudes. Gunn, indeed, has consistently denied that there was ever such a thing as the Movement.

Thomson William Gunn[3] (b. 1929) came up to Trinity in 1950 to read English, residing for all three years in Whewell's Court. The son of a London journalist (later editor of the *Daily Sketch*), Gunn had spent his national service teaching in the Army Educational Corps. His expectations of Cambridge were largely formed by reading Forster and he arrived expecting 'a lot of Ansells and Rickies, and exciting talk about ideas'. He first began seriously writing poetry at Cambridge, and published his first work in no fewer than nine different undergraduate magazines. By the end of his second year he was justifiably established as the Cambridge Poet, with profiles of him appearing in *Granta*, *Varsity*, and *Chequer* – though in retrospect he is modest about how he came to fill that particular niche:

> Looking back on that time, I can see it all as a bit incestuous: we promoted each other consistently. For example, the university newspaper *Varsity* featured a profile of a local celebrity each week, and it seems to me that we all wrote each other's profiles, thus creating and perpetuating each other's celebrity.

Gunn also put in hard academic work (he took a first in Part I of his tripos), attended all Leavis's lectures, and became President of the university's English Club. He and his friend Karl Miller (b. 1931) of Downing (later to found and edit the *London Review of Books*) in turn edited successive editions of an anthology, *Poetry from Cambridge*. Gunn also for a while acted as literary assistant to Mark Boxer (1931–88) of King's (the cartoonist 'Marc') as editor of *Granta*, then entering on a particularly sophisticated phase of its long career.

The chief event of Boxer's editorship, however, was the furore that blew up

---

[3] He was born William Guinneach Gunn, but changed his name by deed poll in 1949. Thomson was his mother's maiden name.

over a poem he printed in the issue for 2 May 1953, 'Aubade' by Anthony de Hoghton, which included such sentiments as

> You drunken gluttonous seedy God,
> You son of a bitch, you snotty old sod.

Possibly the proctors' exaggerated show of outrage over the poem (which they called 'uncomplimentary to God') is explained by the jitteriness over Boxer's threat of an 'anti-Coronation' number for the final May Week issue. Whatever their motivation, and despite a petition signed by E. M. Forster and others, they took the opportunity to rusticate Boxer (the first Cambridge student to be sent down for blasphemy since William Waller, author of *David's Prophecy*, in 1752) and ban *Granta* for the rest of the year. The result was that Boxer was accorded a tremendous mock funeral, travelling to the station in a horse-drawn coffin, while his successor as editor, Nicholas Tomalin of Trinity Hall, remembering the ploy by which the magazine had started in 1889, cocked a snook at the authorities by changing the title back to *The Gadfly* and continuing publication without other alteration throughout the ban.

Described by *Varsity* as 'resembling a lumberjack in dress and build, a Left-Bank, ironside lumberjack', who 'may be seen stepping, open-necked and check-shirted from college to college and back home to Trinity, and breaking now and then into a whimsy of headlong running', Gunn by his third year was thoroughly enjoying Cambridge. He recalls being so drunk at a party at Newnham that

> a don had to be specially brought from her bed, in her nightdress and dressing-gown, to open a side gate, normally locked, so that I could be carried more easily to a waiting taxi. She stood there in pained silence, waiting to give permission for the closing of the gate, and it seems that as I was being hauled past her my unconscious body gave a terrific fart, as if adding the sin of ingratitude to that of gluttony.

On another occasion, his ear-splitting laugh is said to have 'drawn the proctors to the scene of a crime, and had a friend arrested'. Perhaps as a result of such exuberance, Gunn took only a second in his final exams, but on the strength of his poetry he was awarded the Harper-Wood Studentship for English Poetry and Literature, awarded since 1950 by St John's – a possibly unique university award that allows the holder to travel overseas in the furtherance of creative writing. (Frederic Raphael won it the following year.) Its monetary value at that time was small, and Gunn remembers having been very hungry in Rome, though he was able to write much poetry there. In 1954 he returned to Cambridge for a while, partly to be with his close American friend Mike Kitay of Fitzwilliam House, with whom he subsequently left for the United States and with whom he has lived ever since. (Like Forster and Isherwood before him, Gunn first came to terms with his homosexuality at Cambridge.) Meanwhile, he had already as an undergraduate appeared on the radio reading his own poems; and the publication in 1954 of his first collection, *Fighting Terms* (all the contents of which had been written and mostly published at Cambridge), finally consolidated his reputation beyond Cambridge. His 'Forsterian fantasy' about the university had been more than fulfilled; but in a 'Letter from Cambridge' in the *London Magazine* Gunn argued that although Cambridge is not a backwater and is as 'central' as anywhere else (a question debated by Forster's characters in *The Longest Journey*), to stay beyond the point of success is to invite 'jellifying'. One's best hope lies rather in 'keeping on the move, "travelling light", with less congenial associates, with less attractive surroundings, with less leisure' – words that interestingly anticipate his famous poem 'On the Move', written in California.

Six poems by Gunn (including 'The Beach Head') found themselves juxtaposed in Karl Miller's anthology *Poetry from Cambridge 1952–4* with three by the future Poet Laureate Ted Hughes (including 'The Jaguar'); but though distantly aware of each other at Cambridge, the two poets belonged to different circles and did not become friends till years later. Gunn describes Hughes at this date as 'very retiring'; Hughes published nothing until the very end of his undergraduate career and even then published his first poem, in *Granta*, under a pseudonym. Nor did he make the social splash that Gunn did – his main claim to prominence was his title of University Champion at archery.

Edward James Hughes (b. 1930), son of a Yorkshire carpenter, had, like Gunn, done his national service before he came up to Pembroke in 1951 with an Open Exhibition in English. Unlike Gunn, he seems to have found the study of English repressive, if an anecdote allegedly recounted by Hughes to the American critic W. S. Merwin can really be believed.

> At Cambridge he set out to study English Literature. Hated it. Groaned having to write those essays. Felt he was dying of it in some essential place. Sweated late at night over the paper on Dr Johnson et al. – things he didn't want to read. One night, very late, very tired, he went to sleep. Saw the door open and someone like himself come in with a fox's head. The visitor went over to his desk, where an unfinished essay was lying, and put his paw on the papers, leaving a bloody mark; then he came over to the bed, looked down on Ted and said, 'You're killing us', and went out the door.[4]

Whatever the reason, after taking a good second in Part I, he switched in his third year to archaeology and anthropology (in which he took a third). It was only after graduating and leaving Cambridge (he supported himself as a gardener, night-watchman, zoo attendant, schoolteacher, and reader for J. Arthur Rank) that he

---

[4] On another occasion, in January 1955, Hughes was sitting in the bitterly cold room of a Cambridge friend, working on the first draft of 'The Jaguar'. Trying to find an image to describe the particular snarl of the animal in question, he wrote: 'as if he had a biting fly right up inside his nostril'. At that moment a large fly flew out of nowhere straight up Hughes's right nostril. 'I extricated it, and pressed it, like a flower, sealed under Sellotape, in my Complete Shakespeare, where it remained, for verification, as long as that book lasted.'

began to contribute his first poems to the Cambridge magazines *Granta*, *Chequer*, *Delta*, and *Gemini*, as well as one grandly calling itself the *Saint Botolph's Review* which he and five younger Cambridge friends united to produce (it ran for one issue).[5]

It was at the party to launch the *Saint Botolph's Review* (26 February 1956) that Hughes first met a tall, slender Bostonian, in her first year as a Fulbright Scholar reading English at Newnham. Sylvia Plath (1932–63), whose letters home and private journal had been plaintive about the immature boys around her and the depressing difficulty of meeting someone she could look up to, was overwhelmed by Hughes, who seemed to her impressive in every way: toweringly tall, bursting with creative energy, knowledgeable about literature and natural life. 'Met, by the way, a brilliant ex-Cambridge poet at the wild *St Botolph's Review* party last week', she told her mother; 'will probably never see him again . . . but wrote my best poem about him afterwards – the only man I've met yet here who'd be strong enough to be equal with – such is life'. (She didn't mention how, both being drunk, she bit his face when he tried to kiss her.) They did meet again, and soon she was writing that it was all 'most miraculous and thundering and terrifying . . . It is this man, this poet, this Ted Hughes . . . For the first time in my life I can use *all* my knowing and laughing and force and writing to the hilt all the time.'

Hughes abandoned plans to emigrate to Australia and moved back to Cambridge, where they cooked steaks and trout over her college gas ring, quoted poetry to each other, and hiked over the Cambridgeshire countryside: '15 miles yesterday through woods, field, and fen, and came home through moonlit Grantchester and fields of sleeping cows'. That summer term she was signed up by *Varsity* to do features and interviews, and a May Week fashion spread showed her posing in swimsuits and ball gowns. Her poems were appearing in magazines alongside Hughes's, and she was also working on a first novel, about Cambridge life, to be called *Falcon Yard* after the venue of the party where she and Hughes had met (the manuscript has apparently not survived, apart from the section 'Stone Boy with Dolphin', a vivid evocation of the night of the party, published in 1979).

Hughes and Plath were secretly married that summer in London. She was afraid of the reaction of her college authorities, but after spending the vacation together in Spain and Yorkshire they found it impossible, when her second October term came round, to live apart. To her surprise, the college was understanding, the Fulbright sponsors positively congratulatory. But she was obliged to leave her hostel (Whitstead in Barton Road) and so, in December, they moved into a nearby flat at 55 Eltisley Avenue, a 'dusty, dirty, gloomy coal-bin of a house', as she rather unfairly called it. Hughes found work at Coleridge secondary modern

---

[5] Named after St Botolph's rectory, Newnham, where some of the contributors lodged. The poet Anne Stevenson, whose mother-in-law ran the rectory, remembers it as 'crammed with poets'.

school (where, according to the then headmaster, he was given a free hand and 'did a wonderful job with some awkward boys'), and from then until her exams in June 1957 they lived in penurious contentment, rising at five to write, walking frequently over Grantchester Meadows, 'where the spires of King's Chapel looked like glistening pink sugar spikes on a little cake . . . What a lovely walk to have at the end of the street!' She marshalled her husband's poems, typed and retyped them, submitted them unflaggingly to editors and competitions (mainly in America); and it was at Eltisley Avenue that the telegram came announcing that his first collection, *The Hawk in the Rain*, had won an important American prize. They were both starting to make their names.

They left Cambridge the moment her exams were finished.[6] Five years of collaborative life together followed – America, London, prizes, and acclaim – before the finally fracturing marriage and the eruption of buried psychoses brought Plath to her premature end in a gas-filled London flat.

While Gunn's activity centred on *Granta* and *Varsity*, and Hughes's on St Botolph's rectory and the Anchor pub (where, according to *Broadsheet*, 'the landlord has set aside a room for the display of poetry'), a third circle centred on Peter Redgrove, Philip Hobsbaum, and the 'Group' (though it was not yet called that). Redgrove (b. 1932), who had come up to Queens' in 1951 with a science scholarship, experienced a kind of epiphany one day in a local bookshop when, fed up with science books, he opened a poetry anthology instead. 'I read the first lines: "In a somer seson when softe was the sonne . . . " and my hair stood on end, my skin felt sunny inside my clothes.' Instead of completing his science course, he began to attend the poetry group run by Hobsbaum (who was reading English at Downing) at which the Richards/Leavis 'practical criticism' technique was being used experimentally on new poems. These were circulated in a duplicated pamphlet called *Workshop* before being read to the group by the poets themselves and communally criticised (generally with Leavisite severity). This, the original 'poetry workshop', provided the nucleus for the later, more famous 'Group' in London.

It was Redgrove who founded a new poetry magazine, *Delta*, which, originally sold around the streets and colleges of Cambridge, later went on to achieve a national readership. (It survived until 1981, although from 1972 it was no longer edited from Cambridge.) This was the longest surviving in an age swarming with ephemeral little magazines of the same kind. *Cambridge Writing*, founded in 1948 by the undergraduate Young Writers' Group, published early poems by Donald Davie and Frederic Raphael. The short-lived *Imprint* (1949–50) was already by Gunn's time looked back to as the ideal magazine of the sort. *Oasis*, founded in 1950 by John Mander of Trinity and David Stone of Queens' in conjunction with

---

6 She submitted a collection of her poems, *Two Lovers and a Beachcomber*, as part of her tripos (she got a good second). The typescript, containing several unpublished poems, turned up in the English Faculty Library in 1969.

a series of readings at the Union, was sold directly on the streets by what Gunn called 'a kind of suicide squad' of enthusiasts. It was bought in remarkable numbers (up to three thousand per issue), giving it the largest circulation of any poetry magazine in England. The first issues were devoted to major poets like Yeats and Eliot, later ones to undergraduate work. Fifteen hundred poems were submitted for the *Oasis* poetry competition. One of the winners was Thom Gunn (who was also on the editorial board). The shorter-lived *Concern*, with a political–religious slant, sold seven hundred copies of its first issue. *Chequer*, founded in 1953 by a group that included Harry Guest and Ronald Hayman of Trinity Hall with Karl Miller and (again) Thom Gunn, was the most catholic, printing poems by Gunn, Hughes, and Redgrove. *Pawn*, edited from King's, lasted from 1956 until 1972 and was more experimental. *Gemini* (1957–9) was an up-market joint Oxford and Cambridge production, which mixed the work of young poets like Hughes and Plath with that of established writers.

Thom Gunn and Sylvia Plath, if not to the same extent Ted Hughes, exemplified a new urgency for 'success' among the young. The title of one of Kingsley Amis's novels, *I Want It Now*, might stand as motto for the post-war middle-class generation now filling the universities. Their discovery that the traditional Cambridge voice – dry, self-qualifying, clipped with understated self-esteem – could, with only a tiny adjustment, become a medium of high comedy was the start of a whole new era of creativity – the era of *Beyond the Fringe*, *That Was the Week That Was*, and eventually *Monty Python*, all emanating originally from the annual revues put on by the Cambridge Footlights Dramatic Club, the nursery in the 1950s for such talents as Jonathan Miller, Peter Cook, and David Frost. This sudden eruption into showbiz success was remarkable in providing an unexpected victory (Cambridge's first since Bloomsbury) in Davie's putative 'Varsity Match' – on Oxford's own terms of sophistication.

The alleged urgency, cynicism, and ethical betrayals involved in that victory are exposed in Frederic Raphael's television serial *The Glittering Prizes* (1976), subsequently turned into a novel. Raphael (b. 1931) came up to St John's in 1950 to read classics and was active, along with his college contemporary Jonathan Miller (who read medicine two years later), in the Footlights. Raphael and Miller took part in the 1954 revue *Out of the Blue* and the following year's *Between the Lines* (Raphael writing much of their more satirical material), both of which transferred to London (the club's first direct connection with professional show-business since its foundation in 1883). Miller, while still an undergraduate, also took part in a radio comedy programme which included a take-off of Bertrand Russell and G. E. Moore.

The Glittering Prizes chronicles the careers of a group of contemporaries who become friends at Cambridge in the early fifties mainly through their association in a leading dramatic club. Adam Morris, like Raphael himself from a middle-class London Jewish background, goes on to become a bestselling novelist, while other characters become a television personality, a trendy film director, and a professor of interdisciplinary studies at a new university. (None of them, however, seems ultimately much more content with what Cambridge brings them than their beggarly Elizabethan counterparts, Philomusus and Studioso in *The Return from Parnassus*.) Cambridge's main role seems to be to equip them with ambition, self-assurance, the cachet of privileged prestige, and marriage partners (and their marriages, mostly hatched at the May Ball, prove as volatile as their careers). Dons are as markedly absent from Raphael's pages as students from those of C. P. Snow. 'So this is the city of dreaming spires', says Adam Morris's naive girlfriend Sheila, on a day-trip from London in his first term, as they eat in the Taj Mahal restaurant. 'Theoretically that's Oxford', Adam corrects her. 'This is the city of perspiring dreams.' Her own dreams – of married respectability somewhere between Mill Hill and Hendon – are evidently insufficiently perspiring for him; besides, she refuses to stay the night. Already, in the restaurant, Adam is sizing up the available talent.

Whether or not his generation was really as crawlingly eager for fame as Raphael makes out (Jonathan Miller does not recall their Cambridge as quite such a 'bowl of piranha fish'), certainly the annual generations of students that beat, wave on wave, over Cambridge through the fifties seemed destined for glittering prizes of some sort. When Raphael came up in 1950, those already in residence included the novelists Elaine Feinstein (Newnham), Tom Sharpe (Pembroke), J. G. Ballard, and Simon Raven (King's; he was to use the college, as 'Lancaster College', as background for two of his novels and, as 'Tertullian College', for a television play, *Royal Foundation*). The dramatist Peter Shaffer (Trinity) and the journalist Katharine Whitehorn (Newnham) had just gone down. Raphael's freshman contemporaries included Thom Gunn, Mark Boxer, the dramatist John Arden (reading architecture at King's), the poet Harry Guest (Trinity Hall), and the future National Theatre Director Peter Hall (St Catharine's). (Hall had lived in Blinco Grove during his teens and attended the Perse School; he remembers being filled with almost suicidal depression by Cambridge at that time. St Catharine's he used as little more than a lodging-house, being already busy directing plays for the ADC and the Marlowe Society.) The following year saw the arrival of Ted Hughes, Peter Redgrove, Karl Miller, the drama critic Ronald Hayman (Trinity Hall), and the foreign correspondent Nicholas Tomalin (Trinity Hall); 1952 brought Jonathan Miller, Philip Hobsbaum, and the film director Michael Winner (Downing); 1953 brought the novelist and playwright Michael Frayn (Emmanuel); 1954 the poet Peter Scupham (Emmanuel), who had previously attended the Perse School. The 1955 intake included Sylvia Plath, Bamber Gascoigne (Magdalene), and the novelist Andrew Sinclair (Trinity); that of 1956 included the playwright and novelist Simon Gray (Trinity), and the cartoonist Timothy Birdsall (Christ's), and the poet and critic Francis Warner (St Catharine's). A. S. Byatt (b. 1936), the 1990 Booker Prize winner, arrived at Newnham in 1954 to take a first in English; her sister and fellow novelist Margaret Drabble (b. 1939) arrived in 1957 and outdid her by taking a starred first. ('I said to my dons in my final year at Cambridge', Byatt recalls, 'I must leave, my sister's coming. They said, "Oh, she can't do as well as you", but she did. She went one better.') Drabble played leads at the ADC, where she met her future husband, the actor Clive Swift (Caius, 1956). Drabble's 1957 contemporaries included Footlights stars Peter Cook (Pembroke) and Eleanor Bron (Newnham), the actor Derek Jacobi (St John's), and the journalist Christopher Booker (Corpus). David Frost (Caius) and the actor Ian McKellen (St Catharine's) arrived in 1958 (Frost edited *Granta* in 1960 and was Secretary of the Footlights in 1961; his first ever television appearance was in a 'Town and Gown' skit on Anglia in his second year). Those arriving in 1959 included the actor Trevor Nunn (Downing) and the novelists Piers Paul Read (St John's) and Alexis Lykiard (King's).

Among more established writers, C. S. Lewis (1898–1963), having been passed over for professorships at Oxford, was elected in 1954 to the new professorship of medieval and Renaissance English at Cambridge and migrated from Magdalen, Oxford, to Magdalene, Cambridge. A diverse and prolific writer who encompassed many genres from science fiction to works of literary scholarship, Lewis described himself with dramatic exaggeration in his inaugural lecture as Old Western Man and a dinosaur. Although he enjoyed Cambridge (comparing it to pre-industrial Oxford) he hurried home to Oxford at weekends and vacations, travelling on the train he called the 'Cantab Crawler'. Kathleen Raine, then working on Blake as a Research Fellow of Girton, remembered the astonishing range of Lewis's conversation, and thought him practically alone in the Cambridge of that time in understanding that poetry existed 'to serve ends which are not literary'. Lewis remained professor until shortly before his death, and his *Studies in Words* and *An Experiment in Criticism* were both issued by the University Press.

Robert Graves (1895–1985), coming from Oxford in 1923, had been 'scared' by Cambridge: 'everything was so much the same and yet so disturbingly different' – porters in top hats, colleges built of brick instead of stone, the punts propelled the wrong way, 'it was all Looking-Glassy'. In October 1954 when he delivered the Clark Lectures (published as *The Crowning Privilege*) he enjoyed himself better. 'Hordes of devoted students turned away at the door', he wrote from 4 Mortimer Road after the first lecture. But his small son, punting, asked: 'When are we going to get somewhere *really* pretty?' (he was used to 'cliffs five hundred feet high, rich in sea-eagles' nests . . . and pinewood headlands crowned by medieval watchtowers of golden limestone'). In King's College Chapel one day Graves bumped into Siegfried Sassoon, and the two were able to heal a long-standing breach; 'all the years and misunderstandings' melted away, according to Sassoon.

John Betjeman tackled with success that most risky of poetic challenges, another poem on King's College Chapel (drafted on Armistice Day 1947, published in 1954); in a backhanded compliment he once called King's 'the most

Oxfordlike' of Cambridge colleges. In 1948 John Osborne, working as assistant stage manager with a touring company, lodged in a doss-house in Portugal Place. When Dylan Thomas visited Cambridge in 1951 to record a word game for the BBC Light Programme, Karl Miller found in him 'a quality of good manners which rarely figures in the memorials of his life'; his word for a collection of undergraduates was 'a falutin'. The poet and novelist D. M. Thomas, aged nineteen, spent 1954 in Cambridge doing a Russian course as part of his National Service (the dramatist Alan Bennett had attended the same course in 1952); a poor linguist, he diligently learnt the various Russian terms for tanks or shells but 'far more thrilling was learning how to masturbate': this occurred in a Cambridge cinema while watching Marlene Dietrich's 'black-stockinged scything thighs' in *The Blue Angel*. The poet Edwin Muir lived at Swaffham Prior from 1956 until his death in Cambridge in 1959, receiving an honorary degree in 1958. The American poet Robert Frost lectured in Cambridge in 1957, on the occasion of receiving an honorary degree. The Russian poet Yevgeny Yevtushenko gave a reading at the Union in 1962; hosted around Cambridge by Kingsley Amis, he mistook cricket for soccer, played ping-pong, and inspected King's College Chapel with 'the courteous interest . . . of a man looking at something impressive that the Other Side had done'. The American novelist Norman Mailer, lecturing in Cambridge around the same time, disappointed undergraduates expecting a 'prophet of the new message': dressed in a crumpled suit, he is alleged to have 'lost his hold on the audience' before ever he reached the podium and his talk to have been 'mainly inarticulate', punctuated by 'a flurry of punches in the direction of the audience . . . At other times he simply stood, his arms hanging down and his face thrust out, in what seemed a positive stupor of stupidity.' Georges Simenon, sent by his publisher on a day trip to see Cambridge, went in the first pub he came to and stayed there until it was time to go back.

Kingsley Amis (b. 1922), despite his send-up of academics in *Lucky Jim* (1954), was appointed to a fellowship at Peterhouse in 1961, for what his friend Donald Davie has called a 'brief but eventful and unhappy period'. The appointment may have been popular with the students but Amis the bestselling novelist, the comedian, the man of the world, felt at odds with the ritualised and over-formal academic establishment, hating in particular the donnish dinner parties and college feasts – though he found Peterhouse itself 'an oasis of good nature and common sense'. He was disillusioned to find that his colleagues' talk consisted mainly of intra-faculty squabbles rather than Donne and Dickens; he was denigrated as a 'pornographer' by an outraged Leavis,[7] and even branded as homosexual for his unCambridge habit of fraternising with students in pubs. He found his students 'an amiable and tolerant lot' but his teaching duties interfered with his writing and he was appalled by the lack of contact between students and

---

[7] Ironically, since Leavis had himself been called a pornographer back in the thirties, in the wake of the *Ulysses* affair. *The Granta* had even once offered a 'Leavis Prize for Pornography'.

dons. Living first at West Wratting, then in 'a rather posh house' in Madingley Road, he recalls convivial occasions in Miller's Wine Bar and elsewhere with the Scottish poet James Burns Singer (1928–64), then living in Newnham, and the 'often hugely drunk' John Davenport, then living at Duxford; and a less convivial one when the novelist Andrew Sinclair, having invited Amis for drinks at the Merton Arms, allegedly failed to pay: 'I must have left my wallet in my other jacket'.[8] He left in anger and disappointment after two years, having found Cambridge generally

> a town whose most characteristic images – King's Chapel, say, at dusk in a thin mist – seemed cold and lonely, a setting more appropriate to an unhappy love-affair than the bustling exchange of ideas that is supposed to go on: inhospitable despite the ceaseless ceremonial parade of hospitality. Arrival at that curious railway station, with its endless single platform like something out of Kafka or Chirico, ought to tip off the sensitive.

The latter sentiment is echoed by Simon Gray, who languished at Trinity from 1956 to 1965 as student, research student, and supervisor: 'There is the moment, as the London train slides along the interminable Cambridge platform, when my stomach lurches . . .'[9] Gray has nevertheless used Cambridge as the setting for two early novels and two plays – *Quartermaine's Terms* and *The Common Pursuit*.

The novelist Anthony Burgess (1917–93) discovered in 1968, after the death of his first wife, that an Italian admirer he had met briefly four years before, Contessa Liliana Macellari, had borne him a son and was currently researching in applied linguistics at Cambridge. Finding her living with an unemployed actor in a house in Victoria Road 'full of rent-paying Iranians', he persuaded her to relinquish house, lodgers, lover, and Cambridge, and marry him.

The turbulent 1960s are reflected in the work of two dramatists, Howard Brenton (b. 1942), who read English at St Catharine's in 1962–5, and David Hare (b. 1947), who read English at Jesus in 1965–8. Brenton, who went on to achieve some notoriety as the author of such plays as *The Romans in Britain*, seems in retrospect an unlikely winner of the Chancellor's Medal (for 'Lazarus: A Sequence'). His first play, *Ladder of Fools*, was produced at Cambridge in 1965. Hare, who remembers Jesus as 'the dimmest and silliest educational establishment I've ever known', thought the dons of his time 'arrogant and lazy' and out of touch with the radical political feelings of students like himself. He had chosen Jesus in

---

[8] Bryan Appleyard records Bill Buford, editor of *Granta*, similarly welching during a £91 lunch session at Midsummer House in 1989: 'Er I left my wallet at home.'

[9] E. M. Forster also noted his depression on arriving at 'that eel-like platform'. But the singularity of platform is deceptive, as Forster discovered one day in 1966 when setting off to receive an Italian gold medal for literature. He mistakenly boarded the 3.35 to Liverpool Street from the main platform; the Italian ambassador waited at King's Cross to meet him off the 3.40. 'Can you imagine a more mischievous arrangement?' his companion J. R. Ackerley fumed.

order to study under Raymond Williams (by now 'Britain's leading Marxist'), only to be farmed out to junior tutors. Williams himself was occasionally glimpsed across the court, 'books under his arm, a Dylan cap worn at an unlikely angle on his head, entirely in a world of his own', more concerned with compiling *The May Day Manifesto* than teaching students. Hare was soon in any case disillusioned with the prescriptively moral tone of English studies at Cambridge – 'I had no desire to train to be a non-commissioned officer in the arts police, patrolling literature for capital offences such as "failure of seriousness"' (unlike, presumably, his Jesus contemporary Terry Eagleton, a Marxist who rose to be professor of English at Oxford). His play *Teeth 'n' Smiles* (1975) is set at the Jesus College Ball of 1969 and features a disintegrating rock band in collision with the snob society it despises. (The play was partly based on the behaviour of the group Manfred Mann at the Magdalene College Ball of 1967.) Like the character Arthur, Hare was himself once fined for having a girl in his room ('They build walls here to stop undergraduates making love,' Arthur snarls). If Cambridge for the 1950s generation was an escape route from suburbia, by Hare's time it seems to have become indistinguishable from suburbia (the college porter who catches Arthur is described as 'an English suburban stormführer'). Hare's rock group find their escape through drugs, sex, and booze, but with no more ultimate sense of liberation than Raphael's television stars. Desperation leads them to violence – symbolised by their setting light to the ball marquee.

Clive James (b. 1939), poet, novelist, critic, television performer, studied at Pembroke in 1964–8, though he describes in his 'unreliable' memoirs how academic study (estimated at about 'one hour per month') tended to take a back seat to running the Footlights (President 1967), film-acting in London, writing for *Granta* (of which he was literary editor), *The Cambridge Review* (film critic), the *New Statesman* (art criticism), and the *Times Literary Supplement* (poetry reviews), not to mention hitch-hiking through Italy (he regarded Florence as 'my unofficial university'), appearing on University Challenge (he caused Pembroke to lose), and watching every film in the six Cambridge cinemas. Living at Friar's House in Benet Street, he could hear fellow Australian Germaine Greer (b. 1939) pounding out on 'a typewriter the size of a printing press', for ten hours a day, early drafts of her bestselling first book *The Female Eunuch*. 'Through the trembling partition dividing our rooms came the frenzied uproar of a belt-fed Mauser MG42 firing long bursts from a concrete pillbox.'

Four prize-winning novelists were at Cambridge in this period: Anita Brookner, a distinguished art historian long before she wrote her first novel, was Slade Professor in 1967–8, and a Fellow of New Hall; Salman Rushdie studied at King's (1965–8), Graham Swift at Queens' (1967–70), Peter Ackroyd at Clare (1968–71). Rushdie, born in Bombay in 1947, went from Rugby (which he hated) to his father's old college, King's, to read history. While working on a special paper on Islam he first read about the incident which was to inspire his controversial 1988 novel *The Satanic Verses*. He took part in a number of drama productions – 'a tiny bulb in the Footlights' – and his first ambition was to act professionally. At Cambridge he lost his Anglo-Indian conservatism and became radical, though a King's contemporary felt he was now 'trying to have it both ways – be a representative of the oppressed people of the Third World and yet also glory in the public school gloss around him.' Rushdie himself recalls his student days being spent 'under the spell of Buñuel, Godard, Ray, Wajda, Welles, Bergman, Kurosawa, Jancsó, Antonioni, Dylan, Lennon, Jagger, Laing, Marcuse and, inevitably, the two-headed fellow known to Grass readers as Marxengels'. In February 1993 Rushdie marked the fourth anniversary of the *fatwa* which had forced him into hiding by delivering a speech in King's College Chapel.

Cambridge poetry in the sixties tended to diversify, under the influence of such teachers as Davie at Caius and George Steiner, Extraordinary Fellow and later Director of English Studies at Churchill. Among Davie's pupils was J. H. Prynne of Jesus, who later became a Fellow of Caius. His difficult and severe poetry gathered to him a coterie of equally uncompromising disciples, including John Wilkinson (another somewhat unlikely Chancellor's Medallist, who refused to excise a four-letter word from his poem when he recited it in the Senate House) and the poet and critic Veronica Forrest-Thomson (1947–75). By the middle sixties the *avant-garde* was in full swing, mounting exhibitions of concrete poetry and kinetic art and producing the usual ephemeral magazines and editions. But it had little popular support: when the 'Prynnites' took over the Cambridge Poetry Society in the late seventies, membership fell away until the society dissolved.[10]

George Steiner (b. 1929), with his polyglot internationalism and charismatic energies, was by contrast among the most popular lecturers of the sixties, with students from all faculties queueing to hear him. Slighted, like Leavis, by the academic establishment ('Instead of lecturing, as perhaps I ought to have, on Dryden's middle period, I lectured in the first year on "How do we read a poem after Marx, Freud and Lévi-Strauss?" – with pretty fatal results': a senior faculty member, a former prisoner on the Burmese death railways, walked out when Steiner quoted Adorno's line 'No poetry after Auschwitz'), he became in some ways the guru critic to replace Leavis, though with a breadth of reference much more in tune with the times than Leavis's pre-war insularity of English tradition. Like Leavis, Steiner vigorously defends literary cultural values against the depredations of modern society; but whereas Leavis could be criticised (by A. L. Rowse) for being 'not widely read, even in English', Steiner appears to be fluent in most European tongues and intimate with all of European literature. Malcolm Bradbury has described a typical Steiner lecture 'given without notes, as he summoned his extensive materials, covering literary theory, philosophy and politics, from the massive card-catalogue of his mind. The manner was quiet but

---

10 The Eastern Arts Association withdrew its grant, and in 1981 the society was reformed on a much broader basis, with town/gown membership and non-college venues.

charismatic, a great commanding of the audience through the power of language'. Steiner's polymathic interests are evident in such works as *The Death of Tragedy* (1960), *After Babel* (1975), *Antigones* (1984), and *Real Presences* (1989); he has held a professorship in comparative literature at Geneva University from 1974, at Oxford from 1994. But as with Leavis, the powerful idealism is accompanied by difficulties of style and character: one reviewer calls the prose style 'archaic mandarin'; an interviewer records how 'in his peaceful drawing room in Cambridge . . . Steiner rapidly converts interview into tutorial, answer into exegesis, and never lets you forget that he is not only cleverer than most but, in a way that is part ordained, part deliberate, ostentatiously set apart'. As with Leavis, what begins as a concern to open up literature begins to resemble a new elitism.

The poet Richard Burns (b. 1943) may exemplify Steiner's influence. Having studied under Steiner while a student at Pembroke in the early sixties, Burns returned to Cambridge in 1969 to teach at the Cambridgeshire College of Arts and Technology (CCAT) – itself becoming something of an alternative literary centre at this time with Tom Sharpe, John James, and Omar Pound (son of Ezra Pound) also on the teaching staff. Burns has translated Italian and Greek poets and his interest in poetry is international, so that when, in 1975, he founded the first Cambridge Poetry Festival (he claims the idea came to him one morning as he was nursing a hangover on the 103 bus from Shelford) it was natural that the emphasis would be very broad (participants came from more than a dozen countries). The biennial Festival, last held in 1985, was said to be the largest in Europe and maintained its internationalism, its town/gown basis, and its disregard of London literary dictates. (A smaller-scale avant-garde replacement, the Cambridge Conference of Contemporary Poetry, has been held since 1991.)

International in tone, too, has become *Granta*, the student magazine revived in 1979 as a paperback literary quarterly by Bill Buford (b. 1954), a King's postgraduate from California. The grainy first issue of the new series, devoted to new American writing, received a fulsome review from David Lodge in *The Guardian*. The second issue was largely devoted to Steiner's fiction *The Portage to San Cristobal of A.H.* At the time, Buford was living in a Cambridge slum. 'The place was appalling, damp was crawling all over the walls, there was a prostitute next door who would stick her kid in the back yard whenever she had a client, someone once came crashing through the window after a fight, and we were publishing George! It was completely mad.' The third issue had an extract from Salman Rushdie's *Midnight's Children*, lifted without the author's knowledge. The seventh issue, featuring the 'Best of Young British Novelists', was the first to be published by arrangement with Penguin Books. Although initially the name *Granta* 'didn't work in the magazine's favour: I had to keep telling people it wasn't a student magazine and I wasn't an undergraduate', *Granta* soon established itself as one of the most successful publications of its kind, selling 140,000 copies (two-thirds in North America). A showcase for trenchant new work from a galaxy of fashionable writers (if latterly rather set in its winning formula), *Granta* continued to be edited from above a hairdressers in Hobson Street until 1990, when its editorial offices moved to London.[11]

The Chancellor's Medal for poetry has also latterly developed an international bias, tending to go, on the occasions it has been awarded, to students from overseas. Of recent winners, several have been American, one from South Africa, one from New Zealand, one from Holland. The paucity of native British winners remains unexplained.

Meanwhile the English faculty was bitterly divided in 1981 between its more conservative teachers and those who wished to introduce radical 'structuralist' approaches to literary study; the faculty's refusal to promote the left-wing structuralist Colin MacCabe of King's to a lectureship sparked a major row, with Professors Raymond Williams and Frank Kermode supporting the radicals. (McCabe was subsequently appointed professor at Strathclyde University.) An echo of this dispute came in 1992 when the university's proposal to award an honorary degree to Jacques Derrida, French doyen of deconstructionists, was only narrowly passed.

Writers in residence of various sorts began to appear in the 1980s. Holders of the English faculty's Judith E. Wilson Visiting Fellowship (usually with attachment to Magdalene) have included Adrian Mitchell (1980–1), David Benedictus (1981–2), Paul Muldoon (1986–7), Adam Mars-Jones (1987–8) and Jo Shapcott (1990–1). Mitchell recalls lecturing on rock lyrics, oral poetry and music theatre, 'riding round Cambridge on a butcher's boy bike', attending political demonstrations (the title-poem of his 1984 collection *On the Beach at Cambridge*, portraying Cambridge devastated by nuclear war, was recited at one such), and sitting in Belinda's café 'so people could find me/meet me/feed me'. Benedictus produced a Cambridge novel; Muldoon married the 1985 Chancellor's Medallist. King's has had the novelist David Plante as Visiting Fellow (1984–8), Trinity the poet Kit Wright and the 1991 Booker Prize winner Ben Okri as Fellow Commoners in the Creative Arts. The Mexican novelist Carlos Fuentes held the Simón Bolívar chair, 1986–7, lecturing on Latin American literature; the American novelist Toni Morrison (winner of the 1993 Nobel Prize) delivered the 1990 Clark Lectures.

Whereas Cambridge town used to consist largely of a working-class population dependent on the university, recent years have seen an influx of professional people and a general increase in the town's autonomy from the colleges. Within easy reach of London yet sufficiently distant from the capital's distracting pressures, and supposedly full of intelligent and cultured people, Cambridge has

---

[11] Another American who studied at King's and went on to edit a prestigious international literary magazine is George Plimpton, who since 1953 has edited the *Paris Review*, best known for its interviews with eminent authors (the first issue featured E. M. Forster, whom Plimpton had met at King's).

begun to attract a number of resident writers not necessarily connected with the university. These include the poets Burns, Holbrook, Geoffrey Hill (Fellow of Emmanuel 1981-8, Honorary Fellow since 1990), Glen Cavaliero (a Fellow of St Catharine's), Arthur Sale (a Fellow of Magdalene), and Clive Wilmer, as well as the Swedish poet Goran Printz-Påhlson and the Hungarian poet George Gömöri; the biographers Peter Brent, Constance Babington Smith, Piers Brendon, and Daphne Bennett; the critics Clive James and Russell Davies; the stage dramatist Edward Bond, the radio dramatist N. J. Warburton and the television dramatist Michael J. Bird; and the novelists Storm Jameson (who lived at 11 Larchfield from 1953 until her death in 1986), Elaine Feinstein, Graham Coster, John Lennox Cook, and Jeffrey Archer (who bought the Old Vicarage, Grantchester, in 1979). Colleen McCullough wrote her bestselling novel *The Thorn Birds* in a flat at 20 Lyndewode Road while working as a typist with Pye. Rowland Parker (1912-89), a Cambridge schoolmaster for thirty years, wrote his bestselling *The Common Stream* about the thousand-year history of Foxton, the village where he lived; *Town and Gown* chronicled Cambridge town and university relations. John Treherne (1929-89), President of Downing, was an insect neurobiologist who in his spare time wrote three well-received works of 'faction' and two novels; through his friendship with P. D. James (an Associate Fellow of the college since 1986) he was instrumental in setting up the P. D. James Prize for creative writing by undergraduates. The bestselling novelist Susan Howatch in 1993 set up the university's Starbridge Lectureship in Theology and Natural Science (named after her fictional cathedral town) in an attempt to show that religion and science are not incompatible. The novelist Maggie Hemingway (1946-93) lived and went to school in Cambridge from the age of nine. Douglas Adams, creator of *The Hitch Hiker's Guide to the Galaxy*, was born in Cambridge in 1952 and educated at St John's; the younger humorist Stephen Fry was at Queens'. The poet and critic John Holloway (b. 1920), a Fellow of Queens' since 1955, in 1993 published a celebration of Cambridge, *Civitatula: The Little City: A Poem in Six Parts*, hailed by A. L. Rowse as 'the finest and most remarkable long poem since T. S. Eliot's *Four Quartets*. A signal and unique tribute to Cambridge in the history and landscape of England.'

Perhaps the best-known among this group has been Tom Sharpe (b. 1928), who after reading history at Pembroke emigrated to South Africa. Expelled from that country in 1961, he returned to Cambridge and taught at the CCAT for eight years, living in Mill Road. He met his American wife in Cambridge and wrote his first novel, *Riotous Assembly*, in three weeks to raise money for their marriage. It proved a bestseller and they moved to 33 Highfield Avenue. *Wilt* and *The Wilt Alternative* are based on his experiences at the 'Tech', while *Porterhouse Blue* (1974, televised 1987), Sharpe's portrait of a backward, elitist Cambridge college and the attempts of a progressive new Master to reform it, is, Sharpe claims, equally solidly based in its comic detail on actual incident (though the college itself is an invention). Sharpe abandoned Cambridge for Dorset in 1978 but returned in 1985, apparently because he felt he could write better in Cambridge; and in a way his *Porterhouse Blue*, with its bawdy humour and close observation of local type, looks back across the crowded span of six centuries to *The Reeve's Tale*. The shade of Chaucer, one feels, recognising some vestige of continuity amid the ever quickening cycles of movements, schools, coteries, and controversies, would nod approval.

'The high, invisible bridge'

> Would you commence a poet, sir, and be
> A graduate in the threadbare mystery?
> The Ox's ford will no man thither bring
> Where the horse-hoof raised the Pegasian spring;
> Nor will the bridge through which low Cam doth run
> Direct you to the banks of Helicon.
> If in that art you mean to take degrees,
> Bedlam's the best of universities . . .

Thomas Randolph was joking, of course: had not Cambridge brought Nashe and Greene, Marlowe and Spenser, Herbert and Herrick, Milton and Quarles and all the Fletchers safely to the 'banks of Helicon', and was not Randolph himself as firmly established as the Cambridge Poet of his day as Christopher Smart, Alfred Tennyson, Rupert Brooke, or Thom Gunn were to be in theirs?

Yet in implying that a touch of madness sooner makes a poet than academic sanity, Randolph endorses a traditional myth that poetry is quickest achieved by a disordering of the senses:

> There is no true Parnassus but the third loft in a wine tavern, no true Helicon but
> a cup of brown bastard. Will you travel quickly to Parnassus? Do but carry your
> dry feet . . . into the Half Moon or the Rose . . . then call for a cup of pure
> Helicon . . . that will make you speak leaping lines and dancing periods.[1]

Smart, graduating from Cambridge to the literal Bedlam, seems to substantiate Randolph's claim. Wordsworth's fellow students called him mad when he escaped from the university to wander in an ecstasy of identification with the dull fenland scene; so too, no doubt, did the contemporaries of Cowper Powys. Coleridge the Pantisocrat was threatened with the asylum. Housman called Cambridge itself 'an asylum in more senses than one' – though not, one infers from his own

---

[1] *The Pilgrimage to Parnassus*, Act II

output, in Randolph's creative sense. The Mortmere characters of Isherwood's poem – crackling with insane creativity – whoop with joy as they abandon Cambridge's 'pleasant snuggeries', fit only for 'academic buggeries'. If one turns to as recent a work as Donald Davie's *The Shires* (in which one poem is devoted to each English county) to see what local aspect he singles out for analysis, one finds a dialogue between Housman, Gray, Smart, Blake, and (as representative of the sanely uninspired) Harold Monro on the nature of madness. Virginia Woolf once observed that 'common sense and Cambridge are not enough'.

The rationalist wind that sweeps Cambridge streets and courts may numb the imagination in the end, but limited exposure to it (as to Bedlam) may strengthen an artist, offering not a disordering of the senses but a disciplining of the perceptions. Even Bedlam is more likely to be positively productive if it succeeds academic rigour (Smart's *Jubilate Agno* is full of learning as well as inconsequence, as is Lowry's *Under the Volcano*). At a certain stage in most writers' development, the university (if it is doing its job; but for long stretches of time Cambridge was not) provides an ideally stimulating milieu – even though it is unlikely to provide a long-term setting for creative activity of any intensity. As Thom Gunn, who perhaps got as much from Cambridge (not least from Leavis's practical criticism classes) as any poet can hope, has summed up: 'I am grateful to Cambridge for many things. It enriched my life enormously, it gave me the security and advantages that everybody ought to have, but it also brought me up against someone who could eventually teach me that the real business was elsewhere completely.'

Yet though Tennyson or Forster might have said much the same, the careers of most 'Cambridge writers' fall short of this ideal. Marlowe and Milton were beneficially imbued with the intellectual training, Lowry with a symbolic Cambridge of the unconscious; but Wordsworth and Coleridge left unprepossessed, for Isherwood Cambridge seemed an irksome extension of school. Vernon Watkins and Kathleen Raine found the ethos of their day killing to their imaginations, Henry Kirke White actually was killed by the ethos of his. Even so, no one has looked back on Cambridge with quite the acerbity of some Oxonians on Oxford – Gibbon for example ('To the university of Oxford I acknowledge no obligation'), or Southey ('I never dream of Oxford'), or De Quincey ('Oxford, I owe thee nothing').

Although Cambridge possibly has more literary associations than anywhere outside London, few of them have been associations of any duration. Most 'Cambridge writers' have been youthful birds of passage, acquiring influences, knowledge, and friendships, wrinkling their noses at systems and dogmas, passing on. A few were born in the town (Jeremy Taylor, William Whitehead, Gwen Raverat, Frances and John Cornford, Geoffrey Keynes, F. R. Leavis, a handful of modern poets and novelists), very few from outside have (at least until recent times) roosted. The writer who did roost, moreover, was a definite type –

quirky, ingrown, infertile – that cast no flattering light on the place's inspiring qualities (Housman and Gray; even perhaps A. C. Benson, who concealed beneath his torrent of words a paucity of things to say). C. P. Snow, who made as much literary capital out of Cambridge as anyone, commented: 'Cambridge, after *The Masters* had been written, was too small and the wrong place to stay in. *The Masters* had exhausted the most interesting aspect – college intrigue. Writers simply must not live in isolated places.' Quiller-Couch, for decades a successful Cambridge literary institution, once confided: 'this is never home, and I feel all the time like a changeling who has happened out of the country where he would be and to which he belongs'; E. M. Forster, a later institution, declared it 'not a place in which a writer ought to remain'. When one of Frederic Raphael's characters snorts in a moment of disillusion, 'I sometimes wish I'd stayed in Cambridge', another retorts 'What as? A traffic island?' Thom Gunn's advice was to 'keep on the move'.

Cambridge has accordingly been a bridge to pass over, narrow and one-way ('Cambridge Fame-bridge' in Raphael's phrase) rather than a bridge to look down from or to pass back across. Yet with a growing disenchantment with big-city life, and particularly with modern London's commercialised literary rat-race, there is at least potential for a trend in the other direction. Possibly Cambridge may yet be discovered to offer more than the combination-room warfares or embryonic showbiz ambitions of novelists' depictions.

The poet Anne Stevenson (b. 1933), herself born in Cambridge (of American parents), married in Cambridge, and strangely destined, despite all her wanderings, to keep returning to Cambridge, analyses its attraction in her poem 'Coming Back to Cambridge' (1969). For her, Cambridge is

> A city like any other . . . were it not for the
> order at the centre and the
> high, invisible bridge it is built upon
> with its immense views of an intelligible human landscape
> into which you never look without longing to enter;
> into which you never fall without the curious struggle back.

This catches the ambivalence of a place that seems to offer much and yet give little, that seems to be at the heart of something yet for ever on the periphery of everything.

> The river is the same – conceited,
> historic, full of the young.
> The streets are the same. And around them
> the same figures, the same cast with a
> change of actors, move as if concentric
> to a radiance without location.
> The pupils of their eyes glide sideways,
> apprehensive of martyrdom to which

they might not be central.
They can never be sure.
Great elations could be happening without them.

Forster's Rickie and Ansell argued about Cambridge's 'centrality'. Yet as Ansell (and later Gunn) decided, no place is a backwater, backwaters are states of mind, and for all Anne Stevenson's acquaintance with the town, something of the essential Cambridge – something that could not equally be applied, say, to Oxford – evades her account. 'The same cast with a change of actors' – the metaphor glances at the histrionic Cambridge of the 1950s (the Cambridge she knew best), a period that to some extent relates only invertedly to the traditional Cambridge. At Oxford, perhaps, 'the pupils of their eyes' traditionally 'glide sideways' but not, at any rate according to the most idealistic accounts, at Cambridge.

The river of Oxford is the river of London – grandly rolling, broadly promissory, offering a widening transit to empire and power. The river of Cambridge turns away into the flat hinterland, without hurry, narrow and aseptic, embracing the winds that seem to the eye to turn it back on itself. J. W. Blakesley reported to Tennyson in 1830 that 'Hallam has gone back to Cambridge. He was not well while he was in London; moreover, he was submitting himself to the influences of the outer world more than (I think) a man of his genius ought to do.' Kingsley Amis observed that 'although the two places are almost equidistant from London, I noticed a hostility to it in Cambridge that I had never come across in Oxford'. While Oxford produces successions of prime ministers and literary putsches, Cambridge asks 'What *exactly* do you *mean*?' and is prepared, if necessary, to spend a lifetime finding out. What Forster wrote of societies like the Apostles could apply to the Cambridge archetype in general:

> The young men seek truth rather than victory, they are willing to abjure an opinion when it is proved untenable, they do not try to score off one another, they do not feel diffidence too high a price to pay for integrity; and according to some observers that is why Cambridge has played, comparatively speaking, so small a part in the control of world affairs.

The Cambridge archetype is rationalist, purist, puritan, analytical, and treats language as a tool rather than as a musical instrument. As Davie has written, 'the Cantabrigian ethos . . . leaves no margin for *caprice*, for that free-running, freely-associating, arbitrary and gratuitous play of mind out of which, not exclusively but necessarily, artworks arise'. The 'Cantabrigian ethos' sent Kingsley Amis packing in anger, and what 'caprice' there has been – Brooke's 'Grantchester', Tom Sharpe's *Porterhouse Blue*, Jonathan Miller's caricature of Bertrand Russell – has been a sending up of the ethos rather than a celebration of it. While the Oxford of Evelyn Waugh's *Brideshead Revisited* is portrayed as the very touchstone of reality, the Cambridge of Isherwood's *Lions and Shadows* is a fenland phantasm of surrealist unreality to be guyed and derided. Perhaps one reason why

Snow's Cambridge novels seem so flat is that he treats his academic situations with acquiescence instead of with the satire they might seem to deserve.

Yet in spite of everything – in spite of the fact that the university tends to regard the fostering of creativity as irrelevant to its proper purpose (there is no provision in its curricula for what Raine terms the 'exact learning of the Imagination') – Cambridge continues to throw up its writers. Moreover, that it exerts at times something more than a negative attraction is shown by the existence in its history of productive phases. In the Elizabethan period and early seventeenth century Cambridge was a seminal place generally, the fount of the English Renaissance, and it was inevitable that it should produce a large share of the poets and dramatists of the time. What attracted the Romantics to Cambridge is harder to see – indeed, there was much that repelled them and they might have been better off elsewhere, away from Cambridge's 'mathematical gloom'. (Ironically, the one Romantic poet who went to Oxford, Shelley, was the only one interested in experimental science – though it is doubtful whether he would have benefited any more, or lasted any longer, at Cambridge.) Indeed, the romantic connection has often been felt to be rather anomalous: the mood of the third principal literary period (which began roughly when Forster came up in 1898) looked back to the first rather than the second. It is the Elizabethans and the Metaphysicals who have the greatest influence in the modern period. (Among college societies one finds a Nashe Society at St John's, a Milton Society at Christ's, a Shirley Society at St Catharine's, a Dryden Society at Trinity, a Heywood Society at Peterhouse.)

As to the future – one cannot prophesy, but, as a Deighton Bell advertisement of 1951 boasted, 'the Cambridge Poet of today is generally the Oxford Standard Author of tomorrow'. An emergent major writer may at this moment be an undergraduate at one of the colleges or even growing up in Chesterton or Romsey Town. If, as has happened in the past, he or she receives from Cambridge less than due recognition, one can do worse than bear in mind Oscar Wilde's admonition: 'Education is an admirable thing. But it is well to remember from time to time that nothing that is worth knowing can be taught.'

In a place where the atmosphere of tradition can often be overwhelming (the gilded portraits in college halls, the preserved manuscripts in glass cases), it is also worth bearing in mind what academics sometimes forget – that the ink was once fresh and challenging on the ancient paper, the face now frozen through centuries of assured success was once as hesitant, half-formed, and searching as those that appear annually in the autumnal courts. The most worthwhile traditions are those that remain in the making, and each fresh writer will doubtless continue to recreate Cambridge – and to be recreated by Cambridge – in the same way as those who have gone before.

APPENDIX A

The Chancellor's Medal for an English poem

This prize was founded in 1811 by HRH the Duke of Gloucester, following his installation as Chancellor of the University, to be awarded annually 'for the encouragement of English poetry, to a resident undergraduate who shall compose the best ode, or the best poem in heroic verse' on a set subject. The Newdigate Prize at Oxford, founded a few years earlier, may have been a model, though the Chancellor's Medal was not an endowed prize but in the gift of successive Chancellors. A two-hundred-line limit was introduced in 1826; set subjects were in practice discontinued from 1961, from which time it has also usually been permissible to submit a sequence or collection of poems (within the length limit). The examiners were originally the same eleven as for the classical medals; from 1898 they were the Vice-Chancellor, the Orator, the Regius Professor of Greek, and two annual appointees; from 1937 they were the Orator, or, from 1969, the King Edward VII Professor, and two appointees. The medal was originally gold (Macaulay and Tennyson sold theirs for its monetary value) but since the Second World War it has been bronze; the Victorian design by William Wyon is still used. Medallists are required to recite their poems in the Senate House on the occasion appointed.

The first award was made in 1813. In the following list, where a year is omitted no medal was awarded.

1813   *Columbus*: George Waddington, Trinity
1814   *Boadicea*: William Whewell, Trinity
1815   *Wallace*: Edward Smirke, St John's
1816   *Mahomet*: Hamilton Sydney Beresford, Clare
1817   *Jerusalem*: Chauncy Hare Townshend, Trinity Hall
1818   *Imperial and Papal Rome*: Charles Edward Long, Trinity
1819   *Pompeii*: Thomas Babington Macaulay, Trinity
1820   *Waterloo*: George Erving Scott, Trinity Hall
1821   *Evening*: Thomas Babington Macaulay, Trinity
1822   *Palmyra*: John Henry Bright, St John's
1823   *Australasia*: Winthrop Mackworth Praed, Trinity
1824   *Athens*: Winthrop Mackworth Praed, Trinity
1825   *Sculpture*: Edward George Lytton Bulwer, Trinity Hall
1826   *Venice*: Joseph Sumner Brockhurst, St John's

1827 *The Druids*: Christopher Wordsworth, Trinity
1828 *The Invasion of Russia by Napoleon Buonaparte*: Christopher Wordsworth, Trinity
1829 *Timbuctoo*: Alfred Tennyson, Trinity
1830 *Byzantium*: William Chapman Kinglake, Trinity
1831 *Attempts to Find a North-West Passage*; George Stovin Venables, Jesus
1832 *The Taking of Jerusalem in the First Crusade*: William Chapman Kinglake, Trinity
1833 *Delphi*: Clement Berkley Hue, Trinity
1835 *The Death of HRH the Duke of Gloucester*: Thomas Whytehead, St John's
1836 *The Empire of the Sea*: Thomas Whytehead, St John's
1838 *Luther*: William Spicer Wood, St John's
1839 *Bannockburn*: Charles Sangster, St John's
1840 *Richard the First in Palestine*: John Charles Conybeare, Peterhouse
1841 *The Death of Marquess Camden*: John Charles Conybeare, Peterhouse
1842 *The Birth of the Prince of Wales*: Henry James Sumner Maine, Pembroke
1843 *Plato*: William Johnson, King's
1844 *The Tower of London*: Edward Henry Bickersteth, Trinity
1845 *Caubul*: Edward Henry Bickersteth, Trinity
1846 *Caesar's Invasion of Britain*: Edward Henry Bickersteth, Trinity
1847 *Sir Thomas More*: Henry Day, Trinity Hall
1848 *The Death of Baldur*: George John Cayley, Trinity
1849 *Titus at Jerusalem*: Henry Day, Trinity Hall
1850 *The Death of Adelaide the Queen Dowager*: The Hon. Julian Fane, Trinity
1851 *Gustavus Adolphus*: William Edensor Littlewood, Pembroke
1852 *The Arctic Regions*: Frederic William Farrar, Trinity
1853 *Walmer Castle*: Herbert John Reynolds, King's
1854 *The Chinese Empire*: Herbert John Reynolds, King's
1855 *The War in the Crimea*: John Sumner Gibson, Trinity
1856 *Luther at the Diet of Worms*: Oswald William Wallace, Emmanuel
1858 *Delhi*: Arthur Holmes, St John's
1859 *Lord Clive*: George Alder, Queens'
1860 *The Great Comet of 1858*: The Rev. Alexander James Donald D'Orsey, Corpus
1861 *The Prince of Wales at the Tomb of Washington*: Frederic William Henry Myers, Trinity
1862 *The Death of the Prince Consort*: James Rhoades, Trinity
1863 *The Distress in Lancashire*: Frederic William Henry Myers, Trinity
1864 *The Discovery of the Source of the Nile*: John Jardine, Christ's
1865 *Florence*: Sidney Colvin, Trinity
1866 *Westminster Abbey*: William Edward Hart, St John's
1867 *The Atlantic Cables*: Thomas Moss, St John's
1868 *Dante in Exile*: Edward Anthony Beck, Trinity Hall
1869 *The Lake-Dwellings of Switzerland*: Francis Henry Wood, St John's

1870   *Runnymeade*: Edward Anthony Beck, Trinity Hall

1871   *Sedan*: Henry Elliot Malden, Trinity Hall

1872   *The Destruction of Chicago by Fire*: Thomas Ethelbert Page, St John's

1873   *The Thanksgiving in St Paul's for the Recovery of The Prince of Wales*: Douglas Samuel Boutflower, Caius

1874   *William the Silent*: Frederick William Thurstan, Christ's

1875   *Iceland*: George William Rowntree, Clare

1876   *The Centenary of the Declaration of American Independence*: Alfred William Winterslow Dale, Trinity

1877   *Heroism in Arctic Exploration*: Edmund Whytehead Howson, King's

1878   *Canada*: Alfred William Winterslow Dale, Trinity Hall

1879   *The Obelisk of Thothmes*: William John Sparrow-Simpson, Trinity

1880   *Rienzi*: Henry Francis Wilson, Trinity

1881   *Temple Bar*: Arthur Reed Ropes, King's

1882   *Peter the Hermit*: Claude Herbert Alwyn Faure Field, Corpus

1884   *Savonarola*: Goldsworthy Lowes Dickinson, King's

1885   *Vasco Di Gama*: James Hope Moulton, King's

1886   *Bruges*: Albert Romer Macklin, Caius

1888   *Isaac Newton*: Owen Thompson, Trinity

1889   *Windsor Castle*: Arthur Bernard Cook, Trinity

1891   *Iona*: John Howard Bertram Masterman, St John's

1892   *Raphael*: John Howard Bertram Masterman, St John's

1893   *Delphi*: John Howard Bertram Masterman, St John's

1894   *The English Lakes*: Adolphus Alfred Jack, Peterhouse

1895   *Joan of Arc*: Ronald Brunlees McKerrow, Trinity

1897   *Sir Francis Drake*: Geoffrey Winthrop Young, Trinity

1898   *St Augustine of Canterbury*: Geoffrey Winthrop Young, Trinity

1899   *Alfred the Great*: Arthur Cecil Pigou, King's

1900   *Khartoum*: Frank Sidgwick, Trinity

1901   *The Australian Commonwealth*: George Dean Raffles Tucker, Magdalene

1902   *Ely*: Giles Lytton Strachey, Trinity

1904   *Durham*: Robert Quirk, King's

1905   *Michelangelo*: Arthur Conway Osborne Morgan, Trinity

1906   *Tibet*: Charles Mendell Kohan, Trinity

1907   *Edward the First*: Donald Welldon Corrie, King's

1908   *The Fenland*: George Geoffrey Gilbert Butler, Trinity

1909   *John Milton*: Dennis Holme Robertson, Trinity

1910   *After Novara*: Dennis Holme Robertson, Trinity

1911   *St George's Chapel*: Dennis Holme Robertson, Trinity

1914   *The Southern Pole*: Donald Fredric Goold Johnson, Emmanuel

1915   *Hougomont, 1815*: Philip Carrington, Selwyn

1917   *Galahad*: Harold Obbard Lee, Jesus

1918   *The Holy City*: Hugh I'Anson Fausset, Corpus

1919   *St Louis of France*; Frederick Francis Thomas Pinto, Non-Collegiate

1920   *Joan of Arc*: Colin Hercules Mackenzie, King's

1921   *The Death of Napoleon*: Cecil Roy Leonard Falcy, Queens'

1922 *R. L. Stevenson*: Montague Maurice Simmons, Queens'
1923 *St Francis of Assisi*: David William Alun Llewellyn, St John's
1924 *Buddha*: Edward Falaise Upward, Corpus
1925 *Stonehenge*: Henry Hugh Thomas, Sidney Sussex
1926 *Gallipoli*: Alan Trevor Oldham, Emmanuel
1927 *Orestes*: Frederick John Norton, Pembroke
1928 *Proserpine*: Kenneth Harold Ellis, Trinity
1929 *The Bridge*: Elsie Elizabeth Phare, Newnham
1931 *The Roman Road*: Robert William Victor Gittings, Jesus
1934 *The English Countryside*: Frederick William Clayton, King's
1935 *The Vikings*: Olive Fraser, Girton
1936 *Egypt*: Terence Rogers Tiller, Jesus
1937 *The Thames*: Christopher Thomas Gandy, King's
1938 *A Great Man*: John Darrell Boyd, King's
1939 *Fire*: Reginald Arthur Burrows, St Catharine's
1942 *A Londoner*: Irene Josephine Blanche Snatt, Girton
1948 *The Years To Come*: George James Moor, Downing
1949 *Speed*: Alan John Maurice Bird, Selwyn
1953 *Gloriana Rediviva*: Alasdair Eoin Aston, Pembroke
1964 Howard John Brenton, St Catharine's
1966 William Paul Huw Merchant, Emmanuel
1967 Clive Wilmer, King's
1969 Alexander John Howard Martin, Jesus
1970 Elliot Alexander Grant, Christ's
1974 John Lawton Wilkinson, Jesus
1976 Charles Ellis Leftwich, St John's
1977 David Colles Lloyd, King's
1978 Aidan John Semmens, Trinity
1979 Jacqueline Sue Osherow, Trinity
1980 Michael Thomas Hutchinson, Trinity
1982 Alice Abigail Goodman, Girton
1984 James William Noggle, Fitzwilliam
1985 Jean Hanff Korelitz, Clare
1988 Joanne Marion Weiss, St Edmund's
1989 Simon James Alderson, Trinity
1992 Nicoletta Fotinos, Churchill
1994 Keith Malcolm Sands, Jesus

The Clark Lectures, Trinity College

The Clark Lectures in English Literature were founded in memory of W. G. Clark (1821–78), Vice-Master of Trinity College, Public Orator, editor of Shakespeare. Held in most years since 1883, they have covered a variety of subjects and many have subsequently been published. Edmund Gosse's lectures were published as *From Shakespeare to Pope*, E. M. Forster's as *Aspects of the Novel*, Robert Graves's as *The Crowning Privilege*, F. R. Leavis's as *English Literature in our Time and the University*. T. S. Eliot's lectures (not published until 1993) were on Metaphysical poetry, André Maurois's on the art of biography; Edmund Blunden lectured on Charles Lamb, Lord David Cecil on Thomas Hardy, Louis MacNeice on 'Varieties of Parable', L. P. Hartley on Nathaniel Hawthorne, William Empson on 'The Progress of Criticism', Donald Davie on 'The Literature of Dissent, 1700–1930', David Piper on poets and their portraits, Toni Morrison on 'Studies in American Africanism'.

The following list gives dates of appointment – lectures were normally delivered in the succeeding calendar year (T. S. Eliot's, for example, in Lent term, 1926).

1883	(Sir) Leslie Stephen	1921	J. C. Bailey
1884–8	(Sir) Edmund Gosse	1922	Walter de la Mare
1889–93	J. W. Hales	1923	Lascelles Abercrombie
1894–6	Edward Dowden	1924	John Middleton Murry
1897	D. C. Tovey	1925	T. S. Eliot
1898	(Sir) Walter Raleigh	1926	E. M. Forster
1899	H. C. Beeching	1927	André Maurois
1900	Alfred Ainger	1928	(Sir) Desmond MacCarthy
1901	(Sir) Sidney Lee	1929	Herbert Read
1902	Barrett Wendell	1930	Harley Granville-Barker
1904	F. S. Boas	1931	Edmund Blunden
1905	Alexandre Beljame	1933	G. S. Gordon
1907	William Everett	1934	Ernest de Sélincourt
1909	A. W. Verrall	1935	R. W. Chambers
1910	(Sir) Walter Raleigh	1936	(Sir) Herbert J. C. Grierson
1911	W. P. Ker	1937	Harold Nicolson
1914	A. A. Jack	1938	(Sir) Walter Greg

1940	G. W. Young	1964	John Sparrow
1941	Lord David Cecil	1965	Stephen Spender
1942	John Dover Wilson	1966	F. R. Leavis
1943	C. S. Lewis	1967	Muriel Bradbrook
1944	Raymond Mortimer	1968	V. S. Pritchett
1945	Cecil Day Lewis	1970	L. C. Knights
1946	H. B. Charlton	1971	D. W. Harding
1947	R. W. Chapman	1972	F. T. Prince
1948	Nicol Smith	1973	(Sir) William Empson
1949	Helen Darbishire	1974	I. A. Richards
1950	F. P. Wilson	1976	Donald Davie
1951	A. Humphrey House	1977	David Piper
1952	Bonamy Dobrée	1978	Tom Stoppard
1953	G. M. Trevelyan	1980	Charles Tomlinson
1954	Robert Graves	1982	G. H. Hartman
1955	J. R. Sutherland	1984	Jonathan Miller
1956	Joyce Cary	1985	C. H. Gifford
1957	C. V. Wedgwood	1986	Geoffrey Hill
1958	Nevill Coghill	1987	Richard Rorty
1959	E. M. W. Tillyard	1988	Jerome McGann
1960	Robert Birley	1989	Barbara Everett
1961	G. Wilson Knight	1990	Toni Morrison
1962	Louis MacNeice	1991	Christopher Ricks
1963	L. P. Hartley	1992	Bernard Williams

APPENDIX C

Professors of English

(A date after a title indicates the year the post was created.)

Elrington and Bosworth Professor of Anglo-Saxon

1878–1912	W. W. Skeat
1912–41	H. M. Chadwick
1946–57	Bruce Dickins
1957–69	Dorothy Whitelock
1969–82	P. A. M. Clemoes
1984–91	R. I. Page
1991–	Michael Lapidge

King Edward VII Professor of English Literature

1911–12	A. W. Verrall
1912–44	Sir Arthur Quiller-Couch
1946–64	Basil Willey
1965–73	L. C. Knights
1974–82	Frank Kermode
1982–6	Christopher Ricks
1986–93	Marilyn Butler
1994–	Gillian Beer

Professor of Medieval and Renaissance English

1954–63	C. S. Lewis
1964–78	J. A. W. Bennett
1978–88	J. E. Stevens
1988–	Jill Mann

Professor of English (1966/1)

1966–76	Muriel Bradbrook
1976–89	Ian Jack
1989–94	Gillian Beer
1995–	C. I. E. Donaldson

Professor of English (1966/2)

1966–75	Graham Hough
1975–82	Christopher Ricks
1984–	Anne Barton

Professor of Modern English

1972–82	John Holloway

Professor of Drama

1974–83	Raymond Williams

Professor of English (1983)

1983–90	Derek Brewer

Professor of English (1987)

1987–93	John Beer

Professor of English as an International Language

1988–	Gillian Brown

Professor of English and American Language

1989–	Tony Tanner

APPENDIX D

Honorary degrees

The following writers were awarded degrees *honoris causa* by Cambridge University:

1867 John Ruskin, LL.D.

1868 Henry Wadsworth Longfellow, LL.D.

1879 Robert Browning, LL.D.

1883 Matthew Arnold, LL.D.

1886 Oliver Wendell Holmes, LITT.D.

1892 (Sir) Leslie Stephen (Trinity Hall), LITT.D.

1908 Rudyard Kipling, LITT.D.
Sir George Otto Trevelyan (Trinity), LITT.D.

1913 Thomas Hardy, LITT.D.

1920 Charles Doughty (Caius), LITT.D.
Sir J. G. Frazer (Trinity), LITT.D.
(Sir) Edmund Gosse, LITT.D.

1925 Sir Henry Newbolt, LITT.D.

1930 Lascelles Abercrombie, LITT.D.
Sir J. M. Barrie, LITT.D.
John Galsworthy, LITT.D.

1931 John Masefield, LITT.D.

1933 W. B. Yeats, LITT.D.

1934 M. R. James (King's), D.D.
G. M. Trevelyan (Trinity), LITT.D.

1935 Walter de la Mare, LITT.D.

1938 T. S. Eliot, LITT.D.

1939 Paul Claudel, LITT.D.

1948 (Sir) Winston Churchill, LITT.D.

1950 E. M. Forster (King's), LITT.D.

1951 (Dame) Rose Macaulay, LITT.D.

1953 (Sir) Desmond MacCarthy (Trinity), LITT.D.
Thomas Mann, LITT.D.
G. M. Young, LITT.D.

1955 Sir Charles Tennyson (King's), LITT.D.

1957   Robert Frost, LITT.D.
1958   Edwin Muir, LITT.D.
1960   George Seferis, LITT.D.
1962   Graham Greene, LITT.D.
1965   Sir Geoffrey Keynes (Pembroke), LITT.D.
1977   (Sir) William Empson (Magdalene), LITT.D.
          I. A. Richards (Magdalene), LL.D.
1981   Dame Helen Gardner, LITT.D.
1983   V. S. Naipaul, LITT.D.
1984   Jorge Luís Borges, LITT.D.
1986   Ted Hughes (Pembroke), LITT.D.
1987   Carlos Fuentes, LITT.D.
1988   Alistair Cooke (Jesus), LITT.D.
1991   Stefan Heym, LITT.D.
1992   Nadine Gordimer, LITT.D.
1993   Iris Murdoch, LITT.D.

Magazines

The following are some of the principal Cambridge periodicals:

1750–1	*The Student*
1769	*The Cambridge Magazine or Universal Repository*
1776	*The Reformer*
1795	*The University Magazine*
1804	*The Galvanist*
1819	*The Cambridge Monthly Repository or Literary Miscellany*
1824	*The Cambridge Quarterly Review and Academical Register*
1829–30	*The Snob* and *The Gownsman*
1832–4	*Punch in Cambridge*
1832–6	*Toby in Cambridge*
1833–4	*The Cambridge Quarterly Review and Magazine of Literature, Arts, Sciences*
1835	*The Cambridge University Magazine*
1836	*The Freshman*
	The Fellow
1836–7	*The Individual*
1840–3	*The Cambridge University Magazine*
1840	*Ralph's Bottle*
1845–7	*The Oxford and Cambridge Review*
1855–8	*Cambridge Essays*
1856	*The Oxford and Cambridge Magazine*
1858	*Academica*
1858–9	*The Lion*
1858	*The Bear* and *The Cambridge Dionysia*
1858–9	*The Cambridge Terminal Magazine*
1858–	*The Eagle* (St John's)
1860–73	*College Rhymes*
1866–9	*Momus*
1866–71	*The Light Blue*
1868–75	*The Cambridge Undergraduates' Journal*

1868–9	*The Cambridge University Gazette*
1870–	*The Cambridge University Reporter*
1870–1	*The Moslem in Cambridge*
1871–2	*The Tatler in Cambridge*
1871	*The Lantern of the Cam*
1871	*Fleur-de-Lys* (Christ's)
1872	*The Light Green*
1873	*The Cantab*
1877	*The Cambridge Tatler*
1879–	*The Cambridge Review*
1882	*The Cambridge Meteor*
1882–1973	*The Girton Review*
1883	*Ye True Blue*
1884	*The Blue 'un*
1885	*The May Bee*
1885–	*The Chanticlere* (Jesus)
1886–	*Christ's College Magazine*
1886	*The Cambridge University Magazine*
1888	*The Cambridge Fortnightly*
	The Reflector
	The Gadfly
1889–1978	*The Granta* (later *Granta*)
1889–	*Emmanuel College Magazine*
1889–92	*The Trident* (Trinity)
1890–1907	*The Silver Crescent* (Trinity Hall)
1891	*The Wasp*
1891–	*The Caian* (Gonville and Caius)
1892–3	*The Cambridge Observer*
1893–4	*The Brass Halo* (Trinity Hall)
	The 'K.P.' Illustrated
1893–	*The Pem* (Pembroke)
1894	*The Cambridge ABC* (King's)
1896	*The Rag* (Jesus)
1896–1950	*The Pheon* (Sidney Sussex)
1897–	*The Sex* (Peterhouse)
1898	*The Bubble*
1898–	*Lady Clare*
1898–9	*The Cantab*
1898–1928	*The Benedict* (Corpus)
1899	*The Snarl*
	The Cambridge Magazine
1899–1900	*The Cambridge Gazette*
1900	*Alma Mater*
1900–2	*The Cambridge Graphic*
1900–40	*Basileon* (King's)
1903–	*The Griffin* (Downing)

1906	*The Cam*
	The May Bee
1909–39	*The Gownsman*
1909–	*Magdalene College Magazine*
	The Sell (from 1948 *Seldom*) (Selwyn)
1912–23	*The Cambridge Magazine*
1912–13	*The Tripod*
1913–14	*Mandragora*
1913–34	*St Catharine's College Magazine*
1914–55	*Trinity Magazine*
1928–30	*The Venture*
1928–31	*Experiment*
1931–73	*Varsity* (1939–40 as *Cambridge University Journal*;
	1950–2 as *Cambridge Today*;
	merged with *Stop Press*, 1973)
1932–53	*Scrutiny*
1933–4	*Cambridge Left* (revived 1954–7, 1960)
1937	*The Cam*
1937–9	*The Democrat*
1940	*Cambridge Front*
1947–54	*The Cambridge Journal*
1948–52	*Cambridge Writing*
1949–50	*Imprint*
1949–52	*Panorama*
1951–2	*Concern*
	Oasis
1953–4	*Chequer*
1953–81	*Delta* (after 1972 not edited from Cambridge)
1953–	*Broadsheet*
1956	*Saint Botolph's Review*
1956–72	*Pawn* (King's)
1957–9	*Gemini* (Oxford and Cambridge)
1957–	*Trinity Review*
	Cambridge Opinion
1962–7	*Carcanet* (Oxford and Cambridge; later Oxford only)
1965	*Look We Have Come Through*
1965–	*The Cambridge Quarterly*
1968–75	*The 1/– Paper*
1972–	*Stop Press*
1976–8	*Perfect Bound*
1977–	*Logophile*
1979–	*Granta* (new series: after 1990 not edited from Cambridge)
1982–4	*Cambridge Appeal Magazine*
1983	*Scheherazade*
1983–	*The Cambridge Poetry Magazine*
1986–	*Ampersand*

1986–90	*Numbers*
1993–	*In Verse* (King's)
1993	*Involution* (Magdalene)
1993–	*Xero* (Jesus)

APPENDIX F

Manuscripts and relics

NOTE: College combination rooms and libraries (with the exception of the Wren Library at Trinity and the Pepys Library at Magdalene, which are open to the public at advertised times) cannot normally be visited except by arrangement.

Bulstrode Gardens

No. 12: plaque commemorating F. R. and Q. D. Leavis, who lived here.

Christ's College

Senior Combination Room: bust of Milton. Fellows' Garden: 'Milton's Mulberry Tree'; memorial containing the ashes of C. P. Snow, by the pool.

Corpus Christi College

Library: large collection of Anglo-Saxon manuscripts, mostly donated by Archbishop Parker, including the most important extant copy of the 'Anglo-Saxon Chronicle'. Old Court: plaque commemorating Marlowe and Fletcher. Hall: attributed portrait of Marlowe.

Fitzwilliam Museum

Manuscripts include Keats's 'Ode to a Nightingale', Rupert Brooke's 'The Old Vicarage, Grantchester', A. E. Housman's *Last Poems*, J. E. Flecker's *Samarkand*, Thomas Hardy's *Jude the Obscure*. Also pictures by, and life mask of, William Blake, and Samuel Rogers's court suit (worn successively by Wordsworth and Tennyson for their installations as Poet Laureate).

Grantchester

War memorial including name of Rupert Brooke.

Jesus College

Library: Coleridge manuscripts, including a college exercise and a letter referring to the 'Ancient Mariner'; also a lock of Coleridge's hair. Hall: portraits of Coleridge and Sterne. Senior Combination Room: portraits of Coleridge, Sterne, and Quiller-Couch. Chapel: plaque to Coleridge.

King's College

Library: Rupert Brooke and E. M. Forster archives, as well as a large number of other modern literary manuscripts. Chapel: college's war memorial including Rupert Brooke's name; plaque to J. K. Stephen, just inside south door.

King's Parade

No. 11: plaque commemorating visit of Charles Lamb. No. 19: plaque commemorating residence of Edward Fitzgerald.

Magdalene College

Pepys Library: Pepys's books in their original cases; the manuscript of Pepys's diary; also manuscripts by Hardy, Kipling, and Eliot (not on display). Hall: portraits of Pepys, A. C. Benson, Hardy, Kipling, Eliot.

Market Hill

Former premises of Bacon's the tobacconists (corner of Rose Crescent): plaque with extract from Calverley's 'Ode to Tobacco'.

Pembroke College

Library: Gray manuscripts, including that of the 'Elegy in a Country Churchyard' and his commonplace books. Hall: portrait of Spenser.

Peterhouse

Fire-escape bar on window of room formerly occupied by Gray (overlooking churchyard of Little St Mary's).

St Bene't's Church

Monument to Charles Matthews, Byron's friend, drowned in the Cam.

St Giles' Cemetery, Huntingdon Road

Memorials to A. C. Benson, Frances Cornford, Desmond MacCarthy, G. E. Moore, W. W. Skeat, A. W. Verrall, Ludwig Wittgenstein, and others.

St John's College

Library: Samuel Butler relics. Hall: portraits of Wordsworth and Matthew Prior. Chapel: memorial to Henry Kirke White. The Wordsworth Room (used for conferences) commemorates the location of Wordsworth's old room (demolished).

Trinity College

Wren Library: manuscripts include Milton's *Comus*, Thackeray's *Henry Esmond*, A. A. Milne's *Winnie the Pooh*, Byron's first letter (and the cap he wore in Greece); also an important Tennyson archive; Thorwaldsen's statue of Byron. Chapel: statues of Tennyson, Macaulay, Bacon. Backs: an avenue of cherry trees in memory of A. E. Housman (author of 'Loveliest of trees, the cherry now . . . ').

University Library

J. W. Clark collection of books and publications relating to Cambridge (bequeathed in 1912).

Bibliography

Place of publication of books is London unless otherwise stated.

A. ANTHOLOGIES

(in chronological order)

Musae Seatonianae: A Complete Collection of the Cambridge Prize Poems, from the First Institution of That Premium by Tho. Seaton in 1750 to the Year 1806 (2 vols., Cambridge, 1808).

The Cambridge Tart, ed. 'Socius' [Richard Gooch] (1823).

Facetiae Cantabrigienses, ed. 'Socius' [Richard Gooch] (1825).

In Cap and Gown: Three Centuries of Cambridge Wit, ed. Charles Whibley (Kegan Paul, 1890).

Cambridge Prize Poems: A Complete Collection of the English Poems Which Have Obtained the Chancellor's Medal in the University of Cambridge (2 vols., Gibbings & Co., 1894).

The Book of the Cambridge Review 1879–1897 (Cambridge: Macmillan & Bowes, 1898).

A Book of Cambridge Verse, ed. E. E. Kellett (Cambridge University Press, 1911).

In Praise of Cambridge: An Anthology in Prose and Verse, ed. Sydney Waterlow (Constable, 1912).

Cambridge Poets 1900–1913: An Anthology, ed. Aelfrida Tillyard (Cambridge: Heffer, 1913).

Cambridge Poets 1914–1920: An Anthology, ed. Edward Davison (Cambridge: Heffer, 1920).

The 'Granta' and its Contributors, 1889–1914, ed. F. A. Rice (Constable, 1924).

Cambridge Poetry 1929, ed. Christopher Saltmarshe, John Davenport, and Basil Wright (Hogarth Press, 1929).

Cambridge Poetry 1930, ed. John Davenport, Hugh Sykes, and Michael Redgrave (Hogarth Press, 1930).

An Anthology of Cambridge Women's Verse, ed. Margaret Thomas (Hogarth Press, 1931).

Poets of Tomorrow: Second Selection: Cambridge Poetry 1940 (Hogarth Press, 1940).

Poetry from Cambridge in Wartime, ed. Geoffrey Moore (Fortune Press, 1946).

Poetry from Cambridge, 1947–1950, ed. Peter Morris Green (Fortune Press, 1951).

Poetry from Cambridge, 1951–1952, ed. Thom Gunn (Fortune Press, 1952).

In Praise of Cambridge: An Anthology for Friends, ed. Mervyn Horder (Muller, 1952).

Cambridge Anthology, ed. Peter Townsend (Hogarth Press, 1952).

Poetry from Cambridge, 1952–4, ed. Karl Miller (Swinford: Fantasy Press, 1955).

A Cambridge Scrapbook, ed. Jean Lindsay (Cambridge: Heffer, 1955, 1960).

Poetry from Cambridge, ed. Christopher Levenson (Fortune Press, 1958).

Light Blue, Dark Blue: An Anthology of Recent Writing from Oxford and Cambridge Universities (Macdonald, 1960).

The Best of 'Granta', 1889–1966, ed. Jim Philip, John Simpson, and Nicholas Snowman (Secker & Warburg, 1967).

A Selection from 'Scrutiny', ed. F. R. Leavis (2 vols., Cambridge University Press, 1968).

The Cambridge Mind: Ninety Years of the 'Cambridge Review', 1879–1969, ed. Eric Homberger, William Janeway, and Simon Schama (Cape, 1970).

My Cambridge, ed. Ronald Hayman (Robson Books, 1977).

Cambridge Commemorated: An Anthology of University Life, ed. Laurence and Helen Fowler (Cambridge University Press, 1984).

First Set: Blue Jade: Poetry from Oxford and Cambridge (Libanus Press, 1985).

Second Set: Nomads: Poetry from Oxford and Cambridge (Libanus Press, 1986).

The May Anthology: The Oxford and Cambridge Poetry Anthology (Varsity/Cherwell, 1992).

B. FICTION
(in chronological order)

Francis Coventry, *Pompey the Little* (1751; Oxford University Press, 1974).

Charles MacFarlane, *The Camp of Refuge* (Charles Knight, 1844).

Sir George Stephen, *The Jesuit at Cambridge* (Henry Colburn, 1847).

W. M. Thackeray, *The History of Pendennis* (Bradbury & Evans, 1850).

Charles Kingsley, *Alton Locke* (Chapman & Hall, 1850).

Frank E. Smedley, *Frank Fairlegh: or Scenes from the Life of a Private Pupil* (Ward Lock, 1850).

Edward Fitzgerald, *Euphranor* (William Pickering, 1851).

W. M. Thackeray, *The History of Henry Esmond* (Smith, Elder, 1852).

S. Baring Gould, *The Chorister: A Tale of King's College in the Civil Wars* (Cambridge: Meadows, 1854).

James Payn, *The Foster Brothers* (Arthur Hall, 1859).

F. W. Farrar, *Julian Home: A Tale of College Life* (A. & C. Black, 1859).

Herbert Vaughan [Algernon H. V. Morgan], *The Cambridge Grisette* (Tinsley Bros., 1862).

Charles Kingsley, *Hereward the Wake* (Cambridge and London: Macmillan, 1866).

George L. Tottenham, *Charlie Villars at Cambridge* (Hurst & Blackett, 1868).

S. P. Widnall, *The Miller's Daughter: A Legend of the Granta* (Grantchester, 1871).

Martin Legrand [James Rice], *The Cambridge Freshman: or Memoirs of Mr Golightly* (Diprose & Bateman, 1878).

Anthony Trollope, *John Caldigate* (Chapman & Hall, 1879).

John Bickerdyke [Charles Henry Cook], *With the Best Intentions: A Tale of Undergraduate Life at Cambridge* (Sonnenschein, 1884).

James Payn, *The Canon's Ward* (Chatto & Windus, 1884).

Mrs Annie Edwardes, *A Girton Girl* (Bentley & Son, 1885).

Christopher Carr [A. C. Benson], *The Memoirs of Arthur Hamilton, BA* (Kegan Paul, 1886).

Alan St Aubyn [Mrs Frances Marshall], *Trollope's Dilemma: The Story of a Cambridge Quad* (Simpkin, Marshall, 1889); republished as *The Senior Tutor: A Story of a Cambridge Court* (F. V. White, 1904).

R. C. Lehmann, *Harry Fludyer in Cambridge* (Chatto & Windus, 1890).

Alan St Aubyn, *A Fellow of Trinity* (Chatto & Windus, 1890).

   The Junior Dean (Chatto & Windus, 1891).

   The Master of St Benedict's (Chatto & Windus, 1893).

[Sussanah Venn], *Some Married Fellows* (Bentley & Son, 1893).

W. H. Wilkins [W. H. de Winton], *A Green Bay Tree* (Hutchinson, 1894).

E. F. Benson, *Limitations* (Ward Lock, 1896).

   The Babe, BA (Putnam, 1897).

Alan St Aubyn, *A Proctor's Wooing* (F. V. White, 1897).

Archibald Marshall, *Peter Binney, Undergraduate* (Alston Rivers, 1899).

Alice Stronach, *A Newnham Friendship* (Blackie, 1901).

Samuel Butler, *The Way of All Flesh* (Grant Richards, 1903).

C. Kent-Harkway, *Dog Tails from Cambridge* (Jarrold, 1904).

Sir Arthur Conan-Doyle, 'The Missing Three-Quarter', in *The Return of Sherlock Holmes* (Newnes, 1905).

T. Bevan, *The Fen Robbers* (Nelson, 1906).

E. M. Forster, *The Longest Journey* (Blackwood, 1907).

Ian Hay, *A Man's Man* (Blackwood, 1909).

H. G. Wells, *The New Machiavelli* (Bodley Head, 1911).

Hugh Walpole, *The Prelude to Adventure* (Macmillan, 1912).

Humfrey Jordan, *Carmen and Mr Dryasdust* (Putnam's, 1914).

H. G. Wells, *The Research Magnificent* (Macmillan, 1915).

Charles Kingsley (completed by Lucas Malet), *The Tutor's Story* (Smith, Elder, 1916).

A. P. Baker, *A College Mystery* (Cambridge: Heffer, 1918).

Arthur Gray, *Tedious Brief Tales of Granta and Gramarye* (Cambridge: Heffer, 1919).

S. C. Roberts, *Doctor Johnson in Cambridge* (Putnam, 1922).

Virginia Woolf, *Jacob's Room* (Hogarth Press, 1922).

E. F. Benson, *David of King's* (Hodder & Stoughton, 1924).

Archibald Marshall, *The Education of Anthony Dare* (Collins, 1924).

Shane Leslie, *The Cantab* (Chatto & Windus, 1926).

Anthony Armstrong, *Patrick, Undergraduate* (Stanley Paul, 1926).

Josephine Elder, *The Scholarship Girl at Cambridge* (W. & R. Chambers, 1926).

Rosamond Lehmann, *Dusty Answer* (Chatto & Windus, 1927).

Aelfrida Tillyard, *The Young Milliner* (Hutchinson, 1929).

E. F. Benson, *The Inheritor* (Hutchinson, 1930).

Margery Allingham, *Police at the Funeral* (Heinemann, 1931).

Aelfrida Tillyard, *Haste to the Wedding* (Hutchinson, 1931).

Patrick Carleton, *Desirable Young Men* (Philip Allan, 1932).

Christopher Isherwood, *The Memorial* (Hogarth Press, 1932).

Rose Macaulay, *They Were Defeated* (Collins, 1932).

T. H. White, *Darkness at Pemberley* (Gollancz, 1932).

Ian Macartney, *Break of Day* (Gerald Howe, 1932).

A. P. Rossiter, *Poor Scholars* (Chatto & Windus, 1932).

Q. Patrick, *Murder at the 'Varsity* (Longman, 1933).

Jack Overhill, *Romantic Youth* (Mitre Press, 1933).

Richard Heron Ward, *The Spring Term is Over* (Jarrolds, 1933).

Noel Macdonald Wilby, *Alexander Tomlyn: A Tale of Old Cambridge* (Burns Oates, 1933).

L. S. Howarth, *Ladies in Residence: A Novel of Cambridge* (Hodder & Stoughton, 1936).

Joseph Gordon Macleod, *Overture to Cambridge: A Satirical Story* (Allen & Unwin, 1936).

Sarah Campion, *Cambridge Blue* (Peter Davies, 1937).

S. C. Roberts, *Distinguished Visitors* (Cambridge, 1937).

Christopher Isherwood, *Lions and Shadows* (Hogarth Press, 1938).

S. C. Roberts, *Zuleika in Cambridge* (Cambridge: Heffer, 1941).

Glyn Daniel, *The Cambridge Murders* (Gollancz, 1945).

Martin Boyd, *Lucinda Brayford* (Cresset Press, 1946).

C. P. Snow, *The Light and the Dark* (Macmillan, 1947).

Gerald Bullett, *Men at High Table* (Dent, 1948).

David D. Lloyd, *Son and Stranger* (Bodley Head, 1950).

C. P. Snow, *The Masters* (Macmillan, 1951).

Margaret Bullard, *A Perch in Paradise* (Hamish Hamilton, 1952).

Jack Overhill, *The Miller of Trumpington* (Staples Press, 1953).

Andrew Sinclair, *My Friend Judas* (Faber, 1959).

C. P. Snow, *The Affair* (Macmillan, 1960).

Frederic Raphael, *The Limits of Love* (Cassell, 1960).

Simon Raven, *Doctors Wear Scarlet* (Blond, 1960).

Helen Foley, *A Handful of Time* (Hodder & Stoughton, 1961).

Peter Skelton, *The Promise of Days* (William Holman, 1962).

Simon Raven, 'The Sconcing Stoup' [radio play] (1964).

Simon Gray, *Simple People* (Faber, 1965).

John Vaizey, *Barometer Man* (Weidenfeld & Nicolson, 1966).

V. C. Clinton-Baddeley, *Death's Bright Dart* (Gollancz, 1967).

Simon Gray, *Little Portia* (Faber, 1967).

Fred Hoyle and Geoffrey Hoyle, *Rockets in Ursa Minor* (Heinemann, 1969).

Robert Lait, *Switched Out* (MacGibbon & Kee, 1970).

Simon Raven, *Places Where They Sing* (Blond, 1970).

Jack Trevor Storey, *Hitler Needs You* (Alison & Busby, 1970).

E. M. Forster, *Maurice* (Edward Arnold, 1971).

Anthony Swerling, *The Cambridge Plague* (Cambridge: Trinity Lane Press, 1971).

P. D. James, *An Unsuitable Job for a Woman* (Faber, 1972).

Vladimir Nabokov, *Glory* (Weidenfeld & Nicolson, 1972).

Désirée Meyler, *The Green Days* (Hurst & Blackett, 1974).

Tom Sharpe, *Porterhouse Blue* (Secker & Warburg, 1974).

Pamela Hansford Johnson, *The Good Listener* (Macmillan, 1975).

Elaine Feinstein, *The Ecstasy of Dr Miriam Garner* (Hutchinson, 1976).

Bibliography

Frederic Raphael, *The Glittering Prizes* (Allen Lane, 1976).

F. T. Unwin, *Pimbo* (Cambridge: The Author, 1976).
  Dew on My Feet (Cambridge: The Author, 1976).

Edward Upward, *No Home but the Struggle* (Heinemann, 1977).

B. V. Bell, *Fragments from an Orange-Scented Garden* (Great Wilbraham: Lunatic Fringe, 1977).

John Rowe Townsend, *The Xanadu Manuscript* (Oxford University Press, 1977).

Raymond Williams, 'The Writing on the Wall', in *Writers of East Anglia* (Secker & Warburg, 1977).

David Holbrook, *A Play of Passion* (W. H. Allen, 1978).

F. T. Unwin, *Pimbo and Jenny in Old Cambridge* (Cambridge: The Author, 1978).
  Knock on Any Door with Pimbo and Jenny (Cambridge: The Author, 1979).

Bryan Forbes, *Familiar Strangers* (Hodder & Stoughton, 1979).

Sylvia Plath, 'Stone Boy with Dolphin', in *Johnny Panic and the Bible of Dreams* (Faber, 1979).

Elaine Feinstein, 'Drought', in *The Silent Areas* (Hutchinson, 1980).

Dorsey Fiske, *Academic Murder* (Cassell, 1980).

André Jute, *Reverse Negative: A Novel of Suspense* (Secker & Warburg, 1980).

Julian Gloag, *Sleeping Dogs Lie* (Secker & Warburg, 1980).

Randall Collins, *The Case of the Philosophers' Ring* (Brighton: Harvester Press, 1980).

F. T. Unwin, *In the Shadow of King's* (Cambridge: The Author, 1981).
  Gentle Tales of Old Cambridge (Cambridge: The Author, 1982).

Victoria Amey, *Cambridge Cavalcade* (New York: Vantage Books, 1982).

F. T. Unwin, *Cambridge Tales of Mystery and Mirth* (Cambridge: The Author, 1983).

David Wurtzel, *Thomas Lyster, a Cambridge Novel* (Brilliance Books, 1983).

Hosanna Brown, *I Spy, You Die* (Gollancz, 1984).

Nora Kelly, *In the Shadow of King's* (Collins, 1984).

A. S. Byatt, *Still Life* (Chatto & Windus, 1985).

Simon Rees, *The Devil's Looking Glass* (Methuen, 1985).

David Benedictus, *Floating Down to Camelot* (Macdonald, 1985).

Simon Raven, *The Face of the Waters* (Blond, 1985).

Catharine Arnold, *Lost Time* (Hodder & Stoughton, 1986).

Douglas Adams, *Dirk Gently's Holistic Detective Agency* (Heinemann, 1987).

Bruce Duffy, *The World as I Found it* (Secker & Warburg, 1987).

Susan Howatch, *Glittering Images* (Collins, 1987).

Elaine Feinstein, *Mother's Girl* (Hutchinson, 1988).

Valerie Grosvenor Myers, *Culture Shock* (Duckworth, 1988).

Andrew Sinclair, *King Ludd* (Hodder, 1988).

Philip J. Davis, *Thomas Gray, Philosopher Cat* (Souvenir Press, 1989).

Anthony Appiah, *Avenging Angel* (Constable, 1990).

Tony Cape, *The Cambridge Theorem* (Hamish Hamilton, 1990).

Penelope Fitzgerald, *The Gate of Angels* (Collins, 1990).

Victoria Petrie Hay, *Forsaking All Others* (Michael Joseph, 1990).

Jonathan Aycliffe, *Naomi's Room* (HarperCollins, 1991).

J. G. Ballard, *The Kindness of Women* (HarperCollins, 1991).

Stephen Fry, *The Liar* (Heinemann, 1991).

Susan Hill, *Air and Angels* (Sinclair-Stevenson, 1991).

Richard Hunt, *Death Sounds Grand* (Constable, 1991).

Simon Sebag Montefiore, *King's Parade* (Hamish Hamilton, 1991).

Erin Pizzey, *Other Lovers* (Collins, 1991).

Elizabeth George, *For the Sake of Elena* (Bantam Books, 1992).

Jill Paton Walsh, *The Wyndham Case* (Hodder, 1993).

C. OTHER PRINCIPAL SOURCES
General

Attwater, Aubrey, *Pembroke College, Cambridge: A Short History* (Cambridge University Press, 1936).

Bartholomew, A. T., *Catalogue of the Books and Papers for the Most Part Relating to the University, Town and County of Cambridge, Bequeathed to the University by John Willis Clark* (Cambridge University Press, 1912).

Bowes, Robert, *A Catalogue of Books Printed at or Relating to the University, Town & County of Cambridge, from 1521 to 1893* (Macmillan & Bowes, 1894).

Chainey, Graham, 'The Chancellor's English Medal', *Cambridge Review*, December 1984. 'From Boniface to Porterhouse: Cambridge in Fiction', *Cambridge Review*, January 1986.

Cooper, C. H., *Annals of Cambridge* (5 vols., Cambridge, 1842–1908).

Cradock, Percy, *Recollections of the Cambridge Union, 1815–1939* (Cambridge: Bowes & Bowes, 1953).

Eagle, Dorothy, and Carnell, Hilary, *The Oxford Literary Guide to the British Isles* (Oxford University Press, 1977).

Gray, Arthur, *Cambridge and Its Story* (Methuen, 1912); reissued as *Cambridge University: An Episodical History* (Cambridge: Heffer, 1926).

Gray, Arthur, and Brittain, Frederick, *A History of Jesus College, Cambridge* (Heinemann, 1979).

Marillier, H. C., *University Magazines and Their Makers* (1902).

Modern Literary Manuscripts from King's College, Cambridge (Cambridge: Fitzwilliam Museum, 1976).

Mullinger, J. B., *The University of Cambridge* (3 vols., Cambridge University Press, 1873–1911).

Proctor, Mortimer R., *The English University Novel* (University of California, 1957).

Rackham, H. (ed.), *Christ's College in Former Days: Being Articles Reprinted from the College Magazine* (Cambridge University Press, 1939).

Roberts, S. C., *Adventures with Authors* (Cambridge University Press, 1966). *A History of the Cambridge University Press* (Cambridge University Press, 1921).

Wilkinson, L. P., *A Century of King's 1873–1972* (Cambridge: King's College, 1980). *Kingsmen of a Century, 1873–1972* (Cambridge: King's College, 1980).

[Willmott, Robert Aris], *Conversations at Cambridge* (J. W. Parker, 1836).

Chapter 1

Bennett, J. A. W., *Chaucer at Oxford and at Cambridge* (Oxford University Press, 1974).

Brewer, Derek, 'The *Reeve's Tale* and the King's Hall, Cambridge', *Chaucer Review*, 5, no. 4, 1971.

Gray, Arthur, 'On the Wandlebury Legend', *Proceedings of the Cambridge Antiquarian Society*, no. LVIII, 1911.

Lethbridge, T. C., *Gogmagog: The Buried Gods* (Routledge & Kegan Paul, 1957).

Chapter 2

Pollet, Maurice, *John Skelton: Poet of Tudor England* (Dent, 1971).

Ryan, Lawrence V., *Roger Ascham* (Stanford and Oxford University Presses, 1963).

Thomson, D. F. S., and Porter, H. C., *Erasmus and Cambridge* (University of Toronto Press, 1963).

Chapter 3

Club Law: A Comedy Acted in Clare Hall, Cambridge, About 1599–1600, ed. G. C. Moore Smith (Cambridge University Press, 1923).

Greene, Robert, *The Life and Complete Works in Prose and Verse*, ed. Alexander B. Grosart (15 vols., New York: Huth Library, 1964).

Leishman, J. B. (ed.), *The Three Parnassus Plays* (Nicholson & Watson, 1949).

Nashe, Thomas, *The Unfortunate Traveller and Other Works*, ed. J. B. Steane (Penguin, 1972).

   The Works, ed. Ronald B. McKerrow (5 vols., Oxford: Blackwell, 1958).

Nelson, Alan H. (ed.), *Records of Early English Drama: Cambridge* (2 vols., University of Toronto Press, 1989).

Purdon, Noel, 'Quod Me Nutrit Me Destruit', *Cambridge Review*, 4 March 1967.

Reed, Edward Bliss, 'The College Element in *Hamlet*', *Modern Philology*, 6, no. 4, April 1909.

Rowse, A. L., *Christopher Marlowe: A Biography* (Macmillan, 1964).

Rylands, George, *A Distraction of Wits Nurtured in Elizabethan Cambridge* (Cambridge University Press, 1958).

Smith, G. C. Moore, *College Plays Performed in the University of Cambridge* (Cambridge University Press, 1923).

Stern, Virginia F., *Gabriel Harvey: His Life, Marginalia and Library* (Oxford University Press, 1979).

Chapter 4

Chute, Marchette, *Two Gentle Men: The Lives of George Herbert and Robert Herrick* (Secker & Warburg, 1960).

Fletcher, Giles, and Fletcher, Phineas, *Poetical Works*, ed. Frederick S. Boas (2 vols., Cambridge University Press, 1909).

Hammond, Paul, 'A Sparke of That Coelestiall Flame', *Trinity Review*, Easter 1973.

Mullinger, J. B., 'Was Ben Jonson Ever a Member of Our College?', *The Eagle* (St John's College), 25, Easter Term 1904, pp. 302–5.

Randolph, Thomas, *The Poems and Amyntas*, ed. John Jay Parry (Yale and Oxford University Presses, 1917).

Ruggle, George, *Ignoramus*, ed. J. S. Hawkins (1787).

Scott, George Walton, *Robert Herrick 1591–1674* (Sidgwick & Jackson, 1974).

Smith, G. C. Moore, *Thomas Randolph* (Warton Lecture, British Academy) (Oxford University Press, 1927).

Bibliography

Chapter 5

Christ's College Magazine, no. 68, Michaelmas 1908 (Milton tercentenary issue).

Coombe, David E., 'Of Milton and Mulberries', Christ's College Magazine, May 1987.

Hill, Christopher, Milton and the English Revolution (Faber, 1977).

Masson, David, The Life of John Milton, vol. I, 1608–39 (Cambridge: Macmillan, 1859).

Parker, W. R., Milton: A Biography (2 vols., Oxford University Press, 1968).

Wilson, A. N., The Life of John Milton (Oxford University Press, 1983).

Chapter 6

Cleveland, John, The Poems, ed. B. Morris and E. Withington (Oxford University Press, 1967).

Cowley, Abraham, Poetry and Prose, ed. L. C. Martin (Oxford University Press, 1949).

Legouis, Pierre, Andrew Marvell: Poet, Puritan, Patriot (Oxford University Press, 1965).

Ward, Charles E., The Life of John Dryden (Chapel Hill: University of North Carolina Press, 1961).

Chapter 7

Bryant, Arthur, Samuel Pepys: The Man in the Making (Collins, 1933).

Ollard, Richard, Pepys: A Biography (Hodder & Stoughton, 1974).

Pepys, Samuel, The Diary, ed. Robert Latham and William Matthews (11 vols., Bell, 1970–83).

Whiteley, D. Pepys, 'Pepys Rides to Cambridge', Country Life, 18 March 1971.

Chapter 8

Cash, Arthur H., Laurence Sterne: The Early and Middle Years (Methuen, 1974).

Cecil, Lord David, The Stricken Deer: The Life of Cowper (Constable, 1929).

Defoe, Daniel, A Tour through the Whole Island of Great Britain (1724; Dent, 1974).

Evelyn, John, The Diary (Everyman, 1952).

Fiennes, Celia, The Journeys (Cresset Press, 1947).

Mayor, J. E. B. (ed.), Cambridge Under Queen Anne (Cambridge University Press, 1911).

Pattison, William, Poetical Works (1728).

P.R., 'The Distressed Poet: A Cambridge Chatterton, William Pattison', Cambridge Review, 29 February 1964.

Stokes, H. P., 'Chatterton and Cambridge', Cambridge Review, 1 December 1910.

Stubbings, F. H., 'Dr Johnson in Cambridge', Emmanuel College Magazine, 48, 1965/6.

[Ward, Edward], A Step to Stir-Bitch Fair: With Remarks Upon the University of Cambridge (1700).

White, R. J., Dr Bentley: A Study in Academic Scarlet (Eyre & Spottiswoode, 1965).

Wordsworth, Christopher, Social Life at the English Universities in the Eighteenth Century (Cambridge: Deighton Bell, 1874); revised by R. Brimley Johnson as The Undergraduate (Stanley Paul, 1928).

Chapter 9

Anstey, Christopher, Poetical Works (1808).

Devlin, Christopher, Poor Kit Smart (Hart-Davis, 1961).

Gray, Thomas, *Correspondence*, ed. Paget Toynbee and Leonard Whibley (3 vols., Oxford University Press, 1935; new edn, 1971).

Ketton-Cremer, R. W., *Thomas Gray: A Biography* (Cambridge University Press, 1955).

Roberts, S. C., *Thomas Gray of Pembroke* (Glasgow, 1952).

Sells, A. L. Lytton, *Thomas Gray: His Life and Works* (Allen & Unwin, 1980).

Stokes, H. P., 'Thomas Gray and his Cambridge Relatives', *Cambridge Review*, 17 January 1917.

Walpole, Horace, *Correspondence*, ed. W. S. Lewis, vols. XIII–XIV (Oxford University Press, 1948).

Chapter 10

The Eagle (St John's College), 54, no. 237, 1950 (Wordsworth centenary issue).

Gunning, Henry, *Reminiscences of the University, Town and County of Cambridge from the Year 1780* (2 vols., 1854).

Moorman, Mary, *William Wordsworth: A Biography* (2 vols., Oxford University Press, 1957–65).

Schneider, Ben Ross, *Wordsworth's Cambridge Education* (Cambridge University Press, 1957).

Wordsworth, William, *Poetical Works*, ed. Thomas Hutchinson (Oxford University Press, 1936).

Chapter 11

Coleridge, Samuel Taylor, *Collected Letters*, ed. E. L. Griggs, vol. 1, *1785–1800* (Oxford University Press, 1956).

Cornwell, John, *Coleridge: Poet and Revolutionary, 1772–1804* (Allen Lane, 1973).

Forster, E. M., 'Trooper Silas Tomkyn Comberbacke', in *Abinger Harvest* (Edward Arnold, 1936).

Gray, Arthur, 'Coleridge at Jesus, 1791–1794', *The Chanticlere* (Jesus College), no. 16, October 1890.

Holmes, Richard, *Coleridge: Early Visions* (Hodder & Stoughton, 1989).

Knight, Frida, *University Rebel: The Life of William Frend, 1757–1841* (Gollancz, 1971).

Lefebure, Molly, *Samuel Taylor Coleridge: A Bondage of Opium* (Gollancz, 1974).

Chapter 12

Byron, Lord, *Letters and Journals*, ed. Leslie A. Marchand (12 vols., John Murray, 1973–82).

Marchand, Leslie A., *Byron: A Biography*, vol. 1 (John Murray, 1957).

Robson, Robert, 'Lord Byron's Rooms Revisited', *Trinity Review*, Easter 1975.

Walker, Keith, 'Byron at Trinity', *Trinity Review*, Michaelmas 1961.

Chapter 13

B.L.H., 'Leigh Hunt on Cambridge', *Cambridge Review*, 20 October 1910.

Clive, John, *Thomas Babington Macaulay: The Shaping of the Historian* (Secker & Warburg, 1973).

[Cox, W. A.], 'Henry Kirke White', *The Eagle* (St John's College), 28, 1906.

Hudson, Derek, *A Poet in Parliament: The Life of Winthrop Mackworth Praed, 1802–1839* (John Murray, 1939).

Lucas, E. V., 'Cambridge and Charles Lamb', *Cambridge Review*, 17 February 1910, 7 June 1911; reprinted in *Cambridge and Charles Lamb*, ed. George Wherry (Cambridge University Press, 1925).

Lytton, Earl of, *The Life of Edward Bulwer, First Lord Lytton* (Macmillan, 1913).

Macaulay, Thomas Babington, *The Letters*, ed. Thomas Pinney, vol. 1 (Cambridge University Press, 1974).

Monsarrat, Ann, *An Uneasy Victorian: Thackeray the Man* (Cassell, 1980).

Pullan, Brian S., 'Macaulay at Trinity', *Trinity Review*, Lent 1959.

Ray, Gordon N., *Thackeray: The Uses of Adversity (1811–46)* (Oxford University Press, 1955).

Terhune, Alfred McKinley, *The Life of Edward Fitzgerald* (Oxford University Press, 1947).

Thackeray, William Makepeace, *The Letters and Private Papers*, ed. Gordon N. Ray, vol. 1 (Oxford University Press, 1945).

Trevelyan, Sir George Otto, *The Life and Letters of Lord Macaulay* (2 vols., Longman, 1876).

White, Henry Kirke, *The Life and Remains*, ed. Robert Southey (3 vols., 1807–22).

Chapter 14

Allen, Peter, *The Cambridge Apostles: The Early Years* (Cambridge University Press, 1978).

Brookfield, Frances M., *The Cambridge 'Apostles'* (Pitman, 1906).

Hallam, Arthur Henry, *The Writings*, ed. T. H. Vail Motter (Oxford University Press, 1943).

Martin, Robert Bernard, *Tennyson: The Unquiet Heart* (Oxford University Press and Faber, 1980).

Miller, Betty, 'Camelot at Cambridge', *Twentieth Century*, February 1958, pp. 133–47.

Parkin, Stephen, 'Tennyson at Trinity', *Trinity Review*, Easter 1976.

Pope-Hennessy, James, *Monckton Milnes: The Years of Promise* (Constable, 1949).

Stanford, C. V., 'In Memoriam: Alfred, Lord Tennyson', *Cambridge Review*, 13 October 1892.

Tennyson, Alfred, *The Letters*, ed. Cecil Y. Lang and Edgar F. Shannon Jr, vol. 1, *1821–1850* (Oxford University Press, 1982).

Tennyson, Charles, *Alfred Tennyson* (Macmillan, 1950).

Tennyson, Hallam, *Alfred Lord Tennyson: A Memoir* (Macmillan, 1897).

Chapter 15

Bartholomew, A. T., 'Samuel Butler and the Simeonites', *Cambridge Magazine*, 1 March 1913.

Besant, Sir Walter, *Autobiography* (Hutchinson, 1902).

Birrell, Augustine, 'Cambridge and the Poets', in *Obiter Dicta*, 2nd ser. (Elliot Stock, 1887).

Burnand, F. C., *The 'ADC': Being Personal Reminiscences of the University Amateur Dramatic Club, Cambridge* (Chapman & Hall, 1880).

Records and Reminiscences: Personal and General (2 vols., Methuen, 1904).

Bibliography

Calverley, C. S., *The Complete Works* (George Bell, 1901).

Colloms, Brenda, *Charles Kingsley* (Constable, 1975).

Haight, Gordon S., *George Eliot: A Biography* (Oxford University Press, 1968).

Hardy, Florence Emily, *The Early Life of Thomas Hardy* (Macmillan, 1928).

Hilton, Arthur Clement, *The Works* (Cambridge: Macmillan & Bowes, 1904).

Ince, Richard B., *Calverley and Some Cambridge Wits of the Nineteenth Century* (Grant Richards, 1929).

James, Henry, 'English Vignettes', *Lippincotts' Magazine*, 1879; reprinted in *Portraits of Places* (1883); and in *English Hours* (1905; Heinemann, 1960).

Jones, Henry Festing, *Samuel Butler, Author of 'Erewhon': A Memoir* (2 vols., Macmillan, 1919).

Robinson, Duncan, and Wildman, Stephen, *Morris & Company in Cambridge* (Cambridge: Fitzwilliam Museum, 1980).

Skeat, Walter W., 'Reminiscences of CSC', *Christ's College Magazine*, no. 24, 1894.

Stephen, J. K., *Lapsus Calami and Other Verses* (Cambridge: Bowes & Bowes, 1912).

[Stephen, Leslie], *Sketches from Cambridge: By a Don* (Macmillan, 1865).

Waddington, Patrick, *Turgenev and England* (Macmillan, 1980).

Chapter 16

Anstruther, Ian, *Oscar Browning* (John Murray, 1983).

Benson, E. F., *As We Were: A Victorian Peepshow* (Longman, 1930).

Borland, Maureen, *Wilde's Devoted Friend: A Life of Robert Ross* (Oxford: Lennard Publishing, 1990).

Cornford, Frances, *Collected Poems* (Cresset Press, 1954).

Dickins, Bruce, 'Robert Ross at King's', *Cambridge Review*, 23 January 1960.

Gosse, Edmund, *Robert Browning: Personalia* (Fisher Unwin, 1890).

Hall, Trevor H., *Sherlock Holmes: Ten Literary Studies* (Duckworth, 1969).

Holmes, Oliver Wendell, *Our Hundred Days in Europe* (Sampson Low, 1887).

Milne, A. A., *It's Too Late Now: The Autobiography of a Writer* (Methuen, 1939).

Powys, John Cowper, *Autobiography* (Macdonald, 1934).

Raverat, Gwen, *Period Piece: A Cambridge Childhood* (Faber, 1952).

The Light is Dark Enough (Sherlock Holmes Society of London Cambridge Expedition, 1989).

Thwaite, Ann, *Edmund Gosse: A Literary Landscape* (Secker & Warburg, 1984).

 A. A. Milne: His Life (Faber, 1990).

Chapter 17

Beauman, Nicola, *Morgan: A Biography of E. M. Forster* (Hodder & Stoughton, 1993).

Bell, Clive, *Old Friends: Personal Recollections* (Chatto & Windus, 1956).

Bell, Quentin, *Virginia Woolf: A Biography* (2 vols., Hogarth Press, 1972).

Dickinson, Goldsworthy Lowes, *Autobiography*, ed. Dennis Proctor (Duckworth, 1973).

Forster, E. M., *Goldsworthy Lowes Dickinson* (Edward Arnold, 1934).

Furbank, P. N., *E. M. Forster: A Life* (2 vols., Secker & Warburg, 1977–8).

Holroyd, Michael, *Lytton Strachey: A Critical Biography* (2 vols., Heinemann, 1967–8).

King, Francis, *E. M. Forster and His World* (Thames & Hudson, 1978).

Levy, Paul, *Moore: G. E. Moore and the Cambridge Apostles* (Weidenfeld & Nicolson, 1979).

Wilkinson, Patrick, 'Forster and King's', in *Aspects of E. M. Forster*, ed. Oliver Stallybrass (Edward Arnold, 1969).

Woolf, Leonard, *Sowing: An Autobiography of the Years 1880 to 1904* (Hogarth Press, 1960).

Chapter 18

Benkovitz, Miriam J., *Ronald Firbank: A Biography* (Weidenfeld & Nicolson, 1970).

Benson, A. C., *The Diary*, ed. Percy Lubbock (Hutchinson, 1926).

Benson, E. F., *Final Edition: Informal Autobiography* (Longman, 1940).

Crowley, Aleister, *The Confessions*, ed. John Symonds and Kenneth Grant (Arkana, 1989).

Hart-Davis, Rupert, *Hugh Walpole: A Biography* (Macmillan, 1952).

Holland, Vyvyan, 'Ronald Firbank', in *An Evergreen Garland* (Cassell, 1968).

Jones, Alun R., *The Life and Opinions of T. E. Hulme* (Gollancz, 1960).

Leslie, Shane, *The End of a Chapter* (Constable, 1916).
    Long Shadows (John Murray, 1966).

Newsome, David, *On the Edge of Paradise: A. C. Benson, the Diarist* (John Murray, 1980).

Oates, J. C. T., 'Charles Edward Sayle', *Transactions of the Cambridge Bibliographical Society*, 8, 1982.

Pfaff, Richard William, *Montague Rhodes James* (Scolar Press, 1980).

Sassoon, Siegfried, *The Old Century: And Seven More Years* (Faber, 1938).

Sherwood, John, *No Golden Journey: A Biography of James Elroy Flecker* (Heinemann, 1973).

Taylor, Brian, *The Green Avenue: The Life and Writings of Forrest Reid* (Cambridge University Press, 1980).

Chapter 19

Archer, Mary, *Rupert Brooke and the Old Vicarage, Grantchester* (Cambridge: Silent Books, 1989).

Brooke, Rupert, *The Letters*, ed. Geoffrey Keynes (Faber, 1968).

Carey, Hugh, *Duet for Two Voices: An Informal Biography of Edward J. Dent Compiled from His Letters to Clive Carey* (Cambridge University Press, 1979).

Cheason, Denis, *The Cambridgeshire of Rupert Brooke* (Cambridge, 1980).

Delany, Paul, *The Neo-Pagans: Friendship and Love in the Rupert Brooke Circle* (Macmillan, 1987).

Hassall, Christopher, *Rupert Brooke: A Biography* (Faber, 1964).

Hastings, Michael, *The Handsomest Young Man in England: Rupert Brooke* (Michael Joseph, 1967).

Keynes, Geoffrey, *Henry James in Cambridge* (Cambridge: Heffer, 1967); republished in *The Gates of Memory* (Oxford University Press, 1981).

Lehmann, John, *Rupert Brooke: His Life and His Legend* (Weidenfeld & Nicolson, 1980).

Macaulay, Rose, *Two Blind Countries* (Sidgwick & Jackson, 1914).

Chapter 20

Barrie, J. M., *Letters* (Peter Davies, 1942).

Brittain, F., *Arthur Quiller-Couch: A Biographical Study of Q* (Cambridge University Press, 1947).

Fausset, Hugh I'Anson, *A Modern Prelude* (Cape, 1933).

Graves, Richard Percival, *A. E. Housman: The Scholar-Poet* (Routledge & Kegan Paul, 1979).

Housman, A. E., *The Letters*, ed. Henry Maas (Hart-Davis, 1971).

   Selected Prose, ed. John Carter (Cambridge University Press, 1961).

Housman Society Journal, 1, 1974.

Keynes, John Maynard, 'My Early Beliefs', in *Two Memoirs* (Hart-Davis, 1949).

Lawrence, D. H., *The Letters*, vol. II (Cambridge University Press, 1981).

Macaulay, Rose, *Three Days* (Constable, 1919).

Nichols, Beverley, *The Unforgiving Minute* (W. H. Allen, 1978).

Quiller-Couch, Sir Arthur, *Q Anthology: A Selection from the Prose and Verse*, ed. F. Brittain (Dent, 1948).

Rosenbaum, S. P., 'Keynes, Lawrence and Cambridge Revisited', *Cambridge Quarterly*, 11, no. 1, 1982.

Rowse, A. L., *Quiller Couch: a Portrait of 'Q'* (Methuen, 1988).

Sassoon, Siegfried, *Memoirs of an Infantry Officer* (Faber, 1930).

Smith, Constance Babington, *Rose Macaulay* (Collins, 1972).

Steel, D. A., 'Escape and Aftermath: Gide in Cambridge, 1918', *The Yearbook of English Studies*, 15 (1985).

Chapter 21

Bowker, Gordon, (ed.), *Malcolm Lowry Remembered* (Ariel Books, 1985).

   Pursued by Furies: a Life of Malcolm Lowry (HarperCollins, 1993).

Bradbrook, M. C., *Malcolm Lowry: His Art and Early Life* (Cambridge University Press, 1974).

Davies, Hugh Sykes, 'Cambridge Poetry', *Twentieth Century*, February 1955.

Eliot, T. S., *The Letters*, ed. Valerie Eliot, vol. 1 (Faber, 1988).

   The Varieties of Metaphysical Poetry, ed. Ronald Schuchard (Faber, 1993).

Field, Andrew, *VN: The Life and Art of Vladimir Nabokov* (Macdonald, 1987).

Finney, Brian, *Christopher Isherwood: A Critical Biography* (Faber, 1979).

Fryer, Jonathan, *Eye of the Camera: A Life of Christopher Isherwood* (Allison & Busby, 1993).

Gill, Roma (ed.), *William Empson: The Man and His Work* (Routledge & Kegan Paul, 1974).

Howarth, T. E. B., *Cambridge Between Two Wars* (Collins, 1978).

Lehmann, John, *The Whispering Gallery: Autobiography I* (Longman, 1955).

Monsarrat, Nicholas, *Life is a Four-Letter Word*, vol. 1 (Cassell, 1966).

Nabokov, Vladimir, *Speak, Memory* (Gollancz, 1951; Weidenfeld & Nicolson, 1967).

Parker, Peter, *Ackerley: A Life of J. R. Ackerley* (Constable, 1989).

Priestley, J. B., foreword to Thomas Thornley, *Cambridge Memories* (Hamish Hamilton, 1936).

Raine, Kathleen, *The Land Unknown* (Hamish Hamilton, 1975).

Richards, I. A., *Practical Criticism: A Study in Literary Judgment* (Routledge & Kegan Paul, 1929).

I. A. Richards: Essays in his Honor (New York: Oxford University Press, 1973).

Roache, Joel, *Richard Eberhart: The Biography of an American Poet* (Oxford University Press, 1971).

Snow, Philip, *Stranger and Brother: A Portrait of C. P. Snow* (Macmillan, 1982).

Stansky, Peter, and Abrahams, William, *Journey to the Frontier: Julian Bell and John Cornford: Their Lives and the 1930s* (Constable, 1966).

Tillyard, E. M. W., *The Muse Unchained: An Intimate Account of the Revolution in English Studies* (Cambridge: Bowes & Bowes, 1958).

Warner, Sylvia Townsend, *T. H. White: A Biography* (Cape with Chatto & Windus, 1967).

Watson, George, 'The Cambridge Lectures of T. S. Eliot', *Sewanee Review*, no. 99, fall 1991.

Willey, Basil, *Cambridge and Other Memories, 1920–1953* (Chatto & Windus, 1968).

Woolf, Virginia, *A Room of One's Own* (Hogarth Press, 1929).

Chapter 22

Bradbrook, M. C., 'Queenie Leavis: The Dynamics of Rejection', *Cambridge Review*, 20 November 1981.

Brewer, Derek, 'Yes, But . . . ', *Cambridge Review*, January 1985.

Chainey, Graham, 'The Other Leavises', *Cambridge Review*, January 1985; postscript, February 1985, p. 64.

Hayman, Ronald, *Leavis* (Heinemann, 1976).

Houghton, Robert, 'The Leavises in the Sixties and Seventies', *Cambridge Quarterly*, 17, no. 1, 1988.

Leavis, F. R., *English Literature in Our Time and the University* (Chatto & Windus, 1969). *Two Cultures? The Significance of C. P. Snow* (Chatto & Windus, 1962).

Snow, C. P., *The Two Cultures and the Scientific Revolution* (Cambridge University Press, 1959).

Steiner, George, 'F. R. Leavis', *Encounter*, 18, no. 5, May 1962; reprinted in *Language and Silence* (Faber, 1967).

Thompson, Denys (ed.), *The Leavises: Recollections and Impressions* (Cambridge University Press, 1984).

Walsh, William, *F. R. Leavis* (Chatto & Windus, 1980).

Chapter 23

Berryman, John, *Love & Fame* (Faber, 1971).

Boyd, Martin, *Day of My Delight: An Anglo-Australian Memoir* (Lansdowne Press, 1965; Penguin Books, 1986).

Ewart, Gavin, *The Collected Ewart* (Hutchinson, 1982).

Gardner, Helen, *The Composition of Four Quartets* (Faber, 1978).

Gow, A. S. F., *Letters from Cambridge 1939–1944* (Cape, 1945).

Haffenden, John, *The Life of John Berryman* (Routledge & Kegan Paul, 1982).

Marr, David, *Patrick White: A Life* (Cape, 1991).

Moore, Nicholas, *Identity* (Cadenza Press, 1969).

O'Casey, Sean, *Sunset and Evening Star* (Macmillan, 1954); reissued in *Autobiographies*, vol. II (Macmillan, 1981).

Powell, Anthony, *Faces in My Time* (Heinemann, 1980).

Prokosch, Frederic, *Voices: A Memoir* (Faber, 1983).

Chapter 24

Amis, Kingsley, 'No More Parades: On Leaving Cambridge', *Encounter*, 22, no. 2, February 1964; reprinted in *What Became of Jane Austen? And Other Questions* (Cape, 1970).

Memoirs (Hutchinson, 1991).

Appleyard, Bryan, 'Buffalo Bill' (profile of Bill Buford), *Sunday Times*, 10 September 1989.

Cambridge Review, 7 February 1969 (Sylvia Plath issue).

Davie, Donald, *These the Companions: Recollections* (Cambridge University Press, 1982).

'The Varsity Match', *Poetry Nation*, no. 2, 1974; reprinted in *Poetry Dimension Annual 3* (Robson Books, 1975).

Forster, E. M., *Commonplace Book*, ed. Philip Gardner (Scolar Press, 1985).

Gunn, Thom, 'Cambridge in the Fifties', in *The Occasions of Poetry* (Faber, 1982).

'*Oasis*: An Experiment in Selling Poetry', *Bookseller*, 15 March 1952.

Hall, Peter, *Making an Exhibition of Myself* (Sinclair-Stevenson, 1993).

Hare, David, *Teeth 'n' Smiles* (Faber, 1976).

'Cycles of Hope: A Memoir of Raymond Williams', in *Writing Left-Handed* (Faber, 1991).

Hewison, Robert, *Footlights! A Hundred Years of Cambridge Comedy* (Methuen, 1983).

James, Clive, *May Week Was in June* (Cape, 1990).

Miller, Karl, *Rebecca's Vest* (Hamish Hamilton, 1993).

Plath, Sylvia, *Letters Home: Correspondence 1950–1963*, ed. Aurelia Schober Plath (Faber, 1975).

Raphael, Frederic, '25 Years Ago in Cambridge', *The Listener*, 5 February 1976; reprinted in *Cracks in the Ice* (W. H. Allen, 1979).

Redgrove, Peter, 'A Poet in Teaching', *New Universities Quarterly*, Spring 1980.

Sagar, Keith, *The Art of Ted Hughes* (Cambridge University Press, 1975).

Stape, J. H. (ed.), *E. M. Forster: Interviews and Recollections* (Macmillan, 1993).

Stevenson, Anne, *Bitter Fame: A Life of Sylvia Plath* (Viking, 1989).

Index